LEADERSHIP AND CULTURAL WEBS IN ORGANISATIONS: WEAVERS' TALES

LEADERSHIP AND CULTURAL WEBS IN ORGANISATIONS: WEAVERS' TALES

BY

ADRIAN McLEAN
The McLean Partnership, Inc., Pawlet, VT, USA

United Kingdom − North America − Japan
India − Malaysia − China

Emerald Group Publishing Limited
Howard House, Wagon Lane, Bingley BD16 1WA, UK

First edition 2013

Copyright © 2013 Emerald Group Publishing Limited

Reprints and permission service
Contact: permissions@emeraldinsight.com

British Library Cataloguing in Publication Data
A catalogue record for this book is available from the British Library

ISBN: 978-1-78350-108-3

Printed and bound by CPI Group (UK) Ltd, Croydon, CR0 4YY

ISOQAR certified
Management System,
awarded to Emerald
for adherence to
Environmental
standard
ISO 14001:2004.

Certificate Number 1985
ISO 14001

INVESTOR IN PEOPLE

For Luke

Contents

Preface

I am a consultant. I help members of organisations find ways of responding to the seemingly incessant pressures to change, to adapt to the ceaselessly shifting contexts in which all organisations, whether commercial or otherwise, find themselves. I began my career as an academic and half way through I became a consultant. I have kept a 'foot in both camps' ever since. As a member of the School of Management in the University of Bath, a colleague, Peter Reason, introduced me to an organisation simulation called ORGsimONE. I have used this simulation many times since and I am both indebted to Peter for the introduction and to its designer Sherman Grinnell (1976). It has taught me more about the dynamics of organisation change than any textbook, article or seminar in a career spanning more than 4 decades.

In introducing the subject of this book, I would like to share two experiences of running the simulation that stand out for me. I have chosen them not simply because they raise some provocative questions about the value of business education, but more significantly because they highlight the immensely powerful way that patterns of behaviour in organisations are the product of unseen and, in any conventional sense, unmanageable phenomena.

Consider the following images:

ORGsimONE Cards

Using a felt tip pen and drawing freehand, how long would it take you to produce one of these cards? Be conservative in your estimation.

Now, estimate how many cards a group of 25 people might produce in the space after 60 minutes.

When I ask groups this question the most common estimate is that each card would take one person an average of a minute to produce. This means that over 60 minutes 25 people might reasonably be expected to produce 1500 cards.

Now, I would like you to estimate how many cards were actually produced by the following two groups in the course of the full simulation, which means four production periods lasting 15 minutes each:

Group 1 — Business Administration undergraduates in the first semester of their four-year course. Their average age was 18.6 years and fresh from 6th form (high school) they were at the very beginning of learning about business administration. There were 50 students in this group.

Group 2 — Senior executives in a motor component manufacturing company employing 60,000 employees. Based in the United Kingdom, they had plants across Europe and North America. The participants were an elite group of senior managers destined for board positions and sat one level beneath that of director. They had been selected to attend a transformation leadership programme designed to empower engineers who were considered to be the change agents at the heart of the business. There were 25 members in this group. Their average age was 42 years.

A brief description of the simulation is described in Box 1.

Box 1: Outline of ORGsimONE.

ORGsimONE*

The greeting cards are hand drawn using felt tip pens and are the 'product' of a simulated company that produces greetings cards in many designs and colours. The designs are not complex. The simulation (called ORGsimONE) is a daylong exercise that recreates the challenges of managing a production company in a lively and competitive marketplace. The simulation lasts a day and participants draw their roles from of a hat.

These are the typical kinds of roles one might expect in a manufacturing company. A simple hierarchy of managers is responsible for design, production and workflow with groups of workers reporting to them. There are staff functions to support them, in particular a Department of Accounting, a Quality Control Department and a Supplies Department. The CEO is supported by a sales and marketing manager. The structure is a simple stripped-down form of a traditional hierarchy.

Some become workers whose job is to do what they are told, others find themselves in middle management positions in both line and staff functions, and a handful have senior leadership roles with responsibility for the overall success and profitability of the business. One of them takes the role of customer to the company. Their job is to source a reliable supply of year-round greetings cards for sale in a chain of retail stores. ORGsimONE is one of their suppliers.

I have run this simulation hundreds of times in different settings and on different continents. It provides rich insights into virtually all aspects of people and business management. There is no correct answer to this simulation, no one right way of doing things. Its value lies in recreating and reflecting on the choices and styles of leading, managing and following that are used in the course of running the 'company'. It is a rare opportunity to see a whole system in interaction with its environment and to hear feedback directly from the customer in an unvarnished way. I have used it as a means of mirroring cultural patterns of behaviour and of revealing the hidden assumptions and values that inform everyday behaviours and decisions. The brief encourages participants to run the business as they see fit and to maximise profit and employee satisfaction. They are asked not to make any changes to the structure during the first (of four) rounds.

---

*ORGsimONE was created by Sherman Grinnell of Grinnell Associates.

The number of greetings cards produced by the two groups under identical conditions are as follows:

Group 1 (first semester undergraduates) — 2000 cards
Group 2 (senior executives) — 0 cards

The neophyte business students managed to produce 2000 cards over the course of the simulation whereas the high potential executives failed to produce a single card that met the specifications of the exercise.

As reader you might care to take a moment to speculate on these startling results. What accounted for such dramatic differences in productivity? How did each group approach the task of maximising profit and employee satisfaction?

In Group 1, the students immediately collapsed the hierarchy and dived into a chaotic process of making the cards, discovering those with artistic and design talent and assigning them the task of coming up with innovative designs after having met with the customer. This was in spite of an explicit request of the facilitators not to make any changes in the organisation structure until the second of four rounds. The noise levels were high and it was some time before any sense of order emerged. Junior employees were dispatched to purchase cigars and a bottle of scotch for the CEO's office. Gradually, clusters of activity formed with most people involved in producing the cards regardless of their formal title or position in the hierarchy. The CEO and his assistants stayed out of the thick of these activities, preferring instead to savour the perks of high office. The customer was given a tour of the company, introduced to people and shown a sample of the designs ahead of production for his approval. At the end of round one the company met the customer's order both in terms of quantity, product mix and quality. They were penalised for some below standard items but came away having made a modest profit.

In subsequent rounds they continued with the designer-producer approach to the production of cards, adopting a form of worker cooperative that emphasised equality and everyone's right to have a say in decisions. The production requirements for each round were posted in full view of all and this enabled the self-forming teams to adjust their production accordingly. As the realisation grew that there was a need to co-ordinate production between divisions, 'runners' moved between them to monitor and adjust production levels and to exchange other information such as helpful tips and resources. On discovering the risk of toxic materials the CEO made an announcement to everyone and dispatched a small team to investigate the problem. Production continued uninterrupted and the investigating team soon discovered the source of the problem and took appropriate action early.

As the day unfolded the CEO discovered that the customer would pay a premium for high quality innovative cards and he passed this information onto the production teams. Gradually a production cluster emerged that contained the most talented artists and they concentrated on producing some highly innovative cards much to the delight and amusement of the customer. By the fourth and last round they were cruising and produced as many cards in one round as they had during the previous three rounds. They hit the final deadline with minutes to spare and celebrated their success in raucous fashion, with several crates of beer.

This was in stark contrast to how events unfolded for Group 2.

The 25 senior executives in the room were high potential managers destined for the most senior positions in the company. They were drawn from the senior ranks of a company that employed 60,000 people. This was an engineering business and everyone in the room was an expert engineer of one kind or another. As people drew their roles there was an exchange of familiar jokes and banter and people quickly migrated to join others of similar rank. The 'workers' seemed relieved, light hearted and playful whereas the mood among the 'management team' quickly became serious. The most senior executives huddled informally, caught up in serious discussions, evidently deferring to the 'CEO's' thoughts and ideas about strategy and direction.

When the exercise began officially at the beginning of round one the CEO summoned his team of senior managers in abrupt fashion. He banged his desk with his fist and barked an order for his deputies to attend a planning meeting. The room fell silent. These senior managers were absorbed by the need to make strategic decisions, what volume of cards to produce, how to allocate the product mix between teams, how many could they produce in the 15 minutes allowed for production?

As they pondered these questions the line managers in the divisions sought to prepare their teams for the first round of production. They emphasised clear task allocation, smooth workflow and simple designs to allow high volume production. Workers awaited specific instructions. In some teams they decided to experiment with card designs until the details of the order for round one came through. Some managers directed their 'workflow workers' to create templates so as to ensure the accuracy in the production of each card. The customer organised himself, patiently awaiting the arrival of a representative from the company to negotiate an order with him.

The Material Resources department immediately counted out the supply of blank cards needed for the game into tidy piles of 10 and audited all the other materials that they were responsible for, including the supply of felt tipped pens. Additionally, and beyond the requirement of the brief, they created a series of order forms that representatives from each of the three divisions were required to fill out and sign together with a counter signature from their Division manager before they could withdraw supplies. Cards would only be issued in units of 10 they announced.

The planning and preparation period lasted 30 minutes, and as the clock ticked away, the Division Managers, with their teams eagerly awaiting instructions, became increasingly nervous at the absence of an order from the customer. Different managers attempted to convey the growing sense of urgency to the members of the top team who were absorbed in their planning. They were met with polite reassurances at first but gradually the politeness turned to irritation, as no decisions were forthcoming.

It was clear that the entire company was hanging on the outcome of the decisions by the top team. Gradually the workers, with nothing specific to do, became restless, some took out a newspaper, others chatted idly and yet others began to ask pointed questions of their local managers. Still the customer sat in his office waiting for a visit from the company representative.

At the end of the planning period of 30 minutes the situation had not changed. The top team were still discussing their plans but with increasing urgency and decreased listening. The rest of the company began to experience a sense of panic — there was only 15 minutes for production and they still did not know what was required in terms of volumes, types and quality of cards.

Five minutes into the production period the top team finally ended their meeting and announced to each of the three divisions their production quota.

Work teams were half way into the brief production period before the marketing manager informed the customer what cards he could expect. This bore little resemblance to what the customer wanted, much to the surprise and consternation of the marketing manager.

The balance of activity had now shifted to the production divisions where the designers were under urgent pressure to come up with simple prototypes that would be easy to replicate. Anxious managers hovered over the designers urging them to complete their designs quickly, offering suggestions with regard to both the content of the design and the efficiency of the process.

In the midst of this frantic activity the 'production workers' appeared as the only calm people. When they were finally given the approved prototype designs and pressed to 'bang them out' they took their time and questioned aspects of the design detail. In the general confusion they made all kinds of errors. The announcement that the production round had ended found all three divisions in a state of excited chaos. None of them had produced the required number of cards. The product mix did not add up which meant that they could not deliver anything to the long-suffering customer.

In the 15-minute reflection period that concluded the first round there was an agitated discussion as to what had gone wrong with numerous suggestions for improvements. Already the CEO was conducting an acrimonious inquest into the failures of the first round with his division managers. They decided that the structure needed to be revised and became drawn into a heated discussion as to how best to reorganise the company.

In the meantime the customer was left to himself.

While this was happening disillusioned 'workers' who were feeling angered by the disorganisation, and by having felt excluded from any decision making until the very last minute, joined in informal conversations. Their mood was dark. They were very critical of 'management's inefficiency' and 'poor communications' and resented being put under so much pressure at the last minute. It was time to protect their rights and to form a union.

When the CEO and his team had finished their plans for the reorganisation, well into the planning period for round two, he called an all-staff-meeting to announce the changes. The meeting was slow to gather and it was evident that the workers were all clustered in a large and boisterous group. The CEO began his explanation of the changes only to be interrupted by a spokesperson for the 'workers' who announced that they had formed the Amalgamated Union of Card Designers and Manufacturers. The union had a number of grievances arising from the first round and would not return to work until these had been settled to their satisfaction. The blood drained from the CEO's face.

The remainder of the day was devoted to these negotiations. Efforts by the remaining managers to manufacture some cards by themselves were blocked by the union. And so it came to pass that no cards were ever delivered to the customer after four hour-long rounds and a break for lunch. The day had been a total disaster.

This experience turned out to be truly shocking, not least for myself, and I wondered how best to facilitate a reflective conversation on what felt like a humiliating and embarrassing result for all.

What is to be made of these two, contrasting experiences? Both groups had received exactly the same briefing, both were charged with exactly the same objectives as a business. Interventions by the facilitators were identical in both cases. How was it that one group succeeded so spectacularly while the other spiraled further and further into difficulty? When we factor in the realisation that the successful group was comprised entirely of neophytes when it came to the business of leading and managing a company, the question becomes even more compelling.

The ironic reason, I would suggest, was that both groups were doing the same thing. They were both behaving in accordance with unnoticed beliefs, unquestioned assumptions and unspoken, yet shared values. They were acting entirely in accordance with norms and customs that were a taken for granted way of behaving in the community or group of which they were a part. It was 'normal' and 'common sense' for them to respond to the ambiguous challenge of the simulation in the ways they did.

The students' response to the top-heavy organisation structure outlined in the brief was to break the rules and to immediately flatten it, preferring instead a system based on equality. In ignoring the requirement not to make any changes they were rebelling against the authority of those who held formal power, both the designer of the simulation and the facilitators who were 'running the simulation'. In collapsing the demarcation between roles and spontaneously forming into self-managing teams they were again re-patterning the company in accordance with democratic principles based on values of fairness and equality.

Instead of looking to those in authority to direct them or give them permission to act, they happily, almost provocatively, threw down a challenge to those in authority to stop them. The ostentatious consumption of Whisky and cigars could be seen both as a parody of executive privilege and as a testing of the tolerance of those holding formal power — namely the faculty who were running the exercise. Their disregard for the 'rules' of the simulation also expressed the rebellious sentiments of adolescents who had only recently escaped the strict regimes of their schools and parents. They were enjoying the exhilaration of their newfound freedom. And they were smart, intelligent, youngsters who were quick to make sense of the situation and to challenge the unhelpful constraints that had been deliberately incorporated into the design of the event.

In debriefing the managers' disastrous experience, to their immense credit, they resisted the easy option of blaming the design or facilitation of the simulation for their performance. They chose instead to face the discomfort of reflecting on the lessons to be drawn from the experience.

In the past they had attributed the rash of strikes, disputes and walkouts that were plaguing their business and industry to militant trade unionists. What they realised through the simulation was that they were party to creating this militancy. All of them were senior managers and all of them had stories of skirmishes with the unions. What they came to see with a sense of genuine dismay was that the disruption in the room was of their own creation. None of the group was, or had been, active trade unionists. The so called militancy of the activists, who by sheer chance had drawn the roles of workers in the simulation, was in response to the hostile and macho stance of those who had drawn senior management roles.

Here, in holographic form, was a perfect recreation of the depressingly familiar dynamics of their industry. The view gradually formed that:

> This is something of our creation. We cannot blame anyone but ourselves for what happened here today. This has held up a sobering mirror of the world we inhabit day in day out.

They came to the realisation that the corporate culture, of which they complained, was also of their creation. *We are the culture* observed one of them.

As it turned out this was a fateful conversation. The Chairman of the company was due to visit them at the end of the week to debrief their learning from the programme. Insights from the simulation experience were top of their agenda. The Company Chairman listened to them with intense interest, agreeing that this was indeed worrying but also pointing out that, if this was of their joint creation, himself included, it was also within their collective grasp to change. Thus began a wholly different conversation and a decision to embark on a different journey of change, a process of second order change, or as some writers would have it, cultural change. This journey began with a full-scale co-operative inquiry into the corporate culture.

This inquiry, using methods that are described in some detail later, (see Chapter 8), focussed not so much on behaviours as on the assumptions and beliefs that informed behaviour. Just as an electro-magnetic field is revealed through the pattern formed by iron filings scattered over a paper that covers a magnet, the inquiry identified the 'unwritten rules' for getting by in the company. It brought into the open the short cuts, the tacit understandings and agreements that were the currency of everyday exchanges. It revealed the hierarchy of values that privileged accuracy over innovation, caution over experimentation and internal expertise over customer requirements. It named the golden rule that 'when in doubt pass it on'; avoid risk, and above all, make sure that 'the monkey never ends up on your back'. It also revealed the 'Action Man Culture' that emphasised busyness, long hours and which regarded stress as a credential, a badge of honour. It shed light on the sclerotic bureaucracy that called for the 21 signatures needed by a manager to obtain a routine replacement for a key engineer. These, and many other long-established and taken for granted patterns of behaviour, amounted to a culture that no longer served the company, its employees or its customers.

In the course of this work the company chairman asked me the show stopping question that has been my professional companion and preoccupation ever since: How do you change a culture?

This book is my answer to this question, some 30 years later. It reflects my journey through the fields of organisation culture and the dynamics of organisational change. I have travelled this terrain as both an academic and as a practising consultant and have been fortunate to encounter many thoughtful, skilled and wise companions on the journey.

I realised that before I could answer the chairman's question I needed to understand the term culture, what it meant. It is a much used term nowadays but in the early 1980s there was limited understanding of either the term or the implications of applying it in organisational contexts.

I was also interested in what was meant by the notion of cultural change. I realised that the question contained an assumption, that cultural change could be managed. Is this the case, and if so, how? If culture could not be managed in the normal sense of the term, then what role the leader or the change agent? A third set of questions concerned the role of senior leaders, managers and change practitioners in respect to the formation of organisation cultures and especially when it comes to the question of change.

What ideas, approaches and theories are helpful in answering this growing collection of questions? What can be learned from efforts and experiments, both successful and otherwise, when attempts have been made to change a culture?

This book is my exploration of these questions. It has been long in gestation.

Like the tales of Chaucer's (Geoffrey Chaucer, c1390) pilgrims, these stories reflect reality as perceived from many different perspectives. For the most part they are ordinary tales of common people in unheralded settings and, like Chaucer's great work, they do not point to an ultimate truth or reality or to a definitive explanation of events. For those of us concerned with the challenges of leading and facilitating processes of cultural change in organisations, the stories highlight the significance and consequences of reality being perceived so differently and from such different perspectives. What matters is not whether there is an ultimate truth or a single reality to be discovered but how we work with the co-existence of multiple understandings, multiple versions of what people take to be reality, and the multiple ways of ordering experience that are found in all forms of social context.

In that sense we are not pilgrims in search of the Holy Grail of cultural change, we are not traveling in the hope of finding a universal answer or blueprint, but rather travelers, fellow journeymen and women, looking to understand each others' stories and the processes by which shared understanding arises and changes. The audience for Chaucer's pilgrims was not just the reader but also the other pilgrims on the journey. In the same way this work is intended for fellow travelers, for those practitioners, managers and leaders who are puzzling the same questions in this complex territory.

The weaver, or 'Webbe', on that pilgrimage to the tomb of Thomas A Beckett in Canterbury Cathedral, was one of five guildsmen who listened to the stories of his fellow travellers but did not tell his own story. This work is in part inspired by a desire to honour the craft of the weaver, to elevate her story and to celebrate the richness of the gift that the metaphor of weaving offers to the field of organisational change.

Adrian McLean

References

Chaucer, G. (c1390). The Canterbury Tales. Originally circulated in hand-copied manuscripts. For a modern translation see Ecker, R. L., & Crook, E. J. (1993). *Geoffrey Chaucer: The Canterbury Tales: A complete translation into modern english.* Palatka, FL: Hodge & Braddock.

Grinnell, S. K. (1976). *Orgsimone: A simulation of the task and people dynamics of a production organization: Participants manual.* Cleveland, OH: Grinnell Associates.

Acknowledgements

This work spans the entirety of my career and accordingly my acknowledgements are directed to those who have played a significant role in shaping my thinking, guiding my reading and inspiring my practice. I feel fortunate to have found myself in the midst of an extraordinarily creative era in the field of organisations development and especially privileged to have been surrounded by so many gifted and influential members of this august community. Within the broad field of organisations development I have benefitted from membership of three exceptional groups.

My early career at the University of Bath owes much to the mentorship of my erstwhile boss, the late and much lamented, Iain Mangham. Iain introduced me to the field of organisations development and took me on as an apprentice of sorts. His encouragement and trust gave me confidence to experiment and develop my own practice. His invaluable gift to me was the realization that I am not, never was and never could be Iain Mangham. My time in the School of Management was further enriched by the friendship of two exceptional colleagues: Peter Reason and Judi Marshall. Peter introduced me to the thinking of Gregory Bateson and the work of his followers, Paul Watzlawick and colleagues at the Palo Alto Institute. Peter is also responsible for linking me to the scholarship of Case Western Reserve University in Cleveland Ohio, and to the idea of inquiry as a collaborative endeavour. Judi Marshall brought her characteristically sparkling intelligence to our work in combining our burgeoning interest in the topic of organisations culture with Peter's pioneering leadership in the practice of Cooperative Inquiry. It was through Peter that I met Bob Graham and was introduced to the genius of Clifford Geertz.

My transition from academic to consultant was helped enormously by a sabbatical spent in the company of Gareth Morgan at York University in Toronto Canada. I am grateful to Gareth for his friendship and support at that time and for the gift of his landmark work, Images of Organizations. This work prepared the ground for much innovation and creativity in our field and proved to be the catalyst of an exceptionally generative era.

More recently I am indebted to my colleagues at Ashridge Consulting with whom I had the honour of founding and facilitating the Ashridge Masters in Organisations Consulting. This has been a high point of my career as a teacher but also as a student of consulting and facilitation. Much of my thinking about processes of change and facilitation has been informed through partnering with colleagues on the programme and in the course of consulting assignments with them.

In particular I want to acknowledge the influence of my dear friend Bill Critchley from whom I have learned much. I am especially indebted to Bill for translating the mysteries of complexity theory, or more accurately, his view of organisations as complex responsive processes. Robin Ladkin read an early draft of this work and his feedback was invaluable in helping me to find its' focus. Hugh Pidgeon, Kamil Kellner and Kathleen King are notable members of this particular community and I have learned much from them about skilful process facilitation.

Among the Alumni of AMOC, three members stand out as having contributed materially to this work. Alistair Moffat and I partnered on an assignment that is described in Chapter 6 of this work. It was a perfect partnership from which I learned much and came away with the added bonus of a strengthened friendship. Kevin Power has been a companion in deepening my understanding of the work of Gregory Bateson, and I have valued his scholarship as much as his friendship. Finally among this community I want to thank Martine Cannon for her perceptive feedback and encouragement in the latter stages of preparing the manuscript.

The third community that has played a significant role in shaping my thinking are colleagues from Case Western Reserve University who pioneered the theory and practice of Appreciative Inquiry. Ron Fry and Frank Barrett have been outstanding colleagues who embody the highest standards of practitioner scholarship and I am proud to count them as friends. They have both read and commented on various drafts of this work and I thank them for their insightful feedback and patient support. Their companionship and quiet, intellectual authority in this area have been invaluable in helping me to develop my own thinking and practice. I must also of course acknowledge the influence and leadership of David Cooperrider whose humility and generosity has been an inspiration to me. I also want to thank Jane McGruder Watkins for her support, but especially for helping me to grasp the profound significance of social constructionist thinking.

As a Professor of Law, Heidi Li Feldman has been an unexpected but delightful source of support and generous encouragement in the later stages of the process. I have shamelessly incorporated some of her specific suggestions and observations into the text.

Above all I must express my profound thanks to my wife, Marsha. As my professional partner on many of the cases described here she has been integral to the thinking and development of the ideas in this work. Her patience with the infinite forms that my procrastination has taken has been legion and her faith in the value of the work has never wavered. She has provided the highest standard of technical and logistical support on the countless administrative tasks that I would never have completed on my own. More than anything she has been a wise and fearless critic of the work. The value of her feedback, as well as her thoughtful discussion of the ideas as they took form, is beyond measure.

Adrian McLean
June, 2013, Vermont

Chapter 1

Beyond the Holy Grail

'Disorder can play a critical role in giving birth to new, higher forms of order. As we leave behind our machine models and look more deeply into the dynamics of living systems, we begin to glimpse an entirely new way of understanding fluctuations, disorder and change.' (Wheatley, 1992)

Three Envelopes

Keen to get off to a running start, the freshly appointed chief executive called by his new office a day early. It was a balmy Sunday afternoon and he wanted to get a feel for the setting before becoming caught up in the inevitable busyness of his new position. His excitement was tempered by a degree of anxiety. As he was leaving, and feeling more settled, he ran into his predecessor who had come to collect the remaining boxes of personal effects sitting in the corner. Both men were embarrassed by the unexpected encounter and they exchanged polite small talk. The final comments of the outgoing head, almost by way of an afterthought, left the new incumbent feeling a mixture of amusement, curiosity and disbelief. He offered his best wishes to his successor and explained that in the top right hand drawer of the imposing desk he had left three envelopes, numbered in sequence.

> 'I was given these envelopes by my predecessor and they contain helpful advice for times when you may be feeling at a loss and wondering what course of action to take for the best. Open these one at a time and only look at them when you really need inspiration.'

The response was courteous and brief. The new incumbent accepted this act of eccentricity with good humour and made a mental note to toss them into the bin the next day. The two shook hands and went their separate ways.

The new chief executive looked back on the early months of his tenure as a golden era. He was feted on all sides, attended countless receptions and events as part of his familiarisation programme and became accustomed to generous if somewhat fawning assessments of his record and abilities. He realised that he was trading off of the goodwill and early halo-effect afforded to an incoming chief executive and knew that, sooner or later, people would be looking to him to do something special, something that signalled that he had completed his assessment and was ready to take decisive action. The pressure of expectations was mounting and he noticed the many subtle, if polite, ways in which they were conveyed.

Weighing his options late one evening, by pure chance, he rediscovered the three envelopes tucked at the back of the top drawer of his desk. He had forgotten all about them and as he examined them he thought that it would be amusing to see what his predecessor had to say. He opened the envelope with number one written on the outside. Inside, there was a single sheet of paper on which was written:

'Blame your predecessor'

He shook the envelope and looked inside in the expectation that there was something more, but that was it. Three words. Nothing else.

Of course! The perfect ploy to buy time! Everyone's expectations took little if any account of the situation that he had inherited. There were, indeed, pockets of the organisation where things were in a far worse state of affairs that he might have been expected to know before joining. Parts of the organisation were condemned as 'unfit for purpose'. Rome wasn't built in day and with things in such a state of disarray how could anyone reasonably expect him to turn them around in such short time? Given the mess that he had inherited it was unreasonable for others to expect miracles.

This line served him well. There was a broad acknowledgment that parts of the organisation were in disarray and those who had voiced impatience at his lack of decisive action early on sheepishly acknowledged that much had indeed been hidden from him during the selection process for fear that he might be put off. He had a point. It was wrong to expect too much too soon.

The chief executive's relief was short-lived, however, and before long he sensed, stronger than before, the rising tide of expectations. Remarks were more pointed and open. When was he going to put his stamp on things and live up to his impressive reputation? What do you have in store for us chief executive? Clearly, the honeymoon was well and truly over. Feeling the heat, he decided to check out the second envelope. The advice in envelope number 2 was even more cursory than its predecessor:

'Restructure'

This confirmed the CEO's own thinking. The case for reform was compelling. Nothing short of whole-scale restructuring was called for. Too many departments were overblown in size and the Heads of Departments had become too powerful, mighty barons, whose preoccupations were to accumulate power and resources to themselves. Links between departments were fraught with conflicts and disagreements, turf wars were rife and staff operated out of a silo mentality. Where was the shared sense of purpose, the alignment with the market place? People had lost sight of what really mattered and needed to be refocused on the essentials he thought to himself.

The new chief executive had an unarguable case for a radical shake-up and saw it as a golden opportunity to finally make his mark, to stamp his authority on things. His announcement was met with overt support but also with covert dismay and intrigue. All of a sudden he found himself at the centre of countless offers of help in conducting the organisation review. He felt that he was in charge once more and noticed that the questions about his style and philosophy, what he had come to describe as the 'whisperings', had been replaced by thinly disguised lobbying, invitations to lunch, dinner and departmental away-days. He decided to forestall this patently political activity by announcing that a prestigious consulting firm, hired expressly for the purpose, would conduct an independent review of the whole organisation's activities.

The review took eight months. Its much-awaited findings were greeted with intense interest. Several senior personnel resigned, having already secured lucrative positions elsewhere. Departments were merged, others reconfigured, talented middle managers were elevated to senior positions, and most staff enjoyed the benefits of an upward re-grading. The rationale for the new structure was crystal clear: to orient the business more to the customer's needs and to position the company for the already emerging trends in the market.

As he convened the first meeting of his new management team the CEO felt a sense of satisfaction. This was a fresh start, the dawning of a new era. Even his critics had been silenced in the face of such decisive action. He basked in the interest and publicity of the new look.

Within 18 months it was as if nothing had changed. The same patterns had re-established themselves albeit with a largely different cast of players. The same departments were being scapegoated, rivalry between departmental heads was as strong as ever and it was clear that new empires had been formed. Sales had increased but costs had mushroomed. Overall performance was consistent with past trends and not much different than it had been for the previous 10 years, give or take.

Once more the CEO's sensors were picking up rumblings of dissent. Where was the much-hyped transformation, the breakthrough in performance, the promised change of culture? He had heard the jokes about 'rearranging the deck chairs on the Titanic', and the references to the 'musical chairs' syndrome. What to do now, he pondered? In an idle moment he remembered the three envelopes and realised that one remained unopened. Retrieving it from the back of the drawer he reached for his gilt embossed letter opener and read the following:

'*Prepare three envelopes*'

I first heard this story nearly 20 years ago while I was consulting to a large county council in the South of England. A new chief executive had been appointed with the brief to 'Change the Culture'. Senior officers recounted the story to the accompaniment of much mirth and nods of recognition. This story, apocryphal as it undoubtedly is, captures something about the received wisdom at the time concerning the thinking and practice of leadership and organisational change. I would even go so far as to suggest that the story illuminates three habits or assumptions that have characterised the practice of change management for more than a generation. The advice contained in the first envelope, 'blame your predecessor' alludes to a predisposition to a faultfinding mentality. Naturally enough, if we are looking to improve things we need to find out what is wrong, and to find out where is there scope for improvement, we need to trouble shoot the problems. The second envelope, 'restructure' is rooted in an assumption that organisation charts represent the very stuff of organisational life, mapping out, as they do, accountabilities, reporting lines and demarcations between different activities and groupings. Clarity is the watchword here, the inference being that confusion and ambiguity are the enemy of efficiency. The third envelope: 'prepare three envelopes' is a weary comment on the frequency with which they are invoked. It points to the paucity of the repertoire of choices exercised in practice and to the cynicism of those subject to such changes.

I continue to be surprised by how often the terms change and restructuring are used interchangeably in organisations, as if structural change is the obvious and inevitable option for those wanting to make a difference. I would not dispute that structural change may be an accompanying and necessary part of an overall strategy for change, but in this book I wish to question not only the common and seemingly unquestioned linking of the two ideas, but to scrutinise the thinking that gives rise to it.

This book is about how we think about organisations, and the links between our ways of thinking and our actions as leaders, managers and facilitators of change. In so doing I am following a trail that was pioneered more than 20 years ago by such writers as Tom Peters (Peters & Waterman, 1982) and Gareth Morgan (1986). Tom was essentially a practitioner who, together with Robert Waterman, questioned the prevailing wisdom of the time. In many ways they turned much of conventional thinking on its head with the publication of their influential book *In Search of Excellence*. In this work, they stepped outside of the dominant ways of thinking about organisations by pointing to the phenomenon of culture as a factor that set apart outstanding performance. While their work has provoked much debate and controversy, its pragmatic and iconoclastic style engendered a huge amount of interest and excitement among practicing managers, and if nothing else, both re-energised and popularised a topic that had hitherto been the exclusive property of MBA programmes.

Gareth Morgan has also been a landmark writer in this territory. As an academic, his classic text, *Images of Organizations* (Morgan 1986) prepared the intellectual ground for a revolution in thinking about organisations, pointing out the underlying metaphors that have informed much of the theorising about the nature of organisations. In so doing, Morgan confronted us with the liberating observation that we have choice in how we think about organisations, the relationship between how we think about them, lead them, manage them and facilitate change in them are not based on universal and immutable laws but are the consequence of largely unconscious and unquestioned habits of perception. 'If the only thing we know about is a hammer then we will treat everything as if it were a nail' observed Abraham Maslow (1943). If the only way we think about organisations is in structural terms then the natural recipe for change is to restructure.

Know Your Maps

How we think about organisations is of consequence. By emphasising the structural elements of an organisation we naturally incline to a view of change that suggests new structural forms. We become preoccupied with clarity of reporting relationships, with questions regarding how best to cluster different activities as well as how to ensure sufficient coordination across boundaries. Such a view casts leaders as designers or architects, locked away in dark rooms poring over blue prints, or as chess players manoeuvring pieces around an imaginary board as if somehow independent of, and untouched by, both the process and the outcome.

By way of contrast, if we regard organisations as self-patterning social settings in which people gossip, where they observe and learn from the behaviour of their colleagues and supervisors, where they share experiences, speculate on events and make sense of organisational life through their membership of both formal and informal networks, then the question of how to effect change shifts. In this view of things, making structural adjustments might easily be seen as an irrelevance, or even worse, as a distraction. Instead, this way of thinking suggests a different question: how to infiltrate, or find a way of re-patterning the conversations of everyday organisational life. These are very different questions that challenge our ingenuity to discover novel approaches.

Alfred Korzybski (1931) famously wrote: 'The map is not the territory'. He proposed that all efforts to make sense of the world draw on maps or images that we borrow, inherit or absorb as a natural part of our formal and informal education. And these maps are just that, maps or representations. They do not directly correspond to the territory itself. They are abstractions, filters that both select *and*, more importantly, exclude. Every map is an act of selection or punctuation, as Gregory Bateson (1972) has put it. And, as Abraham Maslow implied, we base our behaviour on the sense making apparatus at our disposal; our conceptual maps. The choices or options that we draw on when making crucial decisions in organisational life are a function of the repertoire of maps that we have available to us. I wish to extend this argument to suggest that in the realm of managing, leading and changing organisations not only are we developing new ways of mapping the territory that we refer to as organisations, but that the basis on which we construct these maps is in the process of a profound revision, amounting to a revolution.

A Quiet Revolution

I write these introductory comments on the 11th anniversary of the events of September 11th, 2001, the attack on the Twin Towers of the World Trade Center in

New York. The image was as iconic as it was terrifying. The destruction of such immense symbols of Western capitalism could hardly have been more powerful. As many commentators observed at the time, this event changed things in ways that were unimaginable before. It was not just the spectacular act of deliberate destruction that was so shocking to Westerners but also its manner: through the use of civil aircraft as missiles. We now see the world differently and the repercussions of this event have affected the course of world affairs ever since.

The broader symbolism of this tragedy is only now becoming clear. In many ways the old order, the old certainties and the old sources of authority are also collapsing with equally profound consequences for our lives. The destruction of these iconic structures also marked the beginning of a similar breakdown in many aspects of what we took to be life as normal.

The near meltdown of US and European economies has called into question the credibility, viability and integrity of some of the seemingly impregnable bastions of capitalism. Long running uncertainty and instability surrounding the Eurozone contributes to a sense of prolonged crisis. The catastrophic oil spill in the Gulf of Mexico provided a shocking demonstration of the fragility and vulnerability of technology operating in extreme environments, and gave a sobering reminder of the limits of man's ability to conquer nature. The proliferation of extreme weather incidents, flooding, droughts, hurricanes and other manifestations of global warming, lend an added sense of turmoil and unpredictability to our lives.

The capacity of political leaders to enforce their view of reality without the consent of their people is rapidly eroding as witnessed by the cascading collapse of regimes in the Middle East. Here is an example of large-scale social reconfiguration enabled in large part by networking technology and social media.

The economic crisis in late 2008 resulted in widespread economic upheaval, turmoil on stock markets, plummeting values of house prices, shifting patterns of home ownership, widespread austerity measures and the likelihood of a prolonged period of economic recession for many economies.

The political gridlock and partisanship that has been the hallmark of politics in the United States since the election of President Obama has reinforced the sense of powerlessness and the loss of moral authority by politicians in the Western hemisphere. In addition, much of the management and leadership of our corporations, banks, investment houses, as well as our religious institutions are in crisis. Everywhere we turn we see the debris of outmoded, disgraced, defunct and dysfunctional institutions. Alarming scenes of social upheaval accompany and, in some cases, precipitate these events.

The startling role played by social media in these events echoes the effects of the Gutenberg Press in the early 15th century. According to Marshall McLuhan (1962) the invention of a press that could rapidly reproduce texts, making them available to a mass audience, was a crucial catalyst of the Modern era in the Western world: McLuhan argued that the innovation of this modest goldsmith, was key to the rise of democracy, capitalism, individualism and, among other trends, nationalism.

The arrival of the Internet and other forms of instant social connectivity may be the herald of a new social era. These new, virtual, technologies enable self-organising on an unprecedented scale and with unimaginable consequences. Could it be that we are just beginning to witness the scale and nature of the consequences of a hyper-connected, self-organising universe?

Our assumptive world is in flux. The events of the past 10 years have, if anything, confirmed that there are fewer and fewer comforting certainties to shore up our sense of the world as normal, predictable and stable. My sense of what is certain and unthinkable collapsed along with those New York towers.

A Lesson in Hubris

It is easy at such times to submit to feelings of dismay and despair as the social order and fabric of the past century seems to be disintegrating before our eyes. An alternative is to embrace Margaret Wheatley's view, expressed at the opening to this chapter, that such periods of upheaval and disorder are harbingers of new, previously unimaginable, possibilities and developments and that in effect we find ourselves in the midst of a paradigm shift. I incline to this view.

We are both witnesses to, and participants in, the emergence of new social forms and patterns of relating and, as such, find ourselves as parties to the emergence of a new social order. While technology is transforming the lives of so many, parallel developments in the realms of philosophy indicate that we may also be experiencing an equally profound shift of worldview. We may well be witnessing the last, often violent, thrashings of a Cartesian paradigm, a mechanistic worldview of command and control. A view that presumes the possibility of control through force, of engineered outcomes, and of mans' supremacy over nature, is in rapid decline. The implications of the collapse of this worldview and the new possibilities that it allows are infiltrating all of our lives.

In recent decades a quiet revolution has also been occurring in the related fields of philosophy and social science. This revolution has seen the revision of long-held beliefs that represented the cornerstone of scientific endeavour.

Newtonian physics was concerned with understanding the properties of the physical world through a mechanical lens, observing, measuring and predicting the impact of one object or event on others. This cause-effect, billiard ball thinking has held a vice like grip on both the physical and social sciences until comparatively recently. Studies sought to identify key variables that explained important phenomena. The goal was prediction, to be able to say with confidence that under these circumstances, given these conditions, certain outcomes were likely within defined limits of probability.

The challenge for scientists was to ensure that their models and predictive formulae embraced all of the determining variables. The high priests of social science were accomplished statisticians and their rituals were increasingly sophisticated manipulations of the 'data' of social behaviour appropriately translated into numbers.

The social sciences sought to understand and explain human behaviour through the protocols of the physical sciences and with similar intentions of discerning patterns in the service of prediction and control. Mathematics, the universal language and discipline of the physical sciences was the primary means for understanding human behaviour.

The ultimate goals of science, the pursuit of laws governing the universe, and its twin companion, the dream that one day we will be able to control all aspects of our lives and environments, have been thrown into confusion by a growing realisation of the limitations of this aspiration as we awaken to the social and environmental catastrophes we are creating. Partly out of a growing realisation of the limits of the scientific way of seeing, and partly in response to the emergence of new ideas, our worldview is undergoing a revolutionary change.

The current crises in world affairs can be seen as an expression of a crisis in our epistemology, in our way of thinking and making sense of the world. Like all crises however, we can become so preoccupied coping with the practical consequences, its disruptions and disturbances, that we fail to see the gift of crisis. And the gift is that, in the unwelcome disruption of the familiar, new possibilities become available to us. In loosening our attachment to the comfort giving certainties of a scientific worldview, we are forced to search for different ways of explaining and engaging with the world that we have created and which we now inhabit. The term used most frequently to refer to this new mental state or perspective is postmodernism.

This choice of term is telling. In defining a genre of thinking, its primary reference is to what it is not, namely Modernism. Modernism is a reference to the optimistic faith in the capacity of science to solve all of the problems facing mankind, the unwavering belief in 'progress', and along with it a wholesale adoption of scientism, a way of seeing the world that is informed by scientific principles and beliefs.

The term *postmodernism* is by no means an assertive or confident definition and hints at the dilemma of naming itself in any definitive way. It is easier to define itself as what it is not than what it is. Postmodernism is a rejection of Modernist thinking and the acknowledgement that we find ourselves in an era in which multiple worldviews co-exist and at times compete, that the notion of truth has to be understood in the context of the community in which the term is being used.

My argument is that the elevation of science and scientific thinking has infiltrated our thinking and lives to such an extent that we no longer recognise its pervasive influence. We routinely look for the truth in a situation or search for the right answer without questioning the underlying premise that there is a truth to be discovered, a right answer to be found, an ultimate solution or cause to be identified. Postmodernism sees science as one of many ways of knowing, one of many ways of organising and interpreting our experience as well as one of many ways of choosing a course of action. Postmodernism urges us to recognise the validity of multiple explanatory schema, multiple belief systems and perspectives, and challenges the hegemony of the scientific community. Science, according to postmodernism, is *a* way of seeing, not *the* way of seeing.

Once we shed the trappings of Newtonian physics, the analysis of causal forces and the siren promise of control that has held us in its thrall, our approach to the study of human behaviour enters a different realm. In entering this realm we are stepping into a different world, or more appropriately perhaps, different worlds. As well as discarding long-cherished attachments to objectivity and the protocols of a science rooted in mechanistic physics, we are also questioning the whole premise of modern science: that there exists a single, discoverable reality whose laws and properties are to be understood and, ultimately, controlled through the application of the scientific method.

As much as anything the postmodern era has drawn attention to the frameworks by which we understand the world and our everyday lives and forced us to question and revisit these frameworks.

The quiet revolution in the physical and social sciences has filtered through to the field of organisation studies. The search for universal laws and transformational panaceas is losing ground to views of organisations that are rooted in different philosophical soil. In place of a belief that one day we will discover the Holy Grail of organisational success, and in so doing lay hands on the elusive levers of control, we are witnessing the emergence of a generation of theories and perspectives on the nature and processes of organisations that are set in a different ground of assumptions. Like all growth in fresh soil it is prolific and messy. There is much variety and, to stay with the analogy, it is difficult at times to discern between nourishing produce and weeds. However, there are certain common features of this new assumptive ground that distinguishes it from previous terrain.

Just as science has been consumed by the search for scientific laws and truths, so too it is possible to see a parallel with the organisational hunger for answers and solutions and the pursuit of the elusive Holy Grail of organisational salvation. Wheatley (1992), summarises it well:

> 'In our past explorations, the tradition was to discover something and then formulate it into answers and solutions that could be widely transferred. But now we are on a journey of mutual and simultaneous exploration. In my view, all we can expect from one another is new and interesting information. We can not expect answers. Solutions, as quantum reality teaches, are a temporary event specific to a context, developed through the relationship of persons and circumstances.' (Wheatley, 1992)

On many fronts the edifices of knowledge created by traditional scientific assumptions are being questioned. The almost sacred tradition of scientific objectivity, whereby no effort was spared to avoid contamination of the subject under examination by the researcher, has been challenged on a number of levels. Quantum scientists discovered that the act of observation changes the phenomena under scrutiny.[1] The appropriateness of treating people like inanimate objects to be observed, measured and counted, the traditional tools of scientific method, is increasingly

---

[1]See Capra (1982) for an account of Heisenberg and Bohr's fateful insights that lead to the development of quantum physics.

questioned by social scientists, some of whom are suggesting that it is time that we treated the study of people as if they were human beings.

The very concept of objectivity is itself under attack. Critics argue that we live in a participatory universe in which all things are connected in ways we are at present unable to fully understand.[2] From this perspective it is folly to think that we can separate ourselves, bracket ourselves off from the flow of experience as if we were not an integral part of it. Right now, in so many aspects of daily life, we are in the process of learning ways of understanding and acting that acknowledge this. The dawning realisation of global warming is that we, mankind, are a force of nature.[3] We do not stand outside of this ecology. The environment is not something separate from us. All of us make a difference to the world we inhabit, and in turn are changed by it. We are not objective observers or beneficiaries of nature's bounty, but part of an ecology of connections and relationships that we call the environment. We are being called on to face up to the uncomfortable realisation that our actions as individuals and as a global society are disturbing delicate ecological and environmental balances, possibly in unrecoverable ways.

The elevated importance of objectivity has fostered an illusion of detachment, casting us as somehow separate from that which we are interested in. Furthermore, from such a position of detachment, we have been drawn into the hubristic and mistaken belief that we are in a position to exercise control over things. The reasoning is that if we can achieve full understanding of a system from a detached perspective, we are well placed to manipulate and control it since we alone can see its properties as a total system. This, we are learning, is folly and quite literally, misconceived. If we see ourselves as participants and not as detached observers then we have to let go of any belief in our ability to exercise unilateral control. This, in a nutshell, is the simple but profoundly significant premise at the heart of this book. As leaders, managers, consultants and members of organisations we are in the process of learning what it means to be participants in an organisation when none of us has the capacity to unilaterally control it. Abandoning our position as detached actors, as objective onlookers, as architects and system designers, we are forced to re-visit fundamental questions concerning the nature and processes of organisational change and to rethink our agency in these processes.

Bateson's Dog

As the relevance of Newtonian assumptions to our understanding of human systems has come under sustained critical scrutiny, we have been forced to seek out other explanations founded in different assumptive soil. Human beings, it turns out, are not inert variables, factored into complex causal models. To be human is to think,

---

[2]See, for example, Bateson (1972), Skolimowski (1985) and Senge (1990).
[3]'We ourselves have become a force of nature. We are changing the climate and what happens next is up to us'. David Attenborough quoted in the *Observer*, 21st May 2006.

discriminate, interpret, feel and to interact with others. Any discipline that seeks to understand social behaviour needs to allow for these capacities. Thirty years ago Gregory Bateson, a philosopher, anthropologist and cybernetician, pointed out that the distance covered by a dog that has been kicked is not determined by the force and velocity of the kick but by the information that the kick represents. To understand behaviour is to see humans as meaning making beings, social beings that, individually and collectively, make sense of their experience. And the process of sense making, of interpreting the infinite complexity of our lives and experience, can neither be predicted nor controlled.

Early in the 20th century the seeds of a different way of thinking about human behaviour were being sown. In 1928 William Isaac Thomas formulated the following sociological theorem:

'If men define situations as real, they are real in their consequences.'
(Thomas & Thomas, 1928)

If we believe that someone is behaving in a threatening way then we will respond accordingly, such as finding ways of defending ourselves for example. We might look to avoid or hide from a threatening individual. Alternatively we might call the police or even choose to go on the offensive. If we see the same behaviour as a cry for help, or even as an act of comedy, we may choose to respond differently. Thomas was pointing to a simple but profound feature of human behaviour; humans interpret events in their world and base their behaviour on these interpretations. Their actions, in turn, contribute to the situation, as they become no longer passive witnesses but also active participants based on their interpretations. Most significantly, Thomas points out that whether 'accurate' or not, our interpretation of events and the behaviour based on these interpretations are of consequence to ourselves and to others.

The behaviour of stock markets is an everyday example of how our 'reading' of the market affects the investments we make, what we buy and what we sell. Not only are we reading the movement of stocks, the economic conditions and the statements of influential voices, but we are also reading the behaviour of other investors, looking to them for clues as to confidence or fear. Our choices to buy or sell, in turn contribute to the broader pattern of trading, which other traders are reading.

Seeing ourselves as participants, as sense making actors in the midst of events and not as calm and calculating observers manipulating things from the outside, is a profound shift in our way of thinking about human behaviour in general and organisations in particular. Once we entertain the possibility that 'reality' is not 'fixed' and 'out there' the whole agenda shifts. Instead of searching for immutable laws and relationships we are required to learn more about the ways in which individuals and groups make sense of their worlds; about how they conceive of and interpret reality. There is a shift of emphasis away from the lure of truth and 'solutions'. Our concern instead becomes that of understanding the maps and representations through which we make sense of our world and ourselves in it. Our preoccupation is less with what we see than how we see.

Linda Smircich, an organisational anthropologist offers the following observation:

> 'Human actors do not know or perceive *the* world, but know and perceive *their* world, through the medium of culturally specific frames of reference.' (Smircich, 1983)

This book is set in the context of this quiet revolution and the insights that flow when we relinquish concerns for objectivity; when we abandon the search for universal truths; when we set aside the thinking that flows from seeing organisations as machines or structures; when we see ourselves as participants in social settings, not as engineers or architects; and when we accept the humbling realisation that we are part of a complex ecology of connections and relationships that is beyond the ability of any individual to control or to ever fully comprehend. It takes seriously the idea that how we define situations is of consequence for the actions we take as individuals but also as members of a community or peer group.

It is to discover and understand the maps that are in common use within a community and on which people rely to interpret events and to navigate their way through the monotony, puzzles and surprises of everyday organisational life. It is to accept Linda Smircich's notion that what matters is to understand how 'human actors ... know and perceive *their* world' (Smircich, 1983) and the implications of this for how we approach questions of leadership and change.

I explore these questions through a frame that sees organisations as cultures. I begin by setting out my understanding of this term, a term that is in common and casual use but which I believe is not well understood. The early chapters build on this foundation to explore the features and characteristics of collective human behaviour that this metaphor offers us.

The balance of the book is concerned with the tricky question of cultural change; what does this mean and what is the role of organisation leaders and change facilitators in this lofty endeavour?

The work concludes by offering a metaphor that draws together the insights arising from this excursion into the stories and case studies that collectively comprise these Weavers' Tales.

Structure of the Book

The book begins by defining terms. The idea of corporate culture is now a common part of the lexicon of management but, more so than many management terms, its meaning is elusive and difficult to pin down in any tangible or operational sense.

Chapter 2 explores the idea of culture, drawing particularly on the distinguished work of renowned anthropologist Clifford Geertz (1973) who sees culture as 'patterns of meaning' passed from one generation to another. His work emphasises the way that culture serves to mediate between experience and interpretation. In this chapter, we discuss the implications of his evocative image of culture as 'webs of signification man himself has spun'. The idea of culture as a form of socially created web for interpreting experience and for guiding behaviour lies at the heart of this book. Drawing on the image of culture as a web, we explore the implications of this image for all who have an interest in cultural change. How are cultural webs woven and can they be rewoven in accordance with our intentions as leaders managers and consultants?

Chapter 3 pursues the implications of the idea that culture is conveyed, carried and transmitted via the agency of symbols. Symbols are vehicles that carry meaning and to work with organisation culture is to have an understanding of what forms they take and how they can and cannot be used as a 'tool' of management. In particular we offer an important distinction between high and low profile symbols. While anthropologists stress the significance of the mundane, what we term low-profile symbols, as key to understanding a culture, the emphasis of management writers and practitioners has largely been on the use of high-profile symbols, grand gestures, as a means of shaping the development of cultures. We conclude by considering the generative potential in the dynamic relationship between the two forms of symbol.

Chapter 4 develops the idea of culture as webs of signification and suggests that, like webs, cultures are comprised of many threads. The weaving of meaning occurs in many ways in organisational life and this chapter considers some of the more influential and accessible threads available to managers and leaders. It also explores the paradoxical view that while leaders and managers cannot control or direct how others interpret events they cannot not communicate or avoid participating in the processes by which these interpretive frameworks are formed.

Chapter 5 is about the practice of weaving. Working from the premise that organisations are better understood as verbs not nouns, as organisings not organisations, we explore the idea of cultural webs as an inevitable and unending process of weaving in which we all participate. This is explored through four case studies that illustrate the principles and practices of weaving. The chapter identifies practices that make up the craft of cultural weaving and considers the processes and practices through which new meaning emerges. The cases describe how new cultural webs form over time and highlight the role of leaders in these processes.

The challenges and conditions that enable the formation of new understandings and cultural webs are further explored in Chapter 6. Here we examine, in close detail, an example of the formation of a distinctive cultural web in the context of a merger. A feature of this case is the use of Internet-based technology to support a pan global conversation within the newly merged company. This case also illustrates the role of ambiguity and the importance of honouring the 'shadow conversation' in the formation of new cultural pathways. The exchanges and samples of discourse from one of these virtual conversations provide a fascinating insight into the emergence of new meaning and new frameworks of understanding.

Chapter 7 uses Bateson's notion of 'the pattern that connects' to illustrate how cultural webs or patterns recur, showing up in many different guises and contexts within an organisation. Four case illustrations demonstrate how hidden cultural understandings and orientations can lead to habituated and repetitive patterns of behaviour and sense making while, at the same time, they can constrain and can 'blind' members of a culture to alternative ways of seeing, thinking and acting. The cases vividly illustrate the risks associated with being trapped by barely visible cultural threads.

Given the pervasive and consequential nature of cultural webs to organisational life, especially an organisation's ability to change and re-invent itself, an awareness of cultural patterns is essential to both survival and success. Chapter 8 describes principles and methods for revealing cultural understanding.

Chapter 9 offers a pattern of connection, a metaphor that draws together the themes to be found in the stories, theories and commentary of the work. It develops the notion of culture as a web of signification, noting the similarities between spiders' webs and cultures.

The concluding chapter returns to the chief executive pondering the three envelopes. It summarises the implications of these ideas for senior leaders who are charged with the task of effecting some form of shift in the underlying beliefs and practices of their organisations, with 'changing the culture'. The chapter reprises the insights and practical pathways suggested by this fascinating way of viewing organisations.

References

Bateson, G. (1972). *Steps to an ecology of mind: Collected essays in anthropology, psychiatry, evolution, and epistemology*. Chicago, IL: University Of Chicago Press.

Capra, F. (1982). *The turning point. Science, society and the rising culture*. New York, NY: Simon and Schuster.

Geertz, C. (1973). *The interpretation of cultures: Selected essays*. New York, NY: Basic Books.

Korzybski, A. (1931). *A non-aristotelian system and its necessity for rigour in mathematics and physics*. Paper presented before the American Mathematical Society.

Maslow, A. (1943). A theory of human motivation. *Psychological Review, 50*(4), 370–396.

McLuhan, M. (1962). *The gutenberg galaxy: The making of typographic man*. Toronto, ON: University of Toronto Press.

Morgan, G. (1986). *Images of organization*. London: Sage Publications.

Peters, T. J., & Waterman, R. (1982). In Search of Excellence. Warner Books.

Senge, P. M. (1990). *The fifth discipline*. New York, NY: Doubleday.

Skolimowski, H. (1985). *The co-creative mind as a partner of the creative evolution*. Paper presented to the First International Conference on the Mind — Matter Interaction Universidada Estadual De Campinas — Campinas, SP. Brazil.

Smircich, L. (1983). Concepts of culture and organizational analysis. *Administrative Science Quarterly, 28*(3), 339–358.

Thomas, W. T., & Thomas, D. S. (1928). *The child in America: Behavior problems and programs*. New York, NY: Knopf, pp. 571–572.

Wheatley, M. J. (1992). Leadership and the new science: Discovering order in a chaotic world: Berrett-Koehler Publications, Inc., San Francisco, CA.

Chapter 2

Seeing with Our Minds

In Search of Meaning...

Mrs James pushed at the door with her shoulder and heaved a dustbin through the awkward opening. The staff behind reception looked on in astonishment as she proceeded to empty it over the well-polished floor, and recoiled from the putrid stench of rotting household waste. Climbing over this sprawling mound of empty cans, potato peelings, and used nappies, Mrs James approached the reception staff and delivered her well-rehearsed complaint. This was the third time this year that her refuse had not been collected. Yes, she had put it out in time for collection, she always paid her rates punctually and this was not what she considered to be an acceptable standard of service from the local authority. If the council was not going to collect it from her then in future she would continue to deliver it to them.

A member of staff who was stood behind the reception desk made an attempt to engage with Mrs James. Perhaps they could talk about her problem, would she mind stepping to one side into an interview room so that they could discuss things more privately while council staff began clearing up the mess? Mrs James was having none of it:

> 'I know what you're up to, you're trying to fob me off just like the rest of them. I'm not having this, I demand to see the Chief Executive, right now!'

The member of staff walked from behind the reception desk and said:

> 'My name is Roger Paine. I am the Chief Executive. I'm really sorry that you're unhappy with our service. Why don't we go to my office and discuss this some more over a cup of tea?'

There was a silence. Mrs James looked the chief executive up and down, half turned towards the pile of her rubbish, then, as if seeing him for the first time, drew her hand up to cover her open mouth and said:

> 'Oh! I'm terribly sorry — I thought that you were the person on the reception desk.'

'I am' replied Roger Paine, 'I take a turn on reception every Monday morning.'

Roger Paine was Chief Executive of the Wrekin District Council for several years, during which time this hitherto anonymous district council of approximately one thousand employees became renowned in local government circles for its standard of service and its dynamic, innovative culture. Roger's passion and driving commitment was to create an organisation culture that set new standards for service, and which actively sought to improve the quality of life for all residents within the District. Together with my friend and colleague Judi Marshall, I spent more than six months researching the culture of the Wrekin District Council on behalf of the Local Government Training Board (McLean & Marshall, 1989). Our job was to achieve an in-depth understanding of the Wrekin culture and to discover how this remarkable cultural transformation had been accomplished. During this time not only did I learn a great deal about the Wrekin culture but discovered its infectiousness, and found my attitude towards it changing from that of a cautious and sceptical academic to an admirer and advocate of the ideas and approaches used to achieve such a dramatic change.

Roger Paine's presence on the reception desk that Monday morning was not an accident. He spent 1−2 hours there *each week,* receiving visitors, answering queries, operating the telephone exchange, and giving advice and information on the council and its services. He saw this as a routine part of his role in the course of his tenure at the Wrekin and was one of the many ways in which he chose to signal the importance of an outward facing, service-oriented culture to his staff.

Roger's thinking and his behaviour were informed by a particular way of conceiving organisations. He thought of them as cultures and evolved an approach to the development and change of the organisation based on this construction. In this chapter I will be examining this popular metaphor for conceiving organisations and exploring the challenges and possibilities for leading and managing organisations that it offers.

Much has been written about this way of viewing organisations. In the early 1980s a publishing phenomenon emerged with the publication of *In Search of Excellence* (Peters & Waterman, 1982). This best seller shook up the world of business introducing what represented some radical and provocative ideas. The book challenged the orthodox view of organisations as rational settings in which the primary role of managers and leaders is to take decisions based on objective facts and logic. While some academics had been arguing this point for many years, Tom Peters and Robert Waterman brought the ideas out of the academic closet and in spectacular, almost evangelical fashion, presented a new challenge to all organisational leaders while simultaneously launching a new publishing genre, the business best seller. They described the attributes of so-called excellent organisations and argued that one of the defining characteristics of excellent organisations was their corporate cultures:

'Without exception, the dominance and coherence of culture proved to be an essential quality of the excellent companies. Moreover the stronger the culture and the more it was directed toward the market place, the less need was there for policy manuals, organization charts, or detailed procedures and rules.' (Peters & Waterman, 1982)

They saw the highest purpose of organisational leaders as shaping the culture of their organisations, creating the meaning that defines the companies' identity and purpose. Peters and Waterman's book was the herald of a new field of consulting practice and business publication that became referred to among some of my colleagues as 'the excellence industry'.

Simultaneously, academics and business schools began to explore the value of this way of thinking about organisations, spawning a generation of publications. References to corporate culture and cultural change became commonplace not just in business schools but also in boardrooms. Now we find that these terms are in popular, everyday use.

In this chapter I present my understanding of the term culture and consider some of the more significant implications of this way of looking at organisations. My argument will be an unashamedly personal one based on my experience of working with this metaphor for more than 30 years.

I begin by describing a consulting experience from early in my career that triggered my interest in this area before offering my understanding of the concept of culture, inspired and informed as it is by a particular approach to social anthropology known variously as semiotics or the interpretive paradigm. I will then dig deeper into the meaning of the term and begin the process of exploring the implications of these ideas and perspectives for the agendas of those of us whose concern is the management, leadership and development of organisations.

In the mid-1970s I was an eager novice learning about the practice of Organisation Development. I jumped at the chance to serve as apprentice on a major OD project in a shoe manufacturing company. As a consulting team we spent three years working in a non-directive, facilitative way looking to help the client company achieve its espoused desire to become more participative. I soon discovered that a number of managers in the company were uncomfortable with our non-expert stance, having expected that, as university staff, we would advise them on the most appropriate form of participation for their circumstance and Quaker traditions. We resolutely declined invitations to accept the mantle of expert, believing that the most appropriate form of participation needed to emerge through a process that helped members of the company to develop their own considered understanding of the term before deciding how to set about introducing it. We saw our job as facilitating their process based on the view that the process of arriving at recommendations for participation was best achieved in a participative way.

A kind of struggle unfolded in which a number of senior managers sought to prod us into taking an expert stance, telling them how to proceed. We were reluctant to do this partly because it did not fit with our view of our role but also because we increasingly suspected that their real agenda was to discredit any solutions we might devise. In plain language we felt as though they were trying to 'set us up'. This uneasy stalemate never fully resolved itself, and we experienced less and less progress. Eventually, frustrated by the apparent lack of commitment on the part of many in the client organisation, and with our own morale at a low point, we decided to collude with these attempts to cast us as experts and wrote a report setting out three options for them to consider. In part our intention in doing this was to test our hypothesis regarding their desire to cast us as experts. If this was a client-consultant game that was being played out then here would be valuable information for us on which to assess our continued involvement in this exercise.

In the event our fears were confirmed. At a number of open presentations of the options there was little discussion of the spirit of the options we presented. Instead, a small but vocal group of managers attacked the report for small points of detail, minor inconsistencies and typing errors. Dejected and dispirited we concluded that we had failed, and that the company hadn't been serious in its intent. We likened the company to a rice pudding and our own role to that of a finger. While it had been easy enough to introduce a finger into the pudding, and to moving it around, the skin of the pudding sealed over once it was removed, leaving no sign of our presence. We discovered later that within the company it was felt that we were 'punching sponges'. Both images suggested that our efforts were having no lasting effect, our energy was being accepted and absorbed but the system had a resilience enabling it to sustain its' form and identity in a way that negated our efforts.

This dispiriting confirmation effectively marked the end of our involvement with the company. I took a number of salutary lessons from this experience. I learned that organisations do not always operate on the basis of rationality and logic. Strong forces will look to sustain the status quo in spite of any espousals of a desire to change. At the time I was reading about the work of the Milan School of Psychotherapists (Palazzoli, Boscolo, Cecchin, & Prata, 1978) who described similar experiences with families in therapy. They made the point that social systems can be extremely resourceful in sustaining the status quo in spite of everyone's best efforts to change them even when some of their patterns are clearly destructive or damaging for individuals within the family system. Palazzoli's team argued that it is necessary to:

> '...regard the behaviour of an individual member of a system as an
> expression of a dynamic within the broader system and suggest that it
> is futile to try to change the dynamic by directing attention towards
> the individual in isolation. Instead we need to look at the rules that
> underpin the overt behaviour patterns and to direct our interventions
> there.' (Marshall & McLean, 1983)

Rather than attending to the conscious espousals or intent of organisation leaders I had learned directly that there were hidden forces, not immediately apparent to an observer, that powerfully influenced the dynamics and behaviour of individuals within an organisation and that these operate in essentially a conservative, system maintaining way. It was not long before I was using the term culture to describe these phenomena and inquiring into ways of harnessing them to a change effort instead of experiencing them as an impediment to change. My quest took me

on a journey through a number of different fields of literature, organisation development, systemic therapy, popular management writers, academic organisation theorists and into the realms of social anthropology. While I began this quest by
searching the literature for definitions of culture I was also looking for insights that
might provide some clue as to what forms of intervention might be possible for leaders and others with an interest in cultural change.

Early Excursions

The early literature on corporate culture emphasised the role of organisational
values, corporate image, identity and philosophy. This set off a frenzy of activity in
boardrooms (and Country House Hotels) that kept consultants profitably occupied
for many years. The products of their efforts were the identification of 'core values',
the articulation of company mission statements, codes of conduct, and the revision
of company logos and slogans designed to convey the appropriate corporate image
and culture. Companies that had been dogged by a history of poor industrial
relations ditched their old names and logos and employed graphic designers and
advertising experts to re-fashion their image. In England, for example, The British
Motor Company, a by-word for industrial relations turmoil, renamed itself Leyland
with a fresh logo to symbolise a break with the past (Pilkington, 1996). British
Airways similarly was the new name given to the amalgamated and privatised company formed by the merger of BOAC and BEA, notorious for their reputations as
inefficient, publicly owned companies (Campbell Smith, 1986).

These initiatives emphasised the value driven nature of excellent companies identified by Peters and Waterman and the importance of the outward symbols of corporate culture. The production of mission statements and codes of conduct were
considered to be important ways of affirming the identity, values and purpose of an
organisation. They were seen as providing clarity and direction for organisation
members and were intended as much for the consumption of organisation members'
as for their customers.

There was also much discussion about ways of controlling or managing cultures.
In 1982, for example, Siehl and Martin wrote:

> 'The next logical research issue would be the study of how culture can
> be controlled. Culture is a powerful phenomenon, which plays impor-
> tant functions in organisation life. Do managers want to allow such a
> phenomenon with far reaching effects to develop and change in an
> uncontrolled manner? One would think not.'

The zeal and profusion of these early initiatives resulted in some invaluable
learning.

It was clear that such exercises encouraged greater clarity and focus on an organisation's direction and challenged leaders to be clear about their ambitions, their

assumptions about the organisation's purpose and values. At the same time they exposed this thinking to wider scrutiny and debate. Not least of the benefits of such exercises was the clarity of official signals sent to employees concerning the identity, values and direction of an organisation be it a hospital, a school or an airline.

What also became clear however was that there was more to cultural change than the identification of core values and the production of mission statements, codes of conduct and fresh new logos. Inevitably, such products invited a comparison with the 'reality' of an organisation's culture as experienced by those 'in the thick' of organisational life, and often made for unflattering observations on how far the behaviour of senior managers matched the rhetoric of their statements. In my organisational work I encountered a wary scepticism on the part of organisation members towards such activities and in some cases unmitigated cynicism. Far from inspiring cultural change I came to wonder whether such exercises were ultimately counterproductive because of the way in which they drew attention to the discrepancies between the reality experienced by the majority and some idealised future as portrayed by senior management teams who were seen as disconnected from the experiences of their employees.

An additional concern was the way in which such activities, with their ultimate goal of capturing the agreement or shared understanding in the form of a written document, encouraged a view of corporate culture as a thing, or product to be managed, like cash flow, advertising expenditure or inventory levels; as an item for discussion on the board's agenda. In one case I discovered that the board felt that its contribution to cultural change had ceased once they had formulated their mission statement and disseminated it throughout the company.

There was more to this field of inquiry than was apparent from the practice and writing of popular writers on management. I found myself wanting a fuller understanding of the term culture than could be gleaned from the scraps of definitions to be found in popular books and articles, a selection of which are offered here:

> 'How things are done around here.' (Ouchi & Johnson, 1978)
> 'The social glue that holds the organisation together.' (Baker, 1980)
> 'Values and expectations that organisation members come to share.' (Van Maanen & Schein, 1979)
> 'The taken for granted and shared meanings that people assign to their surroundings.' (Wilkins, 1983)
> 'The ways of thinking, speaking and (inter) acting that characterise a certain group.' (Braten, 1983)

I found each of these useful and insightful in different ways, and it was apparent that they were helpful to managers, but I continued to feel that somehow, they were missing something more encompassing. Each of them spoke to an aspect of culture in a way that was valuable but collectively they lacked coherence, rather in the manner of apocryphal blind men describing an elephant. I was looking for something that went beyond what were effectively sound bites, something that helped me to engage with the phenomenon of culture in all of its complexity and wholeness, something that might suggest strategies through which, as a consultant, I might help clients for whom cultural change was an imperative not an option.

My search eventually led me to the field of social anthropology and to the work of Clifford Geertz. As an ethnographer Geertz's interest was in how the world is conceived and understood from 'the native's point of view' (Geertz, 1973), and with the study of the signs and symbols of a culture. He was especially concerned with how members of any given culture attribute meaning to their experiences and with the many different ways in which meaning is organised and conveyed. The title of his major work on these questions is *The Interpretation of Cultures* (Geertz, 1973). The notion of interpretation is key to understanding his approach. To understand a culture is to understand the interpretations that members of a culture place on their experience; it is to understand how they make sense of things. More than this it is to be interested in the interpretive schema, the systems of belief and explanation that underpin their interpretations. Another term for his orientation to the study of cultures is the term semiotics. Semiotics is the study of signs and symbols of a culture. I found it helpful to think of signs and symbols as vehicles through which meaning is conveyed from one member of a culture to another.

In the spirit of traditional anthropologists, Geertz argued that achieving an understanding of a culture called for deep familiarity based on living in or alongside a society or community. He used the term *immersion* to describe this aspect of the anthropologist's method and emphasised the importance of arriving at 'thick descriptions' of a culture through the use of qualitative methods.

Through a close consideration of Clifford Geertz's ideas, I discovered windows that opened up to reveal insights into the world of organisation culture in a way that met my desire for a holistic appreciation and provoked my thinking about the possibility of intervening into this complex territory. The remainder of this chapter and the next one are concerned with elaborating on Geertz's semiotic approach to understanding cultures. In the course of doing this, I interpret his ideas in the context of organisations and begin the journey of examining their implications for leaders and others interested in the question of cultural change. I have supplemented Geertz's thinking with ideas and commentary by other writers, mostly from the field of organisation studies.

I am tempted to apologise for the academic tone of this and considered advising those readers with an aversion to theory to skip to Chapter 4. However, in my view this topic has long suffered from a shortage of good theory and with a subject as elusive as organisational culture I would urge the reader to refrain from taking a short cut. I would commend Kurt Lewin's famous remark that there is nothing as practical as a theory.

I find it ironic that scholars with the most to offer those of us interested in the pragmatics and practicalities of organisational life often come from unlikely sources seemingly unrelated to the field of organisation studies. I consider Clifford Geertz to be such an individual. The quality of his exposition of cultural understanding in so-called primitive cultures has enormous value for those willing to consider organisations as cultural phenomena. My guess is that no one would have been more surprised to learn this than Professor Geertz himself.[1]

I must sound a final word of caution before beginning this exploration. There is a risk of forgetting that this work is itself a construction. It is one of many ways of mapping a field of scholarship that is concerned with understanding the nature of organisations and processes of change in them. This map, like all other maps, is a representation. It is not the territory.

At the heart of Geertz' view of culture is the question of meaning and interpretation. His primary concern is with how we make sense of the world, with how we invest our experience with meaning and how these meanings are expressed, sustained and transferred from one generation to another. He suggests that our understanding of the world and our experiences are based on the conceptual maps we inherit and absorb as members of a community. He argues that the way in which we attribute meaning to events and objects is influenced by the cultures we belong to and the understandings we inherit as part of the natural process of socialisation. The following quotation from his work is perhaps the clearest encapsulation of this thinking and one of my favourite quotes:

> 'Culture denotes an *historically transmitted pattern of meanings embodied in symbols,*[2] a system of inherited conceptions expressed in symbolic form by means of which men communicate, perpetuate, and develop their knowledge about and attitudes towards life.' (Geertz, 1973)

Let us examine these ideas more closely.

Meaning is Neither Universal Nor Fixed

According to Clifford Geertz the achievement of shared meaning is a social accomplishment. This is most easily demonstrated by a simple, everyday example.

In his book on gestures, Desmond Morris (1979) illustrates the variety of interpretations given to commonplace gestures such as the Thumbs Up, the Nose Tap or the Fingers Cross. The meaning of the Fingers Cross gesture, for example, is not universal; it varies between cultures. Whereas in the United Kingdom, it is seen as an expression of hope or good luck, Morris's research discovered that in Corfu and Turkey, for example, the same gesture signifies a couple. Less common interpretations of the same gesture hold that it refers to friendship and copulation. Morris's work shows the different meanings of many other commonplace gestures depending on the culture in which they are used.

---

[1]Sadly, Clifford Geertz died in 2006.
[2]Italicised emphasis added.

The different interpretations of everyday objects and gestures is further illustrated by the following, somewhat alarming story.

Consider the notice below; it was prominently displayed at a railway crossing in the north of England.

'DANGER

THIS IS AN UN-MANNED LEVEL CROSSING.

DO NOT USE WHILE RED LIGHTS ARE FLASHING.'

Tragically, a young farm worker was killed in a collision with a train when attempting to drive a tractor across just such a crossing. Accident investigators confirmed that the signalling equipment was working satisfactorily and were completely puzzled as to why the driver had crossed at precisely the wrong time. The cause of the accident, they discovered after some time, was not mechanical but semantic. In certain parts of northern England the term 'while' holds a specific, local, meaning.

In these areas the meaning of the word 'while' is 'until'. 'I'll wait while 5:00 o'clock', means I will wait for you *until* 5:00 o'clock. To him the sign might just have easily read:

'DO NOT CROSS THIS UNMANNED LEVEL CROSSING
UNTIL RED LIGHTS ARE FLASHING.'

Eye witnesses confirmed that the tractor driver had sat, waiting at the crossing until the red lights had begun to flash. His *interpretation* of the word 'while' was of real and tragic consequence. And this was an interpretation that he had known since birth and took for granted. He absorbed its meaning through its mundane, everyday use in conversation by friends and family.

According to Geertz, culture mediates meaning. The meaning of a gesture depends on the culture in which it is set. Fingers crossed will convey a different meaning in Turkey than it will in Greece just as the term 'while' has a particular meaning in parts of Yorkshire and Lancashire that differentiates it from other regions of the United Kingdom.

To be interested in a culture is to discover the local meanings held by words, gestures and other forms of communication. It is also to be interested in how such taken for granted meaning and understandings arise.

Meaning is not universal but local, and varies from group to group, from community to community and from society to society. Just like the tractor driver, we rely on inherited meanings to make sense of our experience. When understandings or interpretations of common symbols differ, then coordinated social action becomes problematic. This simple observation helps to explain the havoc and confusion that arises when two companies merge. Two communities with different, yet taken for granted sets of understanding, can be a potent recipe for misunderstanding and conflict.

As this story illustrates not only do our interpretations differ but they also matter. We act on the basis of our interpretations, or according to the famous dictum of W. I. Thomas (Thomas & Thomas, 1928):

'If men define situations as real they are real in their consequences.'

This idea suggests that far from experiencing reality, interacting with it as if it were quite independent of us, our experience is, in part, the consequence of how we perceive reality through the inherited conceptions of our culture. We rely on socially learned interpretations to make sense of our environment and our interpretations inform our actions. Our actions in turn have consequences for our experience as was so sadly evident in the case of the tractor driver. The reality of his tragic death was undeniable, but a different reality might have unfolded had he held a different interpretation of the word 'while'. This interplay between our socially inherited definitions, (or constructs) and our experience of 'reality' lies at the heart of Thomas's dictum and is of enormous consequence in organisation settings. We saw this in the very different scenarios that unfolded in the course of the organisation simulation described in the preface.

The Washington Post conducted an experiment in a sub-way station that starkly demonstrates how the way we define a situation can vary depending on circumstances and with very different consequences for our behaviour:

A man stood in the entrance plaza of a Washington, DC metro station and played a violin in the manner of buskers the world over. It was a cold January morning and more than a thousand people passed though the station, most of them on their daily commute to work. It was three minutes before anyone noticed him playing. A minute later, without breaking stride, a woman threw a dollar into the open violin case and continued on her journey.

After nearly three quarters of an hour a total of six people had stopped and listened to the violinist and there was $32 in the violin case. When he stopped playing at the end of an hour it went unnoticed. He quietly packed away his violin and left the station as anonymously as he had arrived. Only a handful of people stopped to listen him for any length of time, one of them had attended a free concert that he had given three weeks earlier and another had abandoned his aspiration to be a concert violinist at the age of 18.

The account of this experiment observes:

'...the fiddler standing against a bare wall outside the Metro in an indoor arcade at the top of the escalators was one of the finest classical musicians in the world, playing some of the most elegant music ever written on one of the most valuable violins ever made.' (Weingarten, 2007)

Joshua Bell was playing a Stradivarius worth $3.5 million and had just completed a series of concerts where tickets averaged $100.00 each.

This is a true story. Joshua Bell playing incognito in the metro station was organised by the Washington Post as part of a social experiment about perception, taste and people's priorities.

As organisational anthropologists we are interested in how people define situations. In particular we are interested in the dominant terms, phrases and language that are used within a community to explain and make sense of the complexity and uncertainties of organisations in their environments. For those of us used to thinking about the world in terms of discovering its underlying laws and truths, this way of thinking represents something of a challenge. This is where the quiet revolution described in Chapter 1 becomes apparent. This way of understanding turns on its head long-held views about the nature of reality and the search for universal truth.

According to two biologists, Maturana and Varela (1980), the view of perception as a process of recording or capturing something that occurs 'out there in reality' is an expression of a Cartesian view of the world, a view that separates subjects and objects and that assumes a single, enduring and fixed reality to be understood. They radically suggest that what we 'perceive' is the result of our internalised perceptual frames and proclivities that we project onto our experience and thereby 'organise' into something that comes to have meaning for us and which we take to be reality. Similar ideas were expressed by Anthropologist Edward Hall (1959) who talks of culture as a 'set of patterns' that 'channel the senses and thoughts of man'.

Henryk Skolimowski (1985) offers a vivid example of how perceptual habits and patterns are learned. He cites a story about Ludwig Fleck, a Polish microbiologist who was interested in understanding the development of what he terms the 'scientific mind'.

> Fleck noticed that when beginning students are given microscopic sections to observe, at first they are unable to do so. They cannot see what is there. How can it be so? The answer is simple—because all perception, particularly sophisticated forms of perception require rigorous training and development. After a while all students begin to see (under the microscope) what is there to be seen: specific forms and configurations *according to the patterns established by microbiology*.[3] Students' perceptions have been sharpened and focussed to perceive according to the rules of one specialised discipline, which means to say that their minds were sharpened to recognise and identify the phenomena which are important for their discipline.
>
> ... microbiological observations require a trained perception, a form of mind which is well acquainted with the universe of bacteria and other microbes. This form of mind is inherently connected with the forms of observation specific to microbiology. At one point it makes sense to say that it is the mind that perceives, not the eye. *The mind provides the framework, specific knowledge and specific assumptions for the eye to see.* The mind constitutes the universe which the eye then sees. Put otherwise: our mind is built into our eyes. (Skolimowski, 1985)

---

[3]Emphasis added.

Anthropologists would add that this is a cultural process. That these ways of perceiving microbiological phenomena are transferred from one generation of scholars to the next, from teachers to students and among colleagues through conferences, learned papers and informal exchanges. In these ways, 'the formation of a framework that is comprised of specific knowledge and assumptions', a professional culture has become established and is sustained.

Flecks' observations about microbiology are also relevant in the context of organisations. In a study of hospital administrators Meyer (1981) found that patterns or habits of perception, those things that people paid attention to and took to be important, were not fixed but varied between different hospitals.

> '...some administrators who value stability ... ignore their hospital's environment and those administrators who value change attend carefully to environments.' (Meyer, 1981)

To understand a culture is to be interested in where people place their attention. It is to uncover the frameworks of knowledge and assumptions that shape the constructs informing their interpretations of what they perceive. This entails attending to the events, activities and developments that routinely represent the focus of their attention and to the dominant constructions they invoke in arriving at an understanding. It is to be interested in how they make sense of the 'blooming, buzzing confusion' (James, 1890) of organisation life and of the events occurring in their environments. It is to attend to what draws the focus of their attention and what they hold to be significant.

Cultures as Webs of Signification

Clifford Geertz suggests that these learned ways of seeing, these inherited conceptions, can be thought of as a conceptual web:

> 'Man is an animal suspended in webs of signification he himself has spun. I take culture to be those webs, and the analysis of it to be therefore not an experimental science in search of law but an interpretive one in search of meaning.' (Geertz, 1973)

Through the phrase 'webs of signification' Geertz is suggesting that, as members of social groups, communities and societies we acquire a complex interconnected conceptual fabric through which we interpret and give meaning to our experience. This is a fabric formed and affirmed over generations through everyday interactions and exchanges and is characterised by an unquestioned and taken for granted sense of normality.

This idea is at the heart of the analysis in this book. Without realising it, through countless, indirect means, we inherit ways of thinking about and making sense of our experiences. By absorbing others' descriptions and ways of making sense of things we gradually acquire an accumulated conceptual vocabulary. We inherit these conceptions from our families, our friends, our teachers, colleagues and professional associations. Like Fleck's microbiologists, we learn to see the world in particular ways and become accomplished in making fine distinctions that others would miss. We learn to see with our minds. We absorb the conventions and values that are shared by these communities and in turn affirm them through our own actions and utterances. In this way we not only participate in a culture but also contribute to its perpetuation as others learn from us. Over time these cultural webs of signification acquire a distinctive and robust pattern.

There are striking similarities between the properties of spiders' webs and the phenomenon of culture. Webs are hard to see, they are durable and resilient. Their elaborate patterns enable rapid passage for those familiar with the network of preformed pathways. They entrap the unwary, entangle strangers who blunder into them and disable adventurers who would ignore them. If ruptured or torn they are quickly repaired. The richness of this imagery has inspired and informed my consulting work over three decades. In later chapters I consider a number of case examples from a wide range of organisations to examine and illustrate each of these and other qualities of cultural webs.

In this sense the notion of culture takes us beyond the realm of semantics and into the much more complex area of epistemology, the guiding beliefs and assumptions that underpin our cognitive processes, the grammar and rules of grammar that allow us to understand and explain the complexity and interconnectedness of phenomena.

Like a spider's web we can think of culture as a connected set of hidden pathways that guide our perceptions, shape our thinking and suggest pathways for behaviour. To understand a culture is to appreciate the complex, interwoven webs of signification that underpin everyday actions, that frame the way people interpret events and that guide their thinking.

In the same way that a spider's web has a distinctive pattern so too a culture can be understood as a paradigm, an all-encompassing framework for perceiving and understanding through which we encounter and engage with the world.

If we examine the concept of paradigm we can see how it closely resembles the idea of culture. This comparison holds important implications when it comes to questions of cultural change and particularly attempts to manage a change of culture.

Thomas Kuhn (1962) argued that each scientific era is characterised by an accepted set of assumptions that act as foundation stones, or tenets, and upon which experimentation and deduction are based. Collectively these tenets constitute an overall framework or superstructure of ideas within which inquiry and experimentation are conducted. They represent an:

> '... entire constellation of beliefs, values, techniques and so on of a shared community.' (Kuhn, 1962)

Kuhn used the term paradigm to describe this constellation of beliefs. The beliefs acquire the character of absolute truths, and are regarded as fixed and immutable.

Such cognitive superstructures enable the pursuit of scientific activity requiring scientists to conduct their work using accepted protocols and justifying their findings by reference to the tenets or basic beliefs and in accordance with the methodological orthodoxy that it demands.

Kuhn noted that, from time to time, crises occur as anomalous findings arise that cannot be explained within the assumptions of the dominant paradigm. Various forms of denial or discrediting of the findings can safeguard the integrity of the overall paradigm until the accumulation of anomalous evidence becomes overwhelming and the balance of support within the scientific community shifts to embrace not only the new evidence but also the revision of fundamental assumptions it demands. The effect is often a radical reconceptualisation of the problems and possibilities of the field and can lead to a burst of fresh creativity and activity.

The notion of paradigm points to the pervasive nature of a belief system. All phenomena can be explained and understood in terms of the philosophical and intellectual framework that it represents. More mundanely it resembles the robustness and unshakeable belief systems of members of a cult whereby all things can be explained according to their interpretative schema, be it based on an interpretation of religious texts or the teachings of a charismatic founder.

If we take these observations on the characteristics of paradigms and transpose them into the context of organisation cultures they reveal an important concern.

Let us consider for a moment an organisation that is faced with the need for radical change. A semiotic view of culture suggests that how members of a culture conceive of the need for change as well as the strategies identified for achieving it are in themselves framed by their culture. Our efforts to change things are informed by our worldview and dominant constructs. This means that the kind of solutions and initiatives we might create or select to make a difference are in themselves, expressions of the same thinking, the same worldview. This includes how we define the problem, who is held responsible for 'solving' the problem of cultural change, the processes adopted, the measures and metrics used for evaluating any initiative are all informed and framed by the same underlying assumptions and world view, the same paradigm. In Chapter 5 we look at four case examples of how hidden cultural patterns have led to 'more of the same solutions' that inadvertently reinforced and perpetuated an unhelpful cultural dynamic.

This analysis highlights the following dilemma for those looking to effect a change of culture:

'How can we, as members of a culture, make a difference from within? Is this at all possible? Or to put in a different way: can we step outside the boundaries of our thinking, and if so, how?'

In later chapters we see how different organisations have dealt with these challenging questions.

We now turn to consider another of Geertz's observations: cultures serve as a form of vacuum filler:

> 'We live ... in an "information gap". Between what our body tells us
> and what we have to know in order to function, there is a vacuum we

must fill ourselves and we must fill it with information (or misinformation) provided by our culture.' (Geertz, 1973)

This is an important feature of cultures: they help us to deal with uncertainty and ambiguity. In particular they help us to resolve the uncertainty and anxiety that arises when we encounter unfamiliar and equivocal experiences. Geertz likens these experiences to a kind of cognitive vacuum.

The story in the preface describing the very different scenarios that unfolded when two groups engaged with the simulation exercise of producing greetings cards illustrates this perfectly. Both groups, undergraduate students and senior executives, were faced with the identical challenge and the same level of ambiguity. Their contrasting responses to the simulation's challenges of organising, managing and leading a company in a competitive business environment were shaped and informed by their respective cultural heritages. The executives brought familiar hierarchical, and engineering thinking to the ambiguous task while rebellious, anarchic and egalitarian principles underpinned the students' response. Both groups' responded to the ambiguous challenges of the simulation in ways that expressed their habitual, taken for granted ways of thinking and being in the world. While their set task was clear — to maximise profits and to ensure employee satisfaction — the manner in which they accomplished this, how they organised themselves, was uncertain and could be considered as a kind of social vacuum. Both groups were required to make sense of the brief and to interpret the unfolding events and developments as the simulation unfolded. Each group brought familiar, habituated and unquestioned ways of interpreting the situation to resolve the vacuum of uncertainty.

Let us set these ideas into the context of everyday organisational life. We begin with an example of the pervasive resilience and hold that these inherited conceptions, these cultural webs, can exert over an entire organisation.

During the 1980s fierce competition between airlines led to attempts by major airlines to win business on the basis of the quality of their service and customer care. In British Airways, the legacy of the Second World War had lingered and insinuated itself into the organisation culture (Bruce, 1987). The heroes were the pilots who brought their aircraft back safely. A good day at the airline was concluded when the Operations Manager could look along the apron of the terminal and see the aircraft tails lined up in tidy formation. Much attention and interest was placed on the performance and capability of new aircraft. Their purchase and introduction into service always sent a ripple of excitement through the company. Internal and external communications extolled the virtues of any new aircraft, its speed, range, capacity, the modernity of its engines and other technological innovations.

These were the *inherited conceptions* within the airline that were passed on from generation to generation. Newcomers would quickly tune into these preoccupations and attitudes.

Driven by a combination of factors, including worsening losses and a poor public image, the new management of British Airways undertook an initiative to change this culture. A key part of the effort was to change the way in which staff thought about the airline. The hope was to get staff to think of the company as being in the business of service. Instead of being preoccupied with the qualities and capabilities of their aircraft and of elevating the status of their pilots, the intention was to place the customer's total journey experience at the heart of the culture. The idea was to encourage them to *think differently* about their company and the business it was in; to encourage them think of it in terms of a positive, seamless experience for their customers.

In cultural terms this represented an attempt to change long-held habits and patterns of perception by staff, to direct their attention to a different and hitherto disregarded area of the field, and to elevate its importance over matters that were formerly regarded as sacrosanct. It represented nothing less than a shift of paradigm in people's thinking. Staff were not just being asked to give attention to the needs and comfort of their passengers, but to think about their activities *in a fundamentally different way*. The shift that the senior managers were striving for was a shift away from thinking about the airline in terms of products and events such as a flight, a new aircraft, or even a new route, what Sir Colin Marshall describes as a 'commodity mindset'. Instead their efforts were designed to encourage them to think of it as a process, a continuous, seamless process.

> 'There are different ways to think about how to compete in a mass market service business such as ours. One is to think that a business is merely performing a function, in our case transporting people from point A to point B on time and at the lowest possible price. That's the commodity mind set, thinking of an airline as the bus of the skies.
>
> Another way to compete is to go beyond the function and compete on the basis of providing an experience. In our case, we want to make the process of flying from point A to point B as effortless and pleasant as possible. Anyone can fly airplanes, but few organisations can excel in serving people. Because its a competence that's hard to build its also hard for competitors to copy.' (Prokesh, 1995)

Let us note that Sir Colin Marshall's intent was to get staff to 'think about how to compete in a mass market service' in a 'different' way. His efforts were intended to change peoples' deep-seated conceptions about their fundamental purpose as a business. It is also instructive to note that he refers to his company as a 'mass market service business' in this context.

British Airways undertook a wide range of initiatives to achieve this change of culture, including major programmes of staff training, restructuring the company, the adoption of new livery and logos, and a fresh approach to publicity. In particular I would like to highlight three subtle ways in which they sought to get staff to think differently about their business, to relinquish what Marshall calls product or commodity thinking and to adopt instead a process-based view. Two of them involved their chief executive and the third was an advertisement.

As chief executive of British Airways Sir Colin Marshall invested a large amount of his time in leading, supporting and encouraging the cultural change. It clearly represented a high priority to him. In the same way as Roger Paine, he drew on his power as a conspicuous cultural symbol to influence how people thought about the company, their 'inherited conceptions', and through his own actions sought to encourage them to adopt new thinking. He used this power shrewdly, effectively, and as far as I can tell, responsibly. Many stories and accounts of the British Airways experience circulated in the training and development community and many of them are about his role and involvement.[4]

For example, he made a point of attending as many of the training events as possible and listened closely to the views of participants. His presence at these events sent a strong signal to staff that the initiative mattered to him. Attendees at these events reported how he took notes on specific actions he could take to support ideas for enhanced service. They also pointed out that he could be relied on to follow up on his promises. In following through on those conversations he signalled his personal commitment to the changes and embodied the idea of service that he was looking to encourage. This won him respect and demonstrated that he was really serious about the changes. This aspect of his behaviour became part of the new folklore of British Airways, and was the topic of many stories told in the pub and the staff restaurant. Through these conversations and exchanges Colin Marshall and his team were gradually weaving a new web of meaning with staff.

Announcements of new aircraft acquired by the airline continued the tradition of describing their technical improvements and enhanced performance capabilities, but, significantly, they also emphasised how these new features would enable the company to *provide an even better quality of service* to their customers, thereby coupling the old pride and passion with the new service priorities.

In his seasonal message to staff one Christmas Sir Colin's message did not end with the traditional wishes for a Merry Christmas and Happy New Year but also looked forward to the continued provision of excellent service in the coming year. I discovered in conversation with one of his advisers that the significance of this additional part of the message lay *not so much in its content as in its form*. There is a sense of completion and closure to the traditional Christmas message. It is the celebration of an event close to the year's end and a time of relaxation for most. Sir Colin's remarks, in their anticipation of the coming year, were intended to impart a sense of a continuous flow of time in a way analogous to the unceasing nature of service provision: to convey the sense of a never-ending process. Rather than thinking of the holiday as a bounded event that reached a conclusion, he was seeking, in subtle and albeit subliminal ways, to encourage the adoption of a mindset that sees events in the context of a continuous flow of experience.

The third example concerns an advertisement for British Airways that was broadcast repeatedly during this period of cultural change and is of particular interest when seen in the context of a desire to foster a different mindset among staff within the airline. Set at night, the advert featured the brightly lit science-fiction style image of the city of Manhattan, passing over the rooftops of British houses with the voice

---

[4]See, for example, Salama (1995), Carleton and Lineberry (2004).

of an air-traffic controller giving approach instructions to it, as if it were an airliner on final approach. As 'astounded' onlookers gaze skywards at this apparition a voice-over informs the viewer:

> 'Every year British Airways fly more people to more countries than any other airline ... in fact every year we bring more people across the Atlantic than the entire population of Manhattan.' (Saatchi & Saatchi, 1983)

What I take to be significant in this advert is the emphasis it places on the transportation of people, the absence of any reference to aircraft, either visually or verbally, and the imaginative way in which the volume of passengers carried is represented. It is hard not to be impressed by the sheer scale of the airlines' activity. While the ostensible intention of advertising is to influence the behaviour of targeted markets, it is tempting to surmise that, in this case, the airline's staff were an equally important audience for the message.

Through the use of these means, the behaviour of the CEO, the form of his speeches, and the images within advertising campaigns, British Airways sought to create a new frame of meaning, to weave a new 'web of signification', among BA staff. Needless to say these examples are a few of the many initiatives undertaken by the airline, a tiny sample of the many threads that formed their new cultural web.

We now turn our focus to consider another important aspect of understanding a culture: the role of symbols:

> 'Culture denotes an historically transmitted pattern of meanings embodied in symbols, a system of inherited conceptions expressed in symbolic form by means of which men communicate, perpetuate, and develop their knowledge about and attitudes towards life.' (Geertz, 1973)

Behaviour Is Symbolic ... Symbols Carry Meaning

Many things have symbolic significance in organisations. Meaning is made of all kinds of unremarkable aspects of organisational life: appointments, departures, promotions, job titles, space, office furnishing and much more.

The behaviour of senior members of an organisation, for example, sends signals about what is held to be important and influences the process of meaning making in the broader organisation. This, of course, is not necessarily news. Many popular nostrums allude to this: 'Walking the talk', the importance of 'role modelling', and 'being the change we want to see in the world', are all phrases that have become commonplace in recent years. The broader point here is that all of these leadership gestures hold symbolic significance. They carry meaning and send messages. They are noticed and draw comment.

As an illustration of this, I recently heard of an IT employee who keeps a record of every time one of the management team visits his building. He works in a newly rented set of offices about a mile away from the head office and adjacent to two buildings that house other 'overspill' projects. So far he has nine entries for the Marketing Director and no entries for the MD or any of the rest of the senior team. This is over a period of six months. The scrutiny afforded to these visits, and perhaps more significantly the lack of them, clearly signals to the inhabitants of this outpost their importance in the eyes of the most senior executives. The absence of visits by the CEO is seen as an indication of the indifference of senior management toward them as a unit.

Both the keeping of the record and the decision to make its existence known to the management team, can be seen as important, if worrying, statements to senior management.

The behaviour of managers, especially senior managers, must be considered as culturally symbolic. It carries meaning, draws scrutiny and provokes comment.

While much emphasis is placed on the importance of language as a medium for conveying meaning and shaping how we interpret the world, anthropologists stress that understanding a culture is achieved by paying close attention to the patterns of people's behaviour. Geertz is firm in the view that to understand a culture we need to pay careful attention to peoples' acts. Ultimately, he argues, it is through behaviour that cultural statements are made, relationships expressed and patterns enacted.

> 'Behaviour must be attended to and with some exactness, because it is through the flow of behaviour, or more precisely, social action, that cultural forms find articulation.' (Geertz, 1973)

This view holds social action as the primary currency of cultures and one of the main tasks of the anthropologist is to:

> '...uncover the conceptual structures that inform our subjects' acts, the "said" of social discourse.' (Geertz, 1973)

In other words, it is through close attention to people's behaviour that we can hope to understand their values, beliefs and assumptions and gain some clues as to their conceptual structures, to their web of signification. Behaviour is expressive, it carries messages often deeply embedded and encoded. As a more immediate and primary form of communication the cultural significance of social acts can be subtle, yet precisely because of this subtlety they can infiltrate and shape the conceptual structures of a culture in potent ways.

Organisation Structures as Symbols...

In addition to their primary role of defining the formal pattern of relationships, organisation structures, sometimes termed organograms, also convey important messages about values, priorities and relationships. As part of his effort to orient his staffs' attention to the concept of service to the community, Roger Paine reviewed the structure of the Wrekin District Council. He realised that out of the nine departments he inherited when he was appointed chief executive, only four were concerned with the direct provision of service to the community. The others either provided support services to the other departments, such as accounts, training or IT, or were concerned with agencies outside of the District. In a subsequent restructuring Roger reduced the number of departments to five, of which four were concerned with the direct provision of services to the community. He took the view that the structure of an organisation does more than arrange people into functional groupings, but that it also holds symbolic significance by expressing the priorities and preoccupations of the culture. In this sense the formal structure of an organisation provides a subtle, background frame that informs how people think and talk about their organisation. As such it contributes to the web of signification that defines the culture.

These two examples point to the important part played by symbols in conveying meaning and in shaping how people think about their organisational lives. The following chapter develops these ideas further and explores different forms of symbol and the extent to which they can be deliberately managed to achieve a desired shift of culture.

Words Make Worlds...

In addition to behaviour the communication of meaning and the transmission of inherited conceptions also occurs through the medium of language. Language is an integral part of the processes whereby members of a culture:

> '...communicate, perpetuate and develop their knowledge about and attitudes towards life.' (Geertz, 1973)

The language we use to describe the world is of consequence, 'Words create worlds' suggest Frank Barrett and Ron Fry (Barrett & Fry, 2005).

Cultural and semiotic studies encourage us to pay careful attention to the language and terms in popular usage. They offer a clue as to the preoccupations and priorities that infiltrate people's thinking and pervade conversations. The following story shows how certain terms and constructs acquire a prominence in the everyday exchanges and conversations in a way that illuminates the preoccupations and dominant mindset of its members.

> A colleague and I were invited as cultural observers to a staff development conference in a large London law practice. We were puzzled by frequent references to "Fiona". Her name cropped up in many of the seminars and discussions. It was only towards the end of the day that the identity of this seemingly popular and ubiquitous person emerged. It turned out that what we had heard as Fiona was in fact

"Fee-earner". The frequent references to fee-earners, was an obvious indication of the commercial imperatives dominating peoples' attention in this company. It also signalled a fundamental status differentiation within the firm. As a fee earner you were a member of a prestigious group that also carried the onerous responsibility for generating the income that everyone relied on. If you were part of the group of non fee earners, it was clear that you were a member of a lesser class, and that your presence was in the service of those superior beings who generated income.

Margaret Thatcher's reform of public services in the United Kingdom sought to introduce a business culture, referred to as an 'internal market', reasoning that there were swathes of waste and inefficiency that would be eradicated by the adoption of more commercial disciplines and practices. Among the many reforms one of the most striking was in the use of language and terminology. Doctors' surgeries and medical practices for example were encouraged to become 'fund holders', with responsibility for the management of their budgets. Participation in this vast enterprise became differentiated according to which side of a fundamental divide you sat, whether you were a 'purchaser' or a 'provider' (Prowle & Harradine, 2013). I vividly recall a conversation with a nurse who was complaining loud and long that she would never refer to patients as 'clients'. There is an interesting if somewhat ironic twist to this discussion. Whereas Sir Colin Marshall, operating in the highly competitive and commercial arena of air travel, was seeking to encourage a shift of mindset away from product based thinking and towards concepts of process and service, Mrs Thatcher, in encouraging the adoption of more business like efficient practices in the public or service sector, was introducing the language of the market place and manufacturing into the service sector. In so doing she was looking to re-configure a long-held view of the provision of health care. Through the imposition of a new vocabulary she was attempting to weave a new web of meaning.

Prowle and Haradine (2013) comment on this change of language:

> 'We now take for granted that there is a "chief executive" or "manager" accountable for the finances and delivery of public services and that that person will be accountable to a board. Prior to Thatcher we had "administrators", "treasurers" and "consensus" management.' (Prowle & Harradine, 2013)

The fallout from the financial crisis in 2008 has provoked a lively conversation as well as some disturbing revelations regarding the ethics of investment, banking and High Finance. Some of these revelations have offered glimpses into the cultures of high-pressure finance houses. The following is an insider's observation on one such setting. It is from an article in the *New York Times*:

> 'Over the last 12 months I have seen five different managing directors refer to their own clients as "muppets".' (Smith, 2012)

We explore the question of language more fully in Chapter 4 and in particular the relationship between language and leadership in the context of cultural change. For now we note the extraordinary and pervasive role that is played by language in contributing to the actions and interpretations of members of a culture. Language reflects our preoccupations, shapes our actions and is key to the formulation of a shared worldview. The question this raises of course is how far the adoption of different language can be promoted or encouraged as part of an effort to fashion a desired culture? We explore these questions in Chapters 4–6 and 9.

Nearly 40 years ago Ed Hall offered the following observation on cultures:

> 'Culture hides much more than it reveals and strangely enough what it hides, it hides most effectively from its own participants. Years of study have convinced me that the real job is not to understand foreign culture but to understand our own.' (Hall, 1966)

Much cultural 'knowledge' can be considered as unconscious, taken for granted or tacit, (Polanyi, 1966) that is, knowledge that we don't realise we are invoking in a situation but which nevertheless informs our behaviour. We often become aware of such tacit or hidden knowledge when we find ourselves in situations where others do not share the same assumptions, when we have the experience of being strangers in a 'foreign' culture.

I will be surprised if the following illustration doesn't echo the experiences of many.

> In the early 1970s I travelled to Canada from my home in England to visit my sister who was living in Toronto. It was a memorable trip not least because of the cultural richness and variety of this vibrant city. It was my first visit to North America and I was wide eyed with curiosity. I can still remember my astonishment at the size of the "gas guzzling" cars parked in the Airport multi-story parking lot. My friend and I chuckled at the unfamiliar signs on the highway into the city: "Squeeze Left" one commanded and another declared: "Dead End". Intrigued by the sign advising "Right Lane Must Exit", we discovered a driving convention that was new to us. Whereas in the UK once you have joined a Motorway you can, more or less, stay in the same lane as long as you wish, in North America you are forced to change lanes to avoid being diverted off the highway and into an exit lane. This struck us as an apt comparison of the two cultures. In the one it required you to proactively work at achieving a goal or destination, while in the other it was much more possible to settle into a comfortable track and coast along at your own pace until arrival at a destination.

> In the course of the trip we were generously loaned a car for our own use and were free to find our own way. The experience was perplexing and stressful, but above all it was informative. I was driving. Stopping

at the first cross roads (or intersection) for a red light I soon found myself the subject of angry glares from passing pedestrians and realised that the sounding horns from other motorists were also directed at me. Drivers were gesturing and shouting at me but I was perplexed as to why. When, finally, the lights turned green and I was able to drive off I pulled over at the first opportunity and realised that I was gripping the steering wheel like a novice on a first driving lesson. My Canadian passenger explained that I had overshot the stop line by some distance which not only meant that I had stopped across the pathway where pedestrians cross but that I had also intruded into the flow of traffic passing through the other light. At first I was at a loss, since I was an experienced driver in the UK and had never experienced this kind of difficulty before. On reflection I realised why there had been such a commotion.

In North American cities traffic lights are commonly suspended on wires high above an intersection, an unfamiliar location for Brits. The general scale of these junctions is altogether larger than those in the UK but, more significantly, the distance between the stop line and the light is almost twice as great in North America as it is in the UK. I realised that, in my general confusion and disorientation, I had stopped at the same distance from the Stoplight, as I would normally do in the UK. Awareness of this gap was something that I had not, consciously considered until this moment. It was a form of tacit knowledge, something I "knew" but hadn't ever consciously thought about. I had learnt about it through lifelong familiarity, having experienced it thousands of times. To my knowledge no one had ever commented on it. In a culture with different conventions it took this faux pas to make me realise that I was operating out of a cultural awareness and knowledge that I didn't realise I had.'

This story illustrates how an activity as commonplace as driving a car is underpinned by a fabric of assumptions and understandings that, for most of us, require little if any conscious thought in order to perform satisfactorily. While we may be able to articulate some of them if asked, there are likely to be others, such as our understanding of spatial relations, that we are unaware of having learned. This is a reality defined through peoples' actions, through our everyday behaviours and is afforded added significance by endless repetition. While trying to navigate the busy Toronto traffic I didn't realise that I was also navigating the much trickier territory of cultural assumptions and tacitly understood conventions.

There is much about the understandings, patterns and routines of organisational life that necessarily remain in the shadows of our consciousness. The tacit understandings, the short-hand conversations, the processes and procedures that have acquired a fixity and familiarity through countless iterations, all contribute to the smooth running and routine of organisational life. They provide the comfort of familiarity and the reassurance of predictability. In this sense they represent a form of 'social glue that holds the organisation together' (Baker, 1980).

However, once we seek to lead, change or develop an organisation we have to consider the fact that the routines and patterns of activity, the mindsets and perceptual habits are, for the most part, beyond conscious awareness. Much of the knowledge, understandings and conventions regarded as normal by members of an organisation will have the same quality of taken for granted familiarity as an experienced driver travelling a very familiar route. This points to a key challenge in working with organisation culture: how to reveal these hidden assumptions and taken for granted interpretations, how to bring them into conscious awareness and how to take them into account when seeking to effect change. Without such an understanding we are at serious risk of being imprisoned by them, by 'structures we have not learned how to see' (Senge, 1990). In Chapter 8, I discuss methods for bringing this hidden understanding into conscious awareness.

Before we continue with this exploration of the phenomenon of culture it might be helpful to pause and summarise some of the main features of culture that we have considered in this chapter.

- Cultures are concerned with meaning, with how we interpret the confusion and complexity of the world we inhabit. But meaning is not fixed or universal, it varies from culture to culture and is something that is socially formed over time.
- Cultures operate so as to guide and shape our thinking and behaviour. They act as hidden forces that guide where we look, how we look, and what we make of that which we attend to. They are the 'webs of meaning' that provide a framework of specific knowledge and assumptions that guide how we interpret our experience and the choices informing our actions. They serve to resolve ambiguity and uncertainty and help us to make sense of complex situations and ambiguous information.
- While language is a medium through which cultural assumptions and understandings are expressed, behaviour is considered to be a more immediate and reliable indicator of cultural understandings and assumptions.
- A key challenge in all of this for leaders and managers of organisations is to become aware of the part they play in creating meaning and in how they direct the attention of their followers — through what they draw attention to by their own preoccupations and priorities. Leaders typically underestimate the extent to which their actions and statements come under intense scrutiny, draw interpretations, provoke storytelling and speculation as to their significance. Much significance is placed on how closely their actions align with their statements. Leaders are more than role models, they are cultural provocateurs, drawing intense scrutiny and sparking continuous meaning making.
- The challenge of influencing a culture is made all the more difficult since cultural knowledge is, for the most part, tacit, taken for granted and beyond the realms of our conscious awareness. We are dealing here with hidden, yet very potent pathways of understanding.

In the next chapter, we build on these ideas, and particularly examine the way in which meaning is conveyed through the medium of symbols. We distinguish between different types of symbol and the implications of these differences for those looking to influence the development of a culture.

References

Baker, E. (1980). Managing organizational culture. *McKinsey Quarterly* (Autumn), 51−61.

Barrett, F., & Fry, R. (2005). *Appreciative inquiry: A positive approach to cooperative capacity.* Chagrin Falls, OH: Taos Institute Publications.

Braten, S. (1983). Hvor gar grensen for bedriftslocale kulturer? In: M. Hoel & B. Hvinden (Eds), *Kollectivteori og Socoilogi.* Oslo: Gyldendal.

Bruce, M. (1987). Managing people first — bringing the service concept to british airways. *Industrial and Commercial Training, 19*(2), 21−26.

Campbell-Smith, D. (1986). *The british airways story: Struggle for take-off.* London: Hodder and Stoughton.

Carleton, J. R., & Lineberry, C. (2004). *Achieving post-merger success: A stakeholder's guide to cultural due diligence, assessment, and integration.* Chichester: John Wiley.

Geertz, C. (1973). *The interpretation of cultures: Selected essays.* New York, NY: Basic Books.

Gene Weingarten. (2007). *Pearls Before Breakfast.* Washington Post, April 8.

Hall, E. (1959). *The silent language.* New York, NY: Random House.

Hall, E. (1966). *The hidden dimension.* New York, NY: Doubleday.

James, W. (1890). *The principles of psychology.* Classics in the history of psychology, an internet resource developed by Christopher D. Green of York University, Toronto, Ontario.

Kuhn, T. S. (1962). *The structure of scientific revolutions.* Chicago, IL: University of Chicago Press.

Marshall J., & McLean, A. (1983). *Intervening in cultures.* Working Paper: Centre for the Study of Orgaizational Change and Development, University of Bath.

Maturana, H., & Varela, F. (1980). Autopoeisis and cognition: The realization of the living. In R. S. Cohen & M. Wartofsky (Eds.), *Boston studies in the philosophy of science 42.* Dordecht: D. Reidel Publishing Co.

McLean, A. J., & Marshall, J. (1989). *The Wrekin District Council: A cultural portrait.* Local Government Training Board, Luton.

Meyer, A. (1981). How ideologies supplant formal structures and shape environments. *Journal of Management Studies, 19,* 45−61.

Morris, D. (1979) (with Collett, P., Marsh, P. and O'Shaugnessy, M.). Gestures: Their origins and distribution. London: Johnathon Cape.

Ouchi, W. G., & Johnson, J. B. (1978). Types of organizational control and their relationship to emotional well-being. *Administrative Science Quarterly, 23,* 292−317.

Palazzoli, M. S., Boscolo, L., Cecchin, G., & Prata, G. (1978). *Paradox and counterparadox: A new model in the therapy of the family in schizophrenic transaction.* Jason Aronson.

Peters, T. J., & Waterman, R. (1982). *In search of excellence.* New York, NY: Warner Books.

Pilkington, A. (1996). *Transforming Rover, renewal against the odds, 1981−1994.* Bristol: Bristol Academic Press.

Polanyi, M. (1966). *The tacit dimension.* Chicago, IL: University of Chicago Press.

Prokesh, E. (1995). *Competing on customer service: An interview with British Airway's Sir Colin Marshall.* HBR. 1st November 1995.

Prowle, M., & Harradine, D. (2013). *The thatcher legacy: The long shadow over public sector reform.* PS Public Service.co.uk

Saatchi and Saatchi. (1983). '*Manhatten*'. Writer: Dempsey, R., Art Director: Mason P. Director: Loncraine, R. Production Company: James Garrett and Partners. Retrieved from http://www.campaignlive.co.uk/thework/905614/

Salama, A. (1995). *The culture change process: British Airways case study*, Cranfield School of Management.

Senge, P. M. (1990). *The fifth discipline.* New York, NY: Doubleday.

Siehl, C., & Martin, J. (1982). *Learning organizational culture.* Research paper 654, Graduate School of Business, Stanford University.

Skolimowski, H. (1985). *The co-creative mind as a partner of the creative evolution.* Paper presented to the First International Conference on the Mind — Matter Interaction Universidada Estadual De Campinas — Campinas, SP. Brazil

Smith, G. (2012). Why I am leaving goldman sachs. Op-ed in *New York Times*, March 14th 2012.

Thomas, W. I., & Thomas, D. S. (1928). The child in America: Behavior problems and programs. New York: Knopf. In R. S. Cohen & M. Wartofsky (Eds.), *Boston studies in the philosophy of science 42.* Dordecht: D. Reidel Publishing Co.

Van Maanen, J., & Schein, E. H. (1979). Toward of theory of organizational socialization. *Research in Organizational Behavior*, *1*, 209−264.

Weingarten, G. (2007). Pearls before breakfast. *Washington Post*, April 8.

Wilkins, A. L. (1983). *Organizational stories as symbols which control the organization.* In: L. R. Pondy, P. Frost, G. Morgan & T. Dandridge (Eds.), *Organizational symbolism.* Greenwich, Ct JAI.

Chapter 3

Symbols and Culture: Terms, Tales and Totems

Plate 1: The Knotted Gun. Exhibit outside the United Nations Building,
New York.Created by Carl Fredrik Reuterswärd.

In Chapter 2 we touched on the role of symbols in the process of meaning making. In this section I would like to look more closely at the significance of symbols in the context of the development, perpetuation and transformation of organisational cultures. Based on this examination I suggest a distinction that has practical implications for organisational leaders, managers and others interested in change processes.

We begin by revisiting the quotation already featured in the previous chapter. This time our emphasis falls on a different part of that quotation:

> 'Culture…denotes an historically transmitted pattern of meanings *embodied in symbols*, a system of inherited conceptions *expressed in symbolic forms* by means of which men communicate, perpetuate and develop their knowledge about and attitudes towards life.' (Geertz, 1973)

Symbols play a crucial role in the formation and transmission of cultural meanings. They embody and express meaning and serve as vehicles that carry meaning. An understanding of symbols in organisational life is therefore an essential part of any understanding of culture and processes of cultural change. In order to explore this idea further let us reflect on the experiences of someone as they first visit, then join a new company, as if we are companions on their journey. As we accompany them let us pay special attention to the different symbolic ways in which they experience the culture of this new company.

Reflecting on the manner in which their understanding unfolds, we will then step back from the detail of their journey of acculturation to suggest a major distinction in the different forms of symbol through which meaning is conveyed in everyday organisational life. This distinction is then used to consider some of the choices and considerations facing managers, leaders and others interested in fostering desired aspects of cultural change.

For now, let us turn to our newcomer as they step into a new cultural setting.

First Impressions — The Public Face of the Culture

Before even applying for a position our candidate is likely to have been exposed to much information about his prospective new employer. Public coverage in the media, conversations with colleagues, publicity, news coverage and advertisements will already have shaped his image of the company. From these multiple sources he will have formed 'a feel' for its culture whether consciously or intuitively.

On his first appointment with the company our visitor will encounter many symbols and absorb much information and many impressions, he is bombarded with information and imagery. Without having to make a special effort he is most likely to be aware of the company name and its logo.[1] The reception area, whether plush or functional, cramped or palatial, will contain a number of symbols, perhaps photographs of employees or chairmen, examples of products manufactured or services provided, plaques indicating awards won. There may be a framed exhibit of the companies' mission statement. The quality of the furnishings in the reception area may be extravagant and opulent, deep leather settees and marble floors. He may sit in hushed silence or noisy busyness. Alternatively he may find himself waiting in a drab room with only industrial posters for company. The setting may feel cramped and busy or expansive and exuding a sense of calmness. The receptionist, if there is one, may be wearing a uniform or may be hidden behind a sliding glass partition. He may be asked for some formal identification.

---

[1]Often clues to cultural phenomena are to be found in unlikely ways. On one occasion I had much difficulty locating the headquarters of a company that was part of a group of businesses. The only outside indication of the companies' identity was a modest brass plaque at its unremarkable entrance. In contrast to other companies in the group there were no billboard signs advertising the name either on the roof for all to see, or even at the street entrance to the building. In the course of my work with this company I came to discover that they saw themselves as occupying a lowly position in the pecking order within the group. Theirs was a business that made its income through countless modest transactions and which, accordingly, had to be very mindful of their profit margins. These factors combined to make for a low profile, 'keep your head down and work hard' culture. The almost unobtrusive signage was an expression of this corporate modesty and lack of commercial confidence.

Quite probably he will be required to fill out a security pass and to be scanned by surveillance cameras, unable to enter the rest of the facility without a swipe card or an escort. The reception area is likely to contain glossy, business magazines and brochures featuring the different products and companies within a corporate group. He may be handed information, such as safety codes, or required to wear some kind of protective clothing. I am sure that all readers will have their own vivid experiences of such settings and the myriad of symbols that characterise them. It can be an illuminating exercise to systematically attend to these symbols while waiting for an appointment. This profusion of symbols creates an impression to a newcomer or outsider. They carry messages and offer clues to the culture. Some, but not all, of these messages are deliberately and carefully fashioned, such as furniture and décor, signage and corporate symbols of success such as awards, photos and product samples. Much care and effort can be invested into the type of impression offered by such an environment:

> 'We are a hi-tech leading-edge company of the 21st Century'
> 'This is a caring, friendly and open organisation that welcomes visitors and is here to serve the community.'

In other settings the symbols convey a different message:

> 'This is a low-cost, no frills, functional organisation that offers exceptional value for money.'
> 'We are a rich, powerful, global conglomerate, comprising many subsidiaries.'

Our visitor absorbs this rush of information as a blur of half formed impressions. His attention is likely to be focussed on his anticipated meeting and his own feelings about the appointment (Table 1, see page 44).

Second Impressions — Encountering the Informal Face of the Culture

Once through reception, our visitor enters the world of daily organisational life and encounters the everyday environment of employees. Here the symbols are often more subtle and their significance less easy to discern. The quality of the furnishings, floor coverings, the layout of offices, cleanliness, wall hangings, signs on doors, notices, spaces, catering facilities and lighting levels all offer pointers about the culture. The quality of furnishings, lighting and space varies from one building to another. In some parts the toilet facilities feel plush and palatial while in others sections they are much more utilitarian. He notices how people dress and how much emphasis they place on personal appearance.

Our visitor may discern a pattern in how offices and office space are allocated. Who occupies the top floor? Who is located in the basement or ground floors? Who has office space and who doesn't? How do ceiling heights differ? How much space

Table 1: Fabric, furnishings and space as symbol.

Symbols can be subtle too
While some symbols are bold and carefully fashioned others are subtle and can convey cultural messages in unexpected ways. On a recent visit to see a client, I was 'processed' by a phalanx of security staff at the entrance to their 'campus' style facility. Once badged, photographed and otherwise verified as a bone fide visitor, I was handed a map of the campus and waved away in the general direction of the building where I had my appointment. Such was the scale of this facility that it took me 10 minutes driving and much trial and error before I successfully located the car park of the designated building.
With a mixture of relief and mild anxiety I approached the reception area of this multi-storied building. The impressive reception desk was completely deserted. It was clear that there was no receptionist at all. A small notice instructed me to use a telephone to call my contact and announce my arrival. I received a recorded message that they were not at their desk and was invited to leave a message. Feeling perplexed, disoriented and stressed, I intercepted the first person that passed through the area. They patiently explained the office location code that had been written on my security pass and gave helpful directions for finding the office of my contact. I found this a novel and unnerving experience, and later, wondered what it was saying about the values, priorities and mindset of this organisation's culture as well as my own expectations. At first I was tempted to judge it harshly as an expression of indifference and as a lack of courtesy towards visitors. On reflection, I began to wonder whether it might instead be an expression of an assumption that employees and visitors are intelligent, resourceful individuals capable of self-direction and problem solving. My impression was of a 'make your own way' culture. As a hi-tech research facility, packed with highly qualified personnel, it seemed reasonable to expect people to be autonomous and to act intelligently and resourcefully.

or privacy is there between workstations? Our newcomer may notice signs restricting access to certain grades or security clearance levels (See table 2 on page 45).

It is through such a myriad of subtle signals that expressions of power, privilege and status are to be found.

It is easy to read significance into such symbols. As outsiders or strangers it is tempting to make hasty or premature interpretations of such phenomena. Students of culture warn against drawing such conclusions too soon cautioning instead a need to resist early interpretation in favour of discovering how cultural 'insiders' vest such symbols with meaning. The meaning of cultural symbols can only be understood from the viewpoint of how they are interpreted by members of a culture, and this is notoriously difficult for a naïve outsider to appreciate.

Such symbols embody cultural phenomena and shape them at the same time. In attending to these symbols a semiotic perspective is concerned with what is being said through them, and what they reveal (See table 3 on page 45).

Table 2: Forms, furnishings and fabrics convey cultural messages.

In the offices of a Magistrates Court in London, a colleague and I were struck by how indications of seniority and status were evident in the building layout and in the range of furnishings and fabrics. Senior clerks occupied private, spacious offices with deep piled carpeting and comfortable furniture. Most enjoyed impressive views of the London landscape from their windows. In sharp contrast their assistants, the junior clerks and administrative appointments, occupied a confined, windowless office in the basement. The low ceiling added to the impression of cramped overcrowding, as did the rows and rows of files that lined the walls. Desks were crammed full with files and people seemed to be 'camping out' wherever they could find the room. The stark contrasts between these physical settings carried unmistakeable messages about professional status and hinted at the daunting barriers to professional mobility that characterise this profession. More subtly, they also carried echoes of class differentiation that still persist in the United Kingdom.

Table 3: High-profile symbols can misfire.

A recently appointed CEO of a global manufacturing company relocated his offices from the eighth floor of the corporate HQ to the ground floor. No expense was spared in the construction of thick glass walls. His intention was to signal transparency, to suggest his accessibility to staff and to show that he operated in the busy heart of the company, not sealed away in a remote executive suite. The intention of his gesture was only half the story. It's broader meaning lay in how others interpreted it. Staff reacted with suspicion, interpreting it as an expensive and unwelcome intrusion into the shared, public space. We cannot be sure what meaning others will make of a gesture. Regardless of its intent, the significance of a gesture will ultimately be decided by the 'audience' it is aimed at. Social meaning is elusive and attempts to control it can be fraught with difficulty.

Early Socialisation

Once appointed, our newcomer gradually becomes aware of other, more subtle symbols in the form of corporate artefacts and induction rituals. He is provided with additional literature by HR setting out the terms and conditions of his employment contract and may also be offered other literature packs and guides, safety codes and so on. He is invited to attend an induction programme where different representatives of the company set out further details of company policy and practices. In addition to exposure to senior members of the organisation and representatives of different functions he meets other newcomers and compares notes, information and impressions. Among other things they note for example which departments and individuals were not represented during the induction presentations. Course participants spend much time sharing their experiences of previous employment and drawing comparisons with their new company, commenting on differences and surprises.

As they relax with each other they begin to joke around, making fun of some of the jargon and shorthand terms used. They hang out together in the canteen and at a formal dinner at the end of the programme. This group is an important means by which our newcomer makes sense of his experience and his understanding of his new company. He finds himself talking about the day with his wife in the evenings and is surprised by how tired he feels at the end of the first week. All the time he is processing a mass of information both formal and informal and at times he feels overwhelmed by it all.

Our newcomer is gradually absorbing an understanding of the company culture. Events such as the induction training are carefully designed to impart the companies' way of doing things, to socialise the newcomer into the culture. Early impressions can have a powerful effect on peoples' perceptions of an organisation, and on their behaviour. These experiences offer more clues as to the formally stated priorities and preoccupations within the company. They are the outward face of the company culture — a representation of an ideal and an idealised culture. In some cases they are closer to being an aspiration for a desired culture. In other cases they closely mirror how things are done on a day-to-day basis.

Secondary Socialisation — Getting into the Swim

Once the formal induction process is more or less completed, our newcomer enters a different phase of acquaintance with the culture and with a different genre of symbols. Suddenly he finds himself in the full flow of daily activity, and like any newcomer, looking to 'read between the lines', he spends time trying to figure out 'how things are done here' when things 'get real'. He discovers how far the previous descriptions of the culture match his direct experience of it. He has become, in effect, a cultural 'fish' and has to learn to swim in this new 'cultural water'. Lessons from his previous companies count for little, and he cannot rely on transferring knowledge and assumptions into the new setting. It can be a disorienting and disheartening period of time. He is a novice, reduced to the status of newcomer and is forced to relearn things that he thought he knew. His professional or technical expertise that he took to be the reason for his recruitment may be downplayed or discounted altogether, as he adapts to what he perceives as the new conventions and defers to the appropriate 'authorities'.

He likens himself to a foreigner learning to speak a new language, and feels out of his depth in discussions, thrown by the profusion of shorthand terms and acronyms.

He feels unusually tired and spends weekends sleeping and catching up on work.

In this state of disorientation he casts around for clues as to how to conduct himself. He finds himself paying special attention to what his boss says, how she says it, what she does, what she pays close attention to and what she ignores. He discovers what he can expect in terms of her availability, and how much guidance and support she is prepared to give. He learns who can be trusted and who cannot. After a period of trial and error, he finds colleagues who will 'show him the ropes' and who are prepared to divulge some of the more carefully guarded company folklore. He begins to reassess his initial impressions of people, particularly senior players. He is given advice on who to 'cultivate', who he must not alienate and who he can safely ignore.

Our newcomer hears stories of previous employees, legendary leaders and tales of triumph as well as disaster. He finds out who is loyal to whom and how to 'deal with' different departments.

Deep Familiarity — Things Get Real

As time progresses he begins to realise that there are patterns to events and he spots recurring themes. He notices perks going to some people and not to others. He discovers what is highly coveted among his colleagues, and he gradually figures out the subtle ways in which certain behaviours are sanctioned and others rewarded. He notices small ways in which status is signalled; he realises that some workspaces are coveted more than others and that the allocation of workspace is a subtle form of map indicating status and influence. He notices who people approach and who they avoid.

He comes to feel a part of the new company, gradually growing in confidence. He has picked up on the 'unwritten rules' that govern the priorities and preoccupations of his colleagues and his boss. He notices that he is more relaxed.

In a compelling account in the *New York Times* Greg Smith (2012) described why he had chosen to resign from a leading investment bank. In part his decision was because of cultural expectations. In his view the route to becoming a leader in the bank required him and his peers to observe three cultural rules:

> 'Execute on the firm's "axes."'

This means persuading clients to invest in stocks that were considered unlikely 'as having a lot of potential profit'.

> 'Hunt Elephants'.

Which he translates as getting clients to trade in 'whatever will bring the biggest profit' to the company.

And thirdly get yourself into a position where you can:

> '... trade any illiquid, opaque product with a three-letter acronym.'
> (Smith, 2012)

From time to time our newcomer screws up, saying the wrong thing, taking the wrong turn to speak, omitting to consult with the 'right people' and feels embarrassed when he gets the dress code wrong. He learns when 'wives welcome' is a polite gesture and when it is de-rigueur.

At training events and company conferences he is exposed to the 'latest thinking' in his field and is addressed by seniors from across the company. Their presentations and humorous asides expose him to a broader awareness of company strategy and future thinking. Awards are presented and he joins in the indiscreet behaviour at the evening's partying.

When a crisis suddenly hits the company he sees a new side to people that he thought he had figured out. Decisions are taken behind closed doors and he finds it difficult to reconcile the draconian measures taken with earlier statements of company values and codes of conduct. Colleagues observe that 'the rulebook has been thrown out of the window'. He sees the reactions of colleagues to the uncertainty and joins in the spontaneous, conspiratorial conversations and email trails that assess the implications and significance of the new situation. People leave. As the dust settles he realises that he is seeing things in a new, more circumspect, way.

Visitors and clients offer passing observations about the company that strike him as shrewd insights and serve to remind him of how much he has stopped noticing the culture himself.

Our subject realises that he has become acculturated, and this is brought home to him when he has a reunion with colleagues from his former company. It is with an ironic smile that he looks back on his previous company and realises how much he had been a 'company man' there.

Through these experiences, and countless other ways, he learns about the informal culture, the lived culture of daily life. He also shifts from being a newcomer who is preoccupied with reading the culture to a participant in the culture, joining in the sense making conversations but also noticing how he is demonstrating cultural norms through his own behaviour.

This is obviously a stylised account, and as such will have many detailed points of difference from individuals' experiences. However, I would suggest that there is much about the various stages of this fictitious account that will have a ring of familiarity to them for many. Figure 1 summarises the different phases of his engagement with the culture. In a way it represents his journey of transformation into becoming an organisational 'fish'.

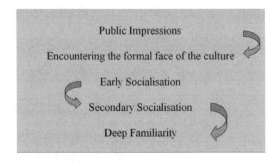

Figure 1:   Phases of acculturation.

High and Low-Profile Symbols (Marshall & McLean, 1985)

I would offer a number of observations on this process of cultural familiarisation. As we proceed through the different phases illustrated here we can discern a shift in emphasis from what we term high-profile symbols to low-profile symbols and from passively reading a culture to becoming an increasingly active participant in it. These distinctions are of real consequence when considering organisations as cultures. They are of particular relevance when it comes to a discussion of cultural change and the role of leaders in that process. It is to a fuller consideration of this distinction and its implications that we now turn.

High-Profile Symbols

These are highly visible phenomena that are readily available for manipulation and stage management and, as such, are subject to careful scrutiny and crafting. Thus, such things as speeches by the CEO or chairman, corporate ceremonies, the publication and dissemination of company value statements, corporate publicity, the choice of logos and the display of mission statements, together with visible artefacts such as can be witnessed in the public spaces of organisational settings — all these might be considered as high-profile symbols. The content, design and delivery of recruitment, induction and training programmes and their associated materials are further vehicles for conveying the high-profile symbols of an organisations' culture.

High-profile symbols are conspicuous phenomena that lend themselves to careful fashioning and polished rehearsal in order to achieve a desired impression. Consider for example formal speeches by politicians. Not only is every word painstakingly crafted, worked and reworked for maximum effect, but an equal amount of time is spent choosing the setting and arranging the background so as to convey an image of a wise and popular person who enjoys the broad support of whichever community is intended as the target audience. Politicians and senior executives commonly employ professional speechwriters and PR experts who not only craft carefully worded speeches but who also coach them in their delivery. On occasion such senior personnel are rehearsed in the use of appropriate hand gestures, and through the judicious use of pauses for dramatic effect. Careful attention is paid to the 'staging' of such set piece speeches. Politicians especially pay careful attention to arranging the location and to selecting the background 'cast', those people who stand or sit behind the speaker and who, by implication, endorse her message. Similarly the timing of such set piece speeches can also carry meaning. The controversy surrounding the timing and location of Fox News presenter Glenn Beck's Washington DC rally to coincide with Martin Luther King Day is an example of this.

Through these carefully choreographed events and highly polished speeches considerable effort is made to craft a desired image, to achieve a desired effect, to send the 'right' message. The importance afforded to the careful fashioning of these messages and symbols has been reinforced by the rise to prominence of branding specialists. These professionals are charged with achieving a coordinated and consistent impression across a range of public images and offerings ranging from product advertisements, to corporate logos and promotional materials. All this is in the service of conveying a desired and consistent image of the company in the eyes of the outside world and, let us remember, those of company members.

Low-Profile Symbols

Anthropologists agree that in order to understand a culture it is necessary to pay careful and sustained attention to the mundane, spontaneous, and unrehearsed gestures of everyday life. They suggest that if we really want to learn about a culture we need to look at the routine protocols, banalities and ordinary exchanges that give texture to what we consider to be life as normal.

They warn against placing too much emphasis on what Stephen Barley (1983) refers to as '*overtly symbolic phenomena*'.

Barley cautions us against being seduced by the exotic and dramatic aspects of a culture:

> 'Clearly logos, stories, colourful terms and arcane rituals are symbolic in nature and it is reasonable to identify and study them.' (Barley, 1983)

However, he issues a memorably colourful warning that is of profound significance to those of us interested in this subject:

> 'From the semiotic perspective ... terms, tales and totems are but lit candles hovering above both the icing and cake of culture.' (Barley, 1983)

Barley urges a shift of attention away from the 'overtly symbolic' and suggests that attention should instead be directed towards:

> '... how members of an organisation or occupation interpret a wide range of phenomena including chairs, air and sunlight — entities so mundane as to appear irrelevant to the well intentioned but culturally ignorant researcher.'[2] (Barley, 1983)

---

[2]Researchers attend to different symbolic forms. For some culture is evident in the *rituals and ceremonies* of organisational life (Deal & Kennedy, 1982). Others are interested in the way in which *the stories* that circulate in all organisations are symbolic, carrying important cultural messages (Martin, 1983; Wilkins, 1983; Mitroff & Kilman, 1976). Yet others have chosen to concentrate on *language* as key symbols for study (Andrews & Hirsch, 1983). Pettigrew (1979) examined *organisational dramas* as highlighting cultural phenomena in his study of a school.

Table 4: Greasy fingerprints.

> On a recent tour of an engineering company that had introduced a Lean Manufacturing approach a colleague observed that metric charts tracking quality information had greasy fingerprints on them, quite a contrast to the pristine conditions that we had found on a previous visit to a high-tech electronics, company. Our hostess was delighted — to her the prints indicated that the charts were in active use by the engineers whose hands inevitably were dirtied in the course of manufacturing the casts that provided the housing for their product.

There are two key ideas here: firstly an injunction to recognise the symbolic significance of the mundane and seemingly insignificant phenomena of organisation life. Secondly we need to attend to how members *interpret* such phenomena. Barley is alerting us to the importance of what we describe as the *low-profile symbols* of organisational culture. His encouragement to attend to how phenomena are interpreted also calls for an understanding of the *interpretive frameworks* that are invoked whenever people make sense of an experience, an utterance or a situation. Low-profile symbols might be thought of as vehicles through which meaning is conveyed, but the meaning that is placed on them is decided through reference to this interpretive framework, or to use Geertz' phrase, web of signification.

This is what we mean by Low-profile symbols. They are the seemingly irrelevant and mundane everyday phenomena that form part of a pervasive context of organisational life. A context so familiar as to be taken for granted and considered normal. Low-profile symbols are like water to a fish. They are both unremarkable and familiar and yet they subtly and insidiously infiltrate our thinking and shape our behaviour (Table 4).[3]

Low-profile symbols are expressed through spontaneous, unrehearsed behaviour when time is short and when there is no obvious concern for an audience. The way in which a member of the public is greeted and received in the reception of the Wrekin District Council when the chief executive in *not* present is every bit as significant an expression of the Wrekin culture as when Roger Paine takes his turn at the desk. It is through the ordinary, the routine, unrehearsed and apparently 'natural' actions and interchanges that cultures are expressed and affirmed.

We may profess, through high-profile symbols, to valuing staff and to achieving a work–life balance, but if a director mandates senior staff to cancel holiday leave this tells a different story, and it is a story that gains in significance as it is told and retold. It is in this way, through the informal sharing of stories, that cultural

---

[3]Pondy et al. suggest that 'unconscious modes of symbolism' represent one of the most challenging realms of study for organisational theorists. Smircich (1983) warns researchers of the 'exclusive reliance on verbal data', and of the risks of losing sight of the broader view or context within which the words of a speaker are interpreted.

understandings emerge and 'patterns of meaning' are transmitted. These patterns of meaning constitute the interpretive framework from which gestures and high-profile symbols are interpreted.

An interesting example of the difference between the two types of symbols is to be found in Paul Bate's excellent book (1994) in which he discusses the use of gifts as symbolic devices. He describes the way in which Jan Carlzon at the Scandinavian Airline SAS used gifts of gold watches to all of his staff as a device for expressing appreciation for their efforts in dramatically improving company performance. The symbolism of the watches was also intended to reinforce the key company value of punctuality. A letter accompanied the gifts from the company president written on 'quality parchment paper' together with an invitation to an all night celebration party.[4]

This positions culture as something within the direct control of leaders (albeit a popular and charismatic leader) and suggests that the careful manipulation of such symbols can foster a desired culture. It casts culture as a means of social control that was exercised through the careful manipulation of such symbols. Paul Bate offers an example of the use of gifts as symbols:

> 'As Carlzon himself says, there is no doubt that symbols are impor-
> tant — for controlling people as well as motivating them. This control
> is exercised by using symbolic devices, such as those described, to
> "trigger" positive emotions about the company and its leaders that
> make people feel submissive and compliant, willing to "go there and
> back" for the people and products they love.' (1994)

This emphasis here is on the conscious use of symbols to control and motivate people, to 'trigger' positive feelings towards the organisation and its leaders and to engender the submission and compliance of loyal employees. It illustrates the thoughtful use of high-profile symbols by a prominent and charismatic leader.

The emphasis of Bate's account is on the use of such symbols on the meaning *intended* by the sender. What is not considered however is the way in which such symbols are *interpreted*, the meaning that organisation members take from them or, more accurately, make with them. It would be helpful to know how well these high-profile symbols are complemented or reinforced by the low-profile symbols of Carlzon and his senior colleagues. To take the question of punctuality for example, the symbolic significance of the watch would be qualified by Carlzon's own habits of punctuality in meetings and appointments and his tolerance for the punctuality, or otherwise of others.

The capacity of Jan Carlzon to control people through the use of symbolic devices is mediated by the low-profile symbols of his own behaviour and by the

---

[4]In the wake of Peters and Waterman's book the use of small gifts (of which mugs, baseball caps, pens and T-shirts must rank as among the most common), exploded in popular use as symbolic icons of corporate culture.

interpretation placed on these high-profile gestures. The power of high-profile gestures is largely determined by the extent to which they are reinforced or qualified by their low-profile counterparts.

If, as Geertz asserts, culture is concerned with interpretations and meaning, then attempts by leaders to manipulate or manage meaning in such a deliberate and direct way can only give us half the picture. The gap between intention and interpretation can be a big one and it is one, I would suggest, that is filled by the existing culture.

Low-profile symbols reside in the subliminal realms of our awareness. We absorb this information experientially.

Dandridge (1979) for example refers to:

> 'informal rituals ... seating at lunch or coffee break, symbolic messages of relationships.'

Like osmosis, we soak them up without realising that we are doing so. Once absorbed they shape the background set of assumptions, expectations and orientations that inform our interpretation of events. They might be considered as resembling the scenery in a theatre. Geertz (1973), makes a similar point, referring to what he terms 'background information'.

> 'Most of what we need to comprehend a particular event, ritual, custom, idea or whatever, *is insinuated as background information*[*] before the thing itself is directly examined.' Geertz

There is a similarity here with the Gestalt distinction between 'figure' and 'ground'.[5] While it is tempting to be drawn to the exotic 'figures' of dramas, the grand gestures, myths, legends, stories, ceremonies and so on, anthropologists focus on the apparent banality of everyday, unrehearsed actions and exchanges. These constitute the 'ground', the backcloth or background set of assumptions that serve as an interpretive framework from which organisation members make sense of their experience and from which they make choices about action. This is what Geertz means when he describes cultures as: '...webs of signification man himself has spun'.

Anthropologists are far less interested in the high-profile symbols of a culture than their low-profile counterparts. It is the low-profile symbols that combine to create a contextual ground of meaning, or 'background information'. Clifford

---

[*]Emphasis added.

[5]'The field of a person's potential awareness at any moment is vast. What a person pays attention to is figural — it comes to the foreground as being most prominent, or has most attraction or urgency. The remainder of their awareness is the "ground" — the background or backcloth. Figure and ground exist together, though, and any figural thought or emotion needs to be viewed in relation to its ground.' (Tosey & Gregory, 2002).

Geertz (1973) suggests that anthropologists make broader interpretations about a culture only after 'exceedingly extended acquaintances with extremely small matters'. It is through the mundane, the seemingly insignificant gestures of organisational life that cultures take their form.

The emphasis afforded by anthropologists to the importance of spontaneous behaviour, the 'flow of behaviour', and the patterns of meaning that they express, contrasts with the interest shown in more stylised expressions of culture by much of the managerial literature on culture.

This is not to say that anthropologists discount the various artefacts, rites and ceremonies of a culture that we refer to as high-profile symbols. However it suggests that they need to be understood from the interpretive framework that is created through the medium of low-profile symbols.

This analysis of the high and low-profile symbols of organisation cultures carries with it some sobering implications for organisational leaders and those who purport to change or manage corporate cultures in some way. If we are interested in understanding and working with corporate cultures, we need to do so through a fuller appreciation of the role played by low-profile symbols in the formation and transmission of cultural knowledge.

While high-profile symbols have the merit and convenience of being within the immediate and tight control of the prominent and the powerful, they do not represent the means through which they can manage, direct, control or even change a culture.

Not only do those in elevated organisation positions not control the interpretation that will be placed on their actions or statements, they cannot control the interpretive frameworks used by organisation members to make meaning of them.

Linda Smircich (1983) makes the point:

> 'The achievement of shared meaning in many areas of organisational life may be problematic since organisational leaders have no monopoly on the development of meaning. All members engage in this process, shaping organisational life through the interpretation and meaning they attach to everyday experience.'

There are important aspects to the processes of understanding and sense making that are beyond the immediate control of organisation leaders. It is not possible to guarantee what meaning employees will take from a gesture such as the gift of a watch or the tolerance of smudged quality metrics. The processes of creating meaning through interpreting such symbols as the donation of a watch, the introduction of quality metrics, a note of thanks from the CEO, or an all night party in a hanger, occur between members of the organisation, as they interact in a myriad of settings. It is in the informal exchanges, the conversations over coffee or in the bar, during journeys or over the phone that reactions to such gestures emerge and agreements on what they 'really mean' begin to form. And this is a complex process influenced by many factors such as the reactions of opinion leaders, the history of such gestures in the past and the presence or absence of the so-called 'feel good factor'.

It is through such informal and spontaneous processes that the fabric of meaning is woven.

I have learned that however carefully a leader or management team might rehearse their behaviour leading up to a meeting with employees, the things that get noticed or talked about afterwards are often the brief asides delivered sotto voce, attempts at jokes that are misinterpreted, or unguarded expressions or mannerisms. These might, for want of a better term, be thought of as symbolic leakage. Consider the following example.

An MD and his team were looking to shape a vision for his manufacturing operation and with it a new approach embracing different values and different patterns of working. A series of workshops were held which had been designed to engage middle to senior staff in the process of developing the vision for the future business. A key part of these workshops was a session during which the MD and his team visited the event and, through a series of lightly structured but informal conversations, reflected on the current situation of the company and exchanged ideas and aspirations for the future of the business. The spirit of the event was informal and conversational but employees were markedly apprehensive at the prospect of such conversations and fearful of how the top managers would react to their honest but sometimes critically expressed views. In spite of these concerns the conversations quickly warmed up and turned into lively and highly engaged exchanges. As one of the co-facilitators I was delighted as the participants visibly relaxed and some important issues were openly debated. The conversations continued beyond the formal sessions as most people adjourned to the bar. When I retired to my room at midnight there were still many lively conversations happening in different clusters.

Next morning, to my dismay, the group was in a grim mood. What was up? Hadn't the previous evening been successful? Surely there had been some really good discussions and some excellent new ideas had emerged. Eventually, someone spoke: No I hadn't been mistaken, the evening had gone really well, much better than they had expected and yes, some excellent ideas had emerged from the conversations. '*So why the glum looks this morning, why the flat energy?*' I inquired.

> 'Well' someone ventured, 'Towards the end of the session, in the bar at about 1.30 am, just as he was about to leave, the MD was saying goodbye and how much he'd enjoyed the evening. He said how important these kind of get-togethers are and that the future success of the company is important to him because: "I am relying on you 'buggers' to pay for my retirement pension".'

This intended joke, a casual remark, had devastated the participants. It was the only thing they talked about and completely overshadowed the ideas that had emerged in the course of the evening. Worse still, after the emotional euphoria of discovering that it was possible to discuss serious matters openly with senior managers without dire consequences, participants felt a sense of betrayal by their MD who, they felt, was not committed to the company for the long term. In their view, he was asking them to give 110% effort, but his own eyes were firmly fixed on the day when he would be retiring from the company. Their emotional bubble had been burst.

In spite of the great lengths taken by the management team to create the right impression by their presence and by the quality of their participation, all of which might be considered as forms of symbol, the enduring interpretation of the event, and the stories that circulated among other staff afterwards, were exclusively about the MD's retirement remark and what it was considered to be saying about his level of commitment to the company.

Meaning, as we have already discussed, is socially constructed not unilaterally determined even in totalitarian regimes. While behaviour can be controlled by coercive methods and brutal enforcement, history teaches us again and again that, even under the harshest regimes, systems of belief and ideologies whether religious, political or artistic find ways of enduring.

Symbolic Alignment or Mixed Messages

It is in the gap between the high and low-profile symbols that the capacity for cynicism and disillusion lies. When the rhetoric of high-profile symbols does not match the 'reality' of peoples' everyday experience it is not long before a toxic, destructive discourse develops that can corrode goodwill and undermine commitment. A harsh, cynical discourse feeds on stories of incongruence, of mixed messages and of double standards. The credibility of senior management is an early casualty when this happens. Over the long term the cost is a loss of optimism and intangible but significant differences to feelings of pride, loyalty and willingness to put in extra effort. In the longer term this puts at risk the psychological contract between employee and the company, with the strong likelihood that any appeal to higher motives invoked through the lofty rhetoric characteristic of high-profile symbols is seen as 'empty rhetoric'. In different ways people revise their expectations downwards, and something important is lost. Newcomers encounter a climate of cynicism and weary resignation, sometimes even, repressed anger.

The Paradox of High and Low-Profile Symbols

The currency of high-profile symbols is weak. Words are cheap, as the saying goes, however well chosen and burnished. Ironically, it is in the low-profile symbols, the mundane, unrehearsed and seemingly inconspicuous acts that the genesis of cultural stories is to be found. This is particularly so when times are inauspicious, and other, more expedient, options beckon. When Sir Colin Marshall showed up at the many training events in British Airways his presence sent a strong signal of his commitment to the reforms that he was advocating. However, what really gave the whole initiative credibility and impetus were the stories, still circulating, of how he followed up on commitments made in the course of the workshops, well after the drama and hoopla of the training sessions had passed. Here was cast iron evidence that he was serious and that he saw himself as a player in making a difference along with everyone else. Roger Paine's presence on the front desk at the Wrekin drew sceptical comment at first, but his sustained presence there every Monday morning in the course of his tenure as chief executive convinced all but the most hardened sceptics that he was serious about standards of service. Ironically, this leadership symbol, clearly a high-profile gesture in the first instance, became a source of pride, and acquired a low-profile normality over time. This gesture increasingly earned the regard of employees:

> 'Of course our chief executive spends Monday mornings at the front
> desk — that's The Wrekin way!'

The paradox here then is that low-profile symbols are the Gold Standard of cultural currency. High-profile symbols are important as public commitments to standards and ambitions. They can do much to provide a sense of identity, purpose and standards of practice. The danger however is to overinvest their significance as cultural signposts or as the prime devices through which any form of cultural change is attempted. From a cultural perspective their significance derives more from their relationship to and congruence with low-profile symbols.

It is in the interweaving of high and low-profile symbols that cultures find form and pattern.

The Craft of Weaving

If we consider the process of weaving a fabric, we can see that the effect is achieved not just through the selection of a particular colour or quality of wool, nor just through the choice of design, the blending of colours or the incorporation of chosen imagery. The achievement of a dense, whole fabric arises through the activity, the process of weaving. This is hard, deliberate and patient work that calls for the full and active involvement of the weaver. And it is salutary to realise that the webs of meaning that we refer to as cultures are collective accomplishments, the achievement of multiple weavers over time.

The making of meaning is an active process in which all members of a culture participate. In this sense it is a form of weaving similar to the creation of the great, mediaeval, tapestries. Multiple weavers work simultaneously to give form to a gradually emerging pattern. The lesson for leaders is clear. It is not sufficient for them to rely on gestures alone. The meaning of a gesture will not make itself. It is not self-evident. Leaders who would seek to influence cultural webs must be prepared for sustained and active participation in multiple processes of meaning making. They need to be prepared to act as weavers of meaning; responding to others' interpretations, challenging and engaging in debate, participating in dialogue as well as looking to act as exemplars of their messages.

Amplification and Magnification — the Goldfish Bowl Effect

The statements and actions of leaders come under close and often intense scrutiny. Frequent reference is made to those in elevated positions of power as occupying a goldfish bowl. Their every gesture is magnified and scrutinised for the finest nuance. Subtle inflections or gestures form the subject of protracted speculation and extensive commentary. Politicians especially enjoy and endure this two-edged phenomenon and, reasonably enough, seek to exploit it to their advantage.

The following account offers a dramatic illustration of this phenomenon.[6] The circumstance was a virtual conference convened to invite discussion of the core values and behaviours to be adopted by a newly formed company. It was a merger between two substantial giants in the communications industry. The new company comprised approximately 60,000 employees and the virtual conference was an attempt to give everyone a voice in the discussions. It was spread over three days so as to allow for contributions from different time zones around the globe and to give time for the conversation threads to evolve and to reach some substantive conclusions. Figure 2 shows levels of participation in the course of the 72-hour event.

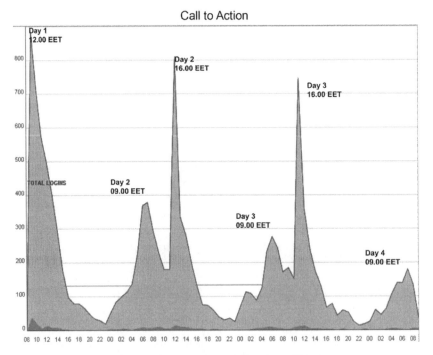

Figure 2:   Participation spikes following CEO comments.

---

[6]This case is described in detail in Chapter 6.

The most dramatic features of this picture are the three 'spikes' in participation. On each occasion they corresponded with a posting by the chief executive.

This is dramatic evidence of the interest shown in a leader's behaviour and thoughts. I would add that on this occasion this was a leader who was well regarded, and who enjoyed a broad level of confidence and the widespread support of his staff. It was evident in the discussions following his contributions that his comments configured the conversation for some time afterwards. This of course was a very high-profile form of contribution by the CEO but it offers dramatic evidence of the visibility of leaders. The gestures of leaders carry a substantially disproportionate weight. The sobering implication of this is that their low-profile gestures also draw a similar level of scrutiny. I very much doubt that the CEO had anticipated this level of interest in his comments, made while he was 'on the road' in a hotel room on an overseas visit.

While leaders are normally very willing to expound and endorse high-profile messaging and to benefit from the attention their participation commands, my experience is that they are less aware that their low-profile symbols, the more mundane aspects of their everyday actions and statements, also draw close scrutiny.

Conclusion

In this chapter I have suggested a number of key features associated with this way of understanding patterned behaviour in organisations.

We have noted that the making of meaning lies at the heart of an organisational culture and that this occurs in the interplay between the expression of official views and the informal processes of interpretation that occur spontaneously in all organisations.

Much cultural knowledge exists as background information, often out of conscious awareness. We absorb cultural knowledge without realising it. Cultural meanings are transmitted both directly (consciously and intentionally) but also indirectly (unconsciously and unintentionally) particularly through indirect, 'analogic' modes of communication.

Meaning making processes occur informally and beyond the direct control of any official leadership. All members of a culture participate in the processes by which meaning arises through social activities of storytelling, informal sense making and enacted patterns of behaviour.

Much of this meaning making is contested, speculative and unstable, iterating through conversation cycles, phone calls and email exchanges as we attempt to make sense of what is going on and seek to influence each others' understanding. It is in the interplay between high and low-profile symbols that cultural webs are woven.

Symbols serve as vehicles of meaning.

We can distinguish between two categories of symbol: high-profile symbols that are conspicuous, amenable to careful rehearsal and fashioning so as to create a particular impression, and low-profile symbols that carry and express meaning in more spontaneous, natural and unrehearsed ways and which constitute the background fabric of organisational assumptions and understandings.

While a heavy emphasis is placed on the spoken and written word in the course of everyday organisational life, anthropologists emphasise the importance of behaviour as playing a crucial role in the process of meaning making, regarding behaviour as the 'said' of social discourse.

Cultures are not separate from the individuals that participate in them but need to be understood as a representation of the totality of their beliefs and behaviour and as living accomplishments that are continuously being created and revised. In the next chapter I propose to build on this analysis of corporate culture by considering how it frames the challenges facing managers and leaders in organisations.

The cultural metaphor challenges all of us to attend to how we participate as co-weavers of a cultural web. It calls on us to consider how our behaviour serves as a form of symbol that conveys meaning, attracts scrutiny and invites interpretation. This is particularly so for those who occupy strategic or conspicuous roles in an organisation. Our concern shifts from questions such as how we might control or engineer a desired culture to considering how, as participants in a culture, we sustain and reinforce cultural patterns or act so as to create possibilities for novelty to arise. This view of organisations as arenas in which meaning is created and recreated on a perpetual basis through constant interactions and conversations holds important implications. If we are seeking to effect some form of change of direction or 'change of culture', then we need to look to those forums and processes in which new understandings, new meanings arise. In terms of the image of culture as a web of signification, we are concerned with the many forms of thread that comprise the complexity that is a web.

It is to a consideration of these questions and challenges that we turn in Chapter 4.

References

Andrews, J. Y., & Hirsch, P. M. (1983). Ambushes, shootouts and knights of the roundtable: The language of corporate take-overs. In R. Pondy, P. Frost, G. Morgan, & T. C. Dandridge (Eds.), *Organizational symbolism*. Greenwich, CT: JAI press.

Barley, S. (1983). Semiotics and the study of occupational and organizational cultures. *Administrative Science Quarterly, 28*(3), 393–413.

Bate, P. (1994). *Strategies for cultural change*. Oxford: Butterworth and Heineman.

Dandridge, T. C. (1979). *Celebrations of corporate anniversaries. An example of modern organizational symbols*. Working Paper, State University of New York at Albany, New York, NY.

Deal, T. E., & Kennedy, A. A. (1982). *Corporate cultures*. Reading, MA: Addison Wesley.

Geertz, C. (1973). *The interpretation of cultures: Selected essays*. New York, NY: Basic Books.

Marshall, J., & McLean, A. (1985). Exploring organisation culture as a route to organisational change. In V. Hammond (Ed.), *Current research in management*. Dover, NH: Frances Pinter.

Martin, J. (1983). Stories and scripts in organizational settings. In A. H. Hastory & A. M. Isen (Eds.), *Cognitive social psychology*. North-Holland: Elsevier.

Mitroff, I., & Kilman, R. H. (1976). On organization stories: An approach to the design and analysis of organizations through myths and stories. In R. Kilmann, L. R. Pondy & D. P. Slevin (Eds.), *The management of organization design: Strategies and implementation* (*Vol. I*, pp. 189–207). New York, NY: Elsevier North-Holland.

Pettigrew, A. M. (1979). On studying organizational paradigms. *Administrative Science Quarterly, 24,* 570–581

Smircich, L. (1983). Concepts of culture and organizational analysis. *Administrative Science Quarterly*, *28*(3), 339–358.

Smith, G. (2012). Why I am leaving Goldman Sachs. *New York Times*, March 14.

Tosey, P., & Gregory, J. (2002). *Dictionary of personal development*. London: Whurr Publishers Ltd.

Wilkins, A. L. (1983). Organizational stories as symbols which control the organization. In L. R. Pondy, P. Frost, G. Morgan & T. Dandridge (Eds.), *Organizational symbolism*. Greenwich, CT: JAI.

Chapter 4

Putting Ourselves in the Picture

Paradoxes, Patterns and Processes in the Selection of Cultural Threads

Plate 1: Magritte: La Reproduction Interdite, c.1937.

This chapter addresses a paradox in the study and practice of how cultures form and change. We have suggested that culture is not a thing to be managed but a way of thinking about the continuous processes of meaning making that gradually coalesce to form frameworks of understanding. These frameworks hold the background assumptions of everyday organisational life and play a crucial, if unnoticed, role in shaping both the thinking and behaviour of its members. We have also suggested that cultures are a collective accomplishment in which all participate. In this sense they are beyond the direct control of organisation leaders. At the same time we are suggesting that leaders *cannot not* participate in processes of meaning making. They are never out of the spotlight and their every act and utterance is subject to intense scrutiny and speculation as to its significance. Leaders are cultural provocateurs, they provoke meaning making and spark conversations. But they do so in the midst of multiple narratives where other voices, other perspectives and alternative inter-pretations compete to define events and to frame understanding. In this sense, we suggest that a leader might more accurately be considered as a weaver among weavers.

This chapter explores this paradox and considers the different ways in which leaders participate in weaving webs of meaning. We examine important ways in which senior members of an organisation play a part in influencing the narratives of everyday organisational life, how they invite organisation members to interpret phenomena and events and how they look to foster the formation of a desired mindset.

This exploration is rooted in Clifford Geertz' evocative notion that cultures can be understood as: 'webs of signification man himself has spun' (Geertz, 1973). We draw a parallel between the many interwoven threads that are required to form a spider's web and the ways in which leaders can draw on a wide range of 'threads' to influence the emergence of a desired cultural pattern.

Viewing cultures as webs offers two perspectives for deepening our interest in this way of understanding organisations and organisational change. Firstly, we can con-sider the nature of the many threads that, in combination, form a web. In this chap-ter we consider 11 threads that are readily available to leaders and others looking to influence the unfolding form and patterns of a culture. This is by no means an exhaustive or comprehensive lexicon of cultural threads. It is offered with the inten-tion of drawing attention to the many ways in which leaders act as weavers among weavers. We examine how leaders can use their role and position to work with these threads while also recognising the limitations of their ability to unilaterally define reality for others.

The second avenue of understanding suggested by the metaphor of cultures as webs is to consider that a web is formed through a process of weaving. The selection of threads is, by itself, not sufficient for a web to form. A web acquires its distinctive form and characteristic qualities as a result of the interweaving of threads to form a remarkably flexible and extraordinarily strong whole. By placing our attention on the activity of weaving we are endorsing a view of organisations that sees them as ongoing and unfolding processes of organising. This contrasts with the Newtonian informed view that has encouraged us to see organisations as objects to be managed or manipulated. The former perspective casts organisations as dynamic, living and unfolding patterns of interaction in which all members participate, while the latter invites us to think of them as objects separate from those who are charged with the responsibility of leading and changing them.

Thinking of cultures as living webs draws our attention to the skills of a weaver and to the nature of their participation in the never-ending processes of meaning making in organisational life.

In following chapters we explore this notion of weaving and we consider the pragmatic implications of what it means to view the formation of a culture as a collective accomplishment on the part of multiple weavers.

For now our attention turns to the many threads that are available for leaders seeking to influence the formation of cultural webs and we examine the challenges of working with these threads in settings over which they do not have unilateral control.

We begin this examination with a brief recapitulation of our view of culture described in previous chapters by way of setting the stage for the discussion that follows. For those readers who are keen to advance to the discussion of specific cultural threads I have indented this section.

> The cultural view considers organisations as interconnecting networks of relationships and communities that rely on a hidden fabric of shared, yet largely tacit, understanding. This background fabric enables, infuses and informs every aspect of their activities, choices and behaviour. The contours of these frameworks emerge over time through social processes of meaning making over which no individual has control.

> There is a reciprocal interconnection here: these background understandings inform our behaviour and, in turn, our behaviour expresses and affirms the web of tacit understandings and assumptions. To be a member of a culture is to co-author the culture.

> It is axiomatic that organisational leaders need to 'manage' the business of the business, to oversee strategy, to allocate resources accordingly and to monitor performance against intentions. The dominance of mechanistic and militaristic metaphors of organisations that has served this aspect of leadership has also encouraged us to think about how we can control or engineer processes of meaning making, to ask the question: how can we 'manage a change of culture'. The formulation of this question reveals the severe limitations of these images of organisations when it comes to an understanding of how organisation cultures form and change.

> The semiotic perspective offers a wholly different framing of this question, inviting us instead to notice the many ways in which we participate with others in the continuously unfolding processes of meaning formation. This perspective encourages leaders to pay close attention to the many ways in which, knowingly and unwittingly, they provoke conversations and influence meaning making through their everyday

behaviour, through the messages conveyed via their low-profile gestures and through the congruence between these and their high-profile gestures. In a context in which all members of a culture are seen as a party to its formulation, maintenance and transformation then a different orientation is called for. In such a context we need to see leaders as cultural weavers and as weavers among weavers. This calls for leaders to embrace a weaver's mindset.

'Culture is not something an organisation has but something it is.' (Smircich, 1983)

If the Cartesian worldview casts culture as an object or phenomenon that is separate from us and leads us to think of it as some 'thing' that can be managed or manipulated, the semiotic perspective holds that we are all participants in a culture and are continuously influenced by it while, simultaneously, shaping it. We are all cultural weavers.

As cultural weavers, we continuously spin cultural threads on a daily basis and repair, reinforce or erode the threads used by others. Some of us are able to work with more threads than others, but none of us has access to all threads and none can guarantee or directly control the pattern that these webs collectively form.

We now turn to a consideration of the many types of thread available for use by a leader as one weaver among many.

'Be the message, just make it clear ...'[1] Embodiment as Intervention

The traditional yardstick of good management has been the capacity to act, to make things happen, to meet objectives. Emphasis is rightly placed on agency, action and achievement. The cultural view of organisations suggests an altogether different, if complementary, emphasis. In contrast to the action orientation with its emphasis on doing, the cultural view draws our attention to the subtle but significant ways in which the actions, statements and orientations of leaders shape how people think about things; how they affect where people place their attention, what they prioritise and how they respond to both predictable and unexpected events. At the risk of caricaturing the two orientations it is the difference between an emphasis on doing and being. The cultural view of organisations suggests that leaders influence and shape 'how things are done around here' (Ouchi & Johnson, 1978) in a

---

[1]This statement was by Roger Paine, CEO at the Wrekin District Council. He used it to describe how he and his management team sought to foster a desired culture (McLean & Marshall, 1989).

myriad of ways. Most obviously we notice *what* leaders do, less apparent are the effects of *how* they do things on the way in which others think about things, and how they participate in the patterns of organisational life.

Achieving a balance between these two orientations, between doing and being, is illustrated by the way in which Roger Paine and his management team chose to progress their efforts to shape the culture of the Wrekin District Council:

> Roger Paine and his management team at the Wrekin District Council asked a cross section of their staff to identify what they felt were the most important values that should serve as a guide and inspiration for all staff in the organisation. After several weeks of discussion and consultation the group settled on four values: Quality, Caring, Fairness and Honesty. Three of these values, Quality Caring and Fairness,[2] met with support from all quarters, staff, managers and elected members (politicians). On completion of the exercise Roger and his team thanked the staff group and discussed with them ways of ensuring that these values became adopted throughout the Council. Initially the management team favoured adopting an internal publicity campaign that promoted the values and that gave them 'the full treatment'. The staff group expressed serious concerns and doubts about this approach. Such an exercise would 'go down like a lead balloon', they were assured. It was likely to engender widespread cynicism and ridicule as another management gimmick.
>
> 'The big talking point was their advice to us, that the words Quality Caring and Fairness ... should not be promoted in the organization in a big bang approach. It would go down like a lead balloon. We must promote these values in more subtle ways: through induction and through Chief Officers just making it clear.' (McLean & Marshall, 1989)
>
> After further reflection and discussion the management team decided that, if they were serious about these values, they ought to be prepared to adopt them as beacons for their own actions and behaviour, and to hold themselves to account against them. To help them do this they agreed that a routine item on their monthly team meetings would be a simple round of hearing from each member what they had done during the month that was an unambiguous expression of support for each of the three values.
>
> At the next team meeting, a month later, when they came to the item on the agenda entitled Values, there was a slight air of embarrassment

---

[2]It was felt that making 'Honesty' a high-profile symbol in the realm of public service and local politics would be to create a hostage to fortune.

when they recalled their commitment a month previously. As they went around the table it quickly became clear that people were struggling to come up with examples of how they had exemplified each of the values. Eventually they admitted to each other that while they still supported the idea in principle, the hurly burly of everyday commitments had meant that this resolution had slipped down their agendas and effectively been 'overtaken by events'. Their preoccupation with the 'doing' part of their jobs had eclipsed their attention to the 'being' part. They resolved to persevere with this idea however and by the next meeting reported on several examples of times when they had spotted opportunities to demonstrate their commitment to the values. One reported on a hospital visit to a staff member who had undergone surgery, another described a thank you note to an amenity manager for the quality of how they conducted a public meeting and so on. They discussed the validity of different stories and applauded the ingenuity of their colleagues. Gradually they found themselves consciously and regularly noticing opportunities to demonstrate and support the values in the course of daily life.

Instead of turning the promulgation of values into a task of publicity, promotion and dissemination, as a series of projects to be managed, the top team accepted it as a challenge to what each of them gave attention to. Instead of asking what can we do, they saw it as reviewing what they drew attention to as managers, to considering what priorities and values their actions expressed. They reasoned that before they could expect others to respect and practice these values they had to be seen to be taking them seriously themselves. In elevating their attention to how they were being in a way that brought it into balance with their formal responsibilities' they opted to embody the code or pattern of the culture that they were seeking to foster.

Research into the Wrekin culture (McLean & Marshall, 1989) revealed that the values of Quality, Caring and Fairness could indeed be witnessed in the daily actions of staff throughout the authority. We discovered that while staff told countless stories illustrating how these values informed their choices and behaviour as Council employees on a daily basis, we were surprised to discover that many staff were not aware of them as a corporate slogan. In short the values, while widely enacted, were not heavily publicised.

By rejecting a strategy of promoting the values as high-profile symbols in favour of embodying them through the routine activities and practices of daily life in the authority, the management team at the Wrekin contributed to their widespread adoption throughout the authority. They trained themselves to notice opportunities that arose in the course of the mundane activities of their daily routine. They cultivated a heightened awareness of the low-profile ways in which they conveyed values and priorities without fanfare. By showing their support for the values through their behaviour, the managers' were communicating analogically,[3] and as such they by-passed the conscious, rational filters of staff members.

The following story from a Wrekin Council employee shows how closely the behaviour of the CEO was scrutinised by rank and file employees and how it provoked a revision of thinking in a particular part of the Council.

> It had been a cold, tough winter. Workers in the depot had been called out on many occasions, to deal with burst water pipes, and the aftermath of flooding in some of the Council-owned properties. Staff had put in long hours and been called out for emergencies at all times of the night and day. Come the spring, Roger Paine and the Depot Manager decided to arrange a gathering to say thank you to the staff for their extra efforts during the winter months. The entire depot was invited to a get-together on a Friday afternoon. Drinks and light refreshments were served and a series of short speeches of appreciation were made. What drew most comment from depot staff was not the fact that the event was being staged but that it was happening at the depot, and not at the Council's main offices in the town and that the chief executive had come to them. They held this to be highly significant. It was unprecedented for the chief executive to come to the depot for any purpose. For him to take time and trouble to do this was seen as especially significant. They felt that it showed respect: that they were cared about and valued.
>
> 'Our new gaffer came and introduced himself. People were pretty shocked. It's unusual for him to come to you. It's a good thing.'
> (McLean & Marshall, 1989)

Our research uncovered an additional consequence of the management team's attention to enactments of the values. As a result of systematically and regularly reviewing their own actions in respect of the values they became increasingly alert to times when their staff took decisions or acted in ways that were informed by the values, as in the following example.

> A housing officer with responsibility for rent arrears was faced with a difficult but common dilemma when deciding how to proceed with a case of serious arrears on the part of a single mother. The choice he

---

[3]This term refers to a more primal form of communication that occurs through our direct experience of phenomena as opposed to digital communication that is concerned with information that is encoded in symbols of some form. Bateson (1972) wrote: 'We are so befuddled by language that we cannot think straight, and it is convenient, sometimes to remember that we are really mammals. The epistemology of the "heart" is that of any non-human mammal. The cat does not say "milk", she simply acts out (or is) her end of an interchange the pattern of which we, in language would call "dependency". He adds: It would seem that analogic communication is in some sense more primitive than digital and that there is a broad evolutionary trend towards the substitution of digital for analogic mechanisms.'

was faced with was either to institute eviction proceedings or to find ways of helping the woman reorganise her finances so as to allow her to recover a seemingly hopeless position. He told us:

> 'I know that we are a caring organisation and that if I go down the route of helping her with debt counselling *I will be supported by my manager.*[4] So this is what I did. We are a caring organisation.' (McLean & Marshall, 1989)

These stories provide examples of managers and staff who took seriously the realisation that they are participants in a culture. Rather than trying to 'manage' the culture, they accepted the challenge of culture as an enacted phenomenon that is expressed through acts: the 'said of social discourse' (Geertz, 1973). The device of reflecting each month on their own behaviour in respect of the values served as an excellent way of heightening awareness of how they participated in the culture and as a way of acquiring new habits of perception and behaviour. If we set this example in the broader context of professional management where much credence and status is afforded those with a proclivity for action, for making things happen, it is interesting to note that so much can spontaneously unfold from the simple but sustained practice of noticing; being mindful of the statements conveyed through ones' behaviour.

This story describes how managers learned about their participation in the culture through attending systematically to a particular aspect of their behaviour. In the process they learned about what they gave attention to and what they ignored as the compelling pressures of daily life in the organisation took hold. Through what might be considered a collective form of meditation or 'mindful attention', they gradually acquired an increasingly acute awareness of opportunities to embody the organisation's values and to notice occasions when others did so. In this way, just like Ludwig Fleck's (Skolimowski, 1985) microbiologists, they trained themselves to see in a particular way. I take it as no accident that what they systematically attended to, both in themselves and in others, became adopted on a widespread basis in the authority as a whole.

This way of thinking calls for a different framing of one of the most challenging questions in the field of organisational change. In place of the often asked: 'How can we manage a change of culture', a number of new questions become relevant. Among them are the following:

- 'How am I already participating in the culture?'
- 'How do things look if I think of myself as a "carrier of the culture", a holographic embodiment or fractal[5] of its defining values, beliefs and underlying assumptions?'

---

[4]Emphasis added.
[5]A fractal is 'a rough or fragmented geometric shape that can be split into parts, each of which is (at least approximately) a reduced-size copy of the whole' (Mandelbrot, 1982).

- 'What do things look like if I consider my everyday actions as the source of cultural stories, as provoking discussion, interpretation and meaning making in the informal conversations of everyday life?'
- What cultural messages am I sending through the way I spend my time, through the things that I give priority to, through the people I engage with and the meetings I attend? What story does my diary tell about my priorities and about where I place my attention?

Rogers' presence on the front desk every Monday morning to receive visitors was an embodiment of the service ethic. In Chapter 2 we described how the only parking privileges at the Wrekin Head Office were for the disabled and the elderly. Each time the CEO and Senior Officers searched for a vacant parking space in the staff car park they were making a cultural statement. They were being the message.

Language, Metaphor and the Formulation of Questions: The Gentle Art of Framing and Reframing

We participate in processes of making of meaning by the questions we ask. Every question sets a frame for how we think about a situation. It extends an invitation to see things through a particular cultural filter and implicitly both defines and constrains the parameters within which it may be answered. In the framing of our questions, in the way we choose to define situations, problems and opportunities, we have the opportunity to shape cultural assumptions. Consider the following story:

'How can we squeeze in an extra lesson of French?'

> Caryn's mobile phone rang. It was Christopher, the Headmaster.
>
> 'We've just finished the parents' evening for the boys in Grade 9, I haven't experienced anything like it before. They wanted to know what is going on.'
>
> 'Oh?' replied Caryn, 'How do you mean?'
>
> 'Well, the boys are so excited and energised. All the parents are talking about it. In fact the energy buzz seems to be contagious. The conversations with them tonight were completely different from other parent's evenings. They seem to have become caught up in the excitement as well. I just thought you'd like to know. It was amazing!'
>
> Caryn had been asked to help the school with a knotty problem. The Head of French was concerned that the group of 13-year-old boys were falling seriously behind. This was the only year when they had some flexibility around the curriculum. Next year they would be preparing for their GCSE exams and there would be little room to adjust the timetable. The difficulty arose from the fact that adding an extra

French class would mean dropping a Maths session and the Head of Maths would not countenance this. The scene was set for some difficult conversations and hard choices.

Caryn called together a group of staff to examine the situation from a fresh perspective. Drawing on the ideas of David Cooperrider and colleagues, she realised how easy it would be to accept the problem as it had been presented.[6] While it might seem obvious to us all that accommodating an extra French lesson in these circumstances is an undeniable problem, Caryn invited the group to experiment with the possibility that the situation might be defined differently. She asked them instead what were they working towards with this group of boys? What was their overarching aspiration, within which the teaching of Maths and French was an important part? What was the opportunity here? What was their overall purpose?

As they warmed to these questions the conversation became enlivened. The group discovered that what felt at first like a statement of a self-evident truth (the further development of skills in both Maths and French) soon turned into a challenging examination of their fundamental values and beliefs. Eventually, after almost two days of discussion and debate, one of the masters summed up the thinking by saying that in his view:

'We are interested in what makes for an excellent whole-life education for thirteen year old boys.'

This was the showstopper. It was the turning point in the conversation and people began using and repeating the phrase. After a while the group agreed that this indeed captured the unstated, but shared, aspiration of the staff team. Caryn then suggested a process of inquiry to discover answers to this compelling question. 'What would it be like if we used this as an opportunity to invite peoples' answers to this question?' She also asked them to consider whom they might usefully ask? Who might have something worthwhile to contribute to this inquiry? Whose ideas might prove illuminating and valid? It was decided to set up a series of conversations involving all staff and boys, but also extending the inquiry to include parents, and former, 'successful' pupils of the school. The suggestion was taken up and a large-scale inquiry was set in motion with the boys asking the questions and gathering stories of notable, high point, learning experiences. The

---

[6]Cooperrider and Srivastva (1987) suggest that we have become so habituated to thinking of organisations as problems to be solved that we tend not to see other possibilities. In a paper to the American Academy of Management Cooperrider posed the question, how would it be if instead, we tried thinking about organisations as places of extraordinary resourcefulness and possibility?

boys embraced this with surprising enthusiasm. Among a host of creative and imaginative ideas to emerge from the process was the audacious proposal for the entire year to spend a week in France learning Maths in French. And this was agreed to.

Such was the interest and enthusiasm generated by the process and the resulting creativity that other school years are exploring how they might incorporate something similar into their curriculum. The ultimate irony is that this experience is now considered as a high-point learning experience.

I find this an inspiring story. Probably my pleasure is a parallel of the delight experienced in the school. This was not just the outcome of the process that is so satisfying but the evident excitement and enthusiasm generated through their participation in the process. And, according to the Headmaster's phone call, it was a contagious enthusiasm. It vividly illustrates the implications of how we frame questions. This case shows that investing the time needed to find an alternative, more generative, way of framing the question led to a novel win–win solution and unleashed extraordinary amounts of creativity and enthusiasm.

The support of the headmaster was vital to this process as was his trust in Caryn. He expressed confidence in her ability as a facilitator to lead them through an unfamiliar process and gave license for the experiment. This was a risk that paid off for everyone involved and it embodied the trusting willingness to experiment that characterised the extraordinarily abundant culture of learning in the school. The episode now stands as a cultural exemplar in the school, a high-point experience for staff and pupils. It signified the spirit of learning, experimentation and trust that has contributed to Worth Abbey School's reputation as one of the foremost private Catholic Schools in the United Kingdom. The process by which an answer was arrived at carried messages about 'how things are done around here' and made a statement about what is valued.

This example also shows that the framing of questions offers important opportunities for weaving the cultural fabric.

Framing and Reframing[7]

The art of framing plays a particularly significant role in the fashioning of a cultural web. Accordingly, we will pause to examine more closely what this term means through a brief excursion into the fascinating world of communications theory.

'Saturday morning was come, and all the summer world was bright and fresh, and brimming with life.'[8] (Twain, 1876)

---

[7] I am grateful to Worth Abbey and to Caryn Vanstone for permission to include this case. Caryn is an organisation consultant who lives in Exeter in the United Kingdom.
[8] From Mark Twain (1876), *The adventures of Tom Sawyer*. Chapter Two.

With these words Mark Twain introduces one of the most celebrated of Tom Sawyers adventures. Tom had been given the onerous task of whitewashing a fence on a beautiful summer's afternoon. It was the last thing that he wanted to do on such a day and almost anything else he could imagine would be preferable.

> 'He surveyed the fence, and all gladness left him and a deep melancholy settled down upon his spirit.'

Drawing on all his legendary cunning and resourcefulness Tom looked to strike a deal with Jim who was on an errand to collect water from the town pump for '*Aunt Polly*'. Just as Tom had tempted Jim to trade places in exchange for a 'white marvel' and the chance to see Tom's sore toe that was wrapped in a bandage, '*Ole missis*' appeared out of nowhere and sent Jim '*flying down the street with his pail and a tingling rear*'.

Tom's scheme had been thwarted. The author writes:

> 'At this dark and hopeless moment an inspiration burst upon him! Nothing less than a great, magnificent inspiration.
>
> He took up his brush and went tranquilly to work. Ben Rogers hove in sight presently — the very boy, of all boys, whose ridicule he had been dreading.' (Twain, 1876)

Ben had been impersonating the Big Missouri, a steamboat on the Mississippi and was eating an apple. He took his time to draw up alongside of Tom:

> 'Tom went on whitewashing — paid no attention to the steamboat. Ben stared a moment and then said: "Hi-yi ! You're up a stump, ain't you!"'
>
> No answer. Tom surveyed his last touch with the eye of an artist, then he gave his brush another gentle sweep and surveyed the result, as before. Ben ranged up alongside of him. Tom's mouth watered for the apple, but he stuck to his work. Ben said: 'Hello, old chap, you got to work, hey?'
>
> Tom wheeled suddenly and said: 'Why, it's you, Ben! I warn't noticing.'
>
> 'Say — I'm going in a-swimming, I am. Don't you wish you could? But of course you'd druther work — wouldn't you? Course you would!'
>
> Tom contemplated the boy a bit, and said: 'What do you call work?'
>
> 'Why, ain't that work?'
>
> Tom resumed his whitewashing, and answered carelessly: 'Well, maybe it is, and maybe it ain't. All I know, is, it suits Tom Sawyer.'
>
> 'Oh come, now, you don't mean to let on that you like it?'
>
> The brush continued to move. 'Like it? Well, I don't see why I oughtn't to like it. Does a boy get a chance to whitewash a fence every day?'

That put the thing in a new light. Ben stopped nibbling his apple. Tom swept his brush daintily back and forth — stepped back to note the effect — added a touch here and there — criticised the effect again — Ben watching every move and getting more and more interested, more and more absorbed. Presently he said:

'Say, Tom, let me whitewash a little.'

To 'frame' something is to make an invitation to view it in a particular way. It is to create a context for perception, to suggest a particular schema of interpretation. This is not an extraordinary event however but something that occurs whenever we engage in conversation, whenever we describe events or anticipate them. Framing is part of the fateful ordinariness of daily life in organisations.

Reframing occurs when we:

'… change the conceptual and or emotional setting or viewpoint in relation to which a situation is experienced and … place it in another frame which fits the "facts" of the same concrete situation equally well or even better, and thereby changes its entire meaning.' (Watzlawick, Weakland, & Fisch, 1974)

'Putting it in a new light' is Mark Twain's description of reframing. Tom Sawyer's clever response to Ben's taunt is a brilliant example of reframing. Ben's perception of the situation was turned on its head as Tom reframed a chore into an irresistible invitation not just for Ben but also for the host of other boys who traded treasures for a turn at whitewashing.

The British poet Stevie Smith shows how reframing can lead to a shocking re-evaluation of a situation. In one of her most celebrated poems, Not Waving but Drowning (Smith, 1983) she invites us to see the gesticulating arms of a swimmer as waving before reframing the situation as that of a man drowning. He wasn't waving but drowning. Our interpretive frame of the same facts will lead to very different responses. Smith doesn't leave things there however but shifts frames again within the poem by suggesting that waving or drowning were metaphors for the man's life struggle:

'I was always much too far out all my life
And not waving but drowning.' (Smith, 1983)

He had been 'drowning' all his life, while we all thought that he was 'waving'. Stevie Smith's life long struggle with depression provides yet another frame for understanding the poem and her work.

Reframing Our View of Organisations

David Cooperrider, together with colleagues at Case Western University,[9] caused a stir at the American Academy of Management when he observed that a dominant

---

[9]The group of scholar practitioners that were part of these early conversations also included Ron Fry, Suresh Srivastva and Frank Barrett.

assumption among practitioners and Business School Academics is that organisations are seen as problems to be solved. The overwhelming framing of much organisation development activity, he suggested, had been concerned with diagnosing and then fixing the problems that are to be found in all organisations. Based on his doctoral research work conducted in the Cleveland Clinic, he offered an alternative, and somewhat provocative, proposition that organisations could equally credibly be seen as the source of extraordinary creativity and possibility, where remarkable things happen on a regular basis.

He suggested an alternative to problem solving as the dominant paradigm for understanding and intervening into them. Instead of looking to fix problems, he suggested an approach to change, growth and development that builds on the strengths and capabilities that are to be found throughout organisations, if we look hard enough. He coined the phrase Appreciative Inquiry as a way of describing an approach that systematically inquires into moments of resourcefulness and exceptional accomplishment in organisations. He observed that when individuals and groups undertook this kind of strength mapping, when they looked for the 'root causes of success', they became more resourceful, more creative and more willing to change.

David's ideas were received with scepticism and laughter at first. In the years since, Appreciative Inquiry has been enthusiastically adopted as one of the foremost approaches to Organisation Development across the globe.

David's paper to the AOM conference, and his contribution to the profession of Organisation Development, was to reframe the field. He revealed a basic assumption that felt like a self-evident truth, that we are in the business of fixing the problems of organisational life, and turned it on its head. This is not to say that problem solving is neither necessary nor vital for improving the operation of complex organisations. What Cooperrider did though, was to open up an extraordinarily fertile new way of thinking about and facilitating organisational change.

He makes two critical claims. Firstly he suggests that to inquire is to intervene. When we give our attention to something we change it in some way. This claim has wide support both from within the field of organisation studies and from quantum mechanics. Studies into worker productivity in the late 1920s and early 1930s, commonly known as the Hawthorne Studies (Mayo, 1949), sought to discover an environment conducive to maximum worker productivity. Worker output was tracked while illumination levels were adjusted, rest breaks introduced and incentive schemes adopted. The landmark discovery of these studies was that increases in productivity were largely the result of the close attention paid to the subjects of the experiment. They felt special and developed a sense of pride as a team at receiving so much sustained attention from the researchers. In quantum mechanics a key breakthrough moment for Heisenberg and Bohr in their studies of particles occurred when they realised that the results they achieved varied depending on the type of measures they used (Capra, 1982).

Gergen (1991) captures the significance of this insight:

> 'The very attempt to measure the position and velocity of a particle will knock the particle about in unpredictable ways. In effect, there is

no basic unit of matter to be observed independent of those who make the observation. Subject and object are inextricably linked.'

Cooperrider's second proposition (2005) builds on the implications of this observation. If inquiry is a form of intervention, then careful consideration needs to be afforded to the subject, or framing of any inquiry. If, as Cooperrider argues, the subject or topic of our inquiry expands under scrutiny, then the focus of an inquiry, the choice or framing, of what he refers to as an 'inquiry topic' becomes highly significant. The following case is an example of this.

Sexual Harassment

The subject of sexual harassment at work is an extremely serious issue. Rita Smith was a highly experienced consultant in this field. She had been leading workshops aimed at addressing the problem of sexual harassment for her client. After running a number of workshops she grew increasingly concerned that the problem of sexual harassment showed little signs of improvement. If anything matters were getting worse. In a conversation with David Cooperrider (Cooperrider & Whitney, 2005), he invited Rita to talk about what it was that she was hoping to achieve. What was the outcome that would tell her she was making progress? Her first reply was to restate her overall goal:

'We want to drastically cut the incidence of sexual harassment. We want to solve this huge problem, or at least make a significant dent in it.' (Cooperrider & Whitney, 2005)

It is hard to argue with this, or with Rita's passionate commitment to making a difference. Persevering with the question 'What is it you want to achieve' led to a different formulation of her aspirations:

'You mean what do I really want? (Long pause…) What we really want is to develop the new organization as a model of high quality cross gender relationships in the workplace!' (Cooperrider & Whitney, 2005)

David Cooperrider then asked her how would it be if they introduced a process that inquired into people's experiences of 'creating and sustaining high quality, cross gender workplace relationships?' (Cooperrider & Whitney, 2005)

This topic framing became the focus for a pilot intervention followed by a major initiative in Avon Mexico. The inquiry unearthed and studied a host of stories about successful cross gender work relationships. As a result of this inquiry many new initiatives were formulated that supported and exemplified cross gender working. Results were dramatic and enduring. In 1997 the companies' achievements were publicly recognised with the Catalyst Award for the best place in the United States for women to work in.

This example reminds us that we have a choice in terms of how we frame or describe situations we face. Are we looking to eradicate sexual harassment, as in this case, or to enhance our capacity for working creatively and successfully in cross gender relationships? Do we want to move away from something or towards something?

These subtle differences in orientation not only triggered the unfolding of a different dynamic in terms of working relationships between men and women, but they also encouraged a different way of thinking about cross gender relations.

Cooperrider suggests that the questions we ask are fateful. They serve as invitations to others to view the world through a conceptual lens or 'frame' of our choosing. For those in positions of power and leadership this is of some consequence. Our framing can propel others into the intractable win—lose dynamics arising from accommodating an extra French lesson at the expense of Maths, or, as this example illustrates, they can unleash unimaginable levels of creativity and contagious enthusiasm.

Colin Marshall's tenure at British Airways was, in part, an effort to reframe how people thought about the business of the airline. He looked to shift the dominant mindset from being preoccupied with aircraft and flying to place travellers' experiences in the forefront of their thinking. He worked to move the focus of peoples' attention away from a celebration of hardware (aircraft) and activity (flying) and to foster instead an obsession with the quality of the process, the end-to-end experience of their passengers in the course of a journey.

Adopting a Social Constructionist worldview confronts us with the sobering realisation that how we describe or interpret things has implications for behaviour, both our own and that of others. More than this, the semiotic view confronts us with the realisation that our constructions of events are not inevitable or fixed. We have an, often unrealised, choice about how we define situations, through the language we use, through the questions we ask and through the interpretations we place on others' statements and actions.

As leaders, managers and consultants we pose questions all the time in the course of daily organisational life. These stories have shown that the formulation of a question can hold considerable significance. Our questions encode assumptions and constrain or enable different possibilities to unfold. The art of asking questions is an important cultural thread. The formulation of questions serves to frame or define how people think about a situation.

We now turn to a related and complementary thread in the weaving of cultural webs: the role of language and metaphor.

Words Make Worlds: Language and Metaphor as Cultural Threads

'We do not describe the world we see, but see the world we describe.'
(Jaworski, 1998)

Scholars and practitioners who write from a Social Constructionist perspective argue that the terms we use when describing phenomena are not neutral devices, empty vessels that merely convey information. Our choice of language, our preference for one term over another; our use of images and metaphors to convey an understanding of things, are in themselves acts of agency. For Social Constructionists language does not simply reflect reality, it shapes our conception of reality.

> '... language for the post modernist is not a reflection of a world exterior to itself, but is world constitutive. Language does not describe action, but is itself a form of action'. (Gergen, 1991)

The language we use, including the metaphors that we invoke, sometimes knowingly and sometimes without conscious reflection, serve as a way of organising our thoughts and perceptions. They also need to be seen as a bid to organise the thoughts of others and as an invitation to them to view the world using our constructs. We have seen earlier that we engage with the world on the basis of these understandings and interpretations. In its capacity to frame and shape others' understanding, perceptions and interpretations of events, language has to be seen as an especially persuasive thread for the fashioning of cultural webs.

The following example is drawn from my consulting experience.

Hunters and Skinners

> The Managing Director of a software company that was aspiring to a reputation for high quality customer service frequently spoke of his marketing staff as 'hunters' and referred to the sales staff as 'skinners'. He was well liked and respected by his staff and regularly enjoyed making play with this imagery in quarterly staff review gatherings and other settings. The language of 'hunters and skinners', enjoyed widespread currency in the company, and was both compelling and amusing, as well as an accurate expression of the aggressive, proactive, attitudes towards the acquisition of business that had been an important feature of the companies' success. However, an unconsidered and unfortunate side effect of this imagery had to do with the way in which it shaped employees' perceptions of their customers. By encouraging them to think of themselves as hunters and skinners he was tacitly casting their clients as quarry or prey. Clearly such imagery does not sit easily with an aspiration for high quality customer service, but it did resonate with disgruntled customers.

By invoking this vivid imagery the Managing Director was inadvertently inviting his staff to adopt a predatory attitude towards their customers. This 'construction' invites people to think of clients as quarry to be pursued, to be outsmarted, entrapped and ultimately captured or worse. It is a construction that sets up a win–lose competition with one party coming out on top following a battle of wits.

It was no surprise that feedback from clients was often highly critical of the poor quality of both products and services they received.

The language and metaphors we use, particularly when we occupy positions of power, serve as micro-invitations to others to interpret events in a particular way. Paul Watzlawick (1978) argues that metaphors are particularly potent invitations since they speak to the right brain[10] and can by-pass the rational filters of our reasoning left-brains. In this sense the use of metaphor resembles a hypnotic suggestion. Attending to the metaphors that pepper the casual conversational exchanges in an organisation can reveal much about a cultural mindset.

The Power of Expectations, the Pygmalion Experiments

The significance of language is no better illustrated than by a series of experiments that took place during the 1960s and 1970s. Research experiments were conducted in the field of education to examine the effects on schoolchildren of the expectations held by their teachers. Known as the Pygmalion experiments (Rosenthal & Jacobson, 1968) over 300 different studies tracked the performance of schoolchildren throughout their school careers and some also extended this to include their early work careers. The studies were concerned with the link between a teacher's expectations and a student's performance. Experts provided teachers with information indicating the capabilities of a group of students. Approximately a third of the class was described as high-potential students. The rest of the group was described as having either average or low potential.

This labelling of students was conducted on a random basis using what were considered to be children within the normal range of ability.

The children's performance in school soon showed marked differences depending on which group they had been allocated to. The results of those described as having high potential showed a statistically significant improvement over the others. Not only were these effects lasting throughout their school careers it emerged that those labelled as 'high potential' students achieved greater and more rapid success in their early careers. Measures of students' IQ were less successful as predictors of success in the classroom than the expectations held by teachers based on these random classifications (Cooperrider, 1990).

These experiments are testimony to the power of expectations, perceptions and the labels we use. The performance of pupils was correlated to the perceptions that their teachers held of their abilities. The behaviour of teachers towards students varied depending on their perceptions of the student's ability. A self-sustaining spiral of causality was in operation. Observational studies discovered that teachers spent more time with high-potential students, were more encouraging in their feedback to them and expected higher standards of performance. Here is hard evidence

---

[10]Paul Watzlawick (1978) speaks of metaphor and imagery as the 'right royal route to the unconscious'.

supporting the dictum that '*If we define situations as real they are real in their consequences*' (Thomas & Thomas, 1928).

Such was the controversy surrounding these studies that the American
Psychological Association declared a moratorium on further experiments of this
nature (Cooperrider, 1990).

Introducing new language and language based in different assumptions, can be a
powerful form of intervention into any system. A related aspect of this exploration
of language and culture is to note that in addition to the introduction of terminology and constructs that support a desired mindset a further consideration is how to
confront what might be thought of as legacy constructs; language and terminology
that invoke and perpetuate attitudes and thinking that is rooted in outdated or
unwanted assumptions, values and attitudes. Roger Paine and his colleagues at the
Wrekin discouraged use of the term 'professional' for example. For them it con-
noted a somewhat detached and expert-based mindset, a kind of 'we know best'
arrogance among officers that ran counter to their desire to foster an ethos of service to the community.

Micro Moments — Interpretations as Cultural Threads

A dirty little secret of organisational life is that followers look to their leaders for
interpretations of ambiguous situations and events. This usually happens in subtle
ways; a slight hesitation that invites the leader to offer their view, their take on
things; a distracted gaze into the middle distance; a furrowing of the eyebrows in a
way that suggests considered reflection; a glance in the direction of the leader with a
look of expectation, or perhaps a direct question soliciting the leader's view. The
reasons for this are neither noble nor surprising, particularly in settings where power
differentials are in play.

It is in these moments that reality is defined. Leaders who 'step up to the mark'
and give their take on things are offering interpretations and defining reality for
their followers, providing an interpretive 'frame' for making sense of an event or a
situation. Such definitions may well be challenged and many leaders invite and welcome such challenge, however, the power inherent in leadership positions always
gives added weight to their interpretations of events. It is in these micro-moments
that reality is defined, a world-view affirmed or the possibility of thinking differently resides. In choosing to give a view, to explain or comment on a situation, leaders invite those present to see the world through their conceptual filters, their
constructs. Every time this happens a leader is either strengthening an existing cultural thread or spinning a new one. Part of the craft of leader as cultural weaver, is
to notice these 'micro moments' and to consider how they are inviting others to
make sense of events through the constructs they invoke.

These stories highlight how language, metaphors and imagery serve to frame our
perceptions and our thinking. They are a ubiquitous feature of everyday organisational life and a vital means of communicating. Their ubiquity can blind us to the
subtle ways in which they shape thinking and their familiarity can anaesthetise us to

the implications of the worldview they encode and the assumptions that they convey. For those leaders, managers and others interested in revising or reshaping cultural assumptions this points to the importance of attending carefully to the language leaders choose and to the metaphors and images they invoke, both in their casual everyday exchanges and in their high-profile communications. Language and metaphors are important cultural threads. They offer an important means by which prominent members of an organisation can influence the interpretative frames by which everyday situations are understood. They also represent an opportunity to introduce new ways of conceiving both the familiar and the novel.

For leaders and those of us concerned with understanding and facilitating change processes these ideas are both liberating and daunting. Liberating in the sense that we are no longer tied to a search for truth but have license to articulate and invoke those images, metaphors and linguistic constructions that support the scenarios we are looking to encourage. Daunting in the sense that we need to accept the responsibilities associated with our constructions and interpretations. If we accept Frank Barrett's provocative assertion that 'words make worlds' (Barrett & Fry, 2005), the implications are immense.

The relevance of these ideas for leaders fall into two broad categories: the use of language and imagery during everyday, impromptu exchanges and conversations, and their use in the broad framing of strategy and cultural intent. We have already considered the former through the imagery of 'hunters and skinners' to portray the complementary roles of marketing and sales staff, and we saw how this inadvertently contributed to a predatory mindset. We turn now to a discussion of framing and reframing in the context of efforts to define or redefine the overall direction, tone and priorities of an organisation. Most commonly this occurs following the appointment of a new CEO.

High-Profile Framing

The appointment of a new chief executive is a natural opportunity to 'frame' the challenges, opportunities and cultural intentions of their appointment. Typically leaders take the opportunity to set out their thinking regarding the nature of the business they are leading and to indicate the kind of cultural hallmarks, priorities and values that they see as configuring how people commit time and resources.

It is common for chief executives to talk publicly about their ambitions for the organisation, both as a business or enterprise but increasingly in terms of the kind of culture that they are looking to foster. Such statements variously refer to values, tenets, beacons, principles, guiding beliefs, a distinctive way of working and other such phrases. So, for example:

- When Paul Sabin was appointed chief executive at Kent County Council, the UK's largest local authority, he identified three cultural 'tenets' that would be the defining principles for his term of office. They were: *Devolution, From Administration to Management and Staying Close to the Customer.*

- Early in Roger Paine's tenure he chose the word '*interventionist*' as a defining principle of the new culture at the Wrekin. Later, and after consultation with staff, the values of *Quality Caring and Fairness* were agreed as being the flagship values of this outstanding District Council.
- The recently appointed new chief executive at Barclays Bank, Anthony Jenkins, laid out five values that would define the new culture in the wake of a series of scandals at the bank: *respect, integrity, service, excellence and stewardship.* (*The Guardian* newspaper, January 2013)

Many organisations formulate their own version of these cultural principles. Such statements are a form of high-profile framing and can be helpful in setting staff expectations and aspirations, in providing an overarching sense of direction and style and in signalling the intent of the incoming leader. They serve to define the broad cultural intent and to set a tone. As such they represent an important and legitimate cultural thread that is readily available to leaders. Their capacity to influence a culture is limited however by how they sit in relation to the many other cultural threads that constitute a web.

More specifically, their impact is qualified by how they are interpreted locally in the narratives and conversations of the informal networks, in what have been described as the 'shadow conversations' (Shaw, 1997) of everyday organisational life. As we will see described in some detail later (Chapter 6) such informal sense making is concerned with how these high-profile framings sit in relation to the 'lived' culture as experienced by participants in the course of their everyday organisational lives. We have seen in an earlier chapter for example the power of informal customs and narratives in an investment bank that urged employees to 'Hunt elephants' or to 'Execute on the firm's axes'.

Such engrained local narratives can and do compete with expressions of corporate values or codes of conduct, often overriding them. Effectively these are two potentially competing narratives: the formal, high-profile framing and the local, informal narratives that interpret and frame these high-profile exhortations. In this context, a key challenge for those looking to heighten the impact of any high-profile framing is how to do so in a way that engages with such powerful local narratives. We explore this interweaving of cultural narratives more fully through case studies in Chapters 5 and 6. Viewed from the perspective of these local narratives, the high-profile framings of incoming leaders can expect to be viewed with 'seen it all before' and 'new broom' scepticism, the tacit question being 'are they serious'?

A further challenge has to do with what might be considered as the sub-text of a high-profile framing; the tacit cultural messages expressed through the way in which the high-profile framing was formulated and communicated. The following case is based on a short article that appeared in the business section of *The Guardian* newspaper.[11]

---

[11]Edited version of an Article in *The Guardian*, Thursday 17 January 2013 entitled: *Barclays Boss Tells Staff: Sign Up to New Values or Leave.*

Looking to 'clean up' the bank's image and culture following a series of highly publicised scandals the newly appointed CEO of Barclays Bank, Anthony Jenkins, announced a 'Purpose and Values' blueprint for bank employees. The announcement was accompanied by a blunt message to those employees who did not feel able to live up to the new statement:

> 'Barclays' reputation was hammered after it was fined £290m in June for rigging Libor interest rates, which unearthed longstanding concerns by Britain's financial regulator about its culture. Jenkins, who took over after Bob Diamond stepped down in the wake of the Libor scandal, said he was putting five values at the heart of his plan: respect, integrity, service, excellence and stewardship.

> "*I have no doubt that the overwhelming majority of you… will enthusiastically support this move. But there might be some who don't feel they can fully buy into an approach which so squarely links performance to the upholding of our values,*" Jenkins said in a memo to his 140,000 staff on Thursday.

> "*My message to those people is simple: Barclays is not the place for you. The rules have changed. You won't feel comfortable at Barclays and, to be frank, we won't feel comfortable with you as colleagues.*"

> Employees' bonuses and performance would be assessed against a new 'purpose and values' blueprint.

> He said bankers pursued short-term profits at the expense of the values and reputation of the organisation, and in the coming weeks more than 1,000 staff would be trained to spread the new values and embed them throughout the bank.'

In this short article we can see at least three high-profile threads being used in the service of effecting a change of culture: the CEO's advocacy of the five new values, a 'spread and embed' training and communications initiative and a re-configuration of bonuses and performance criteria. These are commonly used threads that are readily within the control of most CEOs. On closer inspection I would suggest that at least three other cultural threads are evident. They are less obvious and less readily managed but, from a cultural point of view, of equal significance.

Firstly, the manner in which the five values were arrived at will carry cultural statements. Were they arrived at through consultation with staff or were they chosen by the CEO on his own, or in closed discussion with a group of seniors and possibly a consulting firm? The nature of this process is likely to come under scrutiny locally and to draw informal comment. Such interpretations as are placed on the manner of determining the five values will be further tempered by peoples' experience of similar initiatives in the past.

The 'sign up or leave ultimatum' in particular is likely to provoke much discussion and reaction among staff and carries a cultural message that may lend a particular nuance to how the values are received.

Thirdly, the 'spread and embed' strategy for disseminating these values is itself an expression of a worldview, a further (top-down) statement about 'how things are done around here'.

On the very limited information contained in this article, we can discern at least six cultural threads that are conveying and encoding cultural messages. Their ultimate effect is likely to depend on their cumulative impact as well as the extent to which they complement or contradict each other.

Anthony Jenkins' Purpose and Values framing of the new culture for Barclays is likely to provoke a parallel conversation in the informal or 'shadow' networks of the bank. This example highlights a challenge for any leader who is looking to adopt such forms of high-profile framing: how to interweave the potentially competing narratives of the official framing with the local interpretations and sense making processes that are an inevitable response.

High-profile framings are important and readily managed threads that depend for their impact on their relation, over time, to the many other threads that comprise a cultural web.

We will revisit these questions in the closing chapter where we liken high-profile framings to the radial threads that are architecturally crucial in the early stages of forming a spider's web.

Systems and Procedures as Cultural Threads

We weave cultural webs through the systems and procedures we design and operate. For some this is the sine qua non of organisational life. All organisations rely on such systems. They serve important if not essential operational functions: processing orders, monitoring costs, rewarding and remunerating employees, safeguarding quality and safety standards. These are the routines and formalised protocols of organisational life that give it a defining and rhythmic pattern and momentum. They carry us along with an inevitability that creates the illusion of permanency, certainty and stability. Their functional significance is not our concern here. From a semiotic perspective however we can see that these systems and procedures also carry embedded within them values, assumptions and stances regarding the nature of 'how things are done around here'. In subtle, subliminal ways, they direct our attention and influence our priorities. In the world of academia for example, while faculty are continuously being urged to raise the standards of teaching in the classroom, students complain of ever-increasing class sizes and of unavailable professors. At the same time the allocation of funds to universities in the United Kingdom is based on increasingly competitive, and rigorously scrutinised criteria based on publications and research records.

The 'message' of these systems and procedures to an academic in a British University is as unequivocal as it is traditional: publish or perish! Teaching, while espoused as a primary purpose of the university system, will always take a secondary role to the pursuit of research and publications. The intensity of the funding pressure on university departments to achieve a high ranking in these 'league tables' has led to extraordinary deals and transfers of star academics and their staff from one university to another in a way that increasingly resembles the cut throat world of professional sport.

In the world of software engineering the following case shows how an adjustment to reporting procedures and accountabilities for project teams triggered a shift of mindset among a community of very smart engineers:

> In a specialist software house the business plan set ambitious targets for turnover, and the MD was committed to developing high quality customer relations. The company had tripled its turnover in a period of three years, a truly remarkable achievement. However profitability remained unacceptably modest, hovering at around 10%. Reports of customer satisfaction continued much as before with a characteristic mix of horror stories and delighted customers. Inquiries revealed that the key metrics used to track the progress of projects were concerned with timeliness and budget-spend.

> Project leaders and their managers were preoccupied with meeting project milestones, and with delivering their projects on time and to budget. Both of these might reasonably be considered as highly commendable. However, there were no means for systematically tracking levels of customer satisfaction. In effect they relied on their customers to initiate any feedback, whether in the form of complaints, threats of litigation or glowing letters of commendation. Similarly, project teams, and project leaders in most cases, had no awareness of the profitability of their projects. The concept of profit margin held very little meaning for them.

> Engineers responsible for designing the technical solutions took pride in finding innovative and creative ways of meeting project requirements. The result was a culture of exceptional engineering ingenuity. Too often however their solutions were often considered to be 'gold plated'. The emphasis on innovation was at the expense of a concern for cost effectiveness. Engineers were reluctant to re-use or adapt solutions developed elsewhere, either within the industry or even by a different division within the company. This 'not invented here' norm was a dominant feature of the culture and meant that an inordinate amount of resource was devoted to creating new solutions to familiar challenges, to 're-inventing the wheel'.

> Each month the executive reviewed the performance of the four main operating divisions. Typically these reviews would identify the progress of important projects and give special attention to those that were causing concern for some reason. Essentially they were concerned with technical aspects of projects and with progress against sophisticated project management metrics. A new metric was introduced into the

rhythm of this reporting process. In addition to tracking progress against project management targets, Project Managers were required to report on the profitability of their projects against overall targets for their divisions.

This was hardly a groundbreaking practice and was commonplace in many businesses, but in this company it was one that prompted a significant shift in the thinking of these software engineers. Suddenly, their teams were using their talent for innovation and novel solutions to find ways of cutting costs and adapting existing solutions. Solutions developed on other projects were dusted off and adapted to provide 'good enough' solutions. Cooperation between project teams increased as ideas and shortcuts were exchanged. Something had shifted in their way of working.

The effects of the innovation had repercussions throughout the company.

The introduction of the new metric put pressure on the accounts department to produce the kind of detailed financial information to project teams on a monthly basis that had hitherto been aggregated for the company as a whole at the end of the year. Attitudes of project leaders became much more commercially aware and gradually profit margins began to climb. The culture had changed.

This case highlights the impact of working with two threads in combination. The introduction of additional measures that monitored profit margin represented a change to one cultural thread. However the impact of this innovation was amplified by the low-profile behaviour of the senior managers. By paying sustained attention to this new metric in monthly meetings they signalled that this was indeed a serious expectation. Moreover it later became clear that the selection of project leaders and their allocation to prestigious projects was increasingly influenced by performance against this metric. In this way a third cultural thread was added that reinforced the first two and which provoked much discussion among engineers and project leaders. The incorporation of such discussions into everyday conversations between engineers and project leaders was evidence of a changing culture.

In a recent consulting project I was helping two large companies that had merged to understand both of their corporate cultures and to support an extended conversation intended to help the identification of shared values and cultural intentions for the new, integrated business (Moffat & McLean, 2010). After 12 months of intensive discussions a new set of guiding values had been agreed and endorsed by the board. Different project teams who were developing processes and procedures for the global business used these values to inform their proposals. For example they informed the design of performance evaluation criteria, customer satisfaction surveys, sales and R&D processes, and the syllabus for the companies' academy. In effect they were tailoring these important and formal processes so as to create a context that was conducive to the enactment of the recently endorsed values. This case is discussed in more detail in Chapter 6.

Rewards in the Wrekin:

> 'We were thinking about what sort of rewards would be appropriate, would they be financial or non-financial rewards ... the general consensus was that the organization was not ready for financial rewards. We decided that the system that we were really talking about was non-financial, starting form a simple "thank you" for a job well done, to more tangible but still non-financial things like a bottle of wine. Arranging non-financial rewards, that's now commonplace in the organization' (McLean & Marshall, 1989).

The Medium is the Message: Experience as Thread

Marshall McLuhan's famous dictum (1967) points to another thread in the weaving of meaning. Modern living exposes us to a plethora of information and images to such an extent that we can often feel overwhelmed or saturated (Gergen, 1991). We live in a digital era in which information is coded and transmitted in ever more ingenious ways and at increasingly rapid speeds. McLuhan however was referring to a different form of information. This is the knowing we take from the totality of an experience, when all of our senses simultaneously assimilate many forms of information: tactile, kinaesthetic, olfactory and relational, in a way that leads to an experiential understanding. It is a kind of holistic knowing that resides in our bodies. To take an example, we can read about the thrill, or paralysing fear, of a roller coaster ride and understand it in one sense. To sit on a roller coaster, to feel its body slamming acceleration and the weightless plummeting of its descent followed in an instant by the gravitational pull on muscles and organs as it whips around a tight curve, is a different form of knowing. It is direct, immediate knowing.

This kind of experiential knowing conveys information. We are immersed in this form of knowing throughout our organisational lives, albeit in a less dramatic way, but like background noise, it can be information that we largely ignore as a result of its ever presence. Communication theorists argue that nevertheless, this information provides a form of physiological anchor into our experience of reality.

Polanyi's (1966) work points to a distinction between that which we know and experience through our senses, what he terms visceral knowing, and the formation of abstract concepts that categorise and formalise meaning. The former is experiential knowing through the senses, the latter intellectual or cognitive understanding that describe or names the experience. As we advance through the education system we are concerned increasingly with abstract, conceptual and representative forms of knowing, less and less with the knowing from direct contact or immersion in a phenomenon. By using abstract terms and constructs for our experience: 'scary', 'exciting', 'terrifying', 'thrilling' or 'boring' we are, in fact, invoking social constructs that verbalise our feelings in a way that makes it easier for others to understand. However, Polanyi's point is that, in this translation from primary visceral knowing to conceptual knowing, we are not only shifting realms of understanding but also separating ourselves from the sensual experience of direct immersion. What we risk forgetting here is that the rationality that we place so much value on in the west and in contemporary organisations is a secondary stage in the process of sense making.

In spite of the primacy of rationality in the everyday exchanges of organisational life, together with its emphasis on highly crafted communications, we cannot escape the information of our senses. As members of organisations we all find ourselves immersed in experience that provides a context for interpreting such digitalised information. The dulling effect of familiarity and repetition may anaesthetise our senses, but we cannot deny that we are exposed to visceral stimulation on a continuous basis. Both McLuhan and Polanyi argue that while this form of knowing is mostly tacit, or hidden from our conscious awareness, it is nevertheless an important dimension of how we come to experience the world. Famously Polanyi (1966) wrote that:

'You know more than you think you know'

Berman, commenting on Polanyi's work suggests:

'...on a conscious level we largely spend our lives finding out what we already know on an unconscious level.' (Berman, 1981)

It is as if we have forgotten or discounted our primal, instinctual means of comprehending our worlds in favour of the digitalised and coded transactions that pervade our contemporary lives. The boundary between these two forms of knowing however is not watertight. Information leaks from the visceral to the rational, or from the unconscious to the conscious. More recently writers on emotional intelligence (Goleman, 1996), for example, have signalled that this long neglected realm of understanding is being reclaimed. We are gradually becoming more emotionally literate, more attuned to our senses and bringing this wisdom into organisational arenas.

In the current context I would suggest that the work of Polanyi and others holds considerable significance. If information filters through from a tacit, visceral realm into conscious awareness, then we need to consider the nature of experiential realities in organisations as an important source of meaning making. In short, we are reminded of what might seem like a self-evident, yet often ignored truth, that people make meaning from their experiences of participating in organisations. It may be some time before we attend consciously to the information or knowing that is held in our bodies, before we give it meaning. Rather like someone who feels lethargic, achy and who develops a headache, it can be some time before we begin to wonder whether we are 'off colour' or 'getting sick'.

In the context of organisational life we are constantly exposed to streams of information in the course of our daily activities and in the discharge of our duties.

From time to time various organisation-wide initiatives seek to inform us of, or involve us in a change of some kind: a merger, a continuous improvement process, the introduction of new quality standards and protocols, perhaps a process re-engineering exercise. These will normally be extensively documented, and introduced with accompanying manuals and workshops, company briefings, 'road shows' and other forms of launching events.

Quite often these initiatives are accompanied by bold rhetoric and they invoke terms such as empowerment, autonomy or devolution. Ultimately, what gives these initiatives legitimacy and real significance in the eyes of organisational members is the extent to which they accord with their everyday experience. Do people feel as though they have more autonomy? Can they point to examples of locally devolved decision making powers? Are they supported for taking risks and permitted initiatives that previously would have to have been referred for more senior approval? From a cultural point of view the important question is:

> Has the manner in which a change has been introduced been commensurate with the intent of the initiative?

Have people experienced the process of introducing a change as empowering? Have they been able to interpret it locally? Have they felt encouraged to find their own novel and innovative ways of proceeding? In short:

> Has the medium modelled the message?

The following two cases describe interventions that were designed using these ideas.

How to be Strategic

> Some years ago I was part of a consulting team that worked with a large County Council that had recently been the subject of a 'health check' by one of the top consultancy firms. The verdict came back that the authority scored highly in terms of operational efficiency, discharging its duties dutifully and within tough budgetary constraints. However, it was also reported that the organisation fell short in terms of its capacity to develop strategy. There was no long-term statement of priorities, no sense of unifying vision or identity beyond that of delivering services. The organisation took this feedback seriously and set up a series of seminars led by an eminent professor from a nearby business school that had an enviable reputation. Senior managers spent several days in lecture theatres hearing about different approaches to strategy and the merits of different ways of formulating strategy. They considered a number of case studies of high-profile companies and the merits of their approach to strategic development, debating the wisdom of this formulation over that one. Officers found the seminars fascinating and highly informative. However, by the end of the 18-month series of seminars, when stock was taken of how far

the authority had become more strategic as an organisation, the disappointing conclusion reached by senior officers and elected members
was that no real progress could be discerned.

A second attempt was launched to fulfil the strategic ambition. A firm
of consultants were invited to submit their thoughts on how such a
shift might be achieved in this monolithic organisation. They spoke to
managers who had participated in the programme and heard that
their experience of the original programme carried different messages
than the content of the programme. While rich in information,
superbly presented and led by world-class experts in strategy, the
managers' experience of the process was of feeling like passive recipi-
ents of the wisdom of experts, of feeling intellectually inferior and
talked down to. They described the experience as similar to being
back as undergraduates, sitting at the feet of gurus. While the term
strategic is interpreted differently across business schools there is
some consensus that it entails proactive movement towards a position
within a field of endeavour in such a way as to affirm a particular
image or identity. Inadvertently, it seems, the seminars had created
feelings of inferiority, dependency and passivity, and ironically, had
undermined the confidence and self-image of participants as compe-
tent managers. And it was only in retrospect that they had begun to
realise this and articulate their feelings.

Here we have a stark illustration of a challenge associated with making meaning
in organisations. How to ensure that people experience the difference that is
intended by any change initiative and not just hear about the intention. How can
the medium embody the message?

In this case the consulting firm designed a series of participative workshops
for senior managers. The design was intended to encourage a high degree of self-
directed, discovery learning about the meaning, development and implementation
of strategies. In teams, participants were required to clarify their learning objectives and agendas. What questions did they have? What would constitute a prag-
matically useful outcome for them, their departments and the organisation as a
whole?

A wide and varied range of materials, books, articles and videos were made available to participants and they were encouraged to select from these to help them
develop answers to their questions. In addition a range of managers and leaders
from a wide range of organisational sectors and with extensive experience of working strategically were available to participants for informal conversation. Who participants met with and what they discussed was entirely dependent on their questions
and their learning goals.

Gradually, through immersion in this rich array of materials they formed answers
to their originating questions and new ones surfaced which became the focus for the
next round of their learning cycle. Over the course of three intensive days these
learning communities gradually formulated their own understanding of 'strategy' as

it was most relevant to their circumstances. They were supported and challenged along the way by both the visitors and by the programme facilitators, but essentially they were constructing their own understanding of the pragmatics of strategy formulation for themselves. Their experience, at first confusing and uncomfortable, gradually led to an emerging clarity and a growing sense of what strategy did and did not mean to them. In a way it was a journey of de-mystification and they discovered how they might create their own approach to the subject in a way that felt possible, realistic and organisationally relevant.

While this sketch greatly oversimplifies an extended and complex process, it is intended to illustrate how the fundamental design of the intervention here was predicated on a desire to ensure that the experience of those on the programme was consistent with, and an exemplar of, the outcome that was desired. *The design of the learning process was intended to encourage participants to be strategic in their approach to learning about strategy.* Hence the emphasis on self-directed learning, on proactively scanning for relevant information and on finding or creating their own clarity when faced with a mass of information. The process was an analogue of the desired shift in behaviour on the part of the organisation as a whole. Or more simply put, the medium was intended to be an integral part of the message.

In both experiences, with the business school and then with the self-directed workshops, participants made meaning on the basis of their experiences. In the first example the experiential meaning carried an almost contradictory message from the content of the programme. The second experience helped participants to understand the process of strategy formulation and implementation as a result of their experience during the programme as well as through more traditional forms of learning. They had to *be* strategic in their process of learning and discovery. Their learning was both cognitive and experiential.

Culture Review: Omnishire County Council[12]

> A consulting colleague and I had been asked to help the Social Services Department of this County Council to conduct a study of the department's culture. This was in order to help them think about their long-term staff development agenda. The cultural analysis would provide a kind of basic platform for the development programme and contribute to an identification of those issues that might profitably be addressed. The process adopted was to do the study as a Cooperative Inquiry (Reason & Rowan, 1981). An inquiry team was formed that conducted a series of interviews with staff throughout the large department. The analysis of what had been learned took several meetings. When the work was complete the discussion turned to how the

---

[12]Omnishire is a pseudonym.

information might be shared with the management team. A dominant discovery in the course of the inquiry was that the department comprised many sub-cultures and that there was considerable variety between them. It was more of a patchwork of sub-cultures than something that had any distinctive coherence or defining themes. The question for discussion was how to represent this in the feedback session.

After much discussion the group decided that the only way of honouring this diversity was for the room to be divided into different areas or displays, each one with representations, images and stories that illuminated one of the sub-cultures. Once the management team had assembled for what they imagined would be a presentation they were invited as individuals to visit as many of these tables as they could, to hear the stories and discuss the images with the inquirers before reconvening as a team to reflect on what they had learned. There were three rounds for their visits and they were left to visit whichever display they felt drawn to with the exception of the final round. 'Please use this round to visit a part of the Department with which you are least familiar' was the instruction. The result was an 'eye opening experience' according to several of the team — they had learned things that they hadn't expected and which disturbed them. At the top of their list of insights was the realisation of just how differentiated were the many sub-cultures. 'It was the layout of the room as much as the content of what was said that really brought it home to me' commented the Chief Officer. The medium had endorsed and reinforced the message.

This take on the construction of meaning making in organisations poses a question that I find both illuminating and provocative in my work with clients:

> What meaning do you want people to take from their experience of participating in this process?

No manager can unilaterally determine what meaning will be made of an event or process. Asking this question in itself is not only helpful in clarifying a manager's intent, it can also provide an immensely useful frame for thinking about the design of any process. In my experience this is not a frame that managers and leaders naturally invoke when thinking about the design of processes and events. The messages sent by the medium represent a potent thread in the weaving of cultural webs. Like all threads however its potency lies in how it sits in relation to other threads and in the pattern that they collectively form.

Other Threads

So far in this chapter we have concentrated on seven major forms of cultural thread. We have argued that working with corporate culture means working with many threads. A web, after all, is comprised of hundreds if not thousands of strands. In this section we will look more briefly at some other forms of thread that contribute to the fashioning of a cultural web.

Signage

In the Wrekin District Council there were no signs prohibiting entry, nothing said 'No Entry' — or 'Council Officials Only'. The intention was to make members of the community feel welcome and involved, to think of the offices as part of the community. In the car parks the only signs for reserved parking were for the elderly and handicapped. Everyone else had to take their chances in the main car park including the chief executive, elected members and service directors. This was part of a deliberate intention to signal that the Council Offices were there in the service of the community and to underscore one of the authorities core values: fairness.

At an international terminal in a major US airport, the security scanners and TSA staff are located about 100 yards down a corridor. A moving pedestrian walkway runs the length of this corridor. At the entrance to this walkway a sign reads 'For the use of airline staff and officials only'. Passengers, including those in wheel chairs, have to walk without the benefit of the walkway.

As part of their efforts to develop a stronger sense of a professionalism and friendliness the Inner London Magistrates Courts Service changed the format of the nametags issued to visitors and the doors of staff offices. First names were introduced. Instead of a label reading Mrs Campbell the new labels read Jean Campbell. This could not have been a simpler change and cost pennies to introduce, but it was one of many cultural threads that supported a new way of working (McLean & George McLean, 2002).

Appointments, Promotions and Departures

Much attention and discussion surrounds key appointment and departures. Who is selected to join a company and who is invited to leave carries cultural messages, and often provokes intense speculation. This is never more so than in the days and weeks following a merger. The sub-text of conversations in many mergers has to do with whether this is a true merger of equals or a disguised form of takeover. Who gets the 'key' jobs is a much-scrutinised indicator as to which company has 'come out on top' and accordingly what values and approach people can expect.

The cultural change in a large UK County Council was gathering momentum across the range of services with the major exception of the Education Department. It was only when the Chief Education Officer 'retired' that members of his department acknowledged the possibility of a different culture emerging. He was much loved and respected throughout the service, and according to a member of his management team, his departure signalled the end of an era. The goodbye parties held in celebration of his service were described as a form of wake, not just for their departed leader but also for the cultural habits and traditions that he represented.

More extreme forms of this thread have been used. British Airways famously experienced the 'night of the long knives' (Carleton & Lineberry, 2004) when an entire tier of senior management was removed both as a cost cutting measure but also as a dramatic signal of change. Similarly the popular aphorism: 'If you can't change the people change the people' is another, oft heard mantra. The obvious risk when using such extreme measures is that the cultural message, often a crude signal that 'things are going to be different now' is heavily seasoned with a wave of fear and insecurity. Fear is not an expansive or generative emotion. It triggers a retreat to safety and to familiar coping patterns. In these circumstances the chances of something new emerging are diminished rather than enhanced.

Team Composition

The composition of a senior team, like cabinet appointments, sets the tone for a regime and signals the philosophy and intent of the leadership. This adds an extra consideration to senior appointments. What will their promotion or appointment say about the priorities and values of the new regime? At the same time the retention of certain senior players in a changing scenario also needs to be considered from the perspective of what cultural message will it be sending. At times I have witnessed what amounted to despair and fatalistic resignation in the conversations of staff in one client system on learning that a particular individual would continue as a member of the main board. The central interpretation of a change that didn't happen was that 'as long as this person remains in office nothing will change'.

Chief Officers in the Wrekin

> 'With one, deliberate, exception the team of Chief Officers has changed completely, albeit gradually since Roger Paine's arrival. As the opportunity arose, outgoing departmental heads were replaced with people who shared the Chief Executive's philosophy, in particular the view that people are the key resource. Additionally, they were selected because they did not aspire towards a highly technocratic professionally based style. In the Wrekin the term 'professionalism' has come to connote a concern for systems, procedures and technical competence and a comparatively lower level of concern for people. It is a taboo term.' (McLean & Marshall, 1989)

As much as any cultural thread, promotions can be understood as the hard currency of cultural symbolism. They represent tangible evidence of what attitudes and behaviour are valued by leaders and, as low-profile symbols they either endorse or override high-profile statements of values or intent. They are the trump cards of a cultural change and their potency as cultural threads is enhanced because they occur locally. In my experience however, the cultural significance of appointments is rarely a consideration in the selection of candidates for promotion.

Building Design — Artefacts

Architects understand the power of space, design and setting to promote an atmosphere, a feeling, a zeitgeist. Increasingly companies are seeing that the design of their offices is a means of encouraging particular behaviours and encoding cultural messages. Buildings and their fabric and furnishings are high-profile symbols, bold efforts to embody noble endeavours and ideals through the imaginative use of materials, design, space and artefacts. As the following commentaries demonstrate, they also combine layout with subtle symbolism to foster desired behaviour and attitudes:

> 'The interiors of Waterside, the light beech furniture, the cool colour range, the neat glazing of the meeting room walls, the transparency of the open plan, the comfortable and supportive team spaces, the ready access for everyone to intimate gardens and to wider views of the reconstructed landscape, the textures, amenities and sounds of the busy stimulating street, are beautiful in themselves ... *every physical element, each design feature broadcasts what must be an almost irresistible, Siren-like message about the critical importance of collaborating in and enjoying a new and changing culture of work.*'[*] (Duffy, 1998)

> 'Watersides *is designed for people to interact, to meet casually as well as formally*[*]. A grand covered street is the axis along which the six-office buildings open, filled with coffee shops, banks, grocery stores and florist. All occupants and more can be assembled here for major company events. The training center, management development suite, theatre, corporate library, Internet café, and medical center bring a constant flow of people from all parts of the airline to Waterside, the corporate heart. *Services for the whole person − a gym, a hairdresser, and grocery order and delivery service − help staff to feel valued and loyal to the company.*'[*] (Marmot & Eley, 2000)

The award winning design of British Airways Headquarters Waterside building near Heathrow Airport in London was designed with the intention of encouraging collaboration, casual and random meeting, dialogue and the cross fertilisation of ideas. The Street, a central feature of the complex, is lined with coffee shops, restaurants, meeting places and spaces. The six office buildings are of equal height, deliberately avoiding suggestions of hierarchy and symbolising the continents that the company serves. The provision of so many services such as hairdressers, banks, supermarkets into the Waterside complex was chosen for both sound practical reasons, it saved staff time, but also as a statement to staff that they were valued and their loyalty to the company mattered.

In the course of a consulting assignment with British Airways staff at the Waterside location I was admiring the spectacular architecture and services of this facility. To my surprise people said that they no longer noticed it and that it took the eyes of a newcomer to remind them of what an exceptional environment they

---

[*]Emphasis added.

inhabited. This somewhat sobering discovery made me realise that such symbols, even such impressive ones, lose their impact over time. Perhaps, it is more accurate to see them as becoming part of the taken for granted backdrop against which the activities of daily life occur. When new, they represent impressive high-profile symbols, a spectacular expression of official values and intent, but over time they metamorphose into taken for granted low-profile cultural symbols whose potency depends on complementing the multitude of other cultural threads.

In his biography of Steve Jobs, Walter Isaacson notes how Jobs used the design of a building to encourage a culture of innovation. He describes how Jobs:

> '...had the Pixar building designed to promote encounters and unplanned collaborations. 'If a building doesn't encourage that, you'll lose a lot of innovation and the magic that's sparked by serendipity.' He said. 'So we designed the building to make people get out of their offices and mingle in the central atrium with people they might not otherwise see.' The front doors and main stairs and corridors all led to the atrium, the café and the mailboxes were there, the conference rooms had windows that looked out into it, and the six-hundred-seat theater and two smaller screening rooms all spilled into it.' (Isaacson, 2011)

These images of Google office environments have been heralded as a landmark in innovative design. Full of novel and imaginative features they are intended to foster creativity and to create a 'cool', unorthodox setting for their staff as well as providing a full range of facilities. They make a major statement about Google and its staff.

Plate 2:   Google offices. With kind permission of Scott Brownrigg.

Plate 3:   Google offices. With kind permission of Scott Brownrigg.

Plate 4:   Google offices. With kind permission of Scott Brownrigg.

NSN, a company formed through the merger of Nokia Networks and Siemens Communications, deliberately chose to locate its sales offices close to their major customers as a way of signalling and finessing their intent to be customer focussed.

It is less common these days to hear stories of companies with segregated restaurants and canteens, executive toilet facilities and other such obvious symbols of hierarchy and status. Expressions of status and hierarchy take more subtle forms in this cyber-age. Security passes, knowledge of access codes and other cyber-security information now serve as signals of importance and power.

Like any other cultural thread the design, layout and furnishing of buildings is a means through which intended values can be expressed, symbolic invitations extended and the fabric of meaning shaped. By themselves, the inspirations of modern office design are no more capable of engineering a desired culture than the speeches of a chairman or chief executive. They remain as single, albeit highly conspicuous, threads in the overall web that constitutes a living culture and, like other threads, their power lies in the connections they form with other threads and the coherence of the collective pattern they form.

Concluding Thoughts

In this chapter we have considered some of the ways in which, as members of organisations, we are participants in weaving cultural webs of meaning. As organisational 'fish' that swim in the meaning making milieu of daily organisational life, we should not be surprised that we are blind to the nature of the milieu itself. And yet the capacity of our organisations to develop and change is intimately bound up with our ability to refresh and renew how we understand ourselves and our relationship to the settings in which we operate, be they commercial, political, ecological or whatever.

We have explored a conundrum that confronts those of us who would seek to free up the generative potential of our organisations. While we cannot unilaterally control or define cultural pathways, we need to accept the challenge and responsibility, the inevitability, of being a party to this important process. At the same time we need to understand better our part in perpetuating or disrupting patterns of meaning making within organisational settings. Being a party to these processes means cultivating an awareness of ourselves as agents of meaning making, while accepting the limitations of our capacity to define reality for others.

The challenge has to do with understanding which cultural threads lie within our control and understanding where the limits of our influence lies; in realising as leaders that working with the threads of a cultural web is about issuing multiple invitations as well as engaging in the many meaning making processes of organisational life; participating in the flows and forums, the arenas in which new meanings emerge, allowing ourselves to advocate with passion but also allowing ourselves to be changed, opening ourselves to the possibility of difference and novelty; cultivating an attitude of curiosity and inquiry, of experimentation, innovation and reflexivity. This calls for a capacity constantly to be alert to the statements we are making through our behaviour, our language and the processes we set in motion. This is a significant and important challenge that calls for the cultivation of weavers' mind.

In all of this, the term I wish to emphasise is the notion of mindfulness. As participants in corporate cultures we risk becoming anaesthetised by the familiarity and ultimately the comfort that our habituated ways of seeing represent. We risk becoming corporate sleepwalkers, gradually but inexorably losing good contact with those around us. The challenge of waking up, of seeing with fresh eyes, of stepping beyond the hidden boundaries of our conceptual frameworks is the subject to which we now turn.

References

Barrett, F., & Fry, R. (2005). *Appreciative inquiry: A positive approach to cooperative capacity*. Chagrin Falls, OH: Taos Institute Publications.

Berman, M. (1981). *The reenchantment of the world*. London: Cornell University Press.

Capra, F. (1982). *The turning point: Science, society, and the rising culture*. New York, NY: Simon and Schuster.

Carleton, R. J., & Lineberry, C. (2004). *Achieving post-merger success*. San Francisco, CA: Pfeiffer.

Cooperrider, D. L. (1990). Positive image, positive action: The affirmative basis of organizing. In S. Srivastva & D. L. Cooperrider (Eds.), *Appreciative management and leadership: The power of positive thought and action in organizations* (pp. 91–125). San Francisco, CA: Jossey Bass.

Cooperrider, D., & Whitney, D. (2005). *Appreciative inquiry: A positive revolution in change*. Berrett-Koehler Publishers.

Cooperrider, D. L., & Srivastva, S. (1987). Appreciative inquiry in organizational life. In W. Pasmore & R. Woodman (Eds.), *Research in organization change and development* (Vol. 1, pp. 129–169). Greenwich, CT: JAI Press.

Duffy, F. (1998). Working at Waterside — Conduciveness as a workplace of the British Airways' headquarters in Harmondsworth, England. *The Architectural Review*, August.

Geertz, C. (1973). *The interpretation of cultures: Selected essays*. New York, NY: Basic Books.

Gergen, K. (1991). *The saturated self, dilemmas of identity in contemporary life* (2nd ed.), New York, NY: Basic Books. 2001.

Goleman, D. (1996). *Emotional intelligence: Why it can matter more than IQ*. New York, NY: Bantam Books.

Isaacson, W. (2011). *Steve Jobs*. New York, NY: Simon & Schuster.

Jaworski, J. (1998). *Synchronicity: The inner path of leadership*. San Francisco, CA: Berrett-Koehler Publishers.

Mandelbrot, B. B. (1982). *The fractal geometry of nature*. San Francisco, CA: Freeman.

Marmot, A. F., & Eley, J. (2000). *Office space planning*. New York, NY: McGraw-Hill.

Mayo, E. (1949). *Hawthorne and the western electric company: The social problems of an Industrial civilisation*. Florence, KY: Routledge.

McLean, A., & George McLean, M. (2002). New world wines in old world bottles. *Reflections, The SoL Journal, 4*(2). MIT Press, Boston, MA.

McLean, A. J., & Marshall, J. (1989). *The Wrekin District Council: A cultural portrait*. Luton: Local Government Training Board.

McLuhan, M. (1967). *The medium is the massage*. New York, NY: Bantam Books.

McLuhan, M., Fiore, Q., & Agel, J. (1967). *The medium is the massage: An inventory of effects*. New York, NY: Random House.

Moffat, A , & McLean, A. (2010). Merger as conversation. *The Leadership and Organization Development Journal*, *36*(6), 535–550.

Ouchi, W. G., & Johnson, J. B. (1978). Types of organizational control and their relationship to emotional well-being. *Administrative Science Quarterly*, *23*, 293–317.

Polanyi, M. (1966). *The tacit dimension*. Chicago, IL: University of Chicago Press.

Reason, P., & Rowan, J. (Eds.). (1981). *Human inquiry: A sourcebook of new paradigm research*. Chichester: Wiley.

Reuters. (2013, 17 January). Barclays boss tells staff: Sign up to new values or leave. Guardian Newspapers Ltd.

Rosenthal, R., & Jacobson, L. (1968). *Pygmalion in the classroom*. New York, NY: Holt, Rinehart & Winston.

Shaw, P. (1997). Intervening in the shadow systems of organizations: Consulting from a complexity perspective. *Journal of Organizational Change Management*, *10*(3).

Smircich, L. (1983). Concepts of culture and organization analysis. *Administrative Science Quarterly*, *28*, 339–358.

Smith, S. (1983). *Collected poems*. New York, NY: New Directions Books.

Skolimowski, H. (1985). *The co-creative mind as a partner of the creative evolution*. Paper presented to the First International Conference on the Mind–Matter Interaction, Universidada Estadual De Campinas. Campinas, SP., Brazil.

The Guardian. (2013). *Barclays boss tells staff: sign up to new values or leave*. The Guardian, 17 January 2013.

Thomas, W. I., & Thomas, D. S. (1928). The child in America: Behavior problems and programs. In R. S. Cohen & M. Wartofsky (Eds.), *Boston studies in the philosophy of science* (Vol. 42). Dordecht: D. Reidel Publishing Co.

Twain, M. (1876). *The adventures of Tom Sawyer*. Chicago, IL: The American Publishing Company.

Watzlawick, P. (1978). *The language of change: Elements of therapeutic communication*. New York, NY: W. W. Norton & Company Limited.

Watzlawick, P., Weakland, J. H., & Fisch, R. (1974). *Change: Principles of problem formation and problem resolution*. New York, NY: W.W. Norton & Company.

Chapter 5

The Weaver's Craft

A web comprises many threads or strands and its weaving requires patience and perseverance. It calls for strong anchor points. As structures, webs are both remarkably strong and resilient. Hard to see, its strength comes from its multiple points of connectivity and its elasticity. Stress in one part of the fabric is absorbed across the piece and its natural elasticity ensures the restoration of its form once any interference or stress is dealt with. Webs teach us humility.

Plate 1:   Image of a spider's web.

In previous chapters we have shown how culture can be understood as a 'web of signification', an assumptive framework for understanding the complexities of the world, for interpreting events, framing choices and guiding behaviour. Cultures provide us with our sense of what is 'normal' and 'obvious'. In this sense cultural webs serve us by providing a medium for social behaviour, they allow us the comfort and familiarity of shared conventions and spare us the need to constantly check for understanding and agreement. They provide the pathways by which we navigate organisational life using the briefest of shorthand gestures in the reassuring knowledge that others will readily understand them.

The weaving of a cultural fabric is an active process that occurs through the everyday actions and exchanges of organisational life. The repetition of these exchanges, acts and images provides an essential familiarity, enables continuity and gives a necessary stability to organisational life. For much of the time cultural understandings can happily reside in the realm of taken for granted assumptions as background understandings. This is not to say that disagreements, conflicts and misunderstandings do not occur, but that there is sufficient understanding and agreement about the underlying assumptions and conventions to provide a medium through which conflicts and disagreements can be expressed and understood.

However, times change. Technological innovation is unceasing, established markets shrink and new ones emerge, economic conditions have become far more volatile and the world political order seems to be in a heightened state of flux. At such times long settled assumptions no longer hold, established patterns no longer serve the people who created them. More of the same solutions no longer suffice. Some form of step change becomes an imperative. In these circumstances organisations, and their leaders, face a challenge of a different order: cultural change. Achieving a new cultural pattern calls for a different level of awareness, for different skills and processes. It calls for different levels of attention and intention. It calls for a weaver's mind.

In this chapter we explore what this means. We describe and examine a number of case examples in which new meanings and understandings have been forged, new cultural webs woven. While notoriously robust, cultural frameworks are not fixed. Cultures change. The difficulty arises however when we believe that we might be able to engineer such change in line with our ambitions, that we can directly 'manage cultural change'. Through the cases in this chapter we highlight the circumstances and processes that played a part in the emergence of new patterns of understanding and behaviour and, through these examples, look to illuminate the part played by leaders, managers and facilitators.

We have earlier set out the difficulties that arise when we look to manage or engineer a change of culture. Cultures are social phenomena, a diffuse, collective patterning that forms over time. As such they are not within the direct and immediate control of any individual or group, however powerful. Much cultural knowledge is hidden from everyday awareness and is held in the form of unquestioned and taken for granted habits of perception and behaviour. Unless we are very astute, our 'solutions' are themselves expressions of these tacit assumptive frameworks and, as we have seen in earlier chapters, our efforts to change things inadvertently risks reinforcing the problem.

I explore these examples of cultures that have changed, from my perspective as a consultant, as a coach, as a teacher and mentor to other consultants and of course as a continuing student of organisation change. Some case examples are drawn from my practice. In choosing and presenting them I do not start from an open mind. My map of this territory has formed over years of supporting leaders, organisation members and other consultants in their efforts to understand this complex territory and to make an intended difference. Moments of clarity have emerged from many conversations with colleagues, clients and with practitioner students. These insights and the thinking that informs them have, in turn, influenced my practice.

In presenting these case stories I feel a responsibility to acknowledge these ideas and theories openly, to name their main features; to describe how they inform the contours and pathways of my own map of this territory and to be clear about the navigational tools that I have found helpful in charting a way through this complex territory. In doing so I invite the reader to join me as a companion some way along my own journey of discovery; to travel with me as I attempt to point out the features of the landscape as I see them, as well as the winding pathway that has brought me to my present position.

Accordingly, before exploring case examples of cultural change I set out my understanding of some key terms. Specifically, I wish to begin by drawing attention to some taken for granted terms and constructions, in particular the term 'organisation' and the related question of how to 'manage cultural change'. I follow this with a brief introduction to two ideas that have been key to my unfolding understanding of this material. The first of these ideas was coined in the early 20th century by an Oxford professor named William Bateson. The second idea was developed by his equally influential son, Gregory.

The underlying premise of this section is that if cultures are to change then our thinking about organisations and change processes also needs to change.

Fateful Questions

As times change circumstances call for new thinking, new behaviour and new priorities. We hear talk of needing to find a 'new normal' and of the importance of cultural change. How we frame the question at this point however is of immense importance. If we ask the seemingly innocent question: 'How can we change a culture?' we have already taken a fateful turn. Framing the question in this way is predicated on seeing culture is an 'it', a 'thing' that can be manipulated, a process to be engineered, an 'outcome' to be delivered. It casts culture as something apart from its members and especially its leaders and frames cultural change as a project to be managed. In this formulation of the question leaders become a kind of 'meta-project manager' whose job is to define clear goals, monitor progress and ensure that a desired outcome is delivered.

In this context, I would suggest that it is equally unhelpful to use the term 'organisation'. It also invites us to think in terms of manipulating an object and in so doing to consider it as something separate from its members. If we think of cultural webs as being continuously woven through the everyday behaviours and exchanges of all organisation members, then I would suggest that, in place of the term organisation, we might be better served by using the active verb, organising. Karl Weick (1979) makes this point in characteristically provocative fashion:

> 'Whenever people talk about organizations they are tempted to use lots of nouns, but these seem to impose a spurious stability on the settings being described. In the interest of better organizational understanding we should urge people to stamp out nouns. If students of

organization become stingy in their use of nouns, generous in their use of verbs and extravagant in their use of gerunds, then more attention would be paid to process and we'd learn to see how to see and manage it.'

Weick is here challenging us to take seriously the view that we are all participants in processes of organising rather than members of an organisation. Such a fundamental re-orientation of our thinking prompts us to attend to the living, dynamic and incessant activity and exchanges that occur simultaneously across the fields of activity that we define as an organisation. Organising happens locally, face to face, and is essentially a relational and social phenomenon.

Let us now put these two ideas alongside each other; culture as a collective, social accomplishment that acquires distinctive patterns over time, and a process view of organising instead of seeing organisations as things to be manipulated. Revisiting the topic of cultural change in light of these ideas suggests that we are better served by asking a different question. Instead of asking ourselves: how can we change a culture, it becomes more fruitful to ask:

'How can we create the conditions in which cultural change occurs?'

From this formulation another question follows:

'How can we, as leaders, managers and change facilitators, participate in these settings and processes in ways that enable, support and influence such changes?'

There are two key differences in this way of formulating the question. Firstly, it casts us all as being in the midst of the processes of meaning making. As we have seen earlier, we all participate in these processes whether we realise it or not and whether we choose it or not. The second difference is that this formulation takes the view that no single person or group can unilaterally control what patterns form or how they will emerge. Cultures are collective accomplishments that acquire form and distinctive patterning over time. The challenging, and for some disturbing, implication of this observation is that when it comes to cultural change we can neither engineer nor guarantee an outcome. As Doug Griffin (2002) puts it, we may be in charge but we are not in control. This is a profoundly disturbing proposition for those of us whose understanding of organisational life is rooted in Newtonian, mechanistic thinking and who yearn for predictability and control. Thinking about organising not organisations, is a different way of knowing that calls for a different way of being.

There is an irony in all this. Managers and leaders may not deliberately be able to engineer a desired culture. However, as active participants in the ongoing processes of meaning making, they cannot avoid influencing it. They have influence without control. The question now becomes how to exercise this influence in such a way as to create the conditions in which something close to a desired culture might emerge? For leaders, managers and facilitators this formulation of the question elevates their concern to that of being reflective participants making conscious choices about how they participate in the processes through which meaning, especially new meaning, emerges. This is a central concern in the craft of cultural weaving. In the previous chapter we have explored the many cultural 'threads' through which leaders participate in these processes both consciously and inadvertently. In this chapter we describe and reflect on ways in which these threads are interwoven and the conditions that support the emergence of new cultural patterns. There is more to a web than a collection of threads. A web has to be woven.

By definition, cultural change is concerned with that which is not normal and accordingly calls for leadership that lies outside of conventional expectations and practices.

I now turn to consider two further ideas that have informed my understanding and practice as a consultant concerned with these questions. They originate from the same genetic pool: William and Gregory Bateson, and both are illustrated in the cases described later in the chapter. I offer them as a final prelude, a kind of theoretical appetiser, ahead of the main course, before concluding the chapter with broader reflections on the theory and practice of cultural weaving.

Treasure Your Exceptions

We often hear new leaders proclaim that they prefer evolution to revolution. Darwin's ideas about the evolution of species emphasised the survival of the fittest, and suggested that 'natural selection' ensures the gradual and continuing development of a species. An early critic of Darwin was a Cambridge scholar called William Bateson, a fellow of Saint John's College Cambridge. William Bateson was interested in the ideas of an obscure Belgian monk called Gregor Mendel. In contrast to Darwin's emphasis on continuity, Mendel argued that evolution occurred when there was a *discontinuity* of species variation. William Bateson studied heredity and the emergence of variations from the norm. He was the first to use the term genetics and suggested that organisms adapt to changing environments through deviations from the norm, and pointed to the significance of genetic mutations ('morphological disruptions') in this process. A favourite saying of his was 'Treasure your exceptions'.[1]

In organisational contexts, reward and promotion criteria are essentially Darwinian in their assumptions. We consider it normal to select the 'finest and fittest' and to promote them until, through a process of natural selection, they occupy the most senior and powerful positions. They stand as the lauded embodiments of the most valued talents and attitudes within a system, conspicuous symbols of success for ambitious others to emulate. More than this, these cultural paragons become the guardians of the future, overseeing the formulation of strategy and setting the criteria by which others are selected and assessed. It is a

---

[1] I am indebted to my friend and colleague Kevin Power for background to these insights.

process of continual refinement that can drive out difference and result in closed, self-justificatory thinking. Gradually and imperceptibly this leads to a stifling compliance as difference is dampened, and the capacity for adapting to changing circumstances is diminished. We have recently witnessed the way a latter-day form of Darwinism has significantly contributed to the failure of some of the world's most powerful corporations.

Countless organisation theorists have identified the importance of difference as an essential quality for successful performance. The notion of Requisite Variety first coined by Ashby (1952) states that 'the internal regulatory mechanism of a system must be as diverse as the environment with which it is trying to deal' (Morgan, 1986). Lawrence and Lorsch (1967) suggested that high-performing organisations combine sufficient differentiation necessary to adapt to the complexity of the environment in which they were operating and crucially work hard to achieve integration across these differences. Thomas Kuhn (1962) showed how paradigmatic change occurs when anomalies can no longer be explained or otherwise accommodated within a dominant belief system.

In a different context entirely, Frank Barrett (1998) draws lessons from the conventions of Jazz musicians to suggest that innovation and novelty arise when errors are embraced as a source of learning and difference. There is no such thing as a 'bum note' to improvisational Jazz musicians. An anomaly is repeated, amplified and embellished until a new version of the melody takes form and a new pattern comes into being.

By definition exceptions, anomalies and mutations are a disturbance to the integrity of dominant patterns of thought and behaviour. As such they have the capacity to trigger a reconfiguration of such apparent order. For those whose concern is pattern, or cultural change, such exceptions are to be treasured. We will see in the case studies later in this chapter however that disturbing or interrupting settled patterns unleashes much turbulence that takes many forms. One of the major challenges during such episodes is how to respond to this turbulence in a manner that supports the emergence of new forms while safeguarding the well-being of those involved.

Difference that Makes a Difference

William Bateson's legendary son Gregory was, among other things, one of the early theorists in the field of cybernetics. Drawing on Cybernetic thinking Bateson defines information as 'news of difference' (1972). To consider a thermostat as a simple example of a cybernetic system, a boiler is activated when the temperature falls below a preset threshold. Similarly, a refrigerator motor kicks in when the internal temperature rises sufficiently to trigger the sensor. In both cases the sensors are activated by news of difference. Building on this thinking Bateson memorably suggested that change was 'any difference that makes a difference'. When considered in the context of organisations the wisdom of Bateson's observation lies in the second part of the statement: 'any difference that makes a difference'. A common sense strategy in organisations looking to shake up peoples' attitudes and to stay up to date with thinking elsewhere is to bring in 'fresh blood'. As an attempt to introduce difference into a setting, be it a group a team or department, this device often falls short of expectations because the introduction of difference into a setting ignores the powerful and conservative forces of the prevailing culture.

Not All Difference Makes a Difference

Treasuring exceptions and embracing news of difference have been important ideas that have informed my consulting practice and I would suggest that they represent important pointers for others interested in questions of cultural change. What I have learned is that the elegance of these two phrases belies the challenges of implementing them. On the contrary, I have seen countless examples of how behaviour that is regarded as culturally different is sanctioned. Prevailing cultural norms dampen perceived difference and pressures both subtle and direct are brought to bear in order to restore 'order'. Difference brings and represents a disturbance to that which is regarded as normal even when 'normal' may be dysfunctional and harmful to the long-term viability of a community, company or other forms of organisation. Studies of family systems that are locked into destructive patterns for example tell us that in spite of the distress and suffering associated with pathological conditions such as anorexia, or alcoholism, families are notoriously resilient in the face of efforts to help them.[2] Difference in the form of professional intervention is subtly declined or undermined as the system closes ranks.

Similarly in the context of organisations, I have been struck by the ingenuity with which organisations are able to keep themselves the same in spite of everyone's best efforts to change them. The forces of conservatism, the taken for granted sense of what is right and normal, create a formidable pressure for those who represent difference to 'get in line', to 'get with the program' or 'get on board'.

Two brief stories from my consulting experience illustrate this phenomenon.

New Blood

> At a recent seminar in a global business, my friend and colleague Bill Critchley and I were leading a discussion on the role of leaders during times of radical, discontinuous change. The discussion turned to the importance of bringing in new thinking as a means of provoking new ideas and practices in a global pharmaceutical manufacturing company. At the end of a seminar one of the attendees approached us and said that he had been with the company for 18 months. He was in mid-career and had been brought in because of his expertise but also

---

[2]See, for example Palazzoli, Boscolo, Cecchin, and Prata (1978).

because of his knowledge of practices in his former company, a commercial rival. He was recruited as 'new blood' and because he brought different ways of approaching challenges common to both companies. He told us that in 18 months no one had asked him about his previous experience and that any references he made to how things were done in his previous employment were either ignored or discounted. The message he took from his experience was that his new employer was not serious about change. They were not really open to new ways of doing things. Instead he was expected to adjust to his new companies' ways of working.

Ironically it was in the same seminars that we asked participants, high-level scientists and managers, about the circumstances in which new drugs had been developed. The answer, consistently, was that they were frequently discovered by accident, often as an unexpected side effect of trying to develop a drug for a different purpose.

We see the same reaction to the introduction of news of difference in the next example set in a manufacturing company in the South of England.

Frustration at Foggy Bottom

The marketing director of Cavendish Dyes[3] was an engaging, energetic man. He was a direct, extroverted Yorkshire man who had been appointed a year earlier. His obvious enthusiasm for the companies' products and its commercial potential had been tempered by some puzzling episodes that had left him feeling confused, frustrated and wary. His appointment had been with an explicit brief. It was his clear responsibility to translate the enormous potential of a new range of products developed by the R&D department into commercially successful products. He was charged with getting them off the R&D shelf and into the retail stores.

At first he set about his task energetically, identifying specific products for launch and putting together marketing and advertising programmes. He described his growing dismay and discomfort at the intense scrutiny and 'cross examination' that these plans received from the powerful company Chairman, and at the absence of support from his fellow board members in making the case. He felt isolated in

---

[3]This is a pseudonym. I worked with this company in the mid-1980s when the company was part of a larger holding business. The holding company was subsequently dissolved. While Cavendish Dyes survived this dissolution all of the key players have either left or retired. This made it impossible to obtain permission to use the registered name of the company in this case.

board meetings and frequently put on the spot by the Chairman. As part of a company-wide cost cutting exercise, along with everyone else, he had been asked to submit plans to cut back on expenses. He lost his only assistant in this exercise only to discover that he was the only senior manager not to have 'padded' his budget sufficiently to allow for such cropping. His much-needed assistant was the only casualty of the whole exercise.

The blatant incongruence between his explicit brief and these indirect signals was striking. They pointed to a deep-seated and unhelpful pattern of behaviour in the boardroom. As a newcomer charged with realizing the commercial rewards of newly developed products, he was feeling demoralised and undermined.

Both of these stories highlight ways in which difference is dampened in subtle, often unthinking ways and, on occasion, through simple neglect.

The activities of the newly appointed marketing director, an outsider, not a member of 'the family', could be seen as confronting a very sensitive but masked issue for the company as a whole. His activities represented a threat to the stability of a long established, but hidden, cultural pattern of commercial caution and under-performance that was an unconscious way of protecting the pervasive sense of family that pervaded the company culture. Little wonder that he felt so isolated and challenged in defending his proposals to the chairman. When set in the context of an overall cultural pattern that was described as resembling the stunted growth of a pot-bound plant (described in Chapter 7), it doesn't take much to see why he fell victim to a tacit collusion to remove his support staff through the device of budget cuts. His activities were being pruned back. Even his naturally gregarious and ebullient personality was becoming subdued. In systemic terms he represented a threat to the ongoing stability of the 'game' or pattern of relations, regardless of the fact that it had evidently dysfunctional consequences in important parts of the business.

It is in this respect that human systems are unlike cybernetic circuits. Whereas news of a temperature rise will trigger an adaptive, corrective response in a thermostat to keep the temperature within a certain range, human systems can choose to ignore, reject or interpret news of difference in ways that sustain an ongoing pattern of behaviour or set of beliefs.

We need to exercise caution when bringing in outsiders, appointing people who bring difference, especially if we expect them to make a difference, to stir things up and bring fresh thinking. While they may represent difference, that difference may be no match for the weight of taken for granted traditions and social pressures of an established culture. In order for any difference to make a difference, the provision of exceptional emotional and political support is called for. We need to find ways to 'treasure our exceptions'. While news of difference has the potential to trigger a change in the patterns of thinking and behaviour within an organisation it is in the *response* to such news that the potential for change lies. In my work as a consultant I have come to the conclusion that helping clients discover news of difference is necessary but not sufficient for change to occur. I have learned that at least as much effort needs to be given to supporting clients in processing the emotional and cognitive disruptions that arise when a cherished pattern of behaviour, a cultural nerve, is threatened.

The three cases that follow illustrate a variety of ways in which news of difference was acquired and exceptions treasured in a manner that made a difference. They describe a range of ways in which leaders and managers pursued news of difference, how they responded to this news and the circumstances that led to a reconfiguration of cultural assumptions. At the conclusion of the chapter we use these examples to reflect on different ways in which leaders can become active participants in the emergence of new patterns of understanding and action and we consider other conditions that contribute to the formation of new understandings and cultural patterns.

We have suggested that cultural change occurs when anomalies are embraced, when difference is not pushed away or otherwise dismissed. Cultures change when people are prepared to open themselves to new possibilities, to different ways of thinking and to different points of view. Things change when difference becomes a source of curiosity not ridicule. This is the subject of the first, brief case.

Inquiry and Difference at the Wrekin – Stepping Outside the Boundaries

As part of their efforts to transform the culture of the Wrekin District Council, Roger Paine and his senior management team decided to learn as much as possible about the culture of an organisation which embodied the value of quality. Wanting their authority to be known for high standards of service delivery they chose Marks and Spencer, the retail company, as an organisation that was widely considered to be a hallmark of quality for its products and the standards of its service. Arrangements were made for their assistant personnel manager, Danny Chesterman, to spend six weeks on secondment in a local M&S branch.

For six weeks he immersed himself in the Marks and Spencer way of doing things distributing his time between Corporate HQ, a regional distribution centre, and in a local branch. He attended training events and took temporary positions working in a variety of departments, attending meetings and joining in both formal and informal events. He absorbed the M&S culture as a colleague working alongside regular employees, and by keeping a keen eye open. In all of this he was acting as a kind of cultural anthropologist, an ethnographer interested in the beliefs and customs of a community or society. In this sense his role was not so far removed from the work of legendary anthropologists such as Margaret Mead (1928) and her work in New Guinea or Bronislaw Malinowksi[4] (1922), and his studies of the Trobriand

---

[4]Bronisław Malinowski was a Polish anthropologist who suggested that the goal of the anthropologist, or ethnographer, is: 'to grasp the native's point of view, his relation to life, to realise *his* vision of *his* world'. In other words, the aim of an anthropologist is to experience the everyday life of members of a society along with them, to understand *their* reality in *their* terms.

Islanders. While Danny soaked up the novelty and surprises of this culture, what made his discoveries so significant for the Wrekin was how Roger Paine and his management team colleagues *responded* to his experiences and insights on his return.

Danny's brief was to learn as much as possible about the Marks and Spencer way of doing things. When the six weeks were up Danny returned the Wrekin District Council and was invited to the weekly management team meeting to report back on his experience. Ten minutes had been allocated on the agenda to hear Danny's observations. As it turned out they were so fascinated and inspired by Danny's experiences that the session ended up lasting more than two hours. According to Roger Paine:

> 'That day was a bit of a watershed because we agreed a host of things and one of them was to set up a team of people to come up with what they thought should be the values. The team would be drawn from each department to try to articulate the values that we ought to be following and that started us.' (McLean & Marshall, 1989)

The interest, receptivity and deep curiosity of the senior team to the new ideas and thinking that Danny brought back with him provoked new thinking about how the Wrekin District Council could set about the task of transforming their culture. The willingness of the leadership team to reflect on their own assumptions, to consider different ideas and possibilities and to actively champion and support their incorporation into the routines of daily life in the Wrekin, was key to the emergence of a culture that became renowned for providing exceptional levels of service to their community. Danny brought back news of difference, Roger Paine and his team embraced this as a provocation, a disturbance to their prevailing worldview and in so doing created the conditions in which new understandings could be woven.

When Danny entered the local branch of Marks and Spencer he not only stepped into a new physical space he also stepped into a new cultural setting. In so doing he had also stepped outside of the boundaries of Wrekin District Council thinking. The visit to another organisation had been embraced as a source of new constructs and triggered a host of significant initiatives among staff in the Wrekin. The management team's response to his discoveries ensured that it was a difference that made a difference.

The next example of these ideas in application is set in Cleveland, Ohio, in the United States, and describes a more ambitious project to interrupt a counterproductive cultural pattern that held its members in a vice-like grip.

The Medic Inn — Cultural Immersion

Frank Barrett and David Cooperrider (2001) describe a case of a low-performance hotel that had become enmeshed in seemingly intractable conflicts and rivalries among the management team. Try as they might, none of the more traditional problem solving and conflict resolution approaches were leading to any significant shifts. A more radical course of action was agreed upon. Instead of trying to fix the problems of the current pattern of relationships they collectively decided instead to inquire into the culture, values and modus operandi of another organisation, an award-winning hotel widely recognised for its exceptional standards of service.

> 'Our task was to break out of the current frame altogether. Rather than ask the group members to directly face their tension, to become introspective, and to look at themselves and at their own problems, we proposed that they become active inquirers, focusing on a domain outside their own.' (Barrett & Cooperrider, 2001)

Their approach was partly informed by Petrie's theory of learning (1981) through metaphor, which suggests that:

> '... an anomaly must be introduced that stimulates active thought experimentation and subsequent expansion of cognitive frames.'

A group of about 30 staff participated in this experience. They travelled to a nearby city and checked into the highly regarded hotel for a week. At the time David Cooperrider and Frank Barrett were in the early stages of developing an approach to organisational change that has become known as Appreciative Inquiry.[5] This method deliberately inquires into the most positive, life-giving aspects of the host companies' operation, searching out the root causes of exceptional performance. Their task was to discover those features of hotel's operations and staff behaviour ...

> '... that exhibited fundamental strength and value in terms of the system's people, its management process, its culture, and methods of organization. Deliberately appreciative in nature, the inquiry into the new domain was to revolve around a number of core questions.

> 1. What were the peak moments in the life of the hotel the times when people felt most alive, most energised, most committed and most fulfilled in their involvement?
> 2. What was it that the (hotels' staff) members value most about themselves, their tasks and the organization as a whole?
> 3. Where excellence had been manifested what were the organizational factors (structures, leadership approaches, systems, values, etc.) that most fostered realization of excellence?
> 4. What were the most significant embryonic possibilities, perhaps latent within the system, that signified realistic possibilities for an even better organization? (Barrett & Cooperrider, 2001)

---

[5] There are many texts describing the theory and practice of Appreciative Inquiry. See for instance: Barrett and Fry (2005). Additionally see: Watkins, Mohr, and Kelly (2011).

The team spent two days conducting interviews, asking staff and guests about their high-point experiences, hanging out behind the scenes, observing exchanges between hotel staff and guests as well as reflecting on their own experience as guests in the hotel. The authors write that members of the team:

> '... not only interviewed staff members, but because they stayed at the hotel as guests, they were instructed to note in their journals as many other features as possible. They collected numerous details, for example, on how service was delivered, how their beds were made, how the washrooms were cleaned, how food was delivered, and how employees talked to one another and to guests. In addition to noticing physical layouts, they collected data on how employee meetings were run, who attended and what issues were discussed, and how training programs were conducted.' (Barrett & Cooperrider, 2001)

The facilitators patiently supported members of the team in making sense of what they had discovered. At the same time they encouraged participants to reflect on *how* they were making sense of this material. In doing this they were inviting the visitors to notice the taken for granted assumptions and habitual explanatory frameworks that normally shaped their worldview. This process gradually heightened awareness of the group's preferred constructs and perceptual filters. At the same time they drew attention to the anomalies, the puzzles, the differences and the surprises in what they had found and experienced. What was it that *didn't* make sense to them?

Over the course of many discussions both at the hotel and in the following months, new ideas, new concepts, new terms and phrases began to take form. The group continued to meet for more than 10 months following the visit drawing on their discoveries to formulate a new way of thinking about their business and introducing many 'unique social and physical changes at the Medic Inn'. Gradually, 'through continuing dialogue the group's critical reasoning began to take shape'; a new culture was being painstakingly created, accompanied by a growing sense of excitement and possibility.

> 'There emerged a "four-star" language to reflect images of uniforms, behavioral norms, policies, and procedures. Members from different departments who previously could barely speak to on another began to develop a common language as details for physical revisions and personnel moves were discussed.' (Barrett & Cooperrider, 2001)

The visit resulted in many operational innovations. In the context of cultural change, the significance of this case lies in the fundamental shift that occurred in how the team *conceived* of the management and day-to-day operation of a hotel. The team had begun to think in a fundamentally differently way. Like Danny Chesterman at the Wrekin, they had also stepped outside the boundaries of their thinking. They had left behind the familiar setting and taken for granted routines of their own hotel, both literally and figuratively, and stepped into a different culture with its own very different assumptions, values and traditions. By immersing them-selves in a different culture and with the support of skilled facilitators dedicating time to the process of finding new meaning, they began to formulate new ways of thinking about a business that they thought they understood.

This is an example of weaving. It called for a huge commitment of time and resource as well as exceptional humility and openness to learning. The team amassed an enormous amount of information in the course of their stay and signifi-cantly, they also recognised that an equal amount of time was needed to make sense of what they had learned. Quite literally, they took time out to construct new expla-nations; new ways of thinking about a business that they had been steeped in for the duration of their careers; new ways of thinking about all aspects of how they ran their operation.

This is an example of collective inquiry. They deliberately sought out news of dif-ference before immersing themselves in this alternative reality. The dedication of two days to discovery and two days to making sense of what they had discovered, formulating and articulating to each other what they had learned, meant that the conclusions and insights were forged through debate, discussion and the articulation of new understandings.

This was a process in which new meaning was painstakingly co-created in the heart of a community. It was an example of collectively weaving new webs of mean-ing and understanding from different presuppositions, of working, as it were, with new assumptive thread. It also represented a commitment to discovery, a coura-geous form of humility, perhaps borne of desperation that opened them up to new possibilities, to new ways of thinking and acting. The experience called for a willing-ness to look again, to know in a different way and to set aside the authority of a career. The authors stress the importance of creating 'a deliberately supportive environment' in order to build 'innovative and creative ideas for the future of the organization' (Barrett & Cooperrider, 2001).

The payoff from this investment in time and personnel was dramatic. Within two years their hotel had gone from no stars to four-star status, and went on to win a string of prestigious awards.

One of the more intriguing by-products of this experience was that the long-standing differences among board members were spontaneously resolved. They sim-ply evaporated with the natural discovery of a shared sense of purpose within the top team. Commenting later on this case Cooperrider[6] observed that it represented a validation of a famous quote by Einstein:

> 'No problem can be solved from the same level of consciousness that created it.'

In this case, stepping into a world informed by different understandings, values and taken for granted views of reality, helped the group to relinquish one level of

---

[6]This was an observation made in the course of a seminar.

consciousness and collectively weave another. Through a process of immersion and active inquiry into another culture they were able to introduce transformational changes in their own operation and, at the same time were able to transcend patterns of thinking that had kept them locked in barren conflicts and disputes for so long. The case illustrates the genesis of a new paradigm or culture.

An interesting post-script to this fascinating story lies in the chosen method of inquiry. The team did not read about other, exemplary, hotels. They did not commission experts to talk to them or make elegantly tailored presentations about the management of leading edge hotels. They did not conduct a sophisticated statistical analysis of the key dimensions, or core competencies of outstanding hotel management. They went and stayed on site. They soaked up an understanding through direct contact with people in the setting, listening to all voices and perspectives. They hung out, took a second look at the familiar with fresh eyes, eavesdropped on exchanges between staff and guests and attended to their own experiences of the service as hotel guests. Like Danny Chesterman, they too took on the role of latter-day anthropologists trying to understand another culture in its own terms. This called for a suspension of judgement, for heightened alertness to minutiae and sensitivity to the low-profile symbols of this alternative culture. In order to weave a new fabric of understanding it also called for a willingness to surrender long-held interpretations and explanatory frameworks.

This case shows that cultural weaving calls for bold experimentation, for openness to difference and for a commitment to learning from difference. It requires a willingness to suspend long-held beliefs and practices and to entertain the possibility of new ways of seeing long enough for their practical implications to become apparent. Above all, it calls for direct involvement in these processes as an active participant and a willingness to set aside the comforting cloak of authority. Difference is a fragile and transitory moment of possibility that is all too easily missed, overlooked or dismissed from the illusory vantage point of certainty.

One of the notable features of this case is the realisation by the consulting team that the group risked bringing their normal and familiar ways of understanding and making sense to the situation that they encountered. The facilitators' role in encouraging the group to attend to the anomalies, to the behaviours, language and practices that were out with their familiar experience was key for the emergence of a new, shared understanding of the hospitality business. Here we see the transformative power of news of difference working in combination with a process that encouraged sustained and serious interest in anomalies. It also points to the valuable role played by insightful and skilled facilitators.

The transformative power of stepping outside of a culturally familiar world is a theme in the next, extended, example. In addition to illustrating the value of inquiry as part of a cultural change process the case shows how an initiative that was originally targeted at middle levels of management gradually and progressively interwove the views and contributions of other levels and perspectives. It is particularly interesting because it challenges the common assumption that such processes have to start at the top and require some form of comprehensive, implementation plan. My account of this case is from the perspective of one of two lead facilitators working in close cooperation with the internal head of training. The benefit of this is that it allows for an insider's account of an emergent process. The caution is that it is written from this one perspective, albeit with the endorsement of organisational representatives.[7] In addition to offering a further illustration of the value of news of difference the case illuminates the interweaving of a number of cultural threads described in Chapter 4 and illustrates other phenomena that facilitated the weaving of a different cultural web. We will comment on these in the course of the account and again in reflections at the end of the chapter.

New Ways — The Inner London Magistrate's Courts Service[8]

Background — Changing Times

In the late 1990s The Inner London Magistrate's Courts Service had seen a large portion of their workload eliminated with the introduction of statutory fines for minor offences such as speeding penalties or parking infractions. This reduction in demand was accompanied by a drastic cut in their budgets. Staff cuts accompanied the closure and rationalisation of a number of courts. Remaining staff felt that they were severely under-resourced and that adjusting to the new situation called for new ways of doing things. It was simply not possible to get the business done using the old, familiar, methods that had served them for more than a century. In effect a paradigmatic or cultural change was being called for. The management team responded to this situation by commissioning a training programme that they called New Ways. The idea was to introduce this hard-pressed and demoralised section of middle management to new ways of doing things. Conceived originally as essentially a form of training, the idea was that experts would introduce new practices and processes via a series of workshops. In the event, the client agreed to something very different: a process based on inquiry into other cultures.

Design of the Intervention

The design of the intervention featured the formation of a number of inquiry groups (see Figure 1). These were groups of 15–20 people comprising a cross section of middle managers from across the range of courts and from central administrative functions. The groups met on three, two-day meetings over a period of 8–10 weeks in total. The central idea of the design was that each group would engage in a process of discovery to find new ways of working that would bring fresh thinking and

---

[7]An account of this work was submitted to senior members of the organisation for their comment. A paper based on this case was subsequently published with the full approval of the senior management team.
[8]For a fuller discussion of this case see McLean and George McLean (2002).

ILMCS New Ways Programme

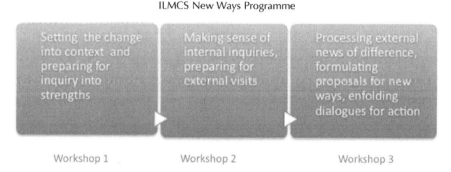

| Setting the change into context and preparing for inquiry into strengths | Making sense of internal inquiries, preparing for external visits | Processing external news of difference, formulating proposals for new ways, enfolding dialogues for action |

Workshop 1   Workshop 2   Workshop 3

Figure 1:   Phases of inquiry and sense making in the Inner London Magistrates Court Service.

practices to the managers of the Courts Service. They were charged with discovering news of difference and using their discoveries to formulate proposals for new ways of managing the service. The design of the process was intended to prepare them for the inquiries, to support them in making sense of what they had discovered and in assessing their potential value to the Service. Finally it was intended to support the assessment of these ideas through conversations that interwove the multiple perspectives, levels of responsibility and professional orientations that collectively comprised the Service. The case describes how the Service came to be reconfigured around different assumptions, different practices and a different pattern of relations between key groups or constituencies. It describes the emergence of a different culture over a period of 18 months.

What follows is a description of each of these three events together with the activities that occurred in between them. This is followed by a discussion of the processes and circumstances that supported the emergence of new, shared understandings and the weaving of new cultural patterns.

Event 1: Current Realities, Context, Contract and Commitment

The first of these two-day meetings began by asking participants to describe their experience of recent changes and encouraged them to express what feelings had been provoked in the course of this period of relative turmoil and change. They drew pictures, listed the many changes they were aware of and wrote newspaper headlines that encapsulated their experience. In addition, they also explored how much say they had over these changes (see Figure 2, from McLean & George McLean, 2002). In this way they built up a multi-layered map of their realities,[9] and compared each other's experiences noting similarities as well as differences.

---

[9]This is akin to Geertz's (1973) notion of 'thick descriptions'.

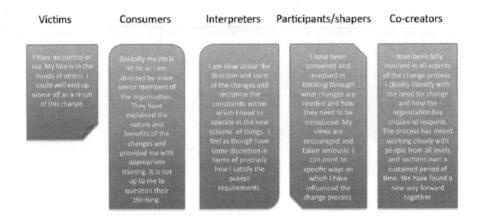

Victims	Consumers	Interpreters	Participants/shapers	Co-creators
I have no control or say. My fate is in the hands of others. I could well end up worse off as a result of this change.	Basically my job is to do as I am directed by more senior members of the organization. They have explained the nature and benefits of the changes and provided me with appropriate training. It is not up to me to question their thinking.	I am clear about the direction and spirit of the changes and recognize the constraints within which I need to operate in the new scheme of things. I feel as though have some discretion in terms of precisely how I satisfy the overall requirements.	I have been consulted and involved in thinking through what changes are needed and how they need to be introduced. My views are encouraged and taken seriously. I can point to specific ways on which I have influenced the change process.	I have been fully involved in all aspects of the change process. I closely identify with the need for change and how the organization has chosen to respond. The process has meant working closely with people from all levels and sections over a sustained period of time. We have found a new way forward together.

•Where would you place yourself on this line right now?
•Where would you like to be?
•What can you do that would help you move closer to your desired position? Three suggestions.

C McLean & George Ltd

Figure 2:   The change continuum.

Looking to the Future — Disruption and Disturbance

Three members of the management team joined the group over a lunch of sandwiches and bites. The senior managers were invited to offer their frank assessment of how things looked for the service as a whole. What did they see as the challenges facing the service and how capable was it of responding to these challenges? Participants were encouraged to contribute their thoughts about these questions in the spirit of dialogue.

The setting was designed to encourage informal conversation at tables scattered through the luncheon area. Each management team member sat among participants and discussed how things looked from their vantage point. The idea was to provide a broad context for the work of the inquiry groups and to give everyone a chance to discuss the implications of the externally imposed changes that the service as a whole was facing. To my surprise this proved to be a disturbing experience for members of the inquiry groups. Following the departure of the 'guests', the group compared notes on the discussions they had been party to. Many of them were angry. It seemed that the management team representatives did not have answers to all of the challenges facing the Service and had admitted to being uncertain as to how things might unfold for the Service in the long term. Feelings of disappointment and shock were expressed. How could these senior managers admit to not knowing how things would work out? Surely this is why they were paid such high salaries!

Others pointed out a contradiction in these reactions. If participants are genuinely being asked to contribute to finding new ways of doing things, to developing new ways of working, then it seemed reasonable that senior executives did NOT have all the answers. The discussion revealed a long established cultural pattern of dependency between staff and their leaders. It became clear that the management team had seen it as part of their role to 'protect' staff from the vicissitudes of the external environment. While staff resented being treated like children, they also looked to their seniors to have the answers and to provide reassurance; a double bind was in operation. The discussion finally shifted when one of the least senior members of the group pointed out that they faced a choice. Did people want to 'continue complaining and keep themselves as passive victims of events', or could they 'treat the request from senior management as genuine', and accept their invitation to play a part in changing the Service?

Each member of the group spoke to this question and most, but not all, chose to accept this novel invitation. Things had begun to change already. This was a fateful moment, a moment of change when a long established cultural pattern was revealed. On this occasion, as on others when I have witnessed out-of-awareness patterns being acknowledged and openly questioned, there were heightened levels of attention, energy and emotionality. Strong feelings were being expressed and with a degree of candour that is rare in public forums. From the perspective of one of two facilitators I sensed an alertness and attentive presence on the part of all members of the group. It felt as though we were teetering on the edge of something. It was a moment of both catharsis and confrontation. The articulation of the options facing the group amounted to a self-administered ultimatum; either we accept the responsibility that accompanies this invitation to contribute, or we stop complaining! Even though there were feelings of anger and fear being expressed it became evident that there was also a growing sense of excitement and of new possibilities. For me, this was a moment of awakening. It was a moment when people sensed a chance to step outside the safety of familiar patterns, to 'wake up' and participate in creating something new. It was to their considerable credit that members of the group chose to accept the invitation. It is my experience that the interruption or dislodgment of cultural patterns invariably triggers this kind of cathartic release.

Engaging in Inquiry

The remainder of the two days was spent in preparation for the process of inquiry. They were introduced to Appreciative Inquiry as a method for discovering new possibilities and welcomed the emphasis that it places on unearthing moments of exceptional performance and resourcefulness. I sensed that they had grown weary of problem finding methods and the deficit discourse that accompanies them. We in the facilitation team had deliberately chosen to offer this strength-based method as a counterpoint to the critical and often adversarial style of discourse so common in the courtroom.

As a first step participants were charged with discovering examples of operational excellence and efficiency that were already happening within the service, both in their own and in each other's courts. This meant becoming familiar with the Appreciative style of inquiry and questions. They interviewed each other in pairs and directly experienced the positive impact of questions that invited reflection on experiences of success and surprising accomplishment. While the intention of these interviews was to familiarise people with the Appreciative method it was clear that helping them to reconnect to positive experiences and stories in the course of their career not only unearthed long forgotten memories but was also an uplifting, positive experience. The mood became more optimistic.

Their first task as inquirers was to conduct interviews in parts of the Service that they were less familiar with in order to discover practices associated with high performance. They were to visit each other's courts and use the Appreciative Inquiry method to discover examples of novel practices that expedited the processing of the workload. They asked about stories of when the courts had been operating at exceptional levels of productivity and efficiency.

The use of questions that inquire into strengths and high-point experiences, was a new experience for these members of the Service.[10]

Event 2: Sharing Discoveries

The second of the two-day meetings was an occasion for them to share with their colleagues what they had discovered in the course of their inquiry visits.

To their considerable surprise, these inter court visits revealed practices that were as valuable as they were unexpected. For example, one court routinely held a 'communications' meeting first thing every Monday morning to anticipate the events of the coming week and to allow everyone a chance to make announcements, offer information or issue a request. This seemingly mundane activity was news for many groups and was eagerly adopted by them into the routines of their own court.

This was more than an exchange of learning however. As the spirit of learning and reflecting grew, increasingly they used the combined ingenuity of the whole group to build on this 'news of difference' to generate fresh possibilities for New Ways. Much interest was generated as people disclosed changes that they had already adopted as a consequence of their visits. New questions and topics of inquiry arose in the course of these exchanges and formed the focus for a second round of inquiry.

After having made sense of their discoveries during the first round of visits the facilitation team suggested a second series of inquiry visits. This time the idea was to visit organisations with a strong reputation in a particular aspect of managing or

---

[10]In the course of these workshops we began to hear accounts of observations made by people not directly involved in the workshops. One such account described a manager witnessing people showing up to an office for their interview. They each approached the office with a somewhat resigned air but left with 'a spring in their step, virtually skipping their way out'. The puzzled observer asked a colleague what was going on in the interview room, because whatever it was, she wanted some of it!

organising and from whom participants felt that they might glean further ideas. For example some members of the group were especially interested in companies that created a great working environment for their staff while other wanted to learn about applications of technology that could expedite data processing. Once the topics of interest had been identified, group members paired up and made plans for their visits.

Visits were made to a wide range of organisations in the three weeks between the second and third workshops. For example one pair spent a day at the 'The Body Shop' where they spent half the time with the personal assistant to the CEO. Others visits were to the headquarters of Virgin Airways, to a Fire Brigade that had recently introduced new technology to expedite the dispatch and routing of their fire tenders. Yet other groups visited Magistrate's Courts Services in other parts of the country that enjoyed a reputation for outstanding service standards.

Event 3: Making Sense and Formulating New Possibilities

There was a twin focus for the third, two-day event. In part it was another opportunity to share the news of difference from visits to other organisations but it was also used as an opportunity to translate them into specific proposals for New Ways of managing the day-to-day operations of the Service. The first day was spent in discussion of what the teams had discovered in the course of their visits to other cultures.

The effect of the visits was electrifying. Each pair returned with fascinating insights, bringing news of difference from their generous hosts. What added impact to their discoveries was the fact that the Magistrate's Service is effectively a closed culture. Once people join the service many remain for their entire careers. As a consequence, they have very little awareness of practices elsewhere. Not only did the visits expose them to new ways of doing things, ways that were literally inconceivable to them prior to the visits, but the visits also helped them become more aware of their self-limiting, culturally held, assumptions. Here again is an example of the value of stepping outside of the physical and cultural boundaries of their organisation and their profession.

As this increasingly rich set of discoveries accumulated, the conversation naturally shifted to considering how these practices and mindsets might be fruitfully applied to the challenges facing their Service. The group split into small teams that worked on developing scenarios for how the Service might incorporate and adapt some of this news of difference and to finding novel ways of representing their scenarios. Independently of the workshops some of the inquiry pairs held meetings to share what they had learned with colleagues in their courts and to invite their thoughts on how the discoveries might make a positive difference in the management of their court.

On day two of the third workshop the scenarios were further honed before sharing them with each other and later with representatives from other sections of the service. These included members of the management team, Stipendiary Magistrates and colleagues of course participants. The idea was to expand the discussion to include representatives from all parts of the Service, but to do so in an informal and inclusive way.

The discoveries and scenarios were shared using a 'marketplace' process. In the same manner as a local market with a collection of stalls there was a buzz of conversation as a number of presentations and conversations occurred simultaneously in different parts of the room. 'Visitors' were encouraged to circulate and engage in these local discussions about the ideas and scenarios[11] in the same manner as someone visiting a market. 'Stallholders' competed to attract passersby and to engage them in conversations about ideas and possibilities.

The inquirers found novel ways of sharing their discoveries and fashioning them into proposals for new ways of operating. They had drawn on the inspiration and learning from their visits to suggests innovations in many aspects of service delivery. Visitors to one of these groups left with a gift bag in the manner of children at a party. In the bag were small artefacts that encapsulated the essence of specific ideas and suggestions. I recall for example the inclusion of a balloon with no colour pigment to signify the value of transparency as well as a toy car to symbolise flexible work/travelling arrangements. Another group had created a version of the game monopoly that engaged their 'visitors' in discovering and discussing many new ideas distributed on the various properties around the edge of the board.

At the end of visiting these displays there was an open discussion in which everyone, participants and 'visitors' together, reflected on the different proposals; what had merit and which ideas were worth pursuing? In the midst of one of these reflective conversations a highly regarded Stipendiary Magistrate commented on his relief at leaving this kind of meeting without feeling that another set of problems had been 'dumped' on him. People were not only coming up with lots of inventive suggestions, but he said, they were not looking to him, or the management team, to make them happen. This was an experience of difference and one that he welcomed. He was delighted to discover that people were ready and eager to run with these ideas. All they needed was support from the management team for the 'big-ticket' items; the rest were adopted locally and without fanfare.

Among other things to emerge from this process was a long considered decision to reequip the courts with new technology. One of the recurring 'Dreams' that featured in many of the presentations was of 'a laptop on every desk'. This became a reality within months enabling the service to make the leap from a Dickensian handwritten set of records to state-of-the-art information technology. In effect their information processing methods went from the 19th century to the 21st in one jump, enabling much more rapid processing of information and freeing staff

---

[11]We call this method a marketplace. In the same spirit of a market there are many stalls, visitors are free to wander and visit may stalls, examining the good on display and engaging in good natured conversation. The intention was to create a relaxed conversational setting conducive to reflection and dialogue.

up to reconfigure their record processing systems and to adopt a more strategic approach to the management of their workload. Not least of the benefits over time was the disappearance of mountains of oppressive files that crowded in on the clerks.

Not all ideas were adopted of course, but the assessment of what should be progressed was openly discussed in the room and open to influence by all.

In addition to service-wide changes such as the adoption of new technology and the introduction of new accounting methods, many local changes occurred spontaneously and did not call for management team approval or even their awareness.

In the course of these multiple inquiries, more and more stakeholders were folded into the conversations, extending the web of connectivity within the Service. A total of five groups undertook these inquiries so that there was a rolling series of inquiries in which later groups built on the ideas of their predecessors. Over a period of approximately 18 months the accumulated discoveries and insights from the visits combined to transform the operating practices within the service. At the same time there were other developments that contributed to the changing pattern of relations within the Service. We now turn to a consideration of these additional threads and how they were interwoven.

An Emergent Process...

This process of repeated cycles of inquiry with each group building on the ideas of their predecessors made for a strong sense of momentum. Not only was the Service transforming itself but interest in the process was also growing and spreading. Formerly sceptical members of the Service began to show up at open meetings and began to volunteer for inquiry groups.

The disarmingly light-hearted manner of the scenario presentations belied the seriousness and transformative potential of the dialogue and ideas that were emerging. Inspired by the enthusiasm and ingenuity of these ideas, and the creative way in which they were shared, the management team were themselves galvanised into action.

The management team found the Appreciative Inquiry approach intriguing and became increasingly prepared to participate in the process, especially as they too realised that staff were not looking to them to make the difference happen. In the course of the many informal conversations that were a feature of the process they repeatedly heard from staff that they did not need to protect them from bad news. 'Treat us like grown ups' was a frequently heard request; 'We can handle bad news as long as you are straight with us and open from the start'.

This represented a challenge to the belief that part of the job of the management team was to manage events on the boundary of the Service and the outside world in a way that protected staff from uncertainty and worry. The realisation that staff did not want to be protected from uncertainty was news of difference that triggered a shift in the pattern of their relations with staff, placing them on more of an adult-to-adult basis. As a result of this insight, the management team ensured that staff members were fully informed of subsequent developments as they unfolded and they invited staff to contribute to the thinking about how they might respond to some of the strategic issues confronting the Service. The culture had shifted.

A final development in this process was the decision by the management team to conduct their own Appreciative Inquiry. They were about to launch some major innovations (among which was the introduction of new IT across the service) and, encouraged by the positive experience of the New Ways process, they wanted to think about how best to approach the management of these changes. Following the example of their staff they chose to inquire into times when change had been managed well in the past. Deliberately choosing to focus on positive experiences of change, they conducted their own Appreciative Inquiry into this topic. They interviewed their own staff but also talked to people from each other's courts. This proved to be both an enlightening and galvanising experience for them. The Appreciative method helped enormously by focussing on experiences of success and thus avoided critical finger pointing and the allocation of blame for things gone awry. Each member of the management team interviewed an average of 10 staff members, drawing out their stories and identifying the specific behaviours and circumstances that had played a part in the successes.

The willingness of senior managers to set substantial time aside to elicit the ideas and views of staff in itself marked a significant shift and sent a strong signal about the new culture. Staff were at first surprised that their views were sought but welcomed the different pattern of relations that it marked. Here were powerful, highly regarded, and in some cases feared, leaders demonstrating a degree of humility and willingness to learn, and to learn from their staff, in a way that challenged long established patterns of hierarchy and deference in a service long on traditions of formality.

Following these interviews the management team spent two days in a hotel making sense of what they had learned and fashioned them into principles to guide them through the upcoming changes. High on their list was consultation and involvement of staff in the process.

Weaving

In these concluding reflections we consider the conditions and actions that comprise what we describe as the craft of cultural weaving.

Inquiry as Cultural Change

At the heart of the changes in the Inner London Magistrate's Service was a preparedness to inquire and to learn. This represented a significant departure from a tradition of didactic, top-down flow of information and expertise.

Embarking on such a journey in the form of an inquiry was a step into the unknown for the management team and for those who commissioned the process. Their willingness to try something new was an encouraging and courageous first step that signalled difference and was entirely consistent with the call to find New Ways of doing things in the Service. This said, their participation in the process was cautious to begin with. It was not until the third iteration of these inquiry cycles that the chief executive came to one of the open sessions for example. Her presence and participation in the marketplace event provoked much conversation and conferred a new legitimacy on the process that was followed by a marked increase in participation from her management team colleagues. Her presence and good-humoured participation represented an unmistakeable low-profile symbol of endorsement. As the caution of the senior team turned to enthusiasm so the process gained momentum.

Connecting Different Worlds — The Lunchtime Conversations

Creating an informal conversation forum between some of those responsible for leading the Service and the clerks responsible for day-to-day operations represented another departure. It was not just the informality of the experience that was new, but also the preparedness of the three directors to offer their frank assessment of the challenges facing the service including voicing their own doubts and concerns that caused such a frisson in the group. As has been described, here was a difference that was, initially at least, disturbing and unwelcome.

Bringing together these two communities for an out-of-the-ordinary conversation proved disturbing in the short term but ultimately generative. This kind of a meta-conversation between groups that normally only connect through hierarchical and operational forums brought together two 'communities of discourse' (Gergen, 1991) in an unusual way. A different kind of conversation took place that interrupted established assumptions and patterns of behaviour.

This exchange, predicated on the assumption that staff would welcome an opportunity to participate in a strategic discussion about the future of the Service, simultaneously revealed and disrupted a long standing cultural pattern, best characterised as a parent–child pattern of dependency (see Harris, 2004). It was this disruption of a familiar pattern, together with the willingness of the group to debate and reflect on their feelings of anger and confusion that led to an early shift in the pattern. The challenge issued by one of the younger female members of the group in the course of this discussion was instrumental in triggering the change of pattern.

The post-luncheon conversation that revealed the discomfort and anger of workshop participants allowed for a significant moment of change. It marked a turning point in the way in which these middle managers participated in the Service, a moment when they chose to relinquish the role of passive victims or interpreters of change.[12] In broader terms it was a moment when they accepted the tacit invitation from senior managers to become active co-weavers of the culture. The introduction of a disturbance by itself was insufficient for pattern change to occur. It was the

---

[12]See McLean and McLean (2002), op. cit.

combination of the disturbance together with the subsequent sense making that allowed for a pattern change to occur. This was an act of weaving. New meaning was being made in the course of that discussion, and it led to new patterns of behaviour.

Importing News of Difference

In a similar manner as the Medic Inn example, the generative source of new possibilities arose through a willingness to step outside the physical and cultural boundaries of the Service. Visits to other courts, and especially to non-related companies and organisations, provided news of difference that expanded the realm of possibilities in the thinking of professionals steeped in the conventions of a closed Service. It is tempting to compare them to explorers who voyaged to far off lands in search of treasure. What they brought back was treasure of a different kind, cultural treasure. They came back with new ideas and ways of thinking that were literally unimaginable within the conceptual confines of the Magistrate's Service. Crucially, I would suggest, the attitudes of interest and curiosity in these new ideas shown by their colleagues and by senior members of the Service created the conditions in which new possibilities could be developed for the Service. Senior managers displayed openness to difference and a willingness to suspend judgement long enough for the ideas to acquire robust sponsorship.

As an added bonus the visits illuminated norms and cultural patterns within the Service that they had become blind to. In so doing they made it possible to question hitherto taken for granted assumptions and conventions. The programme also allowed time for those who participated in the visits to make sense of what they had discovered. Through conversations with their colleagues on the programme and with an ever-expanding network of colleagues in the Service, these new ideas found their way into the broader discourse of the Service. Ideas discovered during visits were showing up spontaneously in the course of day-to-day meetings on an increasingly regular basis. This case illustrates how weaving requires time and space to reflect, to assess and to find new meaning and relevance in novelty.

Process as Container: Creating Space for New Possibilities

This case illustrates the potential of a semi-structured process to helpfully contain and support the weaving of new possibilities and the interruption of old patterns. In the same way as the weaving of a fabric calls for a frame or loom (see Figure 3) that holds the materials in place while they are being woven, there were aspects of this experience that served to temporarily 'hold' participants through a journey of uncertainty and surprise in a way that allowed for reflection on both disturbance and novelty.

The process provided a legitimate space where familiar interpretations could be suspended, allowing for debate and experimentation with alternative explanations and assumptions. People could experience the rare luxury of not knowing. Geertz (1973)

Figure 3:   Weaving loom.

speaks of cultures as filling the vacuum between 'what our body tells us and what we have to know in order to function'. He suggests that culture fills this vacuum with information. I would suggest that the process (a repeated pattern of three two-day workshops, inquiry visits and supported sense making in the interim) served to hold open the vacuum of not knowing long enough for new ways of thinking to develop.

It is suggested that this capacity for organisation members to pause, reflect and discuss significant events, be they welcome or otherwise, was instrumental in creating a generative climate, a climate in which people became ever more willing to entertain new ideas and possibilities, to weave. It was a space in-between, a moment when taken for granted, default interpretations would otherwise have occurred. Typically such conversations occur informally over coffee or lunch breaks, via emails or phone calls, journeys to and from work and so on. Shaw (1997) and others who write from the perspective of organisations as Complex Responsive Processes, suggest that these 'shadow' conversations are the source of innovation and change. This case points to the value of interweaving such shadow conversations with those occurring in the formal management of the Service, and to the generative power of brokering dialogue between the informal and the formal domains, in itself a kind of meta-conversation.

The visits also introduced news of difference into these in-between spaces, introducing novelty into the 'conceptual space' and allowing for new configurations of meaning.

Feeling Safe Enough

Engaging in informal dialogues, even with a clear sense of purpose and supportive facilitation, can provoke as much anxiety in senior participants as is felt by those lower in the hierarchy. As writers on Appreciative Inquiry point out, we have become accustomed to seeing organisations as problems to be solved and we automatically look for the causes of failure or breakdown, especially when seeking to effect more permanent change. The resulting conversation is often fraught with recrimination, finger pointing and fault finding in a way that closes down discussion. Such 'deficit discourse' creates a climate inimical to experimentation and risk taking, and thereby diminishes the chances of new behaviours occurring.

Using Appreciative Inquiry as the primary method for this process made it easier for these conversations to be both constructive and generative. Inquiring into strengths and positive future scenarios contributes to feelings of safety on the part of all participants. In this work as in many others, this was the case regardless of rank or seniority.

Accepting the legitimacy of peoples' feelings, their interpretations and responses to such provocations, albeit the strong expression of dismay, and at times anger, averted the risk of it turning into a subversive discourse. It is suggested that legitimating peoples' feelings in this way marked a step towards an adult–adult pattern of relating. In this case the process modelled a desired cultural shift. The medium carried the message.

Unfolding Process — Building Momentum

The process also ensured that the conclusions, the sense making that emerged from this conversation, served to inform and frame subsequent inquiries. The five iterations of these overlapping inquiry groups provided a rhythm and added further momentum to the entire initiative.

The experience in the Magistrates' Courts Service illustrates that the process of weaving can be a continuing and unfolding process of inquiring, discussing, testing ideas and acting into these new ideas over a period of time. It was a form of Action Inquiry (Reason & Bradbury, 2001). In this instance the five iterations altogether took something in the region of 18 months to complete. All the while new ways of doing things were being folded into the daily practices within the Service. At the heart of the process was the combination of inquiry with an inclusive and an ever-expanding dialogue. It was a continuously unfolding conversation with each group building on the discoveries of its predecessors. New meaning, new ideas and new possibilities were emerging in the course of the process and its five iterations through the conversations and exchanges. News of difference from other courts and outside companies enriched and disturbed the thinking, challenging long-held assumptions and sparking imaginations.

Supporting Sense Making — Creating a Meta-Conversation

Each of the inquiry groups met on three occasions for two days on each occasion (see Figure 1). Participants were active in between these set piece events, conducting interviews and, in small peer groups, sifting through what they had discovered in preparation for sharing with their colleagues and others. These are out-of-the-ordinary activities superimposed onto the day-to-day imperatives of running the service. They added to the workload of those who participated in the process but also introduced a different conversation into the Service. This ever expanding conversation served to encourage consideration of unquestioned and long-held habits and patterns of relating and allowed for the luxury of debating new possibilities. In this sense it might be regarded as a meta-conversation. This was a conversation that hovered above the compelling activities of ordinary business and which brought both context and perspective to these embedded routines. Increasingly insights and ideas from the meta-conversation found their way into the regular round of meetings.

Sustaining this kind of meta-conversation added to peoples' workloads and temporarily increased work pressures for many. A continuing tension throughout the 18 months was balancing the time demands that this process placed on participants and coping with their demanding day jobs. The continuing and active support of leaders for this work within the Service was essential. Fortunately, the evident benefits and changes that began to emerge from the process ensured that this support was forthcoming. However, as a general observation, such work calls for a sustained level of commitment and trust on the part of the organisational leadership. The weaving of cultural change takes time and the long-term support of leaders.

This was a participative process in which the senior management chose to become increasingly involved and to step into the process of weaving. It called for trust and a willingness to explore unknown territory both literally and metaphorically. News of difference, in this case, provided the thread from which the new cultural patterns were woven.

Finally the case illustrates the importance of matching the medium to the message. New processes, new conversations and new forms of participation were used to develop New Ways.

In the following chapter we consider how a new culture was woven when two giant companies decided to merge.

Concluding Comments

Cultural change represents a discontinuous shift, a paradigmatic break and accordingly calls for a different form of leadership than is required during times of continuity, relative stability and even growth. Such change calls on leaders to embrace uncertainty, to tolerate confusion, to live with the discomfort of not knowing and the anxiety of ambiguity. It calls for courage to tolerate periods of emotional turmoil that inevitably accompany uncertainty and experimentation. In many ways this form of leadership sits in direct opposition to orthodox notions of leaders as providing a clear direction, as taking charge and of being in control.

A Weaver's mind calls for qualities not commonly associated with leadership: humility, courage, a capacity to let go, a willingness to yield, to be changed, an attitude of curiosity and appreciation of the unfamiliar, the strange, the dissonant. It calls on leaders to be prepared to follow the lead of others, to attend to weak signals, to experiment with the counter intuitive, to step outside of familiar and comfortable routines and to embrace the unfamiliar and the uncomfortable. It calls on leaders and others to resist the temptation to judge, to dismiss, to ridicule that which is different. Difference is the generative source of Cultural Change.

References

Ashby, R. (1952). *An introduction to cybernetics*. London: Chapman Hall.

Barrett, F. J. (1998). Creativity and improvisation in Jazz and organisations. *Organisation Science, 9*(5), 605−622.

Barrett, F. J., & Cooperrider, D. L. (2001). Generative metaphor intervention: A new approach for working with systems divided by conflict and caught in defensive perception. In L. David, D. L. Cooperrider, P. F. Sorensen, T. F. Yaeger, & D. Whitney (Eds.), *Appreciative inquiry: An emerging direction for organization development*. Champaign, IL: Stipes Publishing LLC.

Barrett, F., & Fry, R. (2005). *Appreciative inquiry: A positive approach to cooperative capacity*. Chagrin Falls, OH: Taos Institute Publications.

Bateson, G. (1972). *Steps to an ecology of mind: Collected essays in anthropology, psychiatry, evolution, and epistemology*. Chicago, IL: University of Chicago Press.

Geertz, C. (1973). *The interpretation of cultures: Selected essays*. New York, NY: Basic Books.

Gergen, K. (1991). *The saturated self*. New York, NY: Basic Books.

Griffin, D. (2002). *The emergence of leadership*. London: Routledge.

Harris, T. (2004). *I'm OK, You're OK*. London: Harper.

Kuhn, T. S. (1962). *The structure of scientific revolutions*. Chicago, IL: University of Chicago Press.

Lawrence, P. R., & Lorsch, J. W. (1967). *Organization and environment: Managing differentiation and integration*. Boston, MA: Harvard University.

Malinowski, B. (1922). *Argonauts of the Western Pacific: An account of native enterprise and adventure in the Archipelagoes of Melanesian New Guinea*. London: Routledge and Kegan Paul.

McLean, A., & George McLean, M. (2002). New world wines in old world bottles. *Reflections: The SoL Journal 4*(2). MIT Press, Boston, MA.

McLean, A. J., & Marshall, J. (1989). *The Wrekin District Council: A cultural portrait*. Luton: Local Government Training Board.

Mead, M. (1928). *Coming of age in Samoa*. New York, NY: William Morrow and Company.

Morgan, G. (1986). *Images of organization*. Sage.

Palazzoli, M. S., Boscolo, L., Cecchin, G., & Prata, G. (1978). *Paradox and counterparadox: A new model in the therapy of the family in schizophrenic transaction*. New York, NY: Jason Aronson.

Petrie, H. (1981). *The dilemma of enquiry and learning* (2nd ed.). Chicago, IL: University of Chicago Press. Revised and updated 2011.

Reason, P. & Bradbury, H. (Eds.). (2001). *Handbook of action research−participative inquiry and practice*. London: Sage.

Shaw, P. (1997). Intervening in the shadow systems of organizations: Consulting from a complexity perspective. *Journal of Organizational Change Management, 10*(3), 235–250.

Watkins, J., Mohr, B., & Kelly, R. (2011). *Appreciative inquiry: Change at the speed of the imagination*. London: Wiley.

Weick, K. E. (1979). *The social psychology of organizing*. Phillipines: Addison Wesley.

Chapter 6

When Cultures Merge

The story goes that architects had designed a new university complex with many state-of-the-art buildings scattered over a large campus. Expanses of freshly laid grass turf offered a lush landscape in which the pristine buildings were set. During one of the many tours of the new campus one visitor questioned an omission. Why were there no pathways between the buildings? Intended as a pedestrian campus, this seemed like a glaring omission. Already sections of the lush turf were showing signs of wear as the new student intake made their way around, creating short cuts.

'That is precisely the point', explained the guide. 'The architects don't want to build the pathways until they see where people walk. It will take some time for the natural patterns formed by pedestrian traffic to become clear. The architects have postponed the installation of pathways until 12 months after the opening of the complex.'

'Years of study have convinced me that the real job is not to understand foreign culture but to understand our own.' (Ed Hall, 1966)

The Challenge

A Meta conversation of a different kind occurs when two companies merge.

Mergers are a time of change, which, as the Chinese remind us, represents both opportunity and danger. While media announcements of company mergers stress the commercial benefits of these strategic moves, the conversation in the corridors of both parties is more often preoccupied with the risks and opportunities that the merger represents to employees.

Decisions to merge companies are invariably commercial: to gain market share, to acquire rights to technology or intellectual property, to re-balance a portfolio and to reduce an unwieldy cost base. In the haste to secure a deal these arguments often push to one side one of the most significant factors that mediates between the operational success and failure of a merger. That factor is culture. Time and again parties to mergers and acquisitions overlook the significance of the deep familiarity, comfort and attachment that comes with cultural habituation. Organisation cultures take years to form. They represent an accumulation of traditions, stories of heroism, betrayal or folly that have been passed on from one generation to the next providing a sense of cohesion, identity and continuity. Mergers and acquisitions bring together two communities with their own weight of tradition, with their own taken for granted customs, habits and attachments. In social terms, a merger is akin to worlds colliding.

In spite of the compelling economic and commercial logic that draws companies into a merger all too often they falter on the hidden rocks of corporate culture. Some researchers estimate that failure rates for M&A activity are as high as 77%, (Carleton & Lineberry, 2004), citing the inability to integrate cultures as a major reason for failure. When we combine the tacit and taken for granted sense of normality and 'rightness' that defines a culture with the potent emotions of uncertainty, fear and rivalry that so often accompany mergers, such high failure rates should not surprise us. Ed Hall's observation, that the real challenge lies in understanding our own cultures before we seek to explore those of others, is especially relevant in merger situations. Without careful attention to such matters the possibilities for misunderstanding and conflict are enormous.

While the notion of merging cultures accords with a managerial view of cultures, as something that can be managed or manipulated, it betrays a limited understanding of the term culture, and may go some way to explaining why failure rates for mergers are so high.

To speak of integrating cultures implies that they can be combined, amalgamated or mixed. I would suggest that this is misconceived, implying as it does the blending of ingredients as if it were some form of cake or other culinary endeavour. Such a view does scant justice to the subtleties of understanding and interpretation that inform the hidden meaning making frameworks characteristic of a culture. It also risks casting leaders as somehow apart from a culture, like a master chef, manipulating it in some way, instead of acknowledging the inevitability of our participation as leaders, facilitators and managers.

The following case examines in some detail a process for supporting the emergence of a shared culture following a merger. In particular it describes the journey that supported first the appreciation of cultural differences followed by an extended meta-conversation that allowed new, shared understandings, new cultural pathways, to form. The case also considers the various forms of weaving that occurred over time and the role of the leadership in this unfolding process.

Weaving a New Cultural Tapestry — the NSN Story

The Context

In 2006 the mobile networks marketplace had been maturing for some time. This prompted the merger of two of the world's largest network providers: Nokia Networks and Siemens Communications. With this merger the new company,

Nokia Siemens Networks (NSN), became one of the world's largest telecommunications infrastructure companies.

The ambition of the chief executive Simon Beresford-Wylie was to create a sense of inclusion and, while wanting the new company to benefit from the strengths and practices of the legacy cultures, he was especially keen to involve employees in co-creating a distinctive culture for the new business.

I was invited to act as consultant on the cultural aspects of the merger by Alistair Moffat, the senior OD specialist appointed to lead the formation of the new culture.

The cultural merger of Nokia Networks and Siemens Communications was informed by our view of culture as a collective accomplishment that emerges over time and through a sustained process of conversation. The intention was to encourage the active participation of all 60,000 members of the new company.

> 'The approach saw the merger as an opportunity to develop a culture distinctive to the new entity and not as an integration of two cultures, based on "best of both" thinking. It was a deliberate attempt to create the conditions in which something novel might emerge. The emphasis was on cultural *formation* not cultural integration. Culture here is seen as an unfolding, emergent accomplishment over time — a multi-voiced conversation. The task was seen as discovering, noticing and capturing the emerging clarity, understandings and agreements as they formed fresh, cultural pathways unique to the new enterprise.'
> (Moffat & McLean, 2010)

This case is an example of an attempt to approach a merger from the perspective of cultural formation, not cultural integration. It illustrates the use of social technology (internet and intranet) to support the weaving of new understandings and the formation over time of agreed cultural principles in a global operation employing 60,000 people.

We saw a number of challenges in achieving this ambition:

- *Elevating Inquiry over Rivalry*: How to acknowledge the cultural traditions of both companies in a way that rendered hidden cultural understandings visible and that contributed to a constructive conversation? The intention was also to encourage a climate of mutual interest and curiosity rather than mistrust and suspicion.
- *Containment*: How to provide a conversation forum with the potential to engage all 60,000 employees in a way that offered sufficient focus while also allowing for an emergent process? How to provide some form of framework or loom to both support and contain the process of emergent meaning making and to accomplish this in the midst of a cauldron of heightened emotions that so often accompany merger processes. How to allow for the expression of legitimate thoughts and feelings at a time of heightened insecurity and uncertainty without unnecessarily amplifying levels of insecurity, mistrust suspicion and competition.
- *Reconciling Operational Imperatives and Emergent Processes*: How to reconcile the pressing need to integrate systems and procedures (in themselves forms of

cultural symbol) with the realisation that cultural pathways would take time to become clear? How to conduct business as usual while allowing for the natural pace of an emergent process? How to do all this while coping with the enormous technical and operational workload associated with a merger?

- *Interweaving the Formal and Shadow Conversations*: How to weave the interconnectivity between the aspirations and formal statements made by leaders with the parallel conversations occurring in the informal or shadow organisation? How to include the legitimate voice of leaders in the conversation while also encouraging all employees to fully participate in the thinking and debate?

All in all a tall order!

As a small OD team we realised that we were limited in what we might accomplish, after all our views about culture and cultural formation suggested that norms and patterns of behaviour would emerge naturally in local settings over time. Complexity theorist Patricia Shaw (1997) suggests that human systems have the capacity to self-organise and that any suggestion of engineering or directing a desired culture is not just mistaken but a delusion.

Shaw and others who write from the perspective of seeing organisations as complex responsive processes (Critchley, 2007; Griffin, Shaw, & Stacey, 1998) point to conversation as lying at the heart of meaning making processes. Inspired by their analysis, our consideration turned to how we might encourage constructive and generative conversations across the new company. How could we create the circumstances in which purposeful weaving of meaning could occur and in a way that sought to capture and highlight the emerging clarity of understanding as it became apparent? A further consideration was how to ensure the full participation of as many voices and perspectives as possible in this conversation.

We were especially concerned to avoid any form of top down process that emphasised the crafting of high-profile statements and that used professional communication initiatives. Our view was that such a process would indeed convey high-profile messages of intent but that these messages would be overshadowed by the low-profile symbols of the process, namely that this was a top down and polished approach. We realised that people would bring intense scrutiny to the early statements, actions and processes in an effort to find or create meaning in the midst of confusion and uncertainty. Small acts, or non-acts, would send big signals. The question for us was how to legitimate an emergent, unfolding sense-making process. We believed that this would be occurring privately anyway. We wanted to create the conditions in a way that invited open and constructive dialogue. Put another way, how could we encourage a healthy, open and inclusive process of weaving, an inclusive exchange and debate?

Combining these constraints together with these beliefs and ambitions we adopted an approach that sought to achieve the following:

Rendering the Invisible Visible: Revealing the taken for granted assumptions and understandings of both legacy cultures in order to make them apparent to both parties and so as to inform the conversation about future cultural intent.

Opening the Conversation: With an early expression of cultural intentions while inviting others to participate in this conversation.

Expanding the Conversation: Creating an inclusive forum for responding to the opening invitation and for participating in the weaving of new understandings.

Punctuating the Process: Finding and naming agreement. Noticing what is becoming evident, what cultural pathways are emerging? Deciding when and how to close the conversation. Transitioning from informal and emergent to formal and fixed.

Encouraging Mindful Weaving: Helping highly conspicuous senior leaders and managers to be thoughtful and intentional in how they participated in the conversation.

The Process Part 1 — Revealing Hidden Understandings

> 'Culture hides much more than it reveals and strangely enough what it hides, it hides most effectively from its own participants.' (Hall, 1959)

We chose to start by developing an appreciation of the legacy cultures of both companies. The intention of this was to surface and reveal the hidden assumptions and understandings that formed the cultural fabric of both companies. The hope was to do so in a way that provoked interest, curiosity and respect. Mergers founder on such hidden understandings and we wanted to ensure that they were, at least, open for all to consider. We also felt that by acknowledging what we might inelegantly term the '-isness' of both cultures any discussions about a future, desired culture could start from a realistic understanding of the inherited traditions of both companies.

We took seriously Ed Hall's caution that before looking to understand another culture it would be wise to understand our own first. What were the assumptions, values and patterns of behaviour that formed the cultural fabric of everyday life in both companies and to which they had become so accustomed as to no longer notice? What were the 'historically transmitted pattern of meanings' (Geertz, 1973, op cit) that guided action and informed their thinking? How were they similar and how different? How were these understandings conveyed through the daily symbols and low-profile exchanges of business as usual? What cultural symbols were held to be significant and what trivial? Who were the heroes in both cultures and what values did they embody through their behaviour? Similarly, who were regarded as anti-heroes or cultural villains and what values did their 'deviant' behaviour illuminate? What were the metaphors that configured the mindset of both cultures?

Surfacing this taken for granted or tacit knowledge was seen as a necessary prelude to any discussions about the future culture. In essence, the requirement was for people to reflect on what they were bringing with them by way of cultural history and to do so in a way that was respectful of both cultural traditions and appreciative of how they had served both companies in the past. We felt the need to respect and honour both of these cultural traditions but also to use such insights as a platform for any discussion about a desired future culture. Equally, our intent was to encourage an attitude of curiosity and inquiry into these cultural legacies, to notice similarities and differences, potential areas of synergy and to set a tone of informed debate.

Munich and Helsinki Workshops

We held two workshops, one in Munich and one in Helsinki. Approximately 40 people showed up at each of these events and they represented employees from a wide variety of departments and organisational seniority. They were, in effect, as diverse a mix of perspectives as it was possible to arrange at short notice.

They shared stories with each other about experiences that highlighted cultural understandings.[1] They worked in pairs initially then combined into groups of four. Each of these groups presented their consolidated sense of themes running through their stories. As part of their presentations each group was asked to create or find an image that captured a sense of the whole picture that was emerging. These were right brain, intuitive representations of their understanding.[2] The entire gathering then reviewed all of this information and reflected on the coherence of the picture that was emerging while also noting any puzzles or anomalies. Further insights emerged in the course of these conversations.

An enormous amount of information was generated in these workshops, and while both groups effectively validated the information generated through this process it was clear that further work was needed to highlight the themes and patterns in this material in a way that gave it sufficient coherence to be helpful to those members of both companies who had not been present at either workshop. How to find a way of summing up such complex information so that it would be recognisable to others, would not oversimplify the subtleties or nuances of each cultural fabric, but which would also provide a helpful departure point for dialogue and inquiry about a desired future culture?

Our professional beliefs meant that we wanted members of both companies to be part of the process of identifying patterns in the data thus generated. The constraints of budget, logistics and above all, work pressure, made this impossible. In the event we took a pragmatic view. At Alistair's suggestion the work of making sense of this mountain of material was undertaken by myself, and a graphic facilitator, Annika Varjonen. For two days we sorted through the wealth of cultural information that had been revealed through the stories and pictures, 'soaking' ourselves in the data. We used a version of Grounded Theory[3] (Glaser & Strauss, 1967) to

---

[1]The principles and methods for revealing hidden cultural understandings are described in Chapter 8.
[2]Paul Watzlawick (1978) argues that such right brain representations are the 'right royal route to the unconscious'.
[3]Grounded Theory is a method that helps to identify patterns and themes in qualitative data sets. See Glaser and Strauss (1967).

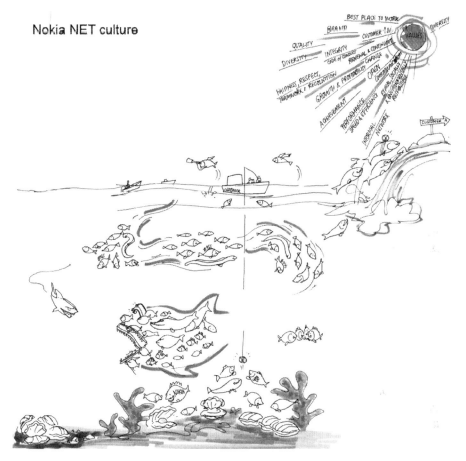

Figure 1:   Visual representation of Nokia Networks culture.

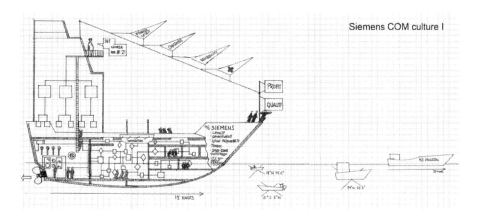

Figure 2:   Visual representation of Siemens Communications culture.

identify themes and patterns in the material. Gradually two cultural metaphors emerged. Annika drew graphic representations of these cultural configurations. They are reproduced in Figures 1 and 2 above.

The Process Part 2: Images Spark Informal Conversations

In addition to the creation of these graphic representations the data from the culture workshops was also captured in the form of a written narrative. In effect, these were two, traditional reports. These written narratives attracted little or no interest, demanding too much executive time.[4] To our surprise however, quite the opposite was true of the artist's imagery. They caught the attention of the new CEO, Simon Beresford Wylie, and his interest was such that he opened one of the early Executive Board meetings with a call to his Board Members to reflect on the significance of these representations for the process of cultural integration. By all accounts the ensuing conversation was lively and engaged with parties from both companies sharing stories that illustrated the imagery in the pictures. The use of imagery that was grounded in the workshop stories proved to be an illuminating and enlivening means of provoking thoughtful conversations about the cultural implications of the merger. They seemed to 'touch a nerve' in both companies and, unbeknown to us, were to be used in workshops across the company to inform and support conversations about the merger.

   The metaphors at the heart of these pictures evoke deeply held understandings that configure patterns of behaviour in both companies. The shoal of fish, an image that occurred in three separate drawings during the workshop in Nokia, captures the self-organising, value-based quality of the culture of Nokia Networks and evoked its capacity to change direction rapidly. It also depicts the strong emphasis placed on team working. The image of a supertanker featured in at least four separate discussion groups in the Siemens workshop. The fact that this image was selected, quite independently, in four out of six groups, pointed to its potency as a dominant metaphor within the business. The image of a supertanker captures the feeling of size and momentum characteristic of such a huge, global organisation. It also hints at the slowness to change direction many identified as a consequence of the companies' size, its consensus based decision-making tradition and its matrix structure. Similarly the layered decks capture something of the sense of hierarchy

---

[4]On reflection, we concluded that there were other qualities associated with the use of narrative that limited its capacity to engage and invite inquiry, especially when compared to the evocative imagery of these representations. There is a definitive quality to a narrative regardless of any caveats or qualifications that might be added. The reader has to decide whether to agree or disagree with the interpretation in the narrative, but is not called on to add their own colour in the same way as when responding to a picture. Narrative has a linear form whereas these pictures provide a sense of a complex, living whole. Finally the ambiguity of imagery invites inquiry and storytelling whereas narrative casts the reader as passive audience.

described in many stories as well the importance placed on observing formal processes. There are many details in both pictures that are not examined here, but which provoked an exchange of stories and cultural understanding throughout the new business.[5]

When viewed from the perspective of weaving, these images, of fish and a supertanker, somewhat serendipitously fostered a climate of interest in the cultural dimension of the merger. They were considered sufficiently valid portraits of both cultures as to allow and encourage constructive conversations and exchanges. They allowed parties from both sides to recognise and give voice to significant differences. For example speed of response to change was a significant point of difference between the companies as were the very different attitudes to hierarchy and decision-making. More importantly these images, and the conversations about them, contributed to a climate where differences were openly acknowledged and discussed. This in itself provided an informed platform for the conversation about the desired future culture for the merged company.

The Process Part 3 — Surfing the Wave of Interest

More important than the accuracy of these representations, however, was the fact that they encouraged non-defensive dialogue between the two companies and created a platform for thinking about the future. At the first two-day meeting of the top 300 new appointees, Alistair encountered a huge interest in the images. They spawned lively conversations that gave rise to the first tentative statements about a desired, future culture. As the leader of the process of cultural integration he was recording 'to camera' reactions to the discussions and came away overwhelmed by the interest and enthusiasm shown. 'This is really important' people said to him over and over again.

This openness to inquiry, the lively interest in similarities and significant differences, created a fertile ground for later discussions. It set a tone that others would follow later. It put cultural questions firmly on the agenda, generated real interest and goodwill and contributed to an atmosphere of co-creation and inquiry rather than competition. A wave of interest in the cultural conversation was gaining momentum.

Once again the challenge of making sense of the material generated in the course of this exercise posed a dilemma for the facilitation team. How to organise several thousand comments into a form that caught the spirit of this group and honoured their aspirations for the future? Once again we felt that the urgency of progressing

---

[5]The reader may notice a somewhat idealised representation of both cultures. The question of cultural 'shadow', the downside of cultural patterns, is not portrayed directly in these images. The shadow aspects of both cultures surfaced in both workshops, however, and were represented in separate images based on the same overall metaphors of fish and tankers. To capture these shadow aspects, Annika also created 'bad weather' drawings. It is interesting that these were not used in the course of workshops and subsequent conversations.

pressing operational matters meant that we had to compromise our desire to involve representatives from the group in identifying themes in the material. With considerable misgivings about the risks of imposing our seemingly arbitrary constructs onto this material three of us undertook the task of 'organising' it into themes.[6] Our analysis of the mass of ideas generated in the course of this meeting centred on five embryonic themes or topics:

Customer Focus: We are passionate about our customers. Customer focus is visible in our strategy, our decisions, our way of working and our behaviour.

Open Communication: We operate in a straightforward, pragmatic and values-based way.

Achieving Together: We, as individuals, influence, contribute to and are responsible for, our teams' achievements.

Being Valued: My team and I are valued members of the NSN community and our contribution increases the company value.

Innovation Leadership: Our customers value our innovation strength and our capability to make the difference.

The Process Part 4 — Widening the Conversation; the Ultimate Challenge

Spiders, in the construction of their webs create interim structures that they use as a kind of scaffolding and as temporary pathways while they in-fill the sticky threads that will ensnare their prey. In the closing stages of web creation they re-ingest these interim pathways.

The question then became, what to do with these embryonic expressions of cultural intent? Such statements commonly are turned over to communications experts for careful polishing and for conversion into High-Profile Symbols before being disseminated or 'rolled out' through a carefully orchestrated communications process. Job done! This is to view culture creation as about the creation of a product, a values statement or a manifesto of some kind, and did not accord with our view of culture as an unfolding process of meaning making that occurs throughout an organisation and which cannot be controlled from the top. In light of Simon Beresford Wylie's desire for an inclusive process and for involving employees in co-creating the culture for the new business, it was clear that a top down dissemination of this

---

[6]Alistair, his colleague Riita and myself ended up doing this work. We took the decision to do this in spite of the risks for pragmatic reasons. Things were moving very quickly and did not allow for protracted processes of consensus building. We took the view that tolerance for such an activity would be low among the cadre of newly appointed managers. We also took the view that the benefits of a 'good enough' summary of the themes was necessary to provide some containment of anxiety at a time when levels of uncertainty and complexity were extremely high.

thinking would not suffice. Furthermore, this was early thinking, not a final position. The challenge was how to open up the conversation to all 60,000 members of the new global business?

The Culture Square

Familiarity with Social Networking technology led Alistair and others to set up an intranet site. This electronic forum or chat room invited anyone to comment on these preliminary statements of cultural intent. The near universal availability of internet technology has enabled the sharing of views and ideas and serves as a novel means of convening a dialogue regardless of status, geographical location or length of tenure. It was decided to call this forum The Culture Square based on the notion of a community space for meeting, for dialogue and for the lively exchange of ideas.

On-line forums are no longer a novelty. The internet has proved to be a revolutionary means of convening shared interest groups. As a technology it bypasses and can subvert attempts by power hierarchies to control information. More and more generations are entering employment for whom membership of pan global, virtual communities is a taken for granted feature of daily life. As we adjust to the possibilities that this technology offers we are also discovering its disadvantages. It offers a platform for the unscrupulous and dishonest, for those who seek to propagandise, to prey on the unwary, and it brings us face to face with challenging questions of authenticity and veracity. The internet is a truly postmodern phenomenon that threatens the hegemony of those groups and individuals who have hitherto exercised editorial and censorship rights over popular media.

While such forums proliferate, the question of how to use them to facilitate and support constructive dialogue is less familiar territory. This represents new territory for those of us in the field of OD consulting and facilitation. In this regard, the experience of facilitating the Culture Square in NSN proved particularly instructive.

As leading players in the field of communications technology, employees of NSN were thoroughly familiar with the use of the internet and its applications. The establishment of an intranet forum as a way of hosting a conversation to support the process of cultural integration following the merger was readily accepted and welcomed.

Our interest was in using the Culture Square to support the formation of cultural patterns, norms and principles. We were also interested in how it could serve as a form of loom or framework for hosting debate and exchange long enough for shared understandings to emerge. *The Culture Square was not just a forum for debate. It was a living manifestation of a culture in formation.* The contributions were not solely ABOUT the new culture, the whole process of engagement, participation and discussion WERE the new culture in the process of formation.

This section of the chapter tracks the subjects and substantive content of discussions in the Square but also describes the dynamic of the unfolding process. It is this dynamic in particular, that illuminates the process of Cultural Weaving.

The Culture Square Is Launched, January 2007

The Culture Square was launched in early January of 2007. Since the legalities of the merger were not completed until early in April, European laws strictly prohibited direct contact between employees of both companies. This meant that two versions of the Culture Square had to be created, one for each set of employees. Comments from each set of employees were then pasted into the other's site. It was a 'clunky' arrangement and far from conducive to a spontaneous exchange. In order to participate in the Square people were required to register using a pseudonym, thus allowing for anonymous contributions. It was made clear that this was not a forum for official announcements but rather an open forum in which anyone could contribute to the debate and be part of the broader conversation.

It was felt that the conversation might benefit from facilitation in its early stages. Previous experience with similar initiatives had been mixed. The concern was that it could degenerate into a forum for petty complaints The intention of facilitating the Culture Square was to set a constructive tone, to foster an attitude of dialogue and inquiry and to encourage an exchange of knowledge and practice between these two industry giants. I agreed to act as facilitator for the early stages.

The invitation to participate described the overall intent and spirit of the exercise, asking people to offer their thoughts about the future culture. The five principles gave focus to the early contributions while also serving as a good enough interim framework that held the conversation open long enough for a more robust agreement and expression of cultural aspiration to develop.

The Culture Square was significant at two levels. It was a forum for hosting a conversation leading to agreement on high-level cultural values and principles. This was its legitimate role. At the same time, the nature and course of the conversation saw the emergence of norms of behaviour in the Square. Conventions or rules for participating in the Square gradually developed in the course of the many exchanges. Rudeness, offensive posts or comments ridiculing others for example were quickly sanctioned, and a generous spirit of sharing and exchange between contributors grew. The new culture was forming in the course of these exchanges. Initially, the Culture Square was intended as a vehicle for an extended, open conversation designed to culminate in a set of values and principles for the new culture. In this sense it was concerned with delivering a *product* — a statement of values. At the same time, through *the process* of debating, through the exchange of ideas and experiences, through the venting of frustration, anger, disappointment, as well as excitement and optimism, new patterns of relating took form. The act of posting a comment and receiving responses from others seemed to help people come to terms with their changed circumstances as evidenced by this comment from a participant:

> 'I believe that everyone (both people from Nokia and Siemens) who participates in this forum, even those who have expressed some cynicism or distrust, has gotten a healthier outlook right after they have expressed their opinion.'

The new culture was taking form as the process of the Culture Square unfolded.

This is another example of Clifford Geertz's (Geertz, 1973, op cit) idea of culture as vacuum filler. He suggests that, when faced with uncertainty, we revert to familiar habits and ways of making sense. The vacuum of uncertainty sucks in the habitual, automatic routines and responses of the familiar culture. In the face of uncertainty, and the anxiety it generates, we fall back on culturally familiar patterns and routines. Mergers are times of exceptional levels of uncertainty and anxiety. Rumours abound and people closely scrutinise morsels of information for clues as to how things will unfold. The desire for clarity and certainty is immense and its absence creates fertile ground for rumour, survival driven behaviour and intense rivalry. Needless to say these are not conditions conducive to a generative dialogue. In these circumstances there is a strong risk of defensive or attacking behaviour, position taking, intense politicking and lobbying, withdrawal and other forms of dysfunctional behaviour. We hoped that, as an intermediate structure or loom, the Culture Square would provide a generative space in which new possibilities and new patterns could take form.

In the following section we take a closer look at some of the exchanges in the Culture Square and see how individual threads of understanding formed and were gradually woven into a pattern. The inclusion of these comments provides a rare glimpse into peoples' feelings and emotional journeys as they make sense of the uncertainty of change and find ways of coping. It also illustrates the twists and turns of a largely self-managing process and how, following a stormy start, it gradually took on an increasingly constructive tone. Finally, and most intriguingly from the perspective of cultural change, it illustrates the questioning of inherited conceptions, the weaving of new understandings, and the emergence of constructs, values and narratives that were to become figural in the emerging culture.

The Culture Square — into the Vacuum

'A bulletin board like this normally has the function of a padded cell. Employees can let off steam internally without doing any harm. So don't set too much hope into the impacts of your contributions in this discussion.' (Kate)

'Ah, but I do have hopes…. Surely how the culture develops is also up to us. Since most of us have only this forum at the moment to voice our views, I can indeed understand the letting off steam aspect. But what is preventing us from also trying to make use of the steam? Or are we all still followers of the jaundiced philosophy "we've always done it like that", or "we've never done it like that"…. Maybe I am an eternal optimist, but rather that than just going back to sleep.' (Eyes Open)

This exchange, early in the history of the Culture Square,[7] expressed a question that hung over the entire project. Was it simply a 'cynical' device by management that encouraged employees to let off steam harmlessly, or did it represent a real opportunity for employees to influence how the culture developed? The answer, ironically, was that it could be either, depending on how employees responded to the invitation to participate. If Kate's view prevailed it is not difficult to imagine how participation would drop away and resentment toward management would build as employees' feelings of being manipulated were confirmed.

Alternatively, if Eyes Open's take on things gained support then perhaps people would participate in the forum with a more optimistic intent and with different expectations. Acting into such a belief would not guarantee that their views would be taken seriously of course, but it would hold open the possibility of something worthwhile emerging from the process. In debating these positions Kate and Eyes Open were most likely giving voice to conversations that were happening throughout the new business. In debating the meaning of the Culture Square as a management 'gesture', they positioned themselves at the heart of the process by which new meaning was emerging.

In embracing the spirit of the Culture Square at face value, Eyes Open was metaphorically 'putting his foot in the door' of the culture formation process and holding it open so as to allow for new possibilities. His decision to 'make use of the steam' could be seen as advocating an alternative interpretation of management's gesture. In this way he was bringing difference. The question was: would it be a difference that made difference?

This important debate captures the essence of weaving. Kate's cautious response to management's gesture, borne out of years of frustration, could have convinced others that this was yet another manifestation of a cynical pattern of containing the emotional fallout from the turmoil of the merger but without the intention of taking their views seriously. Eyes Open chose to challenge her take on things and in so doing sought to interrupt this particular 'historically transmitted pattern of meaning' (Geertz, 1973, op cit) opting instead, to accept a chance to influence things. After all, the alternative, as he so evocatively put it, was to 'just go back to sleep'.

I find this a poignant exchange in which something new became possible. In this micro exchange, we see the earliest moments of a new culture being woven.

The Medium Is the Message

If we pause in this account for a moment, we can see how a number of significant gestures or invitations had already been made through the decision to create the Culture Square and through the way in which it had been set up.

---

[7] All names have been changed to safeguard the identity and privacy of those who participated in this conversation.

Most significant perhaps was the decision to establish the Culture Square. As a gesture it came from a genuine desire to involve as many people as possible in shaping the new culture. It was intended as *an act of inclusion* and an invitation to all employees to *participate in the co-creation of the new culture*. It could also be seen as a means *of fostering feelings of ownership* in the new business.

Secondly, in opening up a discussion that would take time to reach a conclusion (six months in the first estimate), this was signalling the importance of taking time to arrive at important decisions. It was a subtle way of *signalling the importance of quality processes*, in a context where previously the emphasis had been on finding ways to persuade customers to buy the products that the companies had produced. The sub-text of the Culture Square could be seen to be saying: 'Let's take the (considerable) time and resource necessary to reach a quality decision that we can all support.' *Good Process, it is being said, is as important as Good Products.* This complemented the strong and explicit desire by members of the new board to encourage a shift from a product to a solution mindset and to see the adoption of an 'adult-adult' pattern of relating both with clients and each other. As we will shortly see, these intentions would be the subject of intense debate.

Perhaps just as significant here was what didn't happen, namely some version of a communications 'roll out' or 'road show' aimed at disseminating the thinking of top management. The pattern, or analogue, of such processes is akin to selling or persuading and implies the superior wisdom of senior managers to consider such matters. Embedded in such an approach are patriarchal assumptions which infantilise employees and foster patterns of dependence towards their superiors ('elders and betters'). When made in the early days of a new endeavour the impact of such gestures is disproportionate; they represent culturally fateful first steps, the die is cast.

A further intention of the Culture Square was to give everyone a chance to have their say, to *listen to all voices*. This could be seen as analogous with a desire, expressed in the early culture principles, to *be customer centric, to take customers' views and ideas seriously*.

Finally, in issuing an open invite to people, this was intended *as an expression of trust*, stemming from a belief in *the maturity of NSN employees* and in their potential for thoughtful and constructive contribution to an important conversation.

None of these things were openly stated,[8] and to do so would probably have undermined their credibility. They were tacit gestures; messages expressed through the medium of the process and as such were subtle threads that were contributing to an invisible fabric of background assumptions. And, if we accept Mead's notion that the meaning of the gesture is in the response, then how these low-profile symbols were interpreted was not something that could be either controlled or managed by leaders. Ultimately, the test of their credibility would lie in the interplay over time

---

[8]Commenting on a draft of this chapter Alistair offered the view that, at the time, many of these messages were not widely understood by the majority of Executive Board members, 'although the Board were energised by the prevailing parent child dynamic and wanted to move this to Adult-Adult.'

between such gestures and the interpretations placed on them in the informal sense making processes within the broader organisation. This made them extremely fragile threads at the start of the process, easily ruptured, discredited or otherwise damaged.[9]

Early Contributions

The first contributions welcomed the forum and embraced the spirit of participation and co-creation. Contributors commented on the draft principles and added ideas in accordance with the original intent. It was not long however before a second conversation thread emerged, one that questioned the motives and intent behind the Culture Square. Was it a 'padded cell' for merely letting off steam, why was it being facilitated by an outsider and what was his agenda? Where were managers in the conversation, and why was the restructuring taking so long? People felt as though 'the brakes are on'. The tone quickly turned to one of mistrust and cynicism. People denounced the forum as a sham, as a false consultation and warned others against participating.

> 'This is not open communications but announcement by newspaper!'

Some concluded their contributions by announcing their withdrawal, 'leaving in a huff' as one person put it. Interestingly, some of these people reappeared two or three sessions later, drawn it would seem, to the increasingly lively debate. Once again they declared their scorn for the transparency of 'such an obvious form of management manipulation' and departed the Culture Square with another dramatic rhetorical flourish.

This time however other participants implored them to return. 'Your voice is valued and you always make interesting comments', they wrote.

People were hungry for information and were feeling abandoned by their leaders:

> 'We still feel we are in the dark. I would like to see more details, which would make me feel more comfortable going forward. Being left here in the dark is still an unknown, and ultimately affects productivity.'

Many complaints were aimed at the 'clunky' and rudimentary functioning of the Square as a forum. People suspected that contributions were being edited, and that it was difficult to keep up to date with discussions.

---

[9]The credibility of these gestures would be tested over time. People would be attending to the consistency with which they were sustained in different settings, especially when under duress. Meaning would be made of the compatibility of other gestures with these intentions and the actions, statements and language of other seemingly inconspicuous, low profile symbols. Underlying people's response to these gestures was the question: Will the intent hold up over time, across space and under duress?

There was much discussion of announcements and broadcasts by the CEO, Simon Beresford Wylie, and these were broadly approving,

> 'Simon is motivating, he calls a spade a spade.'

Others railed against what they described as 'Management speak' and wrote that

> 'Visions are NOT what we need right now!'

'Is anyone listening to us?' people asked. A fear was expressed that management references to 'benefits' were really code for cost reduction.

Participants worried openly that appointments to newly created posts would be based on local, personal networks and favours and would not be transparent. People felt that they were being kept in the dark and were suspicious of what was happening behind closed doors.

> 'Inform us early about decisions and involve us' came the plea.

There was a lively discussion about which operating language should be used, German or English, and a strongly expressed desire that HR should treat them:

> '... as people and not as topics.'

Concerns were expressed that employees aged 46 years and older would be written off as too old. A lively discussion was provoked by the view that such employees should be seen as 'a casket of competencies'. This is an engaging example of a bid to reframe a dominant construction, ('once you pass 46 you are finished') and as such might be considered as an overture or cultural gambit.[10] This discussion thread was openly questioning a cultural norm.

Some of the discussion threads urged managers to walk the talk and much scrutiny was afforded to their behaviour: Sightings of newly appointed directors on airplanes became the focus for exchanges. Which cabin were they seen in, people wanted to know? There was a muted but unmistakeable sense of surprised approval in peoples' postings on learning that these managers had been spotted travelling coach class.

Suspicions of favouritism in appointments began to surface, the suggestion being that certain senior managers were favouring 'their own people' and that one side was gaining the upper hand. Both sides felt this way, ironically, but being able to express such concerns directly seemed to help allay fears of one side taking over.

As these feelings of suspicion and mistrust surfaced so participation in the Square gradually increased. In particular the number of people who following the

---

[10]The term gambit is used here to suggest a conversational opener or as being akin to an opening move in chess.

discussions but did not contribute comments began to accelerate. Within six weeks there were an average of 7,000 of these 'lurkers' following the discussions.

In the midst of this turmoil, there were thoughtful discussions about the companies' orientation to customers. These centred on how to 'attend to the customer's customer' and to ways of bringing the 'customer's voice inside'. There seemed to be strong support for a more customer-centric culture and many suggestions as to how to achieve this.

Other conversation threads dealt with questions of the company structure, calling for a flatter form that collapsed the hierarchy and for devolution of responsibility and decision making to local project teams.

Under the topic headed 'Being Valued' there was a call for a humane and compassionate attitude towards those who would shortly be losing their jobs,[11] with one contributor asking:

'How can we value people through these layoffs?'

A lively discussion thread expressed the emotional turmoil and roller coaster of feelings experienced when developmental projects are abruptly shut down, a regular feature of fast moving, High-Tech industries. In the midst of this discussion someone made the plaintive statement:

'We need to be allowed time to bury our babies.'

This was a particularly poignant phrase that was adopted by many contributors to this discussion and another example of the origins of an initially fragile cultural thread.

As facilitator of the early weeks of the Culture Square I was apprehensive. Once the early enthusiasm and politeness that greeted the launch had passed it felt as though a lid had been lifted on some raw feelings and old resentments. For a while I sensed hostility directed at me, which I took to be an expression of anger towards the only identifiable figure of authority that was seen as part of the process by which the merger was being managed. In one memorable contribution a participant openly questioned my role, suggesting that I was a management stooge, asked about the phases of the merger process, and what would happen to the comments people were making? Who would I be 'feeding information' to and so on? This was a skilfully written but unmistakeable challenge to my role and neutrality as a facilitator.

I felt the eyes of several thousand 'lurkers' and active participants watching to see how I would respond. I answered the lengthy list of questions as factually and honestly as I could, mindful that my responses would be sending a message to others who had the courage to voice their fears and suspicions. I was especially careful to avoid either an aggressive or a defensive tone in my response.

---

[11]Alistair pointed out that: 'From the outset, it was stated that there would be layoffs and this overshadowed the early period of the merger.'

As a facilitator my concern was to ensure a constructive exchange of experience and ideas and to help both parties understand and learn from each other's rich history. I was looking to keep the conversation focussed on a discussion of the embryonic principles that had emerged from the first meeting of the top 300 managers. I welcomed and encouraged those contributions that addressed these questions, probing for amplification and encouraging others to respond. I realised that my comments were a form of intervention. By simply responding to a comment I was subtly drawing attention to it. I gave careful thought to which comments I addressed and which I ignored. On a number of occasions I felt tempted to admonish or sanction a remark, but realised that in so doing I would be acting as a form of moral authority. I regarded one posting in particular as a sarcastic response to what seemed to be a genuine suggestion. After consultation with Alistair,[12] I deleted my comment that noted (and tacitly disapproved of the sarcasm) before pressing 'send'. To my surprise another posting appeared that made clear the unacceptability of this form of discourse:

'This is not the kind of company that I want to be a part of.'

wrote the contributor. Here was an early sign of the self-regulation that became an increasing feature of the Square and pointed to the emergence of norms of conduct in the new business.

To Edit or Not to Edit...

On several occasions, the anxiety that accompanied the uncertainty and insecurity felt by people awaiting news of a re-structuring found expression in strongly worded criticism of the new, senior management team. The question arose as to whether such outbursts should be edited out of the published version. Alistair and I took the view that to do so would violate the integrity of the process. While it might temporarily ease the discomfort of those senior managers who were the target of criticism, it risked being seen as an act of paternalism and could undermine the credibility of earlier statements of intent. We felt that such an intervention would wreck the burgeoning sense of confidence in the Square as a forum for open debate. Any form of censorship, we felt, would invite an avalanche of protest and destroy the fragile belief that all views were legitimate. The conversation was beginning to self-regulate and for us to censor any posting would interfere with, and possibly destroy the process and the growing ownership of the conversation altogether.

---

[12]Alistair provided me with invaluable support and wise counsel throughout the period when I was facilitating the conversation in the Culture Square. It was a reciprocation of times when I had acted as a 'sea anchor' or co-mentor to him. This points to a broader observation regarding this kind of facilitative work. It is emotionally challenging work and can be stressful. The provision of emotionally intelligent support from colleagues and others who act in a supervisory capacity is enormously important.

Our thinking here was informed by ideas that view organisations as 'Complex Responsive Processes' (Griffin et al., 1998; Shaw, 1997). CRP as it has come to be known:

> '... differentiates between the informal or "shadow" processes of meaning making that occur in all organisations and the official or "formal" pronouncements and version of reality .... This thinking suggests that much meaning making in organisations occurs naturally and spontaneously in the everyday exchanges over coffee, via emails, in corridor conversations and so on, often in response to the "gestures" of its leaders. It is a diffuse process of interpretation and sense making through which opinions are formed and upon which people base their behaviour. It is suggested that the shadow organisation is a rich source of creativity and carries much potential for transformation.' (Moffat & McLean, 2010).

We came to suspect that people were testing out the limits of what could be said without invoking some form of management sanction, retribution or censorship. At times we wondered whether some comments were inviting or looking to provoke such forms of response, a cultural legacy carried over from past experience. This hypothesis was reinforced by a number of developments.

The underlying theme to these exchanges was a concern for safety. The inferred question was 'Can we really say what we think?' Is it safe? At the same time we suspected that a cultural pattern or 'game' (Berne, 1964) was being enacted. We speculated that this 'game' could be seen as a form of 'parent-child' pattern of relations in which the rebellious children (employees) of authoritarian parents (unseen management) were complaining about their powerlessness and the absence of senior managers from the discussions (absent parent).

Complaints took many forms, the 'clunky' nature of the software and the site, the absence of senior managers' voices, the low volume of contributions in the first few weeks ('this forum is not exactly overheating' wrote one participant), and the independence and credentials of the facilitator. There were many comments describing peoples' feelings of impotence and the paralyzing uncertainty of not knowing whether you had a position in the new structure or to whom you would report.

Mergers are frequently times of debilitating uncertainty and the early exchanges in the Culture Square certainly provide evidence of this. There was little about the exchanges in the early weeks that might be considered as constructive contributions to the debate about the future culture of NSN.

The anxiety expressed by contributors to the Culture Square was matched by the feelings of Alistair and myself as well as by those senior managers that had sanctioned and advocated its introduction. The negative and critical tone of some comments during the early weeks made us all wonder about its value. The fear was that the Culture Square may have been fomenting unrest as well as personal, and at times sharp, criticism of senior managers. On several occasions we debated censoring some of the harshest and most inflammatory postings. Our facilitator's instincts told us that this was the early stages of a process and that such cathartic outbursts would gradually make way for more constructive contributions. We also knew that any form of censorship or interference with content would kill the fragile credibility and trustworthiness of the Square in a moment.

Gradually comments began to appear that challenged the negative, complaining and mistrustful tone:

> 'Come on guys, move away from the dark side. Life is good — much light out there! Open your eyes. If it's that bad for you in NSN, don't suffer, don't be a victim, DO something!'

By week five or six there were small signs that the conversation was changing. Three incidents in particular pointed to a shift of pattern.

A core of regular contributors had developed. One of them, still using a pseudonym, made a suggestion that seemingly came out of the blue:

> 'Maybe those who have been active in the Square (from both Siemens and Nokia) could, together with relevant members of designated NSN management, be invited via the forum to take part in a whole-day meeting with Adrian to talk about not only the quality of the platform and urgently needed improvements, but also the status of the discussion on the various themes. Such an event is likely to mean that anonymity for past contributions would be lost (which Kate would welcome); I wouldn't have a problem with that, and of course a new pseudonym could be taken thereafter, if desired.'

He added:

> 'Apart from accelerating necessary change, this meeting would, in itself, contribute towards a common corporate culture. The results could then be published in the — hopefully improved — forum for further comments. Anyone else support the idea?'

There was a cautious welcome for this idea from others but doubts were expressed that it would receive approval from 'senior management'. As quickly as he could Alistair, as a director and as the senior manager responsible for the cultural integration of the merger, welcomed the idea. His only request was that careful thought be given to a venue in order to limit travel costs. This felt like a positive step forward. It signalled a commitment to the Culture Square and to its improvement and, as noted in the posting, would 'in itself' contribute towards a common corporate culture. It would also be experienced, hopefully, as an act of empowerment and would signal that the views of those participating in the Square were indeed valued and being taken seriously.

The meeting was arranged to occur in Munich a little more than two weeks later.

The second development occurred under the topic of 'Open Communications', one of the headline cultural themes. Kate, one of the more active contributors who had hitherto cautioned others against expecting the Square to make any difference, turned her challenge away from those in authority and towards her fellow contributors:

Under the header — **A Question of Trust,** she wrote:

> 'Isn't it cowardice if you fear to lay your identity open? Does it go with a discussion on "Open Communication"?'

In response to this challenge, a discussion thread developed that was concerned with the use of pseudonyms as a requirement for participation in the conversation. First of all there was a clarification of the 'rule':

> After checking …. 'For the e-mail request to join the meeting (in Munich) you don't have to declare your pseudonym, just your real name. If you want, you can even keep silent about your pseudonym at the meeting itself.'

Almost immediately this was followed by the following exchange:

> *This is just excellent* (Hans): I will certainly send that email to be invited. Oh, and by the way: I'm Hans Rebbeck, currently working as a PLM within MN PG. I don't know yet where I will end up in the new organization. And I'm pleased to meet you all. Regards, Hans.

> *Looking forward* (Kate): 'Hi Hans, I'm happy that at least one of you is courageous enough to stand up for his opinion. I hope Eyes Open isn't too shy to do so, too. I believe that defining a culture of trust and open communication and of two-way valuation is an important target not only for the company's sake but also for the people's sake who are working here. When we are able to achieve this, this company will be successful. My name is Kate Eckhardt. I'm working as senior software engineer for FN T in Munich and I'm looking forward to meet you all.'

> *The next 'name dropper'* (Eyes Open) 'I'm coming round to Kate's philosophy: it's probably easier to build a culture with real people rather than with phantoms. So I too am looking forward to meeting both of you! Come to think of it, it would probably make sense for us, and others from Siemens to meet in advance of the official session. What do you think? My name is Martin Green. I'm English and have been with Siemens based in Munich since 1983. I've been in export sales all this time and am now with SN MN as a country manager. I'll continue in the forum from now on as "Martin".'

Here were people taking responsibility and risks. It was a change of pattern from that of being powerless victims, kept in the dark by an absent, and often anonymous, 'management'. In declaring themselves in this way they took responsibility for their statements and stepped out of victim-hood. It was a shift towards proactively looking to influence events and to being 'real people' not 'phantoms' and to making a difference. They were acting in accordance with the culture that they wished to see. It was a glorious moment of active co-creation when they became co-weavers of the new NSN culture.

A third, small indication of the shift towards taking active responsibility showed up under the discussion of the cultural principle of Being Valued:

> 'The wording in Being Valued sounds passive. I or we are being valued — by whom, why should this anonymous thing value me or us? This value starts from every single one of us. I and we have to value ourselves, our colleagues, our environment, etc. and by doing so we also earn the valuing of others.'

This posting, endorsed by others, was another sign that people were taking ownership of the conversation and of the culture. They were shifting from being passive participants to active players in the discussions. In combination, all three of these developments could be seen as contributing to, and as an expression of, an important turn in the conversation. It was beginning to feel as though the invitation to participate in this important conversation was finally being embraced in the spirit of the original intention. The process of weaving was gathering pace.

Munich Revisited

The conversation continued to become more constructive as people gradually embraced the opportunity offered by the Culture Square. The Munich meeting took place approximately seven weeks after the launch of the Square. It was a poignant moment when people introduced themselves first by name and then by alias. It felt akin to a collective unmasking, a stepping out from the anonymity of their nom-de-plumes. There was a sense of relief and pleasure in being face to face with names that had become familiar through the online dialogue. I was struck by the sense of intimacy and warmth between people and by their desire to contribute towards the success of the new business. During the day we identified a number of ways in which the technical platform for the Culture Square could be improved, reviewed the content of the discussions in the Square so far and discussed how best to frame the topics for an upcoming company wide-virtual conference.

This group comprised many of the most active contributors to the discussions so far and had a good a sense of the preoccupations and interests of people across the new business. They represented a cross section of views from the midst of the company and knew what topics would have credibility and hold relevance for people. On the basis of their suggestions, the first version of topics for the forthcoming, pan-organisation conference, (the JAM — discussed more fully below) were drawn up. Members from this group continued to be consulted throughout the build-up to the company wide conference. In terms of Complexity Theory they were at the heart of the shadow conversation and sensitive to how gestures from senior management would be interpreted locally.

To put it in basic terms they ensured that the focus for the conference would be relevant and credible to most people and not something that was seen as having been dreamed up without reference to the 'reality on the ground'.

Alistair and I saw the Munich meeting as an important and symbolic moment in the weaving of the new NSN culture. It was an expression of genuine interest in the views of participants in the forum, an affirmation of their initiative in requesting the meeting and an act of inclusion in the co-creation of the new culture. It suggested a regard for the views of all members of the new company regardless of rank or position and also welcomed the ideas and technical assistance they brought. The 'us-them' sub-text of many contributions early in the history of the Square, along with expressions of mistrust and manipulation that had been a feature of the initial exchanges, gave way to a sense of 'we'. The technical management of the forum now a shared responsibility, and the framing for the landmark, company-wide conference, had its conception in the discussions of that day. The message of the process was that this is something we are all responsible for. All voices are valued and welcome. We are all weavers of the new culture.

Needless to say there was widespread interest in comments about the Munich meeting made in subsequent Square postings by those who had participated. The numbers of 'lurkers' spiked following this session, confirming the interest it held for others. The meeting represented a landmark moment in the weaving of the new culture. It was something that had emerged out of the conversation in the Square and was attended by people who had been at the heart of the early dialogue and as such were considered as credible, as 'one of us'.

The number of postings continued to build. During week 10, there was an exponential increase in the volume of postings such that full-time facilitation was needed to keep up. It was with a sense of satisfaction and relief that I handed this over to Martin, one of the core contributors to the discussions up until that point, and whose suggestion it had been to meet in Munich. Of course, this development, in itself, was a low-profile symbol of the new culture, an expression of co-authorship and self-organisation.

The Culture Square became a forum in which people could ask each other questions, exchange stories, share best practice and lessons learned as well as trade perceptions, rumours and gossip about the merger process. More and more specific suggestions and proposals for how to organise different aspects of the new business became the focus for exchanges as the discussion became more practical and concrete. Below is a sample of the comments and exchanges that took place.[13] The postings have been included as written.

---

[13]These extracts have been included unedited. For many of the contributors English was a second or third language and at times this is evident in their use of grammar. We felt that the spirit of their remarks are clear, however, and far more important than the accuracy of their syntax. The identity of contributors has been disguised.

Part of the debate was about the value and relevance of the Culture Square:

Posting from NC: I've been following the 'Culture Square' since it started. I'm disappointed to see how little attention it appears to have received and how few the contributors are. Maybe the two factors are not unrelated? A few people have had the chance to let off a little steam, but there's very little sign of vigorous debate or exploration of ideas around what should be interesting and important topics. The forum needs to be re-thought and re-launched in a more dynamic format.

Posting from DN: There seems to be the opinion, that posting here is a quite redundant and useless job. Another view is, that our NSN values actually show in the culture square a sign of life. As long as postings need to be anonymous, inclusive yours, we have not implemented those NSN values as they should. But those values are prerequisite to be successful at the end of the day.

Posting from JL: This forum allows the participants to acknowledge their feelings, think about them, process them into what kind of actions they would suggest to take in shaping the new company. I believe that everyone (both people from Nokia and Siemens) who participates in this forum, even those who have expressed some cynicism or distrust, has gotten a healthier outlook right after they have expressed their opinion. The fact that we have acknowledged and processed our emotions is more than enough for us to be able to have peace of mind. Peace of mind is key to moving on and opening up for new opportunities.

Posting from CP: First of all, thank you (Director) for initiating this thread. We at least know that the management of the future NSN take some time to read the threads in this forum.

Posting from SK: It's at most valuable that ex-Nokia managers and directors are visible and discussing in the Culture Square. This proofs the living of NSN values. In addition the Culture Square is a short cut for getting in contact also considered we are looking forward to get one NSN. At least this Square is a place where some footsoldier pioneers are digging to the other side and, like in Switzerland's tunnel building, join together. That's exciting!

There was a lively debate about attitudes towards the competition:

Posting from DB: Respecting our competition is a step towards understanding them, therefore giving us the ability to compete against them. Having worked with or for many of NSN's competitors over the years, I don't believe in simplistic statements of superiority.

Posting from HN: I agree with your idea of valuing or respecting the competition. The Nokia Siemens Merger shows how quickly you can find yourself in the same boat with former competitors. I suspect that as we meet and begin to work with one another, *many of us are starting to throw old pre-conceived notions about the former competition overboard.*[14]

Respecting the competition means acknowledging that our competitors also have great people creating great products and we need to compete and fight hard to take business away from them.

Sometimes the exchanges were particularly sharp as views were expressed and assumptions challenged:

> **Posting from BC:** I am sorry I cannot 'quote' your entire response. You must type really fast or had a pre-prepared answer.
>
> If I try to summarize … you are saying Managers not giving people something to do or not keeping workers motivated has more impact than employees' personal work ethic. That is always possible.
>
> **Response from PS:** Pretty nasty attitude. I've been with the company for more than 7 years; have always achieved 'Target' or 'Exceeds' on my performance ratings; have received raises every single year and bonuses almost every STP, yet my job (and me along with it) has a strong chance of being eliminated due to the cost cutting. However, I do not consider myself dead weight and am personally offended by your nasty assumptions.

One discussion thread was concerned with creating a great working environment:

> **Posting from GM:** I am a former Siemens, and I fully agree with what I read around here. It looks like people have a clear view of the last mile needed to create a great work environment. I would personally summarize the right approach this way:
>
> 'Nokia Siemens Networks' spirit is to be customer focussed. *Let the employees be considered part of the company's customers, and the company be considered part of the employee's customers.*'[15]
>
> By relating the employee to a customer, the company keeps in mind that the deal work/skills for salary is only working if it makes the employee eager to pursue it. What employees need to develop this eagerness is to feel respected, treated with complete fairness, and have a chance to show and grow their potential.

---

[14]Italics have been used to highlight the discarding of 'inherited conceptions' in favour of a different and respectful view of customers. Here is a specific example of weaving new ways of seeing, new understandings.

[15]Here again we see an invitation to see things in a different and specific way. The writer is proposing a particular way of seeing and thinking. This is the minutia of cultural weaving.

The physical environment also drew comment:

> **Posting from RD:** Working environments that are made up of acres of walls will not encourage open communications, casual dialogue and the breaking down of silos. NSN facilities should be inspirational. They must be creative, colorful and energetic. That may not always be easy to achieve with some of our heritage sites, but we must try for it. I've seen the support for this from our most senior management and I am greatly encouraged. To me, that is what Innovation and Leadership is all about.

Not unusually for a merger, much attention was given to who was appointed to key positions and to the manner in which appointments were conducted:

> **Posting from CS:** As far as 'proper guidelines' are concerned, my inputs are as follows: 1. No positions would be filled up and approved behind closed door keeping rest of the relevant work force in darkness.[16]
> Bottom line is to try and make the process more visible, send a clear message to feeling blessed or invincible dudes that no more fooling around and also create atmosphere so that all could participate in the process. Besides, leadership skills that are required for a post merger company like Nokia Siemens Network could be different than it is required for any other conventional company, therefore a blend of old and new blood would be the right way to go forward.

Contributors were much exercised by the question as to where were the managers in the Culture Square. Is anybody listening or paying attention to what is being discussed?

> **Posting from BD:** To respond to Brian's question: what would have to happen for some of the ideas and conversations here to be compelling reading for Management? The first thing that would need to happen is that at least someone in management accesses the forum in the first place and … indicates to us that this is the case.
> **Response Posting from AK:** As a designated future manager I can only tell you so much that between my travels and responding to enquiries and preparing for the launch of our new company there is awfully little time and space left to follow discussions here that are not directly related to the pressing tasks right on my desk. This does not say that

---

[16]The proposal of 'proper guidelines' is of course a bid for general standards of practice. It represents an attempt to establish procedural norms and as such is another form of weaving. And of course the advocacy for transparency is about values.

this discussion in the culture square is not important or relevant, but simply pointing to the fact that a day has only so many hours, that we all are not machines but have families as well who wait for us to come home after 12 or 14 hour days, after a trip to Helsinki or half-way around the world.

Please do not think poorly of management, existing or future, for not finding enough time to follow this discussion but for having to rely on being informed about issues that come up that are relevant to the tasks we are doing now, which are often to continue to fulfill tasks related to the old assignment while simultaneously performing tasks related to the new function in ramping up NSN for the future.

I quite understand how powerless one may feel under the circum-stances, not knowing where the travels will lead us, not knowing one's place on the new ship, with lots of uncertainties and many questions. And yes, I understand that it would be too easy to simply say: just let us do what we need to do, it will work out all right, although it would be nice to answer that way and find one's way home to wife and kids.[17]

Ok, but in this case, you were merely asking for someone from man-agement to actually read this forum and to put in an answer, a sign of life and interest. In light of the simplicity of that request, I think I have done my duty, and shown that I am here, that I am interested, in short, that I care. Ok?

Response from BD: Thanks for your lengthy feedback, AK. Acknowl-edge your workload problem, and appreciate the effort... then it (is)

---

[17]This response from a manager to another expression of a frequently voiced cry by contribu-tors to the Square ('is anyone — managers — listening to us?') is, in my view, a particularly skilful example of weaving. By directly addressing BD's question in a non-judgmental way AK is showing a respect for the legitimacy of the question and the questioner. He is declaring his own reality clearly and unapologetically (and in a non-punitive tone), and is openly addressing the uncertainty and unresolved nature of the many pressing issues and operational realities of managing a merger. In this sense he is treating BD as an adult and making a rela-tional connection. He is weaving a thread of connectivity between the world as experienced by those in the thick of organisational life and those senior managers under pressure to make decisions about operational details in the new company. In declining to reassure him that *'it will work out all right'* he is demonstrating an honesty and realism that in itself is a form of weaving — weaving through being. The response from BD reveals his interpretation of AK's gesture. In this transaction, in this exchange, new meaning was being woven. It was as much in the manner of his response, as in its content, that AK was participating in the process of cultural weaving. In this very brief exchange we witness a demonstration of respect for others, regardless of comparative status, an attitude of openness to the uncertainty and complexity of the current situation (say yes to the mess), and an assumption of maturity on the part of both parties to the exchange. Finally in his willingness to engage with BD's comment AK is demonstrating a preparedness to co-create, to be a co-weaver of the new culture. It is another expression of the idea that 'we create the culture together through our interactions with each other.'

important for us to learn that management as a whole is interested and intends to act on at least some of the ideas discussed. This in itself would encourage more participants, more ideas and a better chance for the creation of a widely accepted common corporate culture.

Questions of organisation structure were also considered:

Posting from MA: The future Nokia Siemens Network organization is a big change for many Siemens colleagues. To walk the talk and achieving together it would be great if Nokia colleagues get more and more in contact with current Siemens colleagues to explain the future organization and offer support for the daily business. I would agree that we have to break the hierarchical approach. This has to be done with respect. We need to find a balance between a flat hierarchical organisation and the need to give employees orientation and that in specific situation someone has to take the lead to solve issues.

Posting from CV: If we want to achieve efficiently together, we need something other than an ever-growing process description. I think, very important aspects of good collaboration are:

— create less organisational boundaries,
— define focused responsibility/authority on the organisational level,
— co-locate people that need to work together closely — instead of co-locating by organisation,
— invest in efficient communication across globalized sites (a common understanding between the PEOPLE, and an efficient information flow should have higher priority than co-operating machines and business tools).

Sometimes the exchanges discussed different cultural assumptions, in this case norms regarding the approachability of upper management:

Posting from JL: To put this right in the beginning: Yes, a culture of open communication between working level and upper management IS desirable as a company culture. And, yes, I believe we can improve that here at Siemens. But I am not sure whether we can all blame that to the managers. I'd never have the idea to call anybody — much less upper management — on a Saturday. I simply can't imagine an emergency that would justify that. But maybe this is the problem? I don't have the opportunity very often to talk to the management but if I have it I use it. And it works.

Maybe that's exactly the point (AJ): *Hi JL, the intention is not to attach blame to management, but rather to show how our current Siemens culture differs from Nokia's. So when you say you would never* have the idea to call anybody on a Saturday, you may be confirming that difference.[18]

Reading leadership signals: By the way, since you mention Simon B-W, my impression from his speech on Dec. 21st in Munich is that he is not actually a big fan of Power-point slides, and can get his point across perfectly well without them: which is refreshing.

As the Culture Square gained momentum senior managers asked for feedback about their part in embodying key values:

Question from a senior leader: What are some things that a manager has done for you in the past which made you feel valued as an individual, and or team member? How did it affect you?[19]

Answer from A: Feeling valued means different things for different people. Listened to my ideas, asked my opinion, gave me the opportunity to perform a task under my responsibility, thanked me for my help, gave me advice on how to behave, made me aware of where I should improve, took time to teach me, spent effort to advance my development without any personal benefit for themselves. Made me feel like I am able to add value to the company.

I have worked on several cross functional projects in the past and one clearly stands out as being the best at making me feel valued as a team member. The overall project lead took the time to have a couple of face-to-face sessions as part of the project even though the team was geographically dispersed we performed formal team building exercises that resulted in the team members understanding each others' responsibilities, tasks and personality. This greatly helped during the project to have an efficient team to accomplish the overall project goals.

---

[18]In my experience of working with cultural understanding one of the most challenging things is to describe cultural phenomena without judging them. This is especially the case in merger situations where the levels of anxiety and uncertainty are elevated. For this reason I was impressed by the wisdom of AJ's comments here. However, the capacity to notice difference without judging it is extraordinarily helpful when it comes to considerations of their relevance and appropriateness to a desired future culture. This attitude of interested non-attachment is an important orientation to bring to the process of weaving.

[19]This is an example of leader as inquirer. As such it flies in the face of traditional views that leaders should show 'strong' leadership, should know the answers and have a firm opinion about things. It models a pulling style of leadership that calls for humility. From a weaving perspective, the posing of the question enfolds a tacit assumption that this is a joint endeavour, a collective process of figuring things out and that we will come to the answer together. These assumptions in themselves are culturally significant. They are weaving gestures that have a presumptive and taken-for-granted quality. The leader who posed this powerful question was already weaving through the assumptions upon which the question was predicated. Weaving was occurring at two levels here, at the level of the content of peoples' responses but also at the more tacit, assumptive level. I would suggest that much is woven into and through these micro transactions. In defining a relationship between a leader and his staff, this exchange is also an analogue for the relationship between the company and its customers.

At the end of the project time was taken to celebrate the project success and to perform a lessons learned. This helped future projects, brought a formal closure to the current project and allowed each team member to digest what they accomplished.

Posting from B: I am excited to see the NSN NAM management taking such an active role here in the Culture Square: that makes us feel valued. However now comes the next stage: us outside the NAM management have to start living these values to make them become reality. Let's start with the one in the mirror.

Sometimes such inquiries took an unexpected turn:

Senior Manager: (The Cultural Principle) 'Being Valued' in my opinion is a difficult subject to be discussed, as it is very personal and perceived differently by each one of us. I also think it is a very important point to talk about, because for me personally adding value to the business is a big part of my daily motivation.

So, my question is: What do you believe the leadership team can do to make you feel being valued? But I also want to ask you very personally: What do you think you can contribute on an everyday basis to create a culture that values the efforts and contributions of your co-workers and team members?

Answer from J: It is difficult to feel valued as an employee when we live in so much fear. Fear that we're going to walk in tomorrow and have no job, fear that (a senior manager) jumped ship before the company even started … fear that we are not going to seize this opportunity to fix procedures that were not working before the merger, and fear of reprisals for voicing our opinions.

Senior Manager Response: *'I am asking myself why I am so shocked after reading your posting?'*[20]

---

[20]The experience of being shocked is an indication that one's taken for granted assumptions and ways of thinking have been disrupted. It is unwelcome and surprising news of difference and another way in which people discovered the differences in each others' sense of reality. Of key importance here is how leaders, especially, respond to such disruptions to their worldview. The authenticity of this leader's response is seen as helpful to the process of weaving. In such a public arena he did not seek to dampen, sanction or in any way deny the reality of J's feelings of fear. As became clear in later postings, this experience was common for a section of the new company. The ability to make and accept such charged comments without sanction was akin to the South Africa Truth and Reconciliation Commission and allowed for the discharge of long held feelings. Accepting these feelings without dismissing or denying them was an important test for the principle of 'Valuing People'. The capacity to respectfully acknowledge such dark emotions and to understand the experiences associated with them was a moment of healing or wholeness and entirely consistent with a cultural ambition to become one company. The exchange of feelings here is a form of emotional weaving. Alistair saw this comment as a subtle form of sanction and an expression of disappointment at the person's response.

This unexpected response drew a number of stories that reinforced the feelings expressed by J. These were vivid accounts of times when the writers had felt afraid to speak up and felt obliged to remain silent. Typical of the responses was one that read:

> 'I can vouch for what you said in your post completely. This is not the culture we should be taking forward. I like to be respected for what I am and what I do and my experience and not for how good I can play politics.'

The uncertainty and anxiety occasioned by mergers provokes many rumours and much speculation: A number of Siemens employees had heard that they were being relocated to Boca Raton and were expressing alarm at this prospect.

> 'You know what is funny? Former Nokia employees are hearing the opposite rumour. Nokia people are being asked to move to Boca Raton .... I just want to know if I can renew the lease for another year and what to do with the wife and kids.'
>
> *'This is indeed funny, The rumours are running wild at both ends, since there hasn't been any communications regarding the site strategy in (this region). For the lack of anything better we can only speculate.'*[21]

Another question invited ideas as to how best to manage across large geographical regions:

> **Question posted:** 'NSN North America is spread across many locations, just like our top competitors. Given the added complexity of working virtually in teams, how can we be better than our competition at balancing the need to give direction and structure to our people, but also enable highly-empowered and customer-focussed teams? How to stay connected to "knowledge teams" while we operate locally in our markets?'
>
> A: I agree with the concepts proposed by X and Y. The exchange of resources to physically separated regions is also good. Creating the exposure of different functions through exchange is also good — our customers love to deal directly with the techies at times and the field resources should understand the demands of R&D. But it also helps to build the personal networks to get things done.
>
> A: I agree with the last response. The most important thing is that we do focus on our daily task to keep our key activities ongoing with customers. We should not spend time with internal politics.

---

[21]The Culture Square allowed for the public processing or exchange of rumours that would normally circulate, and fester, in the shadow conversations. In this way potentially damaging distortions that might radically interfere with peoples' willingness to participate in the weaving conversation were diminished.

Thanks for everyone's response. Let's keep it up and continue to build our new culture together.

Culture Square as Loom

The Culture Square was initiated as a means by which anyone in the new company could participate in the discussion about a desired future culture of the new business.

It was a form of loom or container that hosted the unfolding conversation and through which new understandings, norms of behaviour and values gradually emerged. In this sense the conversation was not just ABOUT the desired culture of the new company, but it also served as a medium through which the culture began to manifest. People used the Culture Square to share interpretations of events including the statements, actions and inactions of their seniors and through their exchanges began to find meaning in the midst of uncertainty and anxiety. Like the trodden pathways that formed between campus buildings, the threads of a shared framework for making sense of events gradually formed. In place of comments directed at the actions and statements of their leaders, contributors began to address their challenges to each other and themselves.

Of particular interest to us was the way in which peoples' participation in the Square evolved over time. The mistrust, misunderstanding, disagreement, contested interpretations, expressions of frustration and resentment that dominated the early exchanges gradually gave way to more constructive contributions and exchanges and to the emergence of new and shared understandings.

We would suggest, with the plentiful benefits of hindsight, that the conversation in the Culture Square unfolded through the following phases:

- Launch, welcome
- Suspicion, mistrust, challenge
- Risk taking, testing
- Catharsis, disclosure, projection
- Engagement, self-regulation, exchange
- Ownership, inquiry, dialogue
- Sounding/grounding board

As a loom, the Culture Square provided sufficient time, space and safety in which a constructive conversation could develop and where, initially fragile, cultural themes could become more robust.

Other factors that contributed to what was ultimately a highly trusted forum were as follows:

'Say yes to the mess' (Barrett, 2012)

The CS and its management and facilitation held open the vacuum of uncertainty long enough for new patterns and ways of thinking to emerge and to gain agreement.

Frank Barrett's observation that skilful improvisation calls for a capacity to 'say yes to the mess' is no better illustrated than the early experience of the Culture Square.[22] In the same way that improvising Jazz musicians trust that form and pattern will emerge from seeming musical chaos, the early turmoil and mistrust that featured so prominently in the early parts of the conversation gradually gave way to more constructive exchanges and the emergence of growing agreement; a found melody.

This can be immensely challenging for leaders and calls for a high tolerance of ambiguity as well as for the considerable anxiety that accompanies uncertainty. Resisting the desire to step in, to edit or censor provocative contributions, to bring a contrived 'clarity' to the often messy discussions, goes against the instincts and is tough for managers and leaders especially. This calls for courage and restraint on the part of leaders as well as the skilful support of colleagues and OD experts. This experience suggests that the rewards from taking such risks can be immense. Instead we increasingly saw leaders participate in the conversation without seeking to control or direct it. These extracts show them inviting ideas, framing thoughtful questions and at times expressing dismay.

Ensuring the Integrity of the Forum — Protecting the Conversational Space

Of particular importance was the decision by Alistair to ensure that the Culture Square was not used for 'official' announcements and communications. Seeing the growing interest in the forum as participation in the conversation grew more lively and constructive, a number of managers wanted to use it to post information and to make announcements. Alistair insisted that this was not the role of this forum. He wanted to keep it as a non-official site and to avoid any accusations that it was being used as a 'managerial' device. His stance was informed by a concern to protect the integrity of the shadow conversation. The Culture Square made public and visible the kind of local conversations that occur informally in all organisations and which provide a continuous commentary on events. The vast number of 'lurkers', who followed the exchanges but who did not participate, were evidence of significant interest across the company. The view was taken that allowing the Culture Square to be used for 'official' business; notices, announcements, surveys and so on, would compromise its status as a 'shadow' forum.

Punctuation and Closure

The conversation had been gaining in momentum and salience for more than six months when a decision was taken to convene a company-wide virtual conversation.

The question arose as to when was enough, enough? Like an artist, sculptor or weaver, how do you know or decide when you are finished or whether this is a

---

[22]This is also consistent with Illya Prigogine's notion of Dissipative Structures Prigogine, Ilya (see Nicolis, 1977).

process that could helpfully continue indefinitely? Alistair took a view in conversation with the Head of HR and the Board that it would be helpful to bring this conversation about culture to a close, to formally describe and articulate those ideas, values and principles that had emerged as having widespread support through this extended process. It was an important act of punctuation, an opportunity to officially endorse those values, patterns, and ideas that were configuring an increasingly stable pattern of conversations, to finally concrete over the well-worn informal pathways of the conversations.

Going Global — The JAM

Alistair had been talking with members of IBM about a Social Networking technology that they were developing for hosting large-scale conferences via the internet. They named this technology a JAM. The name was inspired by the improvisational practice common among musicians, jazz musicians in particular, of assembling in order to perform music.

> The essence of a Jam among musicians is that it is self-organizing and improvisational, calling on highly developed skills of listening as well as musicianship. Such gatherings are characterized by shared assumptions and conventions (Barrett, 2012). Assuming competence on the part of all participants, they place a premium on novelty and on discovering and forming new patterns within familiar melodies. Turn taking is also a feature of such ensembles, as is an expectation that all musicians will accompany or support whichever instrument is leading the melody at any point in time. It calls on all instruments or voices to be given airtime and for others to generously support them. Unexpected departures from the melody or rhythm are embraced and amplified as a source of novelty. There is no such thing as a mistake in a Jam.

> Frank Barrett talks about the practice of what he terms 'provocative leadership' among Jazz ensembles. This is the capacity to disrupt familiar routines and assumptions by, for example, calling for a familiar tune to be played in an unfamiliar key — at the last moment before commencing a performance!

> What provides containment or, to put it another way, allows for improvisation, is the melody. The shared understanding of the melody, between the players and the audience simultaneously provides a focus, and in so doing gives both familiarity and space in which to experiment. This is achieved not just by the melody but also agreements on the key (or key changes) and on the tempo or rhythm at which the piece will be played. Barrett (op cit) speaks of minimum structure and maximum innovation.

The JAM was held early in June 2007. It lasted for 72 hours and invited all 60,000 employees to contribute to the conversation. Four topics gave focus to the conversations. The topics were:

> *Getting Close to Our Customers*: How can we organize ourselves around our customer needs?
> *Enabling Our People to flourish*: How can we make NSN a unique and exceptional place to work?
> *Making NSN Different*: How can we live our brand: pioneering, passionate, different?
> *Becoming ONE Great Company*: How can we create a sustainable future together?

The conversation about the framing of these topics had begun at the Munich meeting and while others, including some senior managers, contributed to their final form, some of the most active participants in the Culture Square were consulted to ensure that they were seen as relevant and current to the conversations in that forum. This represented an interesting interplay between the informal or shadow conversation of the Culture Square and the formal JAM initiative that was sponsored and endorsed by the management team. In this sense the Culture Square served to 'ground' the topics in the reality of peoples' everyday experience in the company.

JAM as Symbol

The JAM was intended to tap into the ideas and suggestions of all 60,000 employees, to invite discussion and debate around these important topics. It also represented a powerful symbol of oneness. It was the first company-wide event since the merger and careful steps were taken to ensure that all employees could participate. This included laying on interpreters in countries where English was not widely spoken at some levels, and arranging for computer terminals and monitors to be accessible in canteens, employee restaurants and other prominent public company spaces. Publicity for the JAM began six weeks before the event and local facilitator teams were recruited and trained to support the conversation and to monitor what themes were emerging in the various discussion forums. Holding this event over 72 hours was intended to allow all regions of the world to participate during their natural work cycle and to allow discussions from one time zone to be considered by those in other zones. In this way the conversations unfolded and iterated over the three days.

A central facilitation and technical team, based in Helsinki, monitored those conversations. Ideas that generated most interest were featured on the opening webpage and this was refreshed every four hours so as to provide a topical summary of the unfolding conversations and to help people find their way to those discussions that interested them. Each participant could personalise their search criteria so as to see rapidly who had responded to their postings and to follow those discussions that interested them most. The intention was to make it easy for people to navigate this massive, unfolding conversation and to help them to find its local relevance.

A Living, Unfolding Conversation

The technical design of the software provided the capability to open new Topic Areas (called 'Areas of Inquiry') in a way that provided room for dedicated discussions of particularly energised and popular topics that had arisen in the course of the discussions. Alistair and other senior managers wanted to ensure that this was a living, unfolding conversation and that the conversation forums needed to be able to accommodate and support these emergent foci. In complexity terms we wanted to allow for the self-organising capability of the conversations, to be alert to those questions and discussions that captured people's attention and which were naturally configuring patterns of participation.

Whereas the Culture Square was a platform for the 'shadow' conversation the informal sense making and interpretation of developments and high-profile gestures, the JAM was an official, high-profile activity in which senior managers actively participated. In this sense it was part of what Griffin et al. (1998), refers to as the 'formal' system. In order to participate employees needed to register, which meant giving full details of identity, location, position and email address.

The interest shown in the views of senior managers and leaders is evident from the following diagram that shows levels of activity throughout the course of the JAM.

The spikes of participation on days two and three coincided with postings from the CEO, Simon Beresford Wylie (see Figure 3), page 172.

Overall, 15,412 people registered for the JAM representing 25% of the companies' total population. Of these 8,034 logged in to the Jam in the course of its 72 hours and there were a total of 3,652 posts. IBM suggest that one measure of participation and engagement for a JAM is the average number of responses to an idea, and, as a rule of thumb, they suggested that an average of 8 was considered to be a favourable indicator. The figure for the NSN JAM was 10.6 suggesting above average levels of engagement.

A number of supplementary topic forums were opened over the course of the three days, one of which was at the request of the CEO. He was keen to use this opportunity to conclude the conversation about cultural values and principles that had been started some six months previously in the Culture Square. This proved to be a lively part of the JAM and gave focus to the closing sessions.

Once the JAM had finished, however, it was clear that further work was called for before the statement of NSN values could be finalised. One suggestion was that this was a task for the directors. This met with strong objections from representatives of the Culture Square on the grounds that the process needed to be transparent and that everyone should have a chance to make final comments.

From Alistair's viewpoint the challenge became:

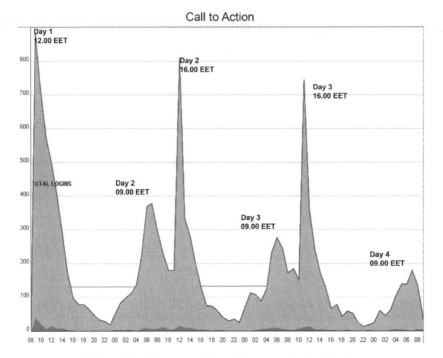

Figure 3:   Patterns of participation in the JAM.

'How do we close this in a way that integrates the outcomes of the Jam into business processes? Not vacuous values but making a difference to what was happening on the ground?'

In the event a small working party drafted a summary of the sentiments and principles that had emerged from this closing conversation. The draft was posted in the Culture Square for two weeks during which time anyone could offer comment and suggest revisions. Finally, after two weeks of comment and discussion in the Square, a final set of values was submitted to the Board for endorsement. This was duly given with the full support of the Board.

The statement of values that was finally endorsed by the board bore little similarity to those that served as an initial focus for the conversations in the Culture Square. The themes had 'migrated' as a consequence of the conversations both in the Culture Square and in the JAM. We see this as an indication of ownership, and as an act of genuine co-creation.

Two hundred and fifty participants in the JAM volunteered to be part of project groups to make sense of the thousands of ideas that had surfaced during the event and to ensure that they found their way to appropriate operational groups. They became known as Values Ambassadors and oversaw their integration into the many business processes and infrastructure projects that were shaping the new business.

The newly agreed values 'gave continuity and focus' to the 'extensive change management activities' (Moffat & McLean, 2010) that were underway including the development of Performance Evaluation Criteria, Customer Satisfaction Surveys, Sales and R&D processes, as well as informing the syllabus for NSN's Academy. They also informed the layout and design of a common approach to workspace throughout the business.[23] Training sessions were held on how to use the output from the JAM in order to identify behavioural metrics that would inform the design of business processes and local activities. One example of how the values were translated into action was the formation of fast response teams that were set up in customer's offices in order to trouble-shoot technical problems.

A year later, in June of 2008, an employment engagement survey found that 82% of employees 'fully supported the values'.

Reflections — Weavers Among Weavers

This case highlights a number of important features of cultural weaving. It reminds us that a web is comprised of both threads and space! Webs are a combination of threads and spaces between threads. Without the spaces the structure would lose its meaning.

The case shows the role of leaders as weavers among weavers in the formation of the new culture. Beside expressing a broad intent and offering early pointers to the discussion, perhaps their most significant contribution was to invite all members of the new company to be part of the conversation and to honour the sovereignty of the process. By sharing their preliminary thoughts in the Square and by inviting responses from all, they provided a focus for the conversation and gave it some impetus. By refraining from editing, censoring or seeking to otherwise control the unfolding conversation they allowed the space necessary for the conversation to take place and for new cultural threads to form. Similarly, by calling for a conclusion to the discussions in the course of the JAM they marked a transition from debate to clarification and action. The closure of the conversation and the naming of the cultural principles and values that had emerged in the course of the exchanges was an important anchor point that provided for containment of the exchanges. All of these actions and non-actions on the part of the new NSN leadership team contributed to the success of a cultural loom that was the Culture Square.

When senior managers contributed to the exchanges they did so as participants, as co-inquirers, as weavers among weavers. We saw in the excerpts of exchanges in the Square how senior managers participated through inquiry, some through advocacy, and by being authentic. They took seriously the views being expressed in the conversation. Most importantly there was no occasion when they sought to force or

---

[23]See Moffat and McLean (2010) for a fuller account of how these values were translated into the formal business processes and informal actions of the company.

direct the conversation by using the strength of their authority as is evident by those times when they were taken aback by some of the responses to their questions.

A form of weaving also took place between the formal system and the shadow conversation on a number of occasions. This occurred first when the views of Culture Square contributors were invited to contribute to the Areas of Inquiry that gave focus to the JAM conference. The decision to post in the Culture Square a draft of the cultural values that had been identified in the course of the JAM was also a moment when the formal and the informal interwove.

Interweaving High and Low-Profile Symbols

The Culture Square served as an important space for reflection, dialogue and the expression of emotions. It also served as a place where distress could be expressed and heard without recrimination, where long held grievances could be acknowledged, risks could be taken and where old emotional wounds could gradually heal. It allowed trust to build and, for some, for it to be re-built. It demonstrated that cultural webs are as much about emotional connectivity as shared understanding

It also demonstrates the capacity of a diverse, globally dispersed group of mature professionals to share thoughts, debate complex technical matters and reach agreement on fundamental principles for organising themselves.

It demonstrates how, given minimal anchor points and foci, the cultural pattern will gradually unfold over time. It also shows how this can be preceded by a period of uncertainty, instability and randomness until a new pattern begins to form. The NSN experience points to the value of a loom for hosting a multi-voiced conversation that holds open the space and vacuum of uncertainty long enough for new threads to form. Holding open this kind of space, without interference, is a major challenge for leaders and facilitators. It calls for courage, confidence and commitment on the part of leaders and senior managers, plus robust emotional support. The reward is ownership.

It also points to the value of starting from an appreciation of the inherited webs that were informing the thinking and orientations of each party. This appreciation served to inform the conversation about a desired future culture but also helped to highlight important differences. It set a tone of inquiry that was to be a feature of the broader conversation.

The foot treads of students and faculty that gradually hardened into discernible pathways between the campus buildings in the story at the opening of this chapter serve as a metaphor for the NSN experience of cultural merger. The threads of connectivity and understanding, random and chaotic at first, slowly formed into increasingly discernible and robust patterns through the conversations and events that unfolded in the months following the merger. These in turn served to shape and inform the more formal policies, procedures and strategic decisions that comprised the governing infrastructure of the new company.

References

Barrett F. (2012). *Say yes to the mess*. Boston, MA: Harvard Press.

Berne E. (1964). *Games people play: The psychology of human relations*. Grove Press, reprinted in 1978.

Carleton, R. J., & Lineberry, C. (2004). *Achieving post-merger success*. San Francisco: Pfeiffer.

Critchley, B. (2007). Consulting in complexity. *British Academy of Management Management Consultancy Special Interest Group*, Manchester, February.

Glaser, B. G., & Strauss A. L. (1967). *The discovery of grounded theory. Strategies for qualitative research*. New Brunswick (USA) and London (UK): Aldine Transaction.

Geertz, C. (1973). *The interpretation of cultures: Selected essays*. New York, NY: Basic Books.

Griffin, D., Shaw, P., & Stacey R. (1998). Speaking of complexity in management theory and practice. *Organization*, *5*, 315–339.

Hall, E. (1959). *The silent language*. New York, NY: Random House.

Hall, E. (1966). *The hidden dimension*. New York, NY: Doubleday.

Moffat, A., & McLean, A. (2010). Merger as conversation. *The Leadership and Organization Development Journal*, *31*(6), 534–550.

Nicolis, G. (1977). *Self-organization in non-equilibrium systems*. Chichester: Wiley. ISBN 0471024015.

Shaw, P. (1997). Intervening in the shadow systems of organizations: Consulting from a complexity perspective. *Journal of Organizational Change Management*, *10*(3), 235–250.

Watzlawick, P. (1978). *The language of change: Elements of therapeutic communication*. New York, NY: W.W. Norton & Company Limited.

Chapter 7

The Pattern That Connects
(On the merits of thinking inside the box)

> 'Human systems may organise their behaviour around a few rules or
> guiding principles that are not at the conscious level. These may
> change without ever entering consciousness. However, bringing these
> rules into conscious awareness offers the opportunity to discuss them,
> investigate their implications and even attempt to change them.'
> (Pratt, Gordon, & Plamping, 2005)

At the beginning of his book *Mind and Nature*, Gregory Bateson (1979) describes a
task that he set to a new cohort of students. He placed a cooked crab in front of a
class of 'Beatniks' and invited them to assume that they were Martians examining
this crab. Their task was to inspect the crab and to arrive at the conclusion that it
was the remains of a living thing. They commented on its symmetry, the resemblance between the left and right sides, and noted that the claws were of unequal
size. For Bateson, the crowning proof that the crab had indeed been a living thing
came when one of the students observed that, even though one of its claws was
much bigger than the other, 'both the claws are made of the same parts'. With this
statement Bateson comments with evident delight:

> 'The speaker politely flung into the trash can the idea that size could
> be of primary or profound importance and went after the pattern
> which connects. He discarded an asymmetry in size in favour of a dee-
> per symmetry in formal relations.' (Bateson, 1979)

In this chapter we are interested in what Bateson terms 'the pattern that connects', the recurring manifestations of cultural patterns that show up in all aspects
of organisational life. Bateson's use of the phrase 'a deeper symmetry of formal relations' is his way of talking about the recurrent expressions of patterns. In the same
way as the claws of Bateson's crab, while asymmetrical, were made of the same
parts, so too in organisational life we observe repeated patterns of thinking and
behaviour. Unlike such readily observable phenomena as the anatomy of a crab's
leg the hidden, tacit and taken for granted nature of cultural patterns makes them
harder to discern and correspondingly more difficult to 'manage'. Like spiders'
webs they remain largely invisible and can only be observed under particular conditions. This makes for a key challenge for those of us concerned with organisational

change: as co-weavers of these webs, and informed as we are by their hidden patterns and pathways, we run the risk re-weaving the same patterns over and over again, *especially* when we set about to change things.

So far in this work we have considered some of the threads that collectively combine to form a cultural web and we have explored some aspects of weaving as a process. In this chapter we describe how these cultural threads combine to form complex but distinctive patterns that configure behaviour in many different contexts. The notion of 'a pattern that connects', points to a discernable and repeated pattern of relationships and discourse that gives a distinctive and characteristic quality to an interconnected whole.

Such an orientation offers a holistic perspective to this exploration of organisation cultures.

This chapter provides examples of such patterns and illustrates how their illumination can unlock historically obsolete patterns in a way that allows for them to reconfigure. My proposition is an echo of the statement at the head of the chapter: once we are able to recognise the pattern that connects we are no longer in its thrall.

This is what I understand by the term organisational transformation and the related notions of cultural or paradigmatic change. For me cultural change occurs when the pattern of connections is configured around different themes.

Before I illustrate these ideas I would like to offer a final assertion that is supported by the cases described in the chapter: the cultural pattern of connections that characterises an organisation is unique to that organisation. Each organisation has its own characteristic 'meta-pattern' or web, and this holds the key to its successful management, leadership and transformation. The implications of this assertion are far reaching and I will explore them in the next chapter.

The first case describes the revelation of a surprising and unique cultural pattern that manifested in numerous settings of a successful business. It also illustrates how the explication, or naming, of the pattern created the possibility of second-order change and triggered a spontaneous reconfiguration of the pattern. An extract from this case, the marketing manager's efforts to launch new products, has been described in Chapter 5 to illustrate how hidden cultural forces can disempower newcomers. It is included in this longer account in order to provide a broader context.

Sleepy Hollow

Cavendish Dyes[1] is a manufacturer of chemical products for the domestic market. Most people who visited its site to the North East of London were surprised at its small size since several of its products were well known brand names. Within the group the Cavendish Dyes

---

[1]Cavendish Dyes is a pseudonym.

site was known as 'Sleepy Hollow', a reference to its modest size and to the rural sense of community and family that characterised its work force. Many employees had worked there throughout their adult lives. Employment with Cavendish was highly prized in the local community but it was difficult to get one of the few vacancies that arose unless you were related to an existing employee. People described it as a friendly and comfortable place to work although some expressed fears that it was beginning to lose its family feel and starting to become more impersonal and bureaucratic.

Physically, the site was cramped and overcrowded and small works were almost continuously underway trying to squeeze in an extra office here and a workroom there. One of the largest and most prestigious departments of the company was the R&D laboratory. Up to a third of total staff were employed in the department developing new forms of product. They were proud of their history and referred to their leading brands with evident pride. Over the past decade or so they had been developing a new class of dyes based on a different chemical principle. They felt certain that the new formulations would herald a revolutionary change in the industry and would not only secure them a position as market leaders but would also prove to be a major commercial success. In the course of my visits I was shown an impressive range of new products that they had developed. However I was puzzled to learn that, with minor exceptions, none of the new products had been launched as commercial products.

The Marketing Director of Cavendish Dyes[2] was an engaging, energetic man. He was a direct, extroverted Yorkshire man who had been appointed a year earlier. His obvious enthusiasm for the companies' products and its commercial potential had been tempered by some puzzling episodes that had left him feeling confused, frustrated and wary. His appointment had been with an explicit brief. It was his clear responsibility to translate the enormous potential of a new range of products developed by the R&D department into commercially successful products. He was charged with getting them off the R&D shelf and into the retail stores.

At first he set about his task energetically, identifying specific products for launch and putting together marketing and advertising programmes. He described his growing dismay and discomfort at the

---

[2] I worked with this company in the mid-1980s when the company was part of a larger holding business. The holding company was subsequently dissolved. While Cavendish Dyes survived this dissolution all of the key players have either left or retired. This made it impossible to obtain permission to use the registered name of the company in this case.

intense scrutiny and 'cross examination' that these plans received from the powerful company Chairman, and at the absence of support from his fellow board members in making the case. He felt isolated in board meetings and frequently put on the spot by the Chairman. As part of a company wide cost cutting exercise, along with everyone else, he had been asked to submit plans to cut back on expenses. He lost his only assistant in this exercise only to discover that he was the only senior manager not to have 'padded' his budget sufficiently to allow for such cropping. His much-needed assistant was the only casualty of the whole exercise.

The blatant incongruence between his explicit brief and these indirect signals was striking. They pointed to a deep-seated and unhelpful pattern of behaviour in the boardroom. As a newcomer charged with realizing the commercial rewards of newly developed products, he was feeling demoralized and undermined.

Board meetings were predictable affairs. Apart from the routine monitoring of performance in different parts of the business certain strategic decisions would regularly present themselves. One part of the business had consistently been losing significant amounts of money. The board would discuss this matter regularly, but always seemed to find good reasons for postponing any action such as closing it down or selling it off. Similarly, board members frequently spoke of the importance of committing to a new commercial push with the launch of the new products sitting on the R&D shelves. Circumstances were never sufficiently propitious to tempt them to cross this threshold however.

This information emerged in the course of a review of the cultures of the different companies within the group. Senior executives discussed recent research into their corporate culture and the conversation turned to these enduring yet seemingly disconnected patterns of behaviour. In the course of the conversation someone offered the observation that there was a connection. He said that the company resembled a pot-bound plant. In the same way as a plant's capacity to grow becomes constrained by the size of its pot these examples all pointed to the presence of some kind of invisible barrier that was holding back the enormous potential for growth that was undoubtedly present.

The reaction to this remark was electrifying. It was as if a light had just been switched on in a dark room. Suddenly everyone was animated, people were all talking at the same time, pointing to examples that illustrated the analogy; the reluctance to convert the product innovations from R&D, the cramped physical conditions, the tendency of the board to back away from major strategic decisions, the desire to retain the friendly, family feel of the work force, the ambivalence towards the new marketing function along with the incongruence between the companies' national reputation and its modest size.

The image of a pot-bound plant perfectly described a pattern that was evident in many aspects of the companies' operations and clearly struck a chord with its senior managers. Here was a pattern that connected many disparate elements of the companies' operations. As the discussion continued various reasons were offered for this pattern: fear of losing the friendly and informal atmosphere of a small company that was tightly linked into the local community; the commercial uncertainty associated with launching new products; the inherently conservative nature of both the staff and management. Someone asked about ways of dealing with a pot-bound plant. What choices or options are there?

Gardeners in the group explained that a pot-bound plant can be transplanted into a larger pot, or its roots can be pruned, Bonsai style, so as to limit its growth. Alternatively it can be removed from the pot and planted into the soil allowing it to grow and flourish naturally. They pointed out that with each of these options it would be necessary to exercise care in order to protect the health of the plant. They spoke of how easily it could be damaged in the course of any change. The conversation also considered how best to prepare a new environment for the plant in order to ensure propitious conditions for its future growth and emphasised the importance of keeping a careful watch during the first few months following the change.

Within six months a new range of products had been successfully launched.

We can see a number of important points illustrated through this case. The power of the image of a pot-bound plant lay in the fact that it expressed a pattern that was common to many relationships and activities within Cavendish Dyes: examples include the cramped site, the overcrowded offices, the abundance of potential for new growth that was frustrated, the reluctance to divest a loss making subsidiary in the face of overwhelming evidence of the need to do so, as well as pruning the power of an energetic director with ambitious plans for expansion. Until the fateful conversation, however, this pattern was unnoticed by staff and leaders within the company. It was beyond their conscious awareness. The identification of this image, at a time of reflection, and when there was a shared realisation of the need for change, surfaced the hidden pattern and provided a common, metaphorical language that allowed managers to engage in a different level of debate. Rather than addressing specific choices and issues they had found a way of engaging in discussion at the level of the pattern of connections. They had engaged in a meta-dialogue.

Moreover, by making explicit patterns of behaviour that had hitherto remained implicit, managers were no longer trapped by the hidden constraints of these patterns. Things changed naturally and spontaneously following this collective insight. Changes did not need to be 'planned', 'engineered' or 'driven through' but took root in fresh soil after some careful tending. These managers were able to assess various strategies for change through the metaphor of a pot-bound plant in a way that spoke to the uniqueness of their situation and which allowed them to express both their hopes and concerns for the future of the business.

The activities of the newly appointed marketing director, an outsider, not a member of 'the family', could be seen as confronting a very sensitive but masked issue for the company as a whole. His activities represented a threat to the stability of a long established, but hidden, cultural pattern of commercial caution and underperformance that was an unconscious way of protecting the sense of family that pervaded the company culture. Little wonder that he felt so isolated and challenged in defending his proposals to the Chairman. When set in the context of an overall cultural pattern of a pot-bound plant it doesn't take much to see why he fell victim to a tacit collusion to remove his support staff through the device of budget cuts. His activities were being pruned back. Even his naturally gregarious and ebullient personality was becoming subdued. In systemic terms he represented a threat to the ongoing stability of the 'game' or pattern of relations, regardless of the fact that it had evidently dysfunctional consequences in important parts of the business.

Understanding the pattern that connects helps to explain how organisations remain stuck at times when they are under extreme pressure to change. Strategies for change or transformation are often themselves further expressions of these hidden patterns of connection. The way in which people think about achieving change is shaped by the hidden ecology of their assumptions and beliefs, their cultural web.

Plus ca change ... plus c'est la meme chose!

In their seminal work on change Watzlawick, Weakland and Fisch (1974), talk about the tendency of individuals and groups to formulate so-called solutions that end up with them feeling that nothing has changed and that, if anything, the original problem has been reinforced. They coined the phrase 'When the solution becomes the problem' to describe this. Their insightful observation is that, in such cases, the chosen 'solutions' are framed by the same unnoticed assumptions that gave rise to the original 'problem'. In the absence of an understanding of the pattern that connects, the use of what seem like common sense solutions can sometimes reinforce the original problem as in the following example. This case was particularly significant to me in my learning about robust, company wide patterns and the role of paradox in enabling change.

Engineering Incorporated — when the solution is the problem

In the late seventies Engineering Incorporated (EI) was in commercial crisis. Sales were nose-diving, labour relations were deteriorating and morale was collapsing.

Share values were in free fall. The company shed 20,000 employees, a third of its work force, in a little less than three years. Through the sixties and seventies EI had been one of the giants of UK manufacturing. In response to these alarming developments senior management realised that some radical changes were in order. At the heart of their strategy for rejuvenating the company was a series of development programmes targeted at the company engineers. The idea was to provoke, inspire and empower these engineers who were seen as being at the professional heart of the business. Their brief was to innovate, to challenge tradition and act as champions of change. They were to be the catalysts of change that would herald a new era.

The rhetoric was bold and the programmes were launched amid feelings of optimism and with the excitement of pioneers charting new territory.

The programmes were staffed by a Business School and much of the detailed design, administration, monitoring and evaluation of the programmes was undertaken by managers from Central Training. A full time university researcher conducted follow-up interviews with participants to assess the impact of the programmes, both for individuals and for the company as a whole. The programmes were aimed at three tiers within the company. The first tier were first line supervisors, the second experienced middle managers. The third tier comprised very senior managers who represented the population from which the next generation of directors would be selected. Several hundred engineers would pass through one or more of these courses.

A central feature of the programme design was a requirement of participants to formulate an 'Action Plan'. These were presented to senior executives towards the end of the programme for endorsement and evaluation. The plans defined participants' personal change agendas on returning to their jobs following the programme. The idea was that participants would draw on their learning from the various sessions to tailor and target specific changes. The Action Plans, it was argued, were a powerful way of synthesising learning and translating it into practical terms that ensured a bridge between the training room and the shop floor. This was widely regarded as a sound, common sense approach.

As one of the team of trainers I noticed how much time and energy participants devoted to formulating their Action Plans and especially to preparing their presentations to the executive at the end of the programme. Many late nights, agonised rehearsals and intensive coaching from Central Training staff ensured that these presentations were both substantive and polished.

Participants' feedback on the programmes was very positive on all the evaluation criteria. Ratings from participants were very favourable. The School of Management took their commitment to the programme very seriously. They assembled a strong and experienced team including many senior professors. The university researcher who was conducting follow up interviews sounded a discordant note. His early findings were that there was little evidence of significant or lasting change. People had found the course very stimulating and enjoyable and had returned from the programmes with enthusiasm and with a commitment to implement their Action Plans. However, a common theme in their reports was that they also described feeling swamped by the pressures and demands of everyday life on their return to their day jobs. Many of them had postponed implementation of their Action Plans until a more propitious window of opportunity presented itself. Participants described feeling like evangelists in the midst of a sea of atheists. They reported that their colleagues, few of whom had been on the programmes, found it hard to understand and even harder to support some of the innovations they were proposing. On the face of it, here was a classic difficulty associated with the transfer of learning from courses. While disappointing, this feedback was interpreted as evidence that a critical mass of key managers had not yet been achieved. The belief among the programme managers was that once a sufficient number of participants had completed the programmes, the innovations would gradually gain an inexorable momentum of their own. With this reassuring interpretation the programme continued.

I was to gain a different perspective on these matters however through my own involvement in the programmes as one of the tutors. Over a period of three years I contributed to the programmes for each of the three tiers of management. Together with a colleague, Judi Marshall, my role in these programmes became more and more focussed on the corporate culture of EI. Judi and I had been developing methods and approaches that were designed to help organisation members identify and reflect on their corporate culture. We began to use these methods with course participants in order to reveal cultural understandings, acting effectively as co-inquirers alongside them, patiently reflecting together on the themes that became apparent through their stories. (See Marshall & McLean, 1985; Marshall & McLean, 1988).[3] Over the course of multiple cohorts of participants we began to see the normally hidden contours of the cultural pattern in increasingly clear relief.[4]

We learned, not surprisingly, that an engineering mind set permeated the company. Precision and standardisation were highly valued qualities, as were clearly defined rules and procedures, preferably set out in manuals. Staff felt like components in a machine, and at risk of being replaced if considered as the cause of a fault. Taking initiative as an individual was frowned on as was risk taking. Among other things participants were asked what advice would they offer to newcomers joining the company. One group's summary of its advice, typical of many, is reproduced below:

* Don't just sit there look busy! Cultivate the impression of busyness.
* Solve problems by doing, never just sit and think. Arrive early and leave late.
* Meet deadlines whatever the cost, even at the expense of quality.
* Keep the monkey off your back. At all costs avoid being landed with responsibility. Whenever possible pass it on.
* Do not take a risk!

In discussion the group summed up their views by saying that EI was an 'Action Man' culture. Above all it was important to cultivate the impression of activity. If

---

[3]These methods are described in some detail in Chapter 8.
[4]For a fuller description of this cultural pattern see Marshall and McLean (1985).

you wanted to take time out for any reason, we were told; 'carry a file with you and walk purposefully wearing an worried expression'. The irony, they added, was that EI was a company in which it was infuriatingly difficult to get anything done. No one would commit to a decision without referring it on ('get the monkey off your back'). Suggestions would be shuffled from one committee to another, and you could expect to be reprimanded for taking a personal initiative to drive things through even if this meant breaking a promise to a customer. The emphasis on engineering had fostered an inward looking, technical culture which privileged the views of internal experts over external voices, most worryingly the voices and views of clients. We heard many stories of new product ideas and requests from key clients going unheard. Huge commercial opportunities had been missed in this way and picked up by their competitors.[5]

After perhaps two years of intensive involvement with this company Judi and I had been reflecting on our role and the extent to which our efforts were making any difference. In the midst of one session we took a walk while participants were busy in discussion groups. The following is an extract from a working paper describing a moment of realisation for us:

> 'During one of these walks the understandings in which we were now soaked bubbled up to connect and interconnect, and a new sense emerged. Each participant had been taking away with him a detailed personal Action Plan, to which considerable energy had been devoted. We realised that the emphasis given to action was an expression of a central element in the culture of the organisation. As an engineering company in a highly competitive mass production industry, the quality of being able to "make things happen" had always been much prized. A recurring phrase used by successive course members to epitomise one aspect of the culture was to "get it out of the door" and another was "output is God." ... Thus, we suddenly appreciated that the importance placed by Central Training on course members completing their Action Plan ... was in itself an expression and affirmation of this cultural characteristic.' (Marshall, & McLean, 1983).

---

[5]This observation was supported by two independent sources. Course participants recounted numerous stories of requests to co-develop new products with leading European manufacturers being neglected such that many opportunities for the development of leading edge innovations were lost. The second manifestation of this inward orientation was evident in the course of the many experiences of the organisation simulation that was used to hold up a mirror to the culture. The simulation requires the manufacturing business to design, manufacture and deliver greetings cards to a customer's specification. As described in the preface, the customer's views were invariably ignored in the course of deciding what card types to manufacture and requests for innovative and creative designs were met with a push for increased precision and the use of templates. The customer's requests for creativity and innovation were interpreted in terms of the engineering culture and did not meet his needs.

Without realising it we were part of a solution that was reinforcing a key feature of the tacit, assumptive fabric of this organisation. The paradox was that in an 'action man culture' it was difficult to get anything done. The common sense solution of placing Action Plans at the heart of the transformation strategy was inadvertently reinforcing the pattern of connections that had contributed to the crisis. Here was an example of a cultural rule or guiding principle referred to in the quotation at the opening of this chapter.

At the time we were particularly interested in the work of a Milan-based group of family therapists who worked with similar, systemic ideas (Palazzoli, Boscolo, Cecchin, & Prata, 1978) in the context of family systems. The paradox at the heart of EI's culture reminded us of the 'paradoxical injunctions'[6] used by Dr. Palazzoli and her team in Milan. Intended to interrupt the self-reinforcing yet hidden beliefs informing dysfunctional family systems, paradoxical injunctions encourage family members not to change a pattern of behaviour but to experiment with exaggerating a chosen aspect of their interactions. In short, they prescribe the symptom.

Drawing on this thinking we considered inviting ...

> '... course members to devise **Inaction Plans**. To encourage them to return from the course with no firm resolve to make changes, indeed with the explicit brief of guarding against changing anything. This idea appealed to us, and course participants, not just for its mischievousness but because, as we began to realise, it would ironically represent a change in the pattern of behaviour of course members returning to their departments and would implicate those colleagues who were (awaiting their return) prepared to neutralise the efforts of the would-be change agent.' (Marshall & McLean, 1983)

We realised that the behaviour and conscious intentions of individuals on the programme were but a small arc in the much broader circuits that characterised the ongoing complexity of life in EI. The well-meaning intentions of a few individuals stood little chance of making a difference to the groundswell of spontaneous and taken for granted ways of conducting themselves that characterised the vast majority of staff. It was clear that Action Plans did not represent difference at all, but were yet another expression of a deep-seated ground rule that was well understood by all staff. Moreover, people were accomplished at receiving their colleagues back from training programmes, at first tolerating, then subtly undermining their plans for change. Action Plans, we realised, represented more of the same. The solution was the problem.

Coincidental to these developments and following a particularly disastrous performance during a business game (see Preface), one of the senior cohorts of managers had begun to reflect on their part in sustaining the culture of EI. Word of the business game disaster, and more importantly the cultural patterns that it revealed,

---

[6]For further information see their fascinating and insightful work described in Boscolo, Cecchin, Palazzoli, and Prata (1978).

reached the Chairman and he commissioned a full review of the EI culture. I was asked to facilitate a group of 18 staff from all levels and sections of the business to conduct a Cooperative Inquiry (Reason & Rowan, 1981) into the EI culture. This included facilitating a meeting with the main board where the group presented their discoveries. The spirit of the inquiry was more about understanding the culture than either judging or trying to fix it and resulted in much thoughtful discussion.

This meant that there were two groups in the company that had a particular interest in the companies' culture: the 'Inaction Plan' cohort of senior managers and the 18 managers who participated in the Cultural Inquiry.

The Inquiry group met on a number of occasions over a period of 6−8 weeks with the consequence that they became steeped in their understanding of the culture. Intriguingly, as the inquiry process unfolded, members of the inquiry group began to describe changes, of small 'out of pattern' experiments that they had spontaneously conducted as managers and which had made a difference.

It was a similar story at a follow-up meeting with the Inaction Plan group. We had made an explicit request that they did not try and introduce changes on their return from the programme, but instead concentrate their attention on noticing examples of the culture 'in action' and learning more about their part in sustaining the cultural patterns they had identified. They told us how they had found it impossible to just notice the culture and their part in it, fascinating though it was, but had felt compelled to intervene and experiment with new ways of doing things. A repeated comment in both groups was: 'Once you see a cultural pattern it is impossible not to act differently'. They expressed surprise at how readily others had accepted their observations and suggestions.

Similar comments were made by members of the Cultural Inquiry group. Many of them reported having become so steeped in understanding the culture that they saw more and more clearly examples of cultural patterns in everyday company life and felt similarly compelled to intervene. To their obvious amusement, their suggestions had also been well received and had clearly been experienced as helpful.

Word began to filter back through the researcher that a number of local, spontaneous changes were occurring, but that these could not be attributed to the courses because they were not part of any Action Plans.

While our suggestion of Inaction Plans was at first a semi playful idea, we soon realised that it was a way of interfering with a stable set of relations that existed between course members and non course members, and it turned out to be both an educative and liberating injunction. It freed people from the tyranny of having to change things and unbalanced the expectations of colleagues adept in the tactics of discounting the efforts of would-be change champions. Finally it encouraged participants to fully attune themselves to the cultural patterns and processes that they had only recently recognised. The effect of this cultural awareness was rather like acquiring the skill of riding a bicycle, once learned it could not be unlearned.

With this cultural knowledge, participants were able to make more judicious and natural use of the ideas, possibilities and innovations gained during the programmes, and with a greater anticipation of the responses and repercussions they could expect in the broader system.

The Main Board and the MD took the results of the cultural inquiry seriously and initiated steps to bring the findings to the attention of all senior and middle managers. Copies of the report were circulated and meetings held. In these ways awareness of the deeply embedded cultural patterns surfaced and became the subject of much debate.

Indeed the impact of the cultural inquiry seemed to shift the tone of the whole change effort towards a more contextually aware process. The freshly surfaced cultural knowledge represented a more considered ground against which future activities and initiatives were developed.

We do not wish to overstate the significance of this intervention in what was a complex, lengthy and multi-faceted initiative. Over time, a range of changes were apparent, some structural, others more procedural and attitudinal. Most notable among them was a shift of attitude towards their clients. People began to pay close attention to clients' requests, paying much more careful attention to their needs and tailoring products accordingly. The new cultural web gradually reconfigured around the customer's needs.

The company gradually transformed itself and reestablished a more modest and sustainable position in a changed and changing marketplace. In view of the disarray and chaos that had precipitated the whole change effort in EI however, this was no small achievement.

Heightening understanding of the pattern that connects, while suspending expectations to change things, was a counterintuitive challenge to the common sense thinking that had led to the Action Plan element of the change strategy. It shifted attention from a solution that represented 'more of the same' and simultaneously highlighted and disrupted the hidden ecology of beliefs and assumptions that had sustained an increasingly dysfunctional pattern of relations. It created space for the reweaving of their cultural web.

In the following case we see how a complex cultural web was spun around the attitudes, preoccupations and technical protocols used by a companies' founders in the development of their products. We see how their way of thinking, heavily influenced by their software and engineering expertise, shaped the development of the company culture. We see again how this web, once woven, had a resilience and pervasive influence on all aspects of the companies' operations and how, overtime, its limitations became increasingly evident.

System Solutions ... Organisation as Algorithm

System Solutions[7] was a manufacturer of computer technology, both hardware and software, with a worldwide presence. Like many others in this emerging industry

---

[7]System Solutions is a pseudonym.

they had enjoyed spectacular growth during the 1970s and 1980s having started from the humblest of origins.

Together with several colleagues I was invited by their training department to participate in the delivery of a training programme about the management of change. The programme had been designed by two freelance consultants in collaboration with the internal training staff based at one of the companies' regional offices. The programme was offered to staff at middle and senior levels.

A thick, and, at first sight, impressive looking course manual had been developed to accompany the programme. It comprised several hundred pages of handouts, short articles and copies of overhead projector slides. This felt somewhat daunting at first. My colleagues and I were not accustomed to running programmes designed by other people and to using their material, but we were reassured in our early meetings that they would welcome any ideas and approaches from our work that could be incorporated into the programmes. For our part we felt excited and privileged to be working with such a prestigious company and one that was so clearly at the leading edge of its industry.

As part of our introduction to the company we were invited to sit in on a meeting of UK training staff. We were perplexed. While English was the first language for most participants and the proceedings were conducted in English, it felt to us as though a foreign language was being used. However hard we listened we found it difficult, and at times impossible, to follow the gist of the discussion. The source of our confusion gradually emerged. Participants were using a short hand code to refer to different programmes, parts of the company and developmental initiatives. A common feature of these codes was that they were comprised of three lettered acronyms or 'TLA's' to use the companies' term. Thus a typical exchange might go:

> 'Have you seen the PCE's for the last AMP? They showed that the PRS has increased by 17%. That excluded ratings from OBP's. When they were included the overall ROC for the PRS was plus 12%.'

In conversation later I queried this particular snippet of TLA speak and discovered that a PCE was a Participant Curriculum Evaluation, that an AMP was an Advanced Management Programme, that PRS represented a Personal Relevance Score. OBPs, it turned out, were Overseas Based Participants and ROC stood for Rate of Change. In order to participate in this company it seemed as if newcomers had to learn a new language.

In the course of running these programmes we gradually learned more and more about the company culture, both through our direct experiences of it and through hearing the stories of its managers. The following themes and patterns began to become clear:

Expert Driven
The company had been founded by technical wizards: part boffins, part entrepreneurs, who began manufacturing components for the computer industry. They gradually expanded into building their own 'boxes' and later into software. Their

products represented clever solutions to some of the complex challenges of the bur-geoning computer industry. The company was populated by extremely bright and capable technicians, some of whom had reputations as mavericks and oddballs. Nearly all were highly qualified experts in their field. The company was stuffed full with experts.

'Over the Wall'
This is a common phrase in the computer industry that refers to the handover of a project on completion of a phase of development. It is metaphorically 'thrown over the wall' to those responsible for the next stage in development or to the user. It also implies an attitude of 'Its your problem now, I've finished my part. Time to move onto the next project.' Course participants reported that as managers they often felt as if they had to catch things that had been thrown over the wall by experts both from inside and outside of the company.

Cascading changes
We discovered that one of the phenomena managers had to cope with was an unending succession of change initiatives that 'cascaded' down through the organisation. The origins and ownership of these initiatives was obscure but managers felt bound by their loyalty to the company to champion them even when they did not fully understand them. They reported that typically, initiatives rarely had time to fully work their way through the organisation before being supplanted by an upgraded version or overtaken by a different approach altogether. They inhabited an organisation in a seemingly continuous state of flux and in which they represented the equivalent of electrical relays, cleaning up a decaying signal and amplifying it as they 'pulsed' it through the remainder of the system.

Flow charts
One of the basic tools used by software (and electrical) engineers is the flow chart. It maps out the different steps and stages in the architecture of a systems solution. The charts define the pathways for the flow of information and energy as it pulses through this network and the symbols indicate different processes, choices and contingencies for the user.

Flux and impermanence
The computing industry is often portrayed as an industry that exemplifies rapid change. Products are being continuously upgraded and technological innovations ensure that most products have short life cycles. The vast majority of software is never used but is superseded by more advanced, or more fully developed versions. Leading companies place a heavy emphasis on learning and research, adopting much of the terminology of universities and institutes. Employees publish formal papers, work sites are often referred to as campuses and some companies adopt a tutor system for coaching and mentoring junior staff.

Disorientation, identification and loyalty
A recurring story told by many managers was their experience of joining the company. They described it as a seemingly interminable process involving up to six or

seven interviews, tests and other assessments that were spread over a number of weeks if not months. By the time a job offer was finally made they felt that they had to be a very special person to have come through such a rigorous and extended process. They felt that they were joining a very exclusive elite. Most people also described a strong sense of disorientation and crisis not long after joining. There were no job descriptions for them, and no induction process to help them assimilate. They were left to their own devices with an empty desk, a telephone and a directory. They soon learned that it was a make-your-own-way culture, and, more disturbingly, that experience and expertise from their previous companies counted for little if anything. Their past, they soon learned, was irrelevant history. To survive and flourish in Systems Solutions they needed to adopt the companies' protocols, stratagems, language and technologies and to forget pretty well everything that they had learned in their previous employment.

Not surprisingly these experiences had a powerful effect on employees of Systems Solutions. Most evidently there was an outward expression of loyalty and pride in working for such a leading-edge company. Staff were highly committed and identified with the companies' success and image. It was like being a member of a very exclusive club. Personal achievement mattered, but always came second to what was best for the business as a whole. Over time we learned that there was another, darker side to club membership. Once we were accepted as trustworthy we began to hear many stories of stress and personal sacrifice. There was an addictive quality to people's involvement. It was commonplace for managers or technicians to work right through several weekends running, to be working day and night in order to complete a particular project. Individual levels of stress were high, as was the incidence of alcoholism, and divorce.

Culture or Cults?
We heard many stories of burnout and of departed employees who were labelled as 'non people'. In our conversations with participants about their experiences of the corporate culture the discussion regularly turned to a consideration of the difference between a culture and a cult. This is a question that had not occurred in other settings and we held it to be significant information. Certainly the driven and selfless quality of peoples' commitment to the company, the tendency for it to infiltrate their family life and the disdain expressed towards those who left, held echoes of cult membership.

As our familiarity with the company and these patterns grew, we were able to set our experience of the culture alongside theirs. As newcomers to the culture we were alert to the differences, surprises and novelties that we experienced in the course of engaging with them. We shared these stories and experiences and described what we saw as a parallel between our experiences of working with System Solutions and our concurrent experience of learning to use a Word Processor. It felt analogous to us. I will describe these experiences in the same manner as the story was told to participants in the programme:

> Our early sense of excitement and pride at the prospect of engaging
> with the technology of the future was followed by a strong sense of

incompetence and bewilderment when confronted by the terms and protocols of the companies' technical and coded language. Just as our new PC would spit back a request if the code for an instruction was incorrect, so too we discovered that Systems Solutions had rejected our first invoice because of a (seemingly minor) error in filling out a job number on the payment request form. Their procedure for authorising payment was both unfamiliar and novel to us.

In order to enjoy the benefits of our new technology we needed to use a software programme. Although such programmes have become very 'user friendly' in recent years the early version of WordStar that we first inherited represented a foreign language to us. Obviously all programmes have been designed by experts and have accompanying manuals to explain their mysteries to newcomers. This particular version however seemed to make few concessions to the neophyte and I was constantly frustrated by my lack of familiarity with the terminology. I found the manual daunting and, unwilling to read it from cover to cover, I began experimenting having learned just enough to perform the most basic tasks.

Gradually I learned useful tips and tricks from others and my confidence and knowledge of the system grew. I was able to make use of more benefits and features of the programme and to develop a sense that it was a tool to support me rather than an intimidating and impenetrable technological mystery. It came as a surprise to learn that others envied my apparent dexterity with the system since I regarded myself as barely having mastered the basics. I became increasingly dependent on my PC and was reluctant to work without it. I found myself staunchly defending the virtues of WordStar in conversations with colleagues using other systems.

Having achieved a basic level of accomplishment I discovered that my version of WordStar was rather dated and that it had been superseded by several later versions that could perform all sorts of wizardry. At this discovery my sense of accomplishment slid down a snake returning me to old feelings of incompetence and naiveté. In time I discovered that not only were WordStar constantly improving and updating their software but that there were countless other software packages all of which were being regularly revised and updated. I became used to these continuous innovations and developed a kind of immunity to the siren calls of their qualities and features as heralded in ever more inventive advertising. I settled on something that suited my needs, something that worked for me.

In the telling of this story the participants nodded knowingly, joining in at different points with anecdotes of their own. The parallels were startlingly clear. The pattern of our experiences with a PC represented an analogue of their membership of

Systems Solutions. There was a similar pattern of connections between the two. It gradually became evident that the style of managing the business, exemplified through its approach to change management, was based on the assumptions, patterns and protocols of systems analysts and electronic engineers. The company was being run as if it were a solution to a complex computing problem. At this point one of the participants offered the observation that there was a phrase, commonly used within the organisation that exemplified this world-view. Managers within Systems Solutions, he informed us, had three preoccupations:

> 'Hardware, Software and Liveware.'

Hardware was, of course, the technology, the boxes and associated bits and pieces. Software refers to the programmes and 'Liveware' is the term used when referring to staff. The fact that the term for staff was in the same genre as that used for technology is of course the point. The dominant, driving priority in the company lay in its technology and associated forms of expertise. Staff were required to adapt to the demands and needs of the technology and their own needs were clearly subordinated to the imperatives of the technology. The point is subtly reinforced by the fact that Liveware is the third item in the list and, by implication, the least important.

The discussions following this conversation were always particularly animated and the sessions were frequently described as 'eye opening' in course appraisals.

Seen from this novel perspective course members began to question some of the assumptions underpinning their approaches to managing change that had hitherto been taken for granted. In particular the consequences of an expert driven, cascade approach to managing change came under close scrutiny. It became clear that managing change was thought about in the same way as developing technology or software. Solutions that had been designed by experts were cascaded through the company and passed along by loyal but barely comprehending managers. Before an initiative had reached the whole of its intended audience another programme was being launched. It was felt that this resulted in many unintended and unwanted consequences for individual managers but also for the business as a whole.

Group Training became drawn into the debate, realising that much of their thinking and approach to the provision of training had been framed by this, hitherto implicit, pattern of connections. The range of programmes on offer had been created by a team of expert Trainers and OD staff, who then commissioned external experts to deliver them. As with our own experience, the delivery of these programmes had often been by people not involved in their design, and not in consultation with those who had designed them. The design had been 'thrown over the wall'. It was not long after these conversations that Group Training effectively closed down its operation for a year and reconceived its approach to the delivery of training. The hallmarks of its revised activities were as follows:

* An emphasis on tailored support to managers.

* An increased use of coaching, mentoring and other live forms of individualised support and development.

* A more demand-driven strategy for the design and provision of courses, based on the expressed needs of managers and integrated into the companies' performance programmes.

* A de-emphasis on mass delivered, company-wide programmes.

Here once more is evidence in support of Peter Senge's (1990), observation regarding patterns, that: 'Once we can see and name them they no longer have the same hold on us.'

The changes introduced by Group Training represented a fundamental shift in their approach to development, one that lay outside of the hitherto predominant mind-set of software engineers. Their revised approach was tailored to meeting the needs of individuals and to responding to their requests for developmental support. This was in strong contrast to the expert designed, trickle down solutions aimed at mass audiences that had informed their previous strategy.

The second feature of this case that merits comment is the extent to which the mind-set of systems engineers had infiltrated and shaped managers' approaches to managing the business. In essence the organisation was being run and managed as if it were an algorithm in which little allowance was made for the needs and idiosyncrasies of employees, the 'liveware'. The high levels of stress, alcoholism, divorce and burnout suggest that here is a system in which individuals were required to make major adjustments and compromises in order to fit into the requirements of the process. The frequent discussion of cults was a further hint at a system in which there were strong pressures for orthodoxy, conformity and loyalty and in which individuality was suppressed. Tailoring training needs to individual requirements was more than the adoption of a different approach, it represented a significant reconfiguration of a long standing cultural pattern.

This case is another example how the identification of the cultural pattern that connects is experienced as both illuminating and liberating and leads to a reconsideration of a hidden yet influential cluster of assumptions.

Dartington Glass

'To listen is to realize that much of our reaction to others comes from memory: it is stored reaction, not fresh response at all. Listening from my predispositions in this way is listening from the "net" of thought that I cast on a particular situation.' (William Isaacs, 1999)

Cultural webs represent the hidden pathways of organisational life. They pattern the coded knowledge and understandings that allow and finesse everyday transactions. For much of the time they serve us and allow us to conduct business with economy and the lightest of interpersonal touches secure in the knowledge that meaning is shared and that we can rely on the subtlest of short hand gestures. For most of the time we rely on these shared understandings and agreements. It is as if cultural webs are the hidden handrails of organisational life. The following case shows how these well-worn pathways and routines pattern our perceptions. It also illustrates how, in shaping and honing our perceptual habits we can become blind to what is happening outside of our 'normal' field of vision. Our cultural webs guide where we look and what we attend to in any particular field. This case reminds us that perception is socially shaped and that our cultural webs can blind as much as they can illuminate.

The Production Manager of Dartington Glass, a 'hand blown' glass manufacturer discovered that the factory was turning out abnormally high levels of 'seconds'. These were glasses in which small specks of dirt in the molten glass blemished the purity of the finished product. Most typically these were wine glasses, goblets and champagne flutes. Quality standards were high and the company considered that a ratio of 70% 'first' quality to 30% 'seconds' was a realistic benchmark for performance. Alarm spread when it emerged that this ratio had inverted itself. The factory was turning out 30% 'firsts' and 70% 'seconds'. Unless the problem could be diagnosed and corrected quickly the commercial implications of this situation would quickly become very serious. Suspicion centred on the furnaces where the molten glass or 'metal' was prepared and gradually brought to the necessary consistency and temperature for the master blowers to demonstrate their considerable skills.

The furnace manager had been in the industry all his life and had developed a famed instinct for his job. He worked through the night, blending the raw material of sand with various chemicals and making careful adjustments to the flow of gas and the speed of the extractor fans that drew off the combusted gases. All the time he kept an experienced eye on the colour and texture of the 'metal'. Through a combination of experience and a celebrated 'feel' for the metal, he brought this mixture to its zenith just in time for the start of the early shift of glass blowers at 6.00 am. He was puzzled by the problem of the bad glass and made a series of adjustments to try to correct things. Nothing made a significant impact. The inverted ratio persisted. He reassured the Production Manager and the MD that he would sort the problem out but as time passed it became clear that they were all stumped.

At the insistence of the managing director, who was under pressure from the board, a technical director was appointed. This man had a scientific background and set about his task systematically. He was sensitive to the status of the furnace manager and respectful of his experience and reputation. He spent days assessing the situation, patiently watching and taking notes. He admired the skill and judgement of the furnace manager and was intrigued at his constant adjustments, like a master chef refining the ingredients of a celebrated dish. Eventually he decided that he needed some technical data on what was happening inside the furnace and attached a cluster of sophisticated monitors. Everything was set and he drove to work the next morning eager to see what story the printouts would tell.

Everything was blank. None of the monitors registered any recordings at all. At first he thought that there had been some kind of electrical failure that interrupted the flow of power to the instruments. On closer examination he discovered that the reason was more elementary. They had been uncoupled. The night staff had disconnected them. It seems that the staff had felt that this degree of scientific probing was unnecessary and would not reveal anything of consequence. Furnaces, they argued, are simple things and the key to making good metal lay in the experience and skill of the furnace manager. How could any gadget measure that? Undaunted, the technical director reconnected all of the equipment and gave strict orders that it was not to be disconnected under any circumstances. As an extra precaution he secured them to the furnace with padlocks. He discovered that there were indeed some inefficiencies in the operation of the furnace. Gas was being drawn off unburned because the fans were too strong and the temperature gradients indicated that the glass could be prepared more quickly. These shortcomings however did not account for the problem of bad glass and the adjustments necessary were more in the nature of fine-tuning. The bad glass problem stubbornly persisted.

It was sixth months before it was discovered where the root of the problem lay. The factory had been using the wrong grade of sand, delivered in error, by their supplier. It emerged that there were no systematic checks on the sand and they had no base data against which they could measure its quality. The problem only cleared after a new batch of sand was delivered and it was realised that the last batch had been of a different, inferior grade.

It was easy to set in place measures that would prevent this problem from recurring and the company did, indeed, introduce thorough checks on sand quality. However, when viewed from a cultural perspective it was clear that this episode revealed a defining feature of the companies' cultural web that explained their reputation for innovative, quality glassware but which also made them vulnerable in other ways. And this was a feature that they had been largely unaware of.

The perceptual habits and preferences of their cultural web privileged sensual and kinaesthetic information. Their cultural map was a craftsman's map and the intuitive, sensory skills of their master craftsmen were highly prized and admired. Their cultural web was configured around the personal skills of craftsmen. It was a craft culture.

The heroes in this culture were the 'master (glass) blowers'. I was told that it took 10 years of training, apprenticeship and experience to achieve the levels of skill evident in their workshops provided the basic talent was present. It was a highly prized status and one that few blowers attained. The master blower's skill comprised a mixture of manual dexterity, a capacity to feel the weight and viscosity of the molten glass, a sense of balance and, of course, a 'good eye'. These, difficult to describe skills ultimately rested on the tactile and kinaesthetic judgements of the individuals concerned. No two products were identical. Few measurements were made during the creation of the products, and yet the final products were stunningly beautiful, and produced in commercial quantities.

The approach of the furnace manager resembled that of the master blowers. He managed the process of preparing the molten glass in the same, intuitive way, preferring to trust his own judgement and reliance on a 'feel' for the furnace above any information provided by sophisticated monitoring equipment.

Scientific gauges mapped their world in a different way, picking up information that could not be seen or directly sensed; the efficiency of gas combustion, the mixture of air and gas and the levels of unburned gases. These monitors traced information over time in a way that revealed patterns harder to discern by relying exclusively on senses, even those of highly experienced craftsmen.

While these kinds of skill are to be expected among glass blowers I learned that essentially the privileging of personal judgement and intuition, hallmarks of the master craftsman, were also to be found in unexpected places.

In the warehouse, for example, the manager was held in high esteem by his staff. This was partly because he was simply very good at his job, ensuring the prompt and accurate shipment of orders and keeping inventory levels low. But mostly he was admired for his encyclopaedic knowledge of the stock. The warehouse had a simple computer system to monitor and record stock levels but staff rarely referred to it and didn't trust it, considering it to be inaccurate and historical. The word in the warehouse was that if you really wanted to know the status of any item in stock you asked the manager and you could rely on his answer. This resulted in a self-fulfilling prophesy. The computer system relied for its accuracy on people updating it as they shipped goods in and out. Staff mistrust of this equipment meant that they frequently forgot to record transactions with the inevitable consequence that it did, indeed, lag behind events. I asked about what happened when the manager took a holiday and was told that he did this only rarely, such was the companies' reliance on him, as well as his own reluctance.

On another occasion I was discussing the process of introducing new products. It turned out to be simple in the extreme. The designer, based in London, who single-handedly designed all of their products, would create a new design that he liked and would visit the factory where a prototype would be made while he observed. The factory manager would consider the new item, weighing it in his hand and examining it from all angles. In this way he reached a judgement as to how much work and materials were required to produce it. On the basis of this examination he declared what it would cost the factory to produce. With this figure in mind the designer would then indicate what he thought the retail price should be and the deal was done, there and then.

'OK so we'll wholesale this at £7.50p per item.'

The entire process would take five minutes or less. This is perhaps a good time to remind ourselves that this was a highly successful and leading manufacturer of hand blown glass in the United Kingdom.

The designer was another of the company heroes, enjoying almost legendary status not just within the company but also throughout the industry. His designs had effectively defined a new genre of glassware that gave the company a distinctive profile in the market. The company depended heavily on his genius and a number of people privately observed that this made the company vulnerable. 'What if he were to be knocked down by a number 9 bus?' was a common but largely rhetorical question.

The near catastrophic experience of using the wrong sand was a shock to the company and with the help of external expertise they used the experience to ask some fundamental questions about their business. The episode had revealed the vulnerability of relying exclusively on the intuition and judgements of their highly gifted craftsmen – both in the manufacturing and management of the business. One measure they took to mitigate their vulnerability was to cultivate and develop a new generation of designers. A competition to identify new design talent led to the appointment of two new, young designers.

A sad post-script to this story is testimony to the wisdom of this strategy. The legendary founding designer died suddenly and prematurely two years after this episode.

This case illustrates a number of features of the companies' culture and powerfully supports Senge's (1990) contention that, as members of a culture we are trapped by forces we have not yet learned to see. In a culture in which intuition, individual judgements and kinaesthetic skills were highly valued, there was suspicion of relying on what might be termed more scientific or 'objective' forms of information. It is tempting to describe this company as having a craft culture. It was clear that the profound respect for the skills of the master blowers, and for the genius of the designer, the elevation of their intuitive and kinaesthetic talents, was equally valued in other parts of the operation where one might expect more rational and administrative skills to prevail such as in the warehouse, the costing of new products or even the management of the furnace.

The resort to the use of padlocks by the new technical director was a particularly vivid illustration of this and a poignant metaphor for the companies' attitude to science and technology. The disconnection of the electronic monitoring devices was as much a rejection of an epistemology, a way of seeing, as anything else. This rejection of more 'scientific' or objective perceptual nets in favour of sensory and intuitive frames was easily understandable. In fact it could be argued that this had been the secret of their commercial success and enviable reputation for contemporary design. Their aversion to more scientific ways of looking and measuring, coupled with their reluctance to use the simplest of technical checks on the quality of their raw material, in this instance had brought them close to commercial disaster.

As often happens in such situations this episode shocked the company into a fundamental review of its operation and underlying assumptions. An unexpected learning to surface from the review was the realisation of how much the craft ethic pervaded all aspects of the companies' operation. Once surfaced, the company began to question its appropriateness in different areas of its operation and a series of changes ensued. With the appointment of the technical director, the introduction of systematic monitoring of materials and the introduction of two new designers, the cultural web gradually was being rewoven in a way that encouraged and supported the co-existence of both craft and scientific ways of seeing.

My erstwhile mentor, Iain Mangham observed that:

'A way of seeing is also a way of not seeing.' (Mangham, 1979)

While our cultural webs provide us with a way of seeing, this example illustrates the potentially catastrophic commercial consequences of how a way of seeing can also blind us to other, potentially crucial, information.

The Pattern that Connects

In each of these four cases insights into cultural patterns surfaced gradually and over time. They were each clients with whom we had a long-term relationship that either allowed or actively encouraged reflection on cultural webs. Anthropologists stress the importance of understanding a *culture in its own terms*. Doing so calls for what Bateson refers to as immersion and calls for an acute sensitivity to participants' interpretive frames.

The insights described here took form through prolonged observation, conversation and reflection as well as through active participation in day-to-day life. In this sense they represented a form of fieldwork or ethnography similar to that of the early anthropologists. We have learned that cultural webs reveal themselves gradually in the manner of an image emerging in the course of a brass rubbing.

Myself and my colleagues who partnered with me during these assignments, brought an interest and expertise in the field of organisational cultures in a way that predisposed us to attend to such phenomena and this expertise formed either an explicit or supplementary part of our contract in all cases. What we noticed in each of these assignments was that, as the focus of attention turned to questions of culture, so interest grew, as did the momentum of the project. This had not been anticipated by either ourselves or by the client. In each case the revealing of cultural patterns was followed by a surge of energy and interest and, in all cases, by a spontaneous change of cultural pattern, sometimes subtle but at other times dramatic. None of these pattern changes had been planned, agreed or even intended in advance. They were spontaneous reconfigurations. This raises the question of intentionality in cultural change and speaks to the debate as to whether or how cultural change can be managed. We return to this question in Chapter 9.

In his studies of complex ecologies Bateson stresses the many circuits of connectivity between phenomena. He also warns that our perception of these circuits is inevitably limited by the threshold of our perception (dogs have an ability to hear higher frequencies than humans for example), and that we are limited in our ability to discern certain phenomena. He also argues that any individual is only capable of perceiving an arc in the broader patterns of connectivity that comprise a complex whole (we can't see beyond the horizon for example). His attitude is one of humility in the face of such complexity. He advocates an appreciation of the complexity of hidden connections between phenomena and cautions against attempting linear interventions into complex circuits of connectivity that we do not fully understand.

My work in the field of organisation cultures has inclined me to the wisdom of Bateson's view. Too often change efforts emphasise the achievement of a desired future state without an appreciation of the current cultural context and how it informs current thinking. Too often, as these cases illustrate, change strategies are informed by the same thinking that gave rise to difficulties in the first place. Cultural patterns are to be respected not overridden. These cases have shown that attending to the idiosyncratic form and reasoning of a culture directly, understanding it in its own terms, without judging or seeking to interfere or interrupt, allows for a different formulation of the problem to emerge. Once the cultural context has been honoured in this way, pattern change often occurs spontaneously.

I would contrast this with what I see as a tendency to look for ways of interrupting patterns, once identified. I would urge a note of caution in this regard. The patterns of connection that comprise a culture have a resilience and robustness developed over many years and represent the accumulated wisdom of many generations. Over time these come to resemble what might be termed a sedimented quality of knowing. Like sediment, it has often hardened and serves as a rock-like foundation of beliefs and practices that have survived long after the logic informing their original adoption has been forgotten. People seem more able to assert cultural knowledge than to explain its origins. An explanation of *how* we do things around here is more readily available than an explanation as to *why* we do things this way. In this sense, attachment to cultural patterns has longevity far beyond knowledge of their origins.

Webs are remarkably strong structures. They yield when under pressure and return to their original form when this pressure is removed. If ruptured or destroyed a new web will soon appear in the same or similar location. To confront a web headlong is to risk becoming entangled. We are all familiar with the fate of an insect or small creature that becomes entangled in a web. As leaders, managers and consultants we ignore cultural webs at our peril. To work with cultural change is to respect these powerful forces, to discover their hidden pathways and to do so with curiosity, acceptance and respect. This chapter demonstrates that, as understanding of cultural knowledge grows and surfaces, so new possibilities for pattern change naturally and spontaneously arise. I would suggest that this represents an ironic inversion of the despairing cry that 'Plus ca change, plus c'est la meme chose'. Instead these stories offer the tantalising thought that 'Plus c'est la meme chose, plus ca change.'

Each of the cultural webs described through these case studies are very different. Configured by historically significant influences each pattern of connections is unique. The significance of this observation is two-fold. Firstly it suggests that attempts to chart cultural phenomena through the use of structured metrics is likely to reveal more about the constructs of those who developed the measuring 'tool' than the cultural patterns they purport to describe. Secondly, the uniqueness of these cultural webs belies any efforts to apply generic principles of cultural change. Rather, any attempt to 'facilitate' cultural change calls for an understanding of these complex ecologies of relationships and embedded belief systems. Once an appreciation of these hidden patterns of connectivity has been achieved then not only do things change spontaneously, but new, second-order options and challenges become much clearer. This was the case with the pattern of the pot-bound plant for example.

A further observation, which at first sight does not apply universally, is how profoundly the core technology seems to have a lingering influence on the mind-set. This was certainly the case with the engineering company EI, and unarguably it seemed to have pervaded the 'craft' culture of Dartington Glass. It was also evident that in System Solutions the management of the business, the attitude towards staff and process for managing change were consistent with a software and algorithmic approach to mapping the world.

In this chapter I have sought to demonstrate that an awareness of the pattern that connects, of the hidden cultural webs that inform the thinking and behaviour of organisation members, is essential. Without this awareness there is a serious risk of reinforcing and recycling old thinking and in a way that leads to more of the same, to first-order solutions. Changing embedded cultural assumptions and patterns of action calls for a degree of reflexivity and awareness that is difficult to achieve from the inside. Ironically, it is especially difficult when the pressure for change is the greatest. At such times our resourcefulness and capacity to step outside the boundaries of our thinking is severely compromised.

In addition to the use of such anthropological methods we have also developed an approach to revealing cultural knowledge that uses storytelling to help organisation members reflect on their taken for granted assumptions, conventions and habits. This approach and its associated methods are described in the next chapter.

References

Bateson, G. (1979). *Mind and nature: A necessary unity*. Advances in Systems Theory, Complexity, and the Human Sciences. Chicago, IL: Hampton Press.

Boscolo, L., Cecchin, G., Palazzoli, M. S., & Prata, G. (1978). *Paradox and counterparadox*. New York, NY: Arinson, Inc.

Isaacs, W. (1999). *Dialogue and the art of thinking together*. New York, NY: Doubleday.

Mangham, I. L. (1979). *The politics of organizational change*. London: Associated Business Press.

Marshall, J., & McLean, A. J. (1983). *Intervening in cultures*. Working Paper, University of Bath, England.

Marshall, J., & McLean, A. (1985). Exploring organisation culture as a route to organisational change. In V. Hammond (Ed.), *Current research in management*. London: Frances Pinter.

Marshall, J., & McLean, A. (1988). Reflections in action: Exploring organizational culture. In P. Reason (Ed.), *Human inquiry in action. Developments in new paradigm research*. London: Sage.

Palazzoli, M. S., Boscolo, L., Cecchin, G., & Prata. G. (1978). *Paradox and counterparadox*. New York, NY: Arinson, Inc.

Pratt, J., Gordon, P., & Plamping, D. (2005). *Working whole systems: Putting theory into practice in organisations*. Oxford, UK: Radcliffe Publishing.

Reason, P., & Rowan, J. (Eds.). (1981). *Human inquiry: A sourcebook of new paradigm research*. Chichester: Wiley.

Senge, P. M. (1990). *The fifth discipline*. New York, NY: Doubleday.

Watzlawick, P., Weakland, J. H., & Fisch, R. (1974). *Change: Principles of problem formation and problem resolution*. London: W.W. Norton & Company.

Chapter 8

Revealing Cultural Patterns

'The fish is the last to know about the sea.'

Ancient Chinese Proverb

'If organisations are seen as mechanical systems with cogs and wheels that need oiling and tend towards disorder, it is the responsibility of those in charge to be continuously fixing and controlling. If, on the other hand, they are understood to be capable of generating their own order — order for free — the role of those in charge is to reveal patterns and engage with guiding principles because this is what enables you to engage at system-wide level.' (Pratt, Gordon, & Plamping, 2005)

One of the challenges of thinking about organisations as cultures is that the term is as elusive to define, as it is to portray. The tacit and taken-for-granted quality of membership of a culture, our sense of 'normalness', makes it difficult for us to describe. Moreover, as we have already noted, a risk when thinking in this way is to slip into turning culture into a noun or a thing to be managed or manipulated, to reify it. If we are to be true to the constructionist view of culture we need to think of the term as a reference to a discernible ongoing pattern of relationships that represent an expression of some form of worldview or epistemology shared by a community. This somewhat unwieldy phrase will have to do for now. It is my way of signalling that when I talk about culture I do not think of it as a thing, but as a continuously evolving, helpful and recognisable way of configuring our understanding of social behaviour. It is important to emphasise that conceiving of organisations as cultures is just one way of 'punctuating' the patterns of activity and affiliation that we term an organisation. So I am reminding myself and the reader that the term culture is in itself a construction and no more truthful, definitive or correct as a way of seeing than any other of the terms that we invoke when seeking to describe and explain behaviour.[1]

---

[1] My interest in culture can be traced to my childhood sense of being a 'foreigner'. Born in Australia, with an Australian father and English mother we moved to England when I was two years old but was always told that one day we would return to what had become, in my imagination, a fabled land where the sun always shone. In the post-war years of the 1950s Australia seemed like a promised land compared to the drab austerity of England. This was a defining time for my sense of identity reinforced by my father's passion for Australian sporting teams and athletes.

Our behaviour as individuals and as members of organisations is informed by inherited conceptions that, once acquired, become for the most part taken for granted and largely out of our conscious awareness much of the time.

As Edward Hall (1959) says of culture, it is:

> '... made up of activities or mannerisms which we once learned but which are so much a part of our everyday life that they are, in fact, often blocked when cerebration takes place.'

Peter Senge (1990) makes a similar observation:

> 'All of us are trapped in structures embedded both in our ways of thinking and in the interpersonal and social milieux in which we live. ... For most of us the structures within which we operate are invisible. We are neither victims nor culprits but human beings controlled by the forces we have not yet learned how to perceive.'

Commenting on scientific writers the philosopher A. N. Whitehead notes a similar difficulty:

> 'The trouble is not with what the author does say, but with what he does not say ... it is not what he knows he has assumed, but with what he has unconsciously assumed. We do not doubt the author's honesty. It is his perspicacity we are criticizing. Each generation criticises the unconscious assumptions made by its parents ...' (Whitehead, 1997)

Sometimes it is hardest to see that which is 'under our nose'. It is notoriously difficult to notice gradual changes in our working or living environments, the fading and increasingly shabby decorations, the gradual fall in standards of service, the increase in workloads, the growth of a child, the ageing of a parent, the spreading of a waistline, the disappearance of migrant species of birds. Sometimes it is only when we visit another organisation, or another country, that we can see our own in a new perspective, with fresh eyes. The following is an account of how my predisposition to 'see' the world in a particular way blinded me to a novel invitation:

> Walking through the beautiful parkland of the Island that lies in Lake Ontario just off downtown Toronto, in the corner of my eye, I caught a glimpse of the familiar rectangular notices at the edge of the lush manicured lawns and dutifully kept to the pathways. A friend prompted me to check out the notices. I confirmed that, 'Yes, I had seen the "Keep off the Grass signs". It was only when prompted to take a second, careful, look at them that I "saw" them for the first time. The notices read: "PLEASE WALK ON THE GRASS". For someone brought up in the UK I had been so accustomed to signs forbidding trespass that I no longer thought to read them. This invitation

was not only a delightful change to a lifetime of stern, civic injunctions, but it also caused me to reflect on the rigidity of my perceptual habits. My behaviour was being governed by unchecked assumptions about the content of the message. And this was an assumption that it did not occur to me to question.

So the challenge of 'seeing' has an added twist. Not only are we challenged to keep our perceptions fresh but, as both Senge and Whitehead allude, we need to be mindful of how we frame what we see. Our perceptual lenses that shape and guide where we look and what we see are just that, perceptual frames that we use without realising that we are using them. Friederich Nietzsche's famous comment is relevant here:

'Truths are illusions of which one has forgotten that they are illusions.' (Friedrich Nietzsche, in Kaufman, 1976)

Perception is not a neutral act. The world we see is not the passive projection of the 'world out there' onto an inner screen. Instead, we need to consider the implications of the fact that where we look, what we see, and what meaning we make of phenomena under scrutiny are the product of our cognitive predispositions and habits. These habits are, in turn, heavily influenced by our upbringing and socialisation or by our acculturation into a corporate, assumptive, world. William Isaacs (1999) suggests that it may be more appropriate to think of our perceptual processes in terms of a 'net' that we cast over the world:

'To listen is to realize that much of our reaction to others comes from memory: it is stored reaction, not fresh response at all. Listening from my predispositions in this way is listening from the "net" of thought that I cast on a particular situation.' (Isaacs, 1999)

We capture information in our net, but what we capture depends on the gauge of the net and where we cast it. If we continue to use the same net we tend to capture the same type of information over and over again, and can end up believing that this is all there is to be captured, this is 'reality'. We 'see' signs forbidding us to walk on the grass regardless of their actual wording. At the same time we can lose our capacity to see novelty and difference, to configure the familiar in unfamiliar ways. We saw in the Dartington Glass case described in the previous chapter how this form of organisational 'blindness' can carry with it serious commercial implications.

Relying on such near catastrophes to bring into relief normally hidden cultural patterns and perceptual habits is a risky strategy. Sadly, this is a familiar background story in some high-profile catastrophes. The inquiry into the NASA Space Shuttle Challenger disaster that occurred on 28 January 1986 revealed a fatal pattern of power relations between engineers and senior managers in a culture in which the goal achievement aspirations of senior managers appeared to override the concern for safety expressed by the companies' engineers (David Sanger, 1986 reprinted in Morgan, 1989).

In a scholarly analysis of this disaster Professor Diane Vaughan from Boston College observed:

> 'What is compelling is how structures of power, history, processes and layered cultures that affected all participants' behaviour at a subtle, operational level combined to produce the outcome ... it is unlikely that the decision they reached (to launch) could have been otherwise, given the multilayered cultures to which they all belonged.'
> (Vaughan, 1996)

The depressing and deeply distressing aspect of this episode is that a very similar conclusion was reached in the aftermath of the Columbia shuttle disaster on 1 February 2003.[2]

The official report of the investigating board found that:

> 'Cultural traits and organizational practices detrimental to safety were allowed to develop', and cited 'reliance on past success as a substitute for sound engineering practices'. It also pointed to 'organizational barriers that prevented effective communication of critical safety information' as problems that contributed to the disaster. (Columbia Accident Investigation Board, Report Volume 1, August 2003)

When disasters strike, it is not uncommon for them to be followed by hand-wringing inquiries, finger pointing or a witch-hunt for those considered negligent or culpable and this is a process that is fuelled by public expectations, outrage and intense media coverage. Resignations and recriminations are the order of the day, seasoned by much, retrospective wisdom and recommendations designed to prevent similar episodes from recurring.

While important lessons are always drawn from these exercises, and while many important measures are put into place to diminish the likelihood of their recurrence, they represent rational and logical interventions into complex patterns that are socially sustained and enacted and which both draw on and express tacit understandings not readily apparent to those of us who participate in them and sustain them. The solutions and faultfinding mentality of inquiries and post mortems is set in a Newtonian cause—effect paradigm.

The view of organisations as cultures invites us to consider that the repeated patterns of system breakdown and failure are expressions of taken for granted

---

[2]Columbia Accident Investigation Board, Report Volume 1, August 2003.
Limited First Printing, August 2003, by the Columbia Accident Investigation Board.
Subsequent Printing and Distribution by the National Aeronautics and Space Administration and the Government Printing Office, Washington, DC.

understandings that are widely shared but poorly perceived or comprehended. We are the enemy. It is our epistemology and our blindness to it that leads us into recurring difficulties. Peter Senge makes a similar observation:

> 'New insights fail to get put into practice because they conflict with deeply held internal images of how the world works, images that limit us to familiar ways of thinking and acting. That is why the discipline of managing mental models — surfacing, testing, and improving our internal pictures of how the world works — promises to be a major breakthrough for building learning organisations.' (Senge, 1990)

The challenge this poses to all organisations and their leaders is to find more benign methods for revealing the hidden, tacit assumptions and perceptual nets that may, at best, unnecessarily constrain the potential of an organisation and at worst can result in catastrophic failures. How can we reveal the mental maps that so powerfully shape and frame our understanding of the world and that guide our behaviour in unobtrusive yet fateful ways?

In addition to the familiar challenges of managing and leading organisations, conducting surveys, gathering information, monitoring performance and so on, we are suggesting that here is a challenge of a different order: how can we notice our noticing? How can we help organisation members to step outside the boundaries of their thinking in a way that brings them into visibility, and allows for an assessment of their relevance and utility?

This is not an easy task, particularly given that a culture represents the interpretive frame through which organisation members make sense of phenomena beyond their current experience and calls for a degree of intellectual dexterity akin to that of a double-jointed acrobat.

Our experience is that it can be both illuminating and liberating for them to delineate the contours of their current ways of mapping reality and an endorsement of Hall's view that the real challenge of understanding a culture is to understand our own. It suggests a paradoxical view of change. Instead of looking to think 'outside of the box', instead of trying to create something new or different, we first need to take a serious interest in the nature of our sameness, our normality. This aligns with the thinking of Gestalt theorists and therapists (Clarkson & MacKewn, 1993), who operate from a view that we cannot help someone become that which they are not, we cannot essentially help them to be different from who they are. The task of therapy from a Gestalt perspective is to encourage people to become more of who they already are, to fully embrace and express their wholeness.

Much of my work as both an academic and as an organisation consultant has been concerned with facilitating processes by which organisation members come to understand their culture. Together with colleagues, I have developed a variety of methods that are designed to surface awareness of a culture. These methods are based on three principles: estrangement, enactment and exemplification.

In the balance of this chapter I will describe each of these principles for revealing the contours of such elusive frameworks of knowledge. They are inspired by the work of a number of classic sociological scholars. This is followed by a description of practical methods based on these principles.

Revealing the Culture — Estrangement

The sociologist Harold Garfinkel (1967) offers one clue as to how we can bring what he terms 'background expectancies' into relief:

> 'One must be a stranger to the life as usual character of everyday scenes, or become estranged from them.'

The experience of being a stranger in a foreign culture not only teaches us about the different ways in which things are done in other cultures but often it brings into sharp relief that which we take for granted in our own. This phenomenon is common in ex-patriot communities where festivals, ceremonies and traditions from one's homeland are adopted with a fervour and enthusiasm that often exceeds anything to be found at home. Even the simplest of settings can hold surprises:

> On taking my 10 month old son to the doctor's office in France while on holiday I was prepared to make a direct payment for the consultation, in itself a radical departure from normal practice in England where such visits are technically 'free' of charge. However I was astonished when the doctor informed me that I was to pay him then and there and he opened a till drawer in his desk, giving me change in the same way as a shopkeeper. For some reason I had expected that the transaction would be more discreet and handled by a receptionist or secretary. This cultural shock led me to reflect on the system of health care in the UK; how accessible it seems regardless of income level and I found myself wondering what it must be like to live in a society in which health care had to be paid for directly like any other service or commodity.

As strangers or foreigners our senses become heightened. We see the world through the eyes of someone for whom nothing is familiar. This can be enchanting, it may be amusing and at times it can feel downright alarming. Knowing how to behave in what would normally be regarded as a familiar setting can become problematic. Even performing some of the more mundane behaviours of everyday life such as crossing the road, can cause us to hesitate and question. The concept of estrangement is discussed by Schuetz (1967) in a graphic analysis of the dilemmas facing a stranger entering a new group:

> 'The stranger ... becomes essentially the man who has to place in question nearly everything that seems to be unquestionable to the

members of the approached group ... The discovery that everything in his new surroundings look quite different from what he expected them to be at home is frequently the first shock to the stranger's confidence in the validity of his habitual thinking as usual. Not only the picture which the stranger has brought along to the cultural pattern of the approached group but the whole hitherto unquestioned scheme of interpretation current within the home group becomes invalidated. It cannot be used as a scheme of orientation within the new social setting.'

The principle of estrangement with its potential for challenging, disrupting or interfering with our taken for granted assumptions has also been adopted by some organisations as part of a deliberate attempt to stimulate creativity and change through the use of internal transfers and secondments. Williams, Dobson, and Walters (1989) describe the use of exchanges and transfers at Abbey National as part of a broader scheme aimed at changing the culture:

'... at Abbey National the decision was made to move managers around more frequently. Those who had been in their posts for more than seven years were, with their agreement, moved to fresh pastures. Normally this involved moving a branch manager to an adjacent branch. Interestingly, in practically all cases, there were reportedly marked improvements in performance, both in the branch left behind and in the one to which they moved.' (Williams et al., 1989)

A similar policy was adopted in the Wrekin District Council where staff were encouraged to take up secondments in other departments. On average 10% of staff were on secondment to another department at any particular time. What was happening in these examples was a form of estrangement, taking people out of profoundly familiar settings in which they could comfortably 'sleepwalk' their way through their day, their week and their year. By a simple act of lateral movement they were required to see the familiar through refreshed eyes.

Interestingly, we can find a theoretical rationale for these experiences in General Systems Theory (Von Bertalanffy, 1968). According to General Systems Theory all systems need to counteract what they term 'entropic' processes in order to survive. If we think of entropy as a state of lack of differentiation, a tendency towards decay and ultimately death, then we can see that such activities as secondments, exchanges and visits serve to counteract entropic processes. Through exposure to difference we disturb settled patterns and create the conditions that allow for creativity and the random connections and coincidences necessary for change and transformation. Ilya Prigogine (Prigogine & Nicolis, 1977) looks at things from a different stance. He suggests that far from tending towards entropy or death, the dissipation of old configurations of established patterns allows for the emergence of novel forms to occur naturally. The introduction of small differences into a stable pattern of activities can lead unpredictably to the emergence of significantly different forms and patterns. Small changes can have big consequences.

Frank Barrett (2012) likens the processes of innovation in organisations to some of the disciplines and conventions that characterise jazz improvisation. A jazz ensemble will look to embrace small 'errors' as a source of novelty, reconfiguring a melody to accommodate what may originally have been an unintended note, played by mistake. The challenge to the jazz ensemble is to provide an accompaniment for the lead instrument in a way that provides a harmonious frame to complement, endorse and garnish the so-called error. In this way a performance is always fresh, always evolving and always mutually adjusting. It requires exceptional qualities of listening and attunement to others, a capacity to simultaneously complement and add value to each other's performance. As a field of musical endeavour, jazz calls for a degree of virtuosity among the members of an ensemble that would challenge and expose the techniques of musicians in many other settings. It is surely an irony that in a context where mastery of an instrument is the sine qua non of membership of this community, one of the defining skills of great jazz musicians according to Barrett, himself an accomplished Jazz pianist, is their capacity to listen, and to do so with exquisite intensity, to the playing of their colleagues. I am of the view that as members of organisations we can learn much from the highly developed listening capacities of Jazz musicians.

In the context of considering how organisation members can find ways of moving beyond the routinised pathways of cultural understandings, the capacity to embrace difference is a rich source of novelty. Excursions into 'foreign' worlds open up routes to new pathways of creativity and expose the stifling and taken for granted assumptions that constrain our thinking. Incorporating such novelty into the every-day normality of organisation life requires courage, persistence and careful protection of these buds of possibility.

New blood

We have described some of the activities that can offer us an insight into our taken for granted worlds. Immersing ourselves in the assumptive worlds of others, being strangers in other worlds, is a powerful way of bringing into relief the assumptions that we no longer notice. Fostering exchanges and secondments similarly reawakens us to the familiar and the habitual. Bringing in strangers, outsiders who import new ideas, and ways of doing things, so-called 'new blood' appointments, can also cause us to reflect on that which we consider to be normal and appropriate. This latter device, importing difference in the form of new people and ideas, is perhaps one of the more common devices adopted as a way of 'shaking up' organisational thinking. 'We need a change so let's bring in some new blood to challenge us' is a common call. Unfortunately this reasoning is set squarely within a Cartesian paradigm, it elevates the individual over the whole, and while disturbing the taken for granted assumptions of a community, inadvertently pits the individual against the weight of taken for granted understandings that support and perpetuate the cultural patterns of a community.

Newcomers who represent difference also represent a challenge to the taken for granted normality and sense of reality held within a community. They are seen as undermining shared beliefs that have been affirmed and reaffirmed in the course of a career and as such are an affront to the historically transmitted pattern of meanings. It should not surprise us that the odds of any individual's thinking supplanting that of an established community are severely unfavourable. Indeed such strategies, by galvanising opposition, are likely to result in an even stronger affirmation of identity and the prevailing epistemology that has supported it. Ruptures to the cultural web caused by newcomers are quickly and quietly repaired.

Here is another paradox, by seeking to disturb, to interrupt and refresh patterns of thinking, by bringing Cartesian solutions to complex ecologies of understanding, we can inadvertently end up reinforcing that which we are looking to change. This provides another explanation for the frequently heard cry that: 'the more things change the more they remain the same.' The cultural perspective provokes us to consider the following: how can we work with the social through the social?

These processes alone allow only part of an answer to how we can ensure the freshness and generative capacity of our organisations. As much as anything the difference that makes a difference lies in how we, as members of an organisation, as participants in its culture, respond to that difference.

The account of Danny Chesterman's visit to Marks and Spencer is an illustration of this. By giving so much time to hearing back from Danny and by the active interest shown by Roger Paine and the management team, they signalled interest in and support for the new possibilities arising from Danny's visit. Their actions and attitude represented a form of positive feedback or amplification, blowing on the embers of possibility that the news from M&S represented.

Roger Paine especially understood this and made the most of the interest and attention that his presence conveyed. Such was his standing in the authority that his presence or absence would be noticed and draw comment. He chose to use this feature of his role judiciously, going out of his way to attend events and meetings that would make little direct difference to the day to day operational functioning of the authority but which, through his presence and his demeanour, sent unmistakable signals about the values and priorities of the authority. He used his presence to amplify that which he wanted to encourage and nurture. I can think of no better example of this than my experience, together with my colleague Judi Marshall, of leading a group that was inquiring into the Wrekin Culture.

> We had been asked by the Local Government Training Board to lead a study into the culture of the Wrekin District Council since it had a reputation for a lively, innovative yet unorthodox approach to local government. Local government is not a setting that is normally associated with high energy and groundbreaking innovation, yet here was an organisation that had everyone's interest and attention including that of the Government and the then Prime Minister Margaret Thatcher.

> Roger and his team, after meeting us and hearing about the intent of the project, had given enthusiastic support for the study. We wanted to do the work as a form of Cooperative inquiry, actively involving members of the authority in the study, conducting interviews and playing a

full part in making sense of the material from the interviews. Roger and the management team were actively helpful in suggesting nominees for membership of this group and in authorising the time requirement.

On the day when we first met with the group, Roger showed up at lunchtime and chatted with members of the team as we ate the buffet lunch. In the post lunch check-in Roger's visit drew comment from the team members. They took his presence as significant, as a sign of approval and interest. People had noticed his evident interest in the topic and, with the added awareness of ethnographers, had been struck by his encouraging manner and use of the phrase: 'Good isn't it!' which he had used on several separate occasions. This, it turns out, was typical of Roger. As we hung out in the authority over the next six months we noticed how diligently and thoughtfully he would casually join a group event or a meeting and quietly show his interest and support. 'Good innit' became our catch phrase when referring to this aspect of his behaviour. In subtle, non-dramatic ways, Roger was choosing to give support to certain activities and individuals, to amplify those attitudes values and behaviours that he wanted to foster.

Those who represent difference within a dominant culture, who bring word of other practices, possibilities and assumptions, find themselves in vulnerable and precarious positions. Whatever they say or advocate by definition represents a departure from the tacitly understood common sense knowledge and understandings that are accepted without question or even conscious thought within the community that comprises a culture. They risk being regarded as either mad or bad and subjected to various forms of social pressure to conform. Others will try to ensure their conformity or will find ways of isolating or rejecting them altogether. Unless these individuals have a strong power base and good support from allies within the system they are likely to find themselves undermined, challenged, side-lined and ultimately rejected. For difference to flourish, to make a difference, especially to the taken for granted assumptive world that is a corporate culture, the requirement is for sustained and significant support from those who have the power or authority to defend or advocate alternative definitions of reality. In short, the strategy of importing difference through new blood or exemplars of other cultures, is tricky territory requiring the serious support of those individuals by power holders and inadvertently risks setting up a power struggle and covert forms of opposition.

The question this begs is who supports the supporters? Roger Paine was a long-term member of an Action Learning Set[3] that was made up of a number of chief

---

[3]Action Learning sets, originated by Reg Revans in the 1940s are on-going learning groups that support each member to both experiment with and learn from different approaches to the problems of organisational life while also serving to reveal the assumptions informing their choices. They are a form of group coaching and using facilitative methods help each member in turn to reflect on issues that they find challenging in their work situation.

executives from other companies and settings. This group brought alternative perspectives to the issues that were preoccupying Roger and exposed the assumptions informing Roger's perceived choices. Not least the group provided invaluable personal and emotional support to Roger during those times when he was feeling vulnerable and at risk of diluting his advocacy. In this way they helped Roger achieve some degree of perspective on his participation in the Wrekin culture. In other contexts we have encouraged the formation of internal networks of such groups to support those who are seeking to foster culturally different ways of working. In this way we have sought to weave a web of supportive relationships and to sustain a community of innovators and experimenters. Here is an example of using a social process to support a social change.

Strangers bring an invaluable perspective to the taken for granted normality of cultural assumptions. They notice things that cultural 'insiders' have come to regard as normal. The fresh eyes of strangers, newcomers or those rejoining a community following an absence, are a rich source of insight into a 'foreign' culture. They have a heightened sensitivity to news of difference and their observations can illuminate the contours of cultural understanding that 'insiders' no longer notice. Later in this chapter we describe a protocol that elicits cultural knowledge through the use of a storytelling method. Several of the questions draw on the principle of estrangement.

Revealing the Culture — Enactment[4]

> 'Experience is the consequence of activity. The manager literally wades into the swarm of "events" that surround him and actively tries to unrandomize them and impose some order. The manager acts physically in the environment, attends to some of it, ignores most of it, talks to other people about what they see and are doing ... As a result the surroundings get sorted into variables and linkages appear more orderly.' (Karl Weick, 1979)

Missing the Mark in a High Street Bank

The setting: A state-of-the-art corporate training facility in the beautiful Cotswold countryside of middle England.

> In a high-windowed stateroom a group of 25 senior bank employees are engrossed in a business simulation. They are running a

---

[4]While the term enactment is commonly used in the context of law, it was introduced into the lexicon of organisation theory by Karl Weick at the University of Michigan. He describes it as: 'Managers construct, rearrange, single out, and demolish many "objective" features of their surroundings. When people act they unrandomize variables, insert vestiges of orderliness, and literally create their own constraints' (Weick, 1979).

manufacturing company that designs and produces greetings cards.[5] They have negotiated a contract with a customer (also part of the simulation) who, while friendly and supportive, is demanding and under pressure to keep his network of retail outlets supplied. He has agreed a minimum order of 100 cards: a variety of Birthday, Get Well Soon and Wedding Anniversary greetings. The Sales and Marketing Manager has negotiated the order and reassured the fretting customer that his supply of cards is secure.

The group has just completed a somewhat hectic period of production and have frantically assembled the fruits of their efforts. They await the final tally of production results from the Quality Control and Accounting Division before the order is shipped to the customer. A huddle of senior managers gathers around the Quality Control and Accounting Division. Finally the Managing Director emerges from the huddle and announces the results to the company:

> 'It went reasonably well. We didn't meet our targets but …
> I expected that. We actually achieved 90/100 … which is very good!'

A small cheer goes up and the managers and workers congratulate themselves. After a while they turn their attention to the task of preparing for the next round of card design and production.

On the face of it this is an unremarkable episode in the midst of a management-training programme. To my colleague, Roy Staughton[6] and myself, who had witnessed countless groups of managers from the bank perform the simulation, the announcement was of telling significance, the embodiment of a cultural pattern of some consequence. Before decoding this somewhat cryptic comment however a few words of background description are in order.

The simulation, while simple and low-tech, invites members of an organisation to find ways of coping with the routine challenges of running a small company that is based in a lively and changing marketplace. Managers have to figure out a strategy, make decisions about where in the market they want to position themselves, decide on the best production arrangements and think about organisational structure, while all the time coping with the varying needs of their employees. The dynamics that unfold from these simple yet familiar ingredients offer a wonderfully rich source of learning at many levels. The context in which this particular episode occurred was that of a weeklong exploration of some of the concepts and thinking in the field of Operations Management. We were using the simulation as a vehicle to illustrate different principles of operations layout and flow.

---

[5]ORGsimONE created by Sherman Grinnel President, Grinnel Associates. This is the same simulation described in the preface.
[6]Roy Staughton is Managing Director of SHAPE international, UK.

We have used the same simulation on many previous occasions and in a wide range of company settings and discovered that it has an interesting property. In the same way as the universally familiar Rorschach tests (1998) provide a projective screen to illuminate inner psychological states, so the simulation also serves as a kind of projective medium through which cultural patterns are expressed. Instructions for role-playing the exercise give sufficient information for participants to understand the conditions and requirements of the game, what the organisation is about, and what the main roles entail. What is not prescribed however is precisely how these challenges are to be achieved. Moreover, active encouragement is given to participants to adapt and change things so as to maximise the conditions for success, however defined. In this way the simulation provides participants with a skeletal form or container, a minimal critical specification,[7] but leaves them to resolve the ambiguities of precisely how to manage, lead and change their organisation in response to the unfolding and often self-generated complexities of normal organisational life.

In short we have found that the ambiguities of the exercise represent a sort of cultural vacuum. Participants interpret the challenges and possibilities of the simulation using familiar interpretive frames, they bring the same web of understanding that they invoke in making sense of their everyday organisational worlds. They resolve the ambiguity using habituated and familiar ways of thinking and acting. Participants deal with the challenges of the simulation by invoking the recipes, routines and perceptual filters that have served them over their corporate years so as to render the challenges of corporate life manageable within their frame of understanding. Put simply, they behave in a way that reenacts their corporate cultures.

So, for example, we find that engineers become preoccupied with the precision with which production cards match design prototypes. They go to great lengths to create templates that will guarantee such precision and they interpret the customer's increasingly desperate requests for more creativity in designs as a call for even greater precision. Groups of Local Government Officers sent the 'interfering' customer on a never-ending series of referrals from one department to another insisting on the adoption of correct procedural protocols and investing much time in designing appropriate forms. Among Malaysian MBA students a common strategy was to acquire copies of competitors' cards and to find ways of reproducing them more cheaply. In the preface to this book we described how one group from the automotive sector managed to last a whole day without producing any cards at all. Within minutes of commencing the simulation the 'managers' had become locked in a labour relations dispute with 'militant workers' that painfully mirrored the ruinously stalemate dynamics of the industry at the time. We contrasted this memorable experience with that of first year undergraduates who joyfully dismantled any semblance of hierarchy and operated as self-managing worker cooperatives.

---

[7]'The principle of minimum critical specification suggests that managers and organizational designers should primarily adopt a facilitating or orchestrating role, creating "enabling conditions" that allow a system to find its own form.' Morgan (1986)

In short, the simulation can serve as a mirror that helps organisation members to stand back and reflect on their self-generated patterns of behaviour: the hidden assumptions, values and beliefs that combine to form their cultural web.

Let us return now to our group of bank managers cosseted in the luxury of the Cotswolds. We rejoin them at the moment when their Managing Director was commenting on their performance against a target of 100 cards:

> 'It went reasonably well. We didn't meet our targets but ...
> I expected that. We actually achieved 90/100 ... which is very good!'

The reaction of Roy and myself to this seemingly innocuous announcement lay in its familiarity to us. In the course of more than 20 iterations of the simulation with groups from this bank we had noticed that their performance in the simulation would almost invariably fall short of modest production targets. On each occasion a senior manager would condone the (under) performance and commend staff for having come so close. No one seemed unduly concerned at the fact that a target had been missed and that this would mean letting the customer down. We began to record these incidents verbatim and as our collection of examples accumulated we shared them with participants as part of debriefing the exercise. What did they make of this remarkable pattern? To what extent was this phenomenon an artefact of the simulation or was it a phenomenon that they witnessed in the course of their daily lives in the bank?

At first their reaction was to discount the significance of the pattern as an accident, a coincidence of no significance. After a while other voices joined the discussion:

> 'Hold on a minute. We never take targets seriously in the bank! I have missed my targets as a manager for three years now and no one pays any attention. I have still been promoted twice in the same period.'

> 'That's right. You know that any new initiative or project will soon lose interest and momentum and people will stop paying attention to any targets. Everyone will be waiting for the next bright idea to come along.'

> 'In my last appraisal I was given a high grading which meant a salary increase even though my section had not fully achieved objectives agreed a year previously.'

And so the conversation unfolded, with speaker after speaker recounting their own examples of this cultural phenomenon to the growing amusement of the rest of the group. It became clear that here was something that was widely 'understood' but had never been voiced, even in private conversations.

Here we have an example of enactment. Enactment refers to the acting out of an assumption in a way that legitimates it as an acceptable and normal form of conduct. Enactment is to define reality through our behaviour or acts. Its significance lies not only at the level of actual conduct or behaviour, what we do, but also operates at the level of what it signifies about what we know to be acceptable or desirable. There is a circular and self reinforcing quality here. In the doing of something, we are also test ing its legitimacy or acceptability within a system. So, consider for instance calling for a waiter in a restaurant. This is an entirely normal and acceptable form of beha-viour. If, however, we were to request that in addition to bringing our meal and drinks that he might care to polish our shoes, then we might expect a different reac-tion. A strange look, perhaps, possibly laughter at a weak attempt at a joke, or maybe an inquiry from the Maitre D, politely informing us of the nearest shoe shin-ing service. In declining our request each of these responses is also carrying a message regarding what is legitimate and appropriate behaviour in this setting.

Behaviour is informed by our understandings of how things are done around here but, in turn, it is also a means through which these understandings become shaped, affirmed and reshaped. To miss a deadline without anything untoward happening to us represents information. This may well inform how we behave the next time we face a deadline. In addition we may also draw on this information when others for whom we have responsibility fall short of their deadline targets. At the very least it is likely to inform how we react. In this way understandings are constantly formed and tested out in the continuous stream of activity of organisational life. And, often under the pressure and busyness of daily life, we have little time or inclination to reflect, to formally notice these emergent understandings. They become taken for granted and half familiar, and may not even feature in our conversations and meet-ings. So, while not part of the pattern of discourse necessarily within an organisation, they nevertheless reside in and inform our behaviour in ways that are out of our con-scious awareness. They are enactments of our culture and we may well struggle to explain them when an outsider draws attention to them.

It is for these reasons that we have found the simulation to be such a valuable device in helping to reveal cultural knowledge. Participants in the simulation enact their cultural patterns, their assumptions and beliefs. The simulation allows us, together with participants, to notice these patterns and to inquire into their signifi-cance and relevance. It allows us the rare opportunity to push the pause button on the helter-skelter stream of activity. It gives us a chance to think again about those patterns that have acquired both familiarity and legitimacy but which have never been openly discussed or questioned. It brings into conscious awareness patterns and understandings that have hitherto resided in the twilight reaches of our con-sciousness and allows for an open dialogue. Once such knowledge is in the con-scious realm we are then free to question and debate its current relevance and usefulness. Moreover, once such patterns have been named and become part of the public discourse, it is more likely that people will notice the different forms and set-tings in which they manifest. Such activities allow us to be in a position to exercise more informed, conscious choices.

In the case of our bank managers the energy of the debate carried over into the bar in the evening and was introduced into conversations with visitors to the pro-gramme, including some of the more senior directors of the bank. The cultural insights thus gleaned found their way into both formal and informal arenas of dis-cussion and debate.

Revealing the Culture — Exemplification

'Cultures are stories we tell ourselves about ourselves and then forget that they are stories.' (Whitney, Cooperrider, Garrison, & Moore, 1996)

When we join an organisation we hear its stories. These stories serve as moral tales, as coded messages that signal expectations, subtly conveying how we do things around here or, less directly, how we do not do things around here. Sometimes these are stories depicting the behaviour of the company heroes, such as Bill Hewlett (Malone, 2007), who on discovering that doors had been locked denying access to tools and materials, was outraged and posted a notice insisting that employees should be allowed access to them at all times including holidays, weekends and night shifts. This became enshrined in the HP way, the 'rules of the garage' that endured for decades and were held as inviolable by HP employees.

Other stories feature less heroic figures. Individuals who, though long departed, still define the culture through their disregard of its expectations and values. A story from local government:

> 'We had a chief executive once who mistook a rehearsal for a nuclear attack as the real thing. He started issuing instructions left right and centre and set himself up as a petty dictator. A right little Hitler he turned out to be. Needless to say when he discovered that it was just a rehearsal he looked a right fool. Nobody took him seriously after that and he was gone within six months.'

I am indebted to my friend James for his insider's account of the cultural dynamics within a leading London law firm. He describes the dynamics of power to isolate and ridicule Peter, an organisational 'deviant', someone who had the temerity to suggest that the accomplishment of significant cultural change for the business also implicated the board:

James' commentary begins

> 'David sets the scene … He makes reference to issues of behaviour and structure. Tony (the board member) chips in with:'
>
> 'You'll never get the behaviour change you want unless you make some very radical changes in structure …'
>
> Peter says: 'Does that apply to the executive lounge?'

James' commentary continues

> 'This is a reference to the luxurious, open plan executive suite, home to the Chairman and his Chief Executives. It is regarded as an exclusive environment and the belief is that senior executives rarely venture outside of this cosseted luxury.

Tony snarls at Peter:

> "You're like the Harry Jones of the company. He keeps asking why people take an instant dislike to him. The simple answer is, Peter, because it saves time!"

James' commentary:

'This is surreal. I try and bring some focus back. I say:'

> 'The note summarises some work that David, Harry, Peter and I did the other day. Since that time, we've sat down and tried to test the ideas out with some practical examples and we're not sure it holds water too well.'

'Tony responds aggressively, still smarting from Peter's goading:'

'Where's the problem?'

David says, 'I'll explain'.

James' commentary:

Rather brave I thought.

For James, this was an illustration of a 'Jester', Peter, taking a swipe at Tony, the 'King' who retaliates by 'squashing' Peter. For James the message from this encounter was unequivocal:

> 'Just remember Peter, you're here because I allow it and for no other reason.'

The story carries important information regarding power relations, and signals the limited scope for dissent or challenge at the top of this company. Tony's 'squashing' of Peter will have been noted by all present and the humorous put down — 'because it saves time', guarantees that the story will be recounted over and over throughout the company.

These stories are the very stuff of organisational life. They constitute the gossip shared during informal encounters over coffee, in the bar or restaurant, via e-mail, while travelling. While they entertain us they also educate us, subtly conveying and affirming the way things are, what is acceptable, what is expected and what is taboo. They define our choices and invite us to see the world in a particular way. They represent cautionary tales for those who would question, challenge or disregard their prescriptions and injunctions, so they serve as a subtle form of social control.

Exemplification stories are stories that feature individuals who in some way highlight key cultural phenomena. Through their behaviour they draw attention to what is regarded as worthwhile and admirable or behaviour to which members of the organisation aspire. They embody or exemplify some aspect of the culture. So the story of Bill Hewlett's actions in breaking the lock and posting the note represents a powerful expression of the need for openness, for free access to information and resources. It also carries a message of profound trust: 'We trust you and do not imagine that you will abuse this trust and we assume that you will always act in a way that is in the service of the companies' best interest.'

Organisational Villains...

Not all exemplification stories feature legendary individuals whose acts stand as a beacon for others to emulate. We have found that on occasion the behaviour of some individuals is seen as an affront to cherished or valued practices or traditions.

> **Creative accounting:** On discovering that she had missed the deadline for submitting her expenses an executive asked someone in the finance department what she should do. Dissatisfied with the answer, she then approached the most senior manager with overall responsibility for the region. His advice was to submit fresh expenses in the next quarter that added up to the amount outstanding, but to be 'creative' in explaining the reason for the expense and the dates on which the expenses were incurred. In this way they would fit into the current accounting period and the executive would get her expenses back. Word of this quickly spread on the internal grapevine. When it reached the ears of a director a decision was taken to dismiss the senior manager. The message of the dismissal was to uphold the strict ethical standards of the company, which was horrified that a senior manager would actively collude in a deception, even though it was intended to help the executive reclaim her money.

In some organisations such action by the senior manager would have cast him as a hero, finding ways to bend the rules to help out a colleague who had missed a deadline. In this particular setting, the integrity of managers is held as an absolute value and the company is draconian in upholding such standards. Needless to say, news of the dismissal spread rapidly through the informal grapevine as did the cultural message it carried.

These individuals, held up as villains in the folklore of company storytelling, inadvertently highlight and affirm that which is regarded as sacrosanct. In defining them as villains, as 'not like us', we are also affirming that which we collectively believe, who we are and how we do things. In this way stories of organisational villains also carry key messages about the culture, what is beyond the bounds of acceptable behaviour.

The Fool or Jester...

A third category of stories also concerns the disregard or misreading of cultural understandings. These are stories of people deemed to be fools. They are fools because they have not 'got it', they are seen as clumsy and insensitive, not necessarily self serving. They fumble their way through, blindly disregarding the subtle messages and coded warnings of others. They provide amusement but at the same time differentiate what is and is not 'us'. We tell these stories as much for our entertainment as for the confirmation that we are not like that. We would not make that mistake, do things in that way or use that kind of language. In savouring their discomfort, their non-membership of a group as outsiders or outlaws, we define ourselves as insiders, as those who know how the world works. Through these stories we are casting ourselves a savvy, wise old hands who know the ropes.

Interestingly, we have often found that when we ask people to spell out what it is that the fools have not 'got', what unwritten rules have been disregarded or overlooked, we find them strangely inarticulate. 'Isn't it obvious?' is a common response. They frequently struggle to put into words that which is taken for granted and 'understood' between them. It is precisely this sense of normality, of obviousness that is characteristic of cultural knowledge. The difficulty in articulating the tacit understanding from these stories is a sign that cultural learnings have become internalised, like the habits and conventions of driving a car.

There is a primal quality to these stories, and storytelling. Stories connect us to the oral tradition that was a defining feature of preliterate societies and which still persists in native cultures. Storytelling, like biblical parables, is a powerful means of education. We remember and retell stories far more readily than we remember power point presentations.

In the service of better understanding how we see, how we can become more aware of our perceptual frames and filters, and more aware of the tacit assumptions we invoke in the course of conducting the normal, the routine affairs of organisational life, we propose that stories offer us an invaluable gateway into this largely unconscious realm.

In the course of many years as a consultant interested in helping organisation members to reveal cultural understanding, together with colleagues I developed a methodology that invites organisation members to tell each other stories that carry cultural messages. These stories draw on the principles of estrangement, exemplification and enactment described above. See Table 1 on page 222.

Estrangement stories invite us to tell what we see when we are strangers to a situation. When stepping into a new culture for the first time we see it with fresh eyes. We can take nothing for granted and find ourselves surprised, amused or confused by events that others not only understand but also consider normal, obvious and often not worthy of comment. When we first join an organisation, for example, as well as learning the technicalities of the new job, the systems and procedures, discovering who is who, we also have to learn at a different level. We have to figure out the tacit and unwritten conventions and expectations. We are learning to read the culture, and, layered on top of all the other novelty, this can make for a tiring and potentially stressful time. Once the protective cloak of being the 'newcomer' disappears, we are largely reliant on our own wits to decode and make sense of this cultural information, often discovering that which is held as sacred and sensitive through mistakes, 'errors' and unwitting faux pas. We feel our way through what

Table 1: Questions for revealing your organisation's culture.

Discovering Your Organisation's Culture **Questions for Interviewers**

Below are seven sets of questions that will help you probe beneath the surface of your company culture. As always, when interviewing, you will need to listen carefully and fashion follow up questions that fill out and probe the answers that you receive. Above all when listening to the answers you need to be asking yourself: what is this saying about the company culture? It is a good idea to take notes. Pay careful attention to the type of language your subject uses and any imagery or metaphors that they may use.

After each of the stories it is important that you establish the 'moral' or 'rule' illustrated through the story. In different ways each of these stories highlight a feature of the organisation culture — they indicate what is considered to be the 'right', 'normal' and 'proper' ways of doing things in your culture. The storyteller is likely to assume that the point of the story is obvious. Even though you might think that you understand it, ask them to spell it out.

On first joining your company …
Can you remember what struck you as being *novel, surprising or different* about the way things happened compared to what you were expecting or what you were used to in your previous organisation?

Compared to another organisation …
with which you are familiar, *what is it about the way in which they do things that you consider to be odd, novel or interesting?* Do they permit or encourage behaviour or attitudes that would be unthinkable in your company? Are there things that you regard as normal that they find odd or unusual for some reason? What does this say about what is considered to be 'normal' in your company.

That sums us up nicely!
Can you think of a recent event, product or process that conveys *in a nutshell,* the essence of how things are done in your company? Describe it in as much detail as you can. How is it typical? What would it be saying to an outsider who wanted to learn about your organisation's way of doing things?

Heroes, villains and fools
Who are the heroes in your company? Tell me about them. What is the most popular story about a hero in your company? Is there someone who has done something heroic recently? What values or behaviours do they embody or exemplify?

Villains. What kind of behaviour will lead others to think of you as a villain? Why is this? Can you describe a specific instance of something someone did (or didn't do) that merited the label villain? What does their behaviour tell us about standards of behaviour here?

Table 1: (*Continued*)

Discovering Your Organisation's Culture **Questions for Interviewers**

Organisational 'fools' are the butt of everyone's jokes. Often they just get it wrong without realising it. Are there, or have there been, people in your company like this? Can you tell me some of the stories that are told about them? What is it that they don't understand?
It is not necessary or desirable to ask people to name villains or fools, particularly if they are still employed in the organisation. The intention here is not to ridicule or demean someone, but to understand what cultural 'rules' their behaviour is illuminating.

How others see you
Sometimes complete strangers or visitors make comments that are very perceptive, or particularly insightful. It is as if they have *put their finger on* an aspect of your company's way of doing things that insiders no longer see. What do outsiders say about your company? What do they remark on when they come to visit, and what overheard or reported comments have you picked up?

Passing on your wisdom — an informal induction programme
Imagine that you have won the lottery and have decided to resign. You are leaving the company next week. Before you leave you have been asked to brief your replacement to take over from you. Assume that he or she is a newcomer and that you want to be as helpful as possible towards them. *What advice would you give them? What is it that they **really need to know** in order to be effective and successful?* How should they behave so that they have a good chance of being accepted and effective? What things should they watch out for? How might they easily slip up? What would earn them the respect of their colleagues?

Reflecting on your answers to all of these questions and the stories you have shared — how would you sum them up in the form of a picture or an image? What would you draw?
Note: You may consider it helpful to offer a prompt to help people find an image. For example: If your organisation were a movie, a form of transport or a sports team … what would you draw?
The important part of this is their explanations for their choice of image. What are the similarities between what they have chosen and their company?

can be a confusing and vulnerable time, all the while soaking up the 'news of difference' absorbing the information sometimes consciously and reflectively, sometimes without realising it. We bring to the new situation old understandings and patterns of behaving that will have served us well in the past but which may have little currency in the new circumstance.

Exemplification stories invite us to notice those individuals whose behaviour highlights what we might consider as cultural 'rules'. They do this either by embodying them in their highest form, thus making them organisational heroes, or by drawing attention to them through deliberately or inadvertently breaking them. The latter might be considered as organisational villains or fools. All of them, heroes, villains and fools, in their own way illuminate cultural understandings.

Exemplification stories invite us to describe those moments when we have a sense of the culture as being most visible, when it is being enacted in a way that feels characteristic, typical of us when we are at our best and at our worst simultaneously.

In my experience learning about a culture is a slow and gradual process of discovery, best conducted in collaboration with members of a culture, patiently reflecting on the significance of multiple 'bits' of information. The analogy that best represents this process is that of brass rubbing. Brass rubbing is popular hobby entailing the tracing of brass plaques often to be found embedded in the floors of English churches and cathedrals. The brass plates are mediaeval images of an eminent person buried beneath the plaque. The process entails covering the brass in white paper and, using charcoal, tracing lightly over the image until its underlying form and contours are revealed.

Plate 1:   'Man in Armour' monumental brass rubbing, ANBR Durham.9
© Ashmolean Museum, University of Oxford.

In the same way, the process of discerning the pattern of connectivity characteristic of a culture requires patient accumulation of information and a preparedness to allow the natural form of the pattern that connects to emerge gradually and naturally.

The principles of estrangement, enactment and exemplification can be invoked in many creative ways to reveal cultural 'rules' and I would encourage the reader to experiment with their own applications of these principles.

In addition to these methods of eliciting cultural understandings a further consideration is how to apply these methods and how to make sense of the information that arises. Early in my practice I conducted interviews using these questions and used a version of Grounded Theory (Glaser & Strauss, 1967) as a method for making sense of the answers. I took the role of a researcher and reflected my findings back to the client in the form of a report often accompanied by a formal presentation. In later years I adopted a form of Cooperative Inquiry as my preferred method for such work. Cooperative Inquiry is a form of Collaborative Inquiry in which members of the client organisation participate in the inquiry, sense making and dissemination phases of the study[8] and participate in decisions about the design of the inquiry process. Cooperative Inquiry supports a cross-section of organisation members to formulate their own understanding of their discoveries in a way that allows for the social construction of shared understanding. Accordingly my role has migrated from that of expert to facilitator and co-inquirer.

Imagery — A Fourth Principle?

In addition to the use of the three principles of enactment, estrangement and exemplification we have also been struck how the use of images and metaphor can bring additional insight into cultural patterns. The two images for example in Chapter 6 that portray the pre-merger cultures of Nokia Networks and Siemens Communications became widely embraced as a representation of their respective cultural patterns. The elements of both images had emerged in the workshops in which representatives of both companies had generated insights by using the storytelling method described (see Figures 1 and 2 in Chapter 6) and by identifying images that expressed their sense of the culture. The final, composite, images were shaped by a professional artist and illustrator in collaboration with myself. The elements and relationships that were portrayed in both of the pictures were visual representations of the 'data' that had emerged through the storytelling process. Validation of these images was evident in the eagerness with which members of both cultures subsequently spoke to the content of the pictures. The fact that the images were rapidly shared across the new global company is further evidence of their

---

[8]For an account of such a Cooperative Inquiry see Marshall and McLean (1998).

intuitive appeal. Finally, their spontaneous use in multiple workshops to inform dialogues about the cultural implications of the merger also points to their value.

This accords with our experience of this work in many other settings. The representation of cultural patterns in visual form not only provokes immense interest and ignites spontaneous dialogue, but our finding is that these images also lead to deeper insights into the patterns themselves. We have noted earlier Paul Watzlawick's observation (1977) that images and metaphor provide a direct route into unconscious knowledge.

A word of caution is in order when considering the use of such imagery. Our view is that it is most helpful as a means of summarizing and providing a holistic depiction of cultural patterns that have already been identified through the methods described above. The power of such imagery is to be found in its ability to offer a simultaneous and visual representation of multiple cultural features. As such it can render subtle phenomena accessible in a manner that allows for them to be more easily discussed by non-experts, by a wide range of organization members. We would caution others interested in using such imagery that its power is derived from being grounded in a 'thick soup' of data and from its resonance with repeated expressions of cultural patterns identified over the course of several cycles of inquiry.[9]

The header to this section poses the question as to whether such imagery can be considered a principle of cultural discovery in the same way as the three principles of estrangement, enactment and exemplification. I see the use of imagery in this context as primarily a powerful means of representing and complementing the cultural contours revealed through these principles. As the saying goes, a picture is worth a thousand words.

References

Barrett, F. (2012). *Yes to the mess: Surprising leadership lessons from Jazz*. Boston, MA: Harvard Business School Publishing.

Clarkson, P., & MacKewn, J. (1993). *Fritz perls*. London: Sage.

Garfinkel, H. (1967). *Studies in ethnomethodology*. Englewood Cliffs, NJ: Prentice-Hall.

Glaser, B. G., & Strauss, A. L. (1967). *The discovery of grounded theory: Strategies for qualitative research*. Chicago, IL: Aldine.

Hall, E. (1959). *The silent language*. New York, NY: Random House.

Isaacs, W. (1999). *Dialogue and the art of thinking together*. New York, NY: Doubleday.

Malone, M. S. (2007). *Bill and Dave*. New York, NY: The Penguin.

Marshall, J., & McLean A. (1998). Reflection in action: Exploring organizational culture. In P. Reason (Ed.), *Human inquiry in action*. London: Sage.

McLean, A., & Marshall, J. (1991). *Cultures at work: How to identify and understand them*. Luton: Local Government Training Board.

Morgan, G. (1986). *Images of organization*. London: Sage.

---

[9]For a practical guide to inquiry into organisation cultures see McLean and Marshall (1991).

Morgan, G. (1989). *Creative organization theory: A resourcebook*. Sage.

Nietzsche, F. (1976). On truth and falsity in their extramoral sense. In W. Kaufman (Ed.), *The portable nietzche*. New York, NY: Viking Press. (Originally unpublished).

Pratt, J., Gordon, P., & Plamping, D. R. (2005). *Working whole systems: Putting theory into practice in organisations*. Oxford, UK: Radcliffe Publishing.

Prigogine, I., & Nicolis, G. (1977). *Self-organization in non-equilibrium systems*. Chichester: Wiley.

Rorschach, H. (1998). *Psychodiagnostics: A diagnostic test based on perception* (10th ed.). Cambridge, MA: Hogrefe Publishing Corp.

Schuetz, A. (1967). *The phenomenology of the social world*. Evanston, IL: Northwestern University Press.

Senge, P. M. (1990). *The fifth discipline*. New York, NY: Doubleday.

Vaughan. (1996). *The challenger launch decision*. Chicago: University of Chicago Press.

Von Bertalanffy, K. L. (1968). *General system theory: Foundations, development, applications*. New York, NY: George Braziller. (Revised edition 1976).

Watzlawick, P. (1977). *The language of change*. New York, NY: W. W. Norton.

Weick, K. (1979). *The social psychology of organizing*. Reading, MA: Addison Wesley Publishing Company.

Whitehead, A. N. (1997). *Science and the modern world*. Free Press (Simon & Schuster).

Whitney, D., Cooperrider, D., Garrison, M. E., & Moore, J. P. (1996). *Appreciative inquiry and culture change at GTE: Giving birth to a positive revolution*. Retrieved from http://appreciativeinquiry.case.edu

Williams, A., Dobson, P., & Walters, M. (1989). *Changing culture*. London: Institute of Personnel Management.

Chapter 9

Web as Metaphor

'And metaphors like cats behind your smile,
Each one wound up to purr,
each one a pride,
Each one a fine gold beast you've hid inside ...'
— (Ray Bradbury, 1992)

From Ordinary to Extraordinary Leadership

During times of paradigmatic change, the hidden and unquestioned beliefs under-pinning our view of the world are thrown into relief. We are forced to question everything that we take to be real, normal and right. And this is a disturbing, disor-ienting experience.

The shift away from a Newtonian, mechanistic world view to a postmodern orientation privileges an appreciation of how we understand and make sense of events over concerns for objectivity and truth and gives a heightened emphasis to *how we see* rather than *what we see*. The same shift is occurring in our understand-ing of organisations, and in how we think about what it means to lead and manage them. The long-held view of organisations as structures and as machines to be con-trolled by detached, omniscient leaders is giving way to seeing them as living, social processes and as conversational routines and exchanges that self-pattern to form distinctive cultures. Yes, leaders influence the nature of these patterns, but as social phenomena in which they are participants, as weavers among weavers, they cannot guarantee how these patterns will unfold or what form they will take. In this view of things leaders influence, they cannot control.

The cases described in this work demonstrate that the patterns of behaviour, values and beliefs that define an organisation culture, gradually acquire distinctive and increasingly resilient forms that both prescribe acceptable pathways for acting and infiltrate every facet of daily life. At the same time such patterns also prohibit and sanction other options and choices. These hidden pathways for action and thought both serve us and constrain us. They serve us by providing a medium for enabling social exchange and transactions using the subtlest of gestures and sym-bols. Through the familiarity accorded by repeated daily experience we come to know how to get things done in a setting and how to navigate our way through the daily, weekly and yearly routines of organisational life. These understandings and expectancies are held as background information, enshrined and coded in artefacts and rituals as well as systems and procedures. They are rarely spelt out explicitly but are tacitly understood by most, if not all, members. They provide a comprehensive framework, a pervasive medium, for making sense of things and for framing our choices when challenges are encountered.

They constrain us however, when we need to do things differently, when the ground rules change, when there are discontinuous structural shifts in the contextual ecologies on which we rely.

Throughout this book I have suggested that an understanding of how cultural understandings form and change is of primary, pragmatic and practical value for businesses and institutions looking to ensure their continuing relevance in a rapidly changing world.

Our postmodern world, a world of flux and uncertainty, places a premium on the capacity to understand the formation and change of these underlying assumptions, mindsets and interpretive frameworks. This capacity is a pre-eminent and distinguishing capability of leaders in the 21st century. It calls for leaders to exercise a heightened sense of reflexivity and to create the conditions in which organisation members can both recognise and step outside the hidden boundaries that constrain their thinking and behaviour. It also calls on leaders to support processes that allow complex communities to reconfigure themselves around different values, assumptions and core understandings. It calls on them to tolerate ambiguity and to become accustomed to the processes whereby new understanding emerges through discourse, inquiry and experimentation. It calls for a heightened sense of self as participant, not as director or commander, and of self as symbol whose every action, non-action, and gesture draws scrutiny, invites interpretation and implies a worldview. It calls for heightened sensitivity and respect for the possibilities inherent in difference.

Writers who view organisations from the perspective of Complex Responsive Processes (Griffin & Stacey, 2005) refer to this as 'extraordinary leadership'. It lies beyond the capacity to ensure the efficient management of a business, relying as it does on the core disciplines of operational efficiency as well as the formulation and implementation of a business strategy. These will always continue to be necessary and relevant. Extraordinary leadership is required when things are far from certain, when environmental turbulence makes it hard to achieve either clarity or consensus on how to proceed, when we are 'in charge but not in control', when familiar assumptions and routines no longer make a desired difference, and when more of the same will no longer suffice. When, in short, some form of cultural change is required.

I am especially interested in what all this means for those with the responsibility for leading and changing organisations, be they communities, companies or other forms of social grouping faced with the need for discontinuous change, with the imperative to respond to the shifting contexts in which they operate.

We constantly hear the call for a change of culture. While it is easy to make such calls, it has proved far more elusive to understand *how* such change happens in any intentional way. The question as to whether cultural change can be 'managed' has proved particularly problematic. This has been an elusive black box in the field of organisation studies and I offer these stories, together with the lessons they suggest, as a contribution to this important question.

Beyond Mechanistic Thinking

This work has brought an anthropological perspective to bear on the challenges familiar to many, if not all, corporations and other forms of organisation. It has drawn on the insights from the developing fields anthropology social constructionism, and particularly on the ideas of Clifford Geertz and Gregory Bateson as well as insights from the field of Complexity Theory.

This book is intended as a contribution to our understanding of organisations as patterned social behaviour, and to developing our understanding of the processes of cultural change, including the role of leaders, managers and facilitators in this endeavour.

In this penultimate chapter I build on Geertz's (Geertz, 1973) metaphor of cultures as 'webs of signification'. I was struck by the power of the metaphor when I first read Geertz's work more than 30 years ago. In the course of my work as a practising consultant and in the process of writing this book, I have found more and more ways in which the metaphor resonates with my understanding of the field and offers insights into processes associated with cultural change. I have sensed a broader pattern of connections becoming apparent in the manner of an image emerging in a photographer's dark room. The value of metaphors is that they connect multiple elements through a unifying motif. The danger is that their compelling appeal can mean that information that sits less naturally with the metaphor is downplayed or ignored. Such devices for organising our understanding are helpful because they provide a broader coherence to what might otherwise be disparate observations. They also allow us simultaneously to see inter-relationships between multiple phenomena, and thus enable a view of a 'whole', to glimpse the 'dance of interacting parts' (Bateson, 1972). In this sense, they help us to better manage complex information sets.

In expanding on this metaphor of culture as web I am mindful of Gregory Bateson's observation that all perception is an act of punctuation. Let me be clear. I am not proposing that this view of thinking about patterns of behaviour in organisations is in anyway superior or more accurate than many of the other metaphors in this increasingly crowded field of research and practice. I am offering it because I think and hope that it may be a helpful device that draws together many of the observations and insights in this work. I also offer it because I believe and hope that it provides novel insights for leaders, for OD professionals and for other students in this fascinating arena.

The remainder of this chapter is concerned with elaborating on the metaphor of organisation cultures as 'webs of signification.' My proposition is that there are many similarities between the structural properties of spiders' webs and those of organisation cultures. I also suggest that the process by which a spider's web is woven can also illuminate our understanding of cultural change and the role of those who would lead or facilitate such processes.

We begin by summarising some of the distinguishing features of webs and follow this by a detailed consideration of how each of these features illuminates our understanding of organisation culture.

On Webs[1]

1. *Webs are strong, resilient and efficient.* They have a greater tensile strength than the same weight of steel. If damaged they are quickly repaired or rewoven. They have much greater elasticity than steel and *yield in response to external pressure. Webs are efficient.* Once woven, the spider doesn't need to expend energy chasing her prey.
2. *Webs rely on secure anchors.*
3. *The construction of a web commences with the weaving of radial threads.*
4. *Spiders use temporary threads in the process of constructing a web.* Once the web is complete they re-ingest these temporary pathways.
5. *Webs are comprised of many interwoven threads.* It is the interconnectivity of threads that provides robustness and distributed strength to the whole.
6. *Webs provide non-sticky pathways by which a spider can travel.* These are in contrast to other, sticky threads through which they entrap their prey.
7. *Webs are hard to see* and are designed to ensnare the unseeing and the unwary.
8. *Webs are comprised of both threads and spaces between threads.* The spaces are as necessary as the threads.
9. *Spiders work with up to seven different kinds of silk when weaving a web.*

1. Webs Are Strong …

Cultural patterns, once formed, are pervasive and remarkably resilient. A vivid example of the strength of a cultural web was evident in the stories of those employees of Systems Solutions, the IT manufacturer that was managed using a mindset resembling an algorithm or flow diagram. It was a culture replete with technical experts who created (and recreated) solutions that were then driven systematically through the business. It was a fast-moving environment where the half-life of solutions was counted in weeks and sometimes days and where reputations were quickly gained and just as quickly lost. With few exceptions, employees described the

---

[1]For a description of the features of spiders webs and weaving processes see, for example, Cranford, Tarakanova, Pugno, and Buehler (2012) and Saravanan (2006).

disorienting experience of a protracted selection process followed by an absence of direction and induction into the company. The disregard for the value of their experience in previous companies was unnerving for them and fostered an attitude of dependency, a need to figure out how to fit into the unspecified protocols and diffuse expectations that characterised this companies' way of doing things.

Newcomers learned that they could not look to others to provide direction but needed to proactively build their own network and create a role for themselves within it.

They discovered that they were the 'live-ware' that interfaced with the hardware and software of this high-tech business and paid a high price in terms of personal stress and ruptured relationships with anyone outside of the company, including their families. The strength of this cyber-culture led many to openly inquire about the similarities between corporate cultures and cults, not least because of the strong norms of loyalty and selflessness that were a distinctive and much lauded feature of the culture. The 'disappearance' of those 'non-people' who resigned or departed for other reasons bore another resemblance to the obligations of loyalty on cult members in religious communities and struck a sinister note in conversations about the corporate culture.

This culture had a strong hold on its members who, of course, were one and the same as those who perpetuated it, recreating it through routine, daily exchanges and conversations.

We saw the same phenomenon in the setting of EI engineering. Their preoccupation with the precise replication of components, a prized quality in high volume manufacturing, also contributed to a 'component' view of employees. 'Problem people' were dealt with in the same way as replacing 'faulty components' and restructuring or 'rebuilding' underperforming departments in the same was as they would dismantle and rebuild an underperforming engine or machine. We also saw how their response to a perceived need to revitalise their struggling business fortunes through high-profile training programmes featured Personal Action Plans as the cornerstone of their recovery plan. We observed how this change strategy was another expression of the existing 'Action Man' culture. Without intending to, the programme was recreating the same values and ways of thinking that was a defining feature of their existing culture and which was no longer serving the changing requirements of their business context. This 'Action Man' culture emphasised the impression of busyness, precision and manufacturing convenience over the flexibility and creativity that the customer craved. Excessive workloads and personal stress were considered to be necessary evidence of dedication to the company.

In these and many of the other cases described we have seen how the hidden orientations and force-fields of their culture informed participants actions, their non-actions, how they defined problems and opportunities, the initiatives and choices they made as well the way they approached change.

We also noted how, in each case, the exercise of surfacing, naming and inquiring into these hidden understandings, these mindsets, seemed to free up energy and often led to a spontaneous shift in patterns of behaviour, allowing for new ways of framing their choices and options for action. In the terms of Korzybski's

(Korzybski, 1931) notion that 'the map is not the territory', it was as if helping members of an organisation recognise their cultural map freed them to explore the territory in new ways, to re-conceive the familiar, to depart from well-worn pathways used to navigate the territory without thinking, as if sleepwalking.

These stories suggest that we need to be respectful of the conservative, pattern sustaining qualities of cultures. They caution an attitude of humility in light of this and point to the wisdom of working with the patterns of culture wherever possible rather than casually and hubristically looking to change them.

Webs are ... flexible and resilient

A recurring theme in many of the stories in this work is just how readily, in the wake of a disturbance, cultural patterns will snap back and restore their original form. This was one of the earliest lessons of my career as an OD consultant in the course of the assignment with a shoe manufacturer described in Chapter 2. The client's observation that as a consulting team we were seen as 'punching sponges' eerily matched our own, private, assessment of the relationship as resembling the self-sealing properties of a rice pudding. Both images describe the restoration of the status quo ante and suggested a resilient capacity to sustain a pattern of relations.

The isolation and subtle disempowerment of the newly appointed and energetic marketing director at Sleepy Hollow illustrates the often irrational and illogical ways in which cultural patterns persist even in the face of compelling, rational arguments for change. His efforts to launch many of the new generation of products sitting on the shelves of the R&D department was systematically, if unwittingly, undermined by his Board colleagues and by the Chairman. It was only when the realisation that this systemic pull-back was part of a broader pattern characterised metaphorically by the stunted growth of a 'pot bound' plant, that these hidden force fields were revealed and lost their potency.

This compares to the poignant story of the highly qualified chemist who was lured from a competitor to a pharmaceutical company in order to introduce new thinking, as a 'new blood' appointment. He discovered to his chagrin that no one was interested in listening to his ideas and he experienced subtle, but overwhelming, pressure to 'get with the program' and to 'fall in line' with what was considered to be 'normal and accepted' practice. He shared his story with us 18 months after joining the company and expressed a kind of puzzled disappointment at what, for him, was completely unexpected and counter intuitive.

Cultural webs are social phenomena, social accomplishments. To rupture or ignore them is to invite social responses that seek to restore the pattern.

We have seen how cultural norms dampen difference and bring pressure to bear on those who represent difference. Those who walk a different path, who seek to interrupt long-held cultural patterns, experience pressures that are both subtle and direct. They can expect to be undermined, sanctioned and otherwise pressured into conformity. This is the shadow side of the facility of social exchange and action that cultural webs enable. Taken for granted customs and meanings make for communicative efficiency and provide the comfort of familiarity. They minimise the need to explain or justify the familiar and routine. When individuals or groups either deliberately or inadvertently depart from these well-worn routines and cultural pathways, they become like insects caught in the cultural web, tangled and immobilised by the ever-tightening mesh of convention. The more they resist and struggle the more entangled they become, the more energy they expend in futile effort.

Individuals might temporarily rupture a cultural web, newly appointed leaders, powerful new comers with a determination to shake things up, those with a brief to 'sweep away' the old. But, as was dramatically illustrated by the decoupling of electronic monitors by the craftsmen glass blowers in the Dartington Glass case, cultural webs are remarkably resilient and will self-repair in ways that isolate or entrap these adventurers.

Viewed from this perspective the chances that a so-called 'new blood' strategy will make any significant or lasting difference, are limited. Perversely, such strategies are just as likely to reinforce cultural patterns as efforts to neutralise a perceived threat to an ongoing pattern actually end up strengthening existing norms. It acts in a manner akin to the bodies' immune system whereby the detection of 'foreign' matter triggers the mobilisation of the bodies' immune system.

Fighting against a culture is energy sapping. To confront a culture is to invite a system-wide response, often characterised by yielding at first as the energy of the potential threat is absorbed, before the would-be reformer becomes slowly but inexorably entangled in its threads. Like spiders' creations, cultural webs have an enormous capacity to absorb the energy of foreigners or would be reformers. Their resilience comes from a deep-seated ingenuity to regroup in the face of perceived 'threats' or disruptions and from their capacity to restore familiar patterns and pathways.

It is little wonder that despairing leaders, faced with such systemic resilience, end up resorting to draconian solutions typified by the phrase: 'If you can't change the people, change the people.'[2]

These stories point to a paradox for those whose interest lies in the field broadly defined as 'cultural change'. The more we try to 'engineer' a change of culture the more we risk reinforcing its resilience, while the more we look to appreciate and understand cultural forces and patterns the less likely are we to be ensnared by them.

2. Webs Rely on Secure Anchors

The tension of a cobweb, as well as its capacity to absorb energy and flex, calls for secure anchor points. When a spider constructs a web her first efforts are concerned with attaching radial threads to secure anchor points before reinforcing the thread

---

[2]This is a phrase that I have heard attributed to the cultural change effort led by Colin Marshall at British Airways. I am unable to verify this in the form of a sourced reference for this but have heard it used often in conversations between OD practitioners.

to ensure that it has sufficient strength. Once a series of radial threads have been created and similarly anchored, then the spider weaves circular threads from the inside out, ensuring that the gaps between threads are close enough for the spider to cross.

These stories suggest that cultural webs also require secure anchor points. The stories in this work point to at least three forms anchor point: commitment and political support, emotional anchors, and process anchors. We now turn to examine each of these.

Commitment and Political Support as Anchor Point

When organisation leaders speak of cultural change people scrutinise their behaviour to determine the strength of their commitment to change. Close scrutiny is brought to the consistency between their behaviour and their statements. There is much interest in the match between their high-profile, public gestures and the statements made by the low-profile symbols of their everyday actions, their spontaneous, unrehearsed statements and asides. Particular attention is paid to the strength of their resolve and to the robustness of the political cover they provide. Stepping into the unknown, letting go of old pathways calls for courage, emotional resilience and a willingness to take risks. The commitment of leadership to a process of cultural change can be seen as an important anchor.

As the NSN case illustrates, once an intention to cultural change has been declared, an early topic of conversation and careful scrutiny among organisation members is concerned with questions such as:

> Are they serious? Will it last? Is this just a flash in the pan, a passing fad or fashion? How committed are they? How much political 'cover' will they provide to those who experiment? Will they lose their nerve or their interest over time?

We have seen in these and other stories that the commitment of leaders to a change will be tested and efforts made to re-assert familiar, if dysfunctional, patterns by other members of the social ecology that is a culture.

It is clear that people look for signs of commitment in small gestures, in the low-profile actions and 'off the record' statements of leaders. Their unexpected presence at a meeting or venue, the content of small talk during informal moments, who they are seen to listen to and spend time with, who they support publicly. We have seen that almost anything can draw scrutiny and trigger a pulse of conversation rippling through the informal sense making communities of an organisation. What class of seat do executives occupy when travelling; how often does an executive visit an outlying office; where in the order of priorities does 'commitment to our people' feature on a slide?

Particular attention is paid to those brave souls who accept the invitation to experiment and who take the risk of departing from well-trodden cultural pathways.

Are they supported, encouraged and rewarded as was the case with Danny Chesterman's secondment to Marks and Spencer, or do their proposals come under intense interrogation from the most senior executive in the company as we saw with the Marketing Director in Sleepy Hollow? In this case the probing and detailed scrutiny of plans to launch new products from the all-powerful Chairman of the Group was taken as an unequivocal warning not to disturb a long established pattern.

Like budgerigars in a coalmine,[3] the fortunes of these early pioneers and pattern-breakers are carefully, if cautiously, watched. News of their fate spreads in an instant.

Nothing is too trivial to send a message of intent, commitment or seriousness. It is through the scrutiny of such low-profile gestures that the assessment of a leader is made. Ultimately, it is through the interpretation of such low-profiles symbols that cultures are woven.

Political Anchors

Another aspect of anchoring support for major change occurs when leaders ensure that they have the necessary support of others who hold power. Roger Paine's first priority on his appointment was to build a strong relationship with the Councillors, the elected members of Wrekin District Council, whose sustained support for his reforms was essential. Similarly, a feature of Paul Sabin's tenure as chief executive of Kent County Council was the close understanding he developed with the Chairman of the County Council, the political head. Colin Marshall had a cast iron ally in Lord King, the then Chairman of British Airways (Carleton & Lineberry, 2004).

The demonstration of commitment to a new cultural pathway by leaders is clearly one form of anchor that is required for cultural transformation. We would also note that this principle operates in the opposite way. In order to weave a new cultural web or pattern, these stories suggest that, on occasion, before new anchor points can be secured, old attachments may need to be severed. In his autobiography Tony Blair refers to this as: 'Taking away the givens'. He writes:

> 'By this I mean as follows. Usually, you operate in any organization within boundaries of thought and practice. These become 'givens'. So in the NHS it is a given that the surgeon performs operations, and the GP is a general practitioner who doesn't touch the surgeon's knife. The nurse doesn't (or didn't then) hand out complicated prescriptions. The more hospital beds, the better the service. In the private sector you pay; in the public sector you don't.

---

[3]This is a reference to the former practice in coal mining of using a budgerigar to test for toxic gases such as carbon monoxide, methane or carbon dioxide. The presence of such gases would either kill or cause distress to the bird before affecting the miners. Its use was discontinued in British mines in 1987. As such it was a form of early warning system.

Challenging these 'givens' within which the system operates can be hard. They are always there for a reason and, historically at least, often a good reason. Changing them can be even harder. A whole web of custom practice and interest has been created around them; yet for the organization to make progress they must be changed.' (Blair, 2010)

When Roger Paine was first appointed to his post as CEO at the Wrekin District Council:

'... he reported that the fiercest debates were over kettles and privileged car parking spaces for Chief Officers. One of his first acts was to abolish parking privileges for everyone, including himself, with the exception of elected members and the disabled.' (McLean & Marshall, 1989)

We saw this demonstrated in the discussion of the symbolic significance of appointments and departures in a County Council. It was only when a number of chief officers of key departments 'retired' that their staff realised that an era had come to an end. Confronting outmoded beliefs head on serves to sever old attachments and prepares the conditions for the formation of fresh cultural configurations.

Emotional Anchors

Upside Down Glasses

'The American psychologist GM Stratton, invented special eye glasses which used mirror systems and telescopes to alter retinal images. These bizarre eyeglasses restructured the world by inverting it both horizontally and vertically. After continuously wearing these lenses for several days, Stratton was amazed to discover that everything he observed became 'normal'. He could even walk with ease and enjoy seeing the natural world. After living for a while in this altered visual world, Stratton decided to remove the spectacles. At that moment he found that 'the reversal of everything from the order to which I had grown accustomed during the last week, gave the scene a surprising, bewildering air which lasted for several hours.' He then had to relearn how to see what to others was an 'undistorted world', which now appeared to him as 'distorted'. (Gregory, 1971)

'A lens, or frame of reference, determines the pattern we see, whether it is up or down, distorted or not. A change of lens always invokes a period of initial confusion or transition. If an observer can endure the crisis of transition, a new frame will result in an alternative order.' (Keeney, 1983).

A theme of many stories in this work is that cultural change, discontinuous shifts in beliefs and patterns of behaviour, can be disturbing and disorienting for all concerned. Strong emotions are stirred and anxieties triggered as people's sense of certainty and stability is disrupted.

We saw how trenchant criticism was directed at leaders early in the exchanges within the Culture Square during the merger process in NSN. While the discourse gradually became more constructive as the weeks passed, there were numerous occasions when serious consideration was given by senior managers to censoring contributions or to closing down the forum altogether. As it turned out, the Culture Square ultimately become a trusted forum and the ideas and exchanges generated over the course of many months served to ease the tensions and misunderstandings that are an inevitable feature of most mergers. The exchanges in the Culture Square forum also became a source of many constructive proposals for how to operationalise the growing consensus around values and operating principles.

Trusting that these exchanges would ultimately prove to be fruitful, and that managerial interventions would instantly destroy the fragile trust that was forming, took courage and extraordinary restraint on the part of the leadership team. This was helped by the skilful work of Alistair Moffat who as Director responsible for the cultural integration of the merger spent much of his time supporting and reassuring his colleagues. Alistair's efforts helped them to stick to their resolve and to trust that the understandings that eventually emerged would be much more robust for the fact that they had been arrived at through a broad based, self-organising dialogue. Once the safety and reliability of the Square had been established the process of creating new threads began from the inside out.

Roger Paine and his team described the many moments of crisis and uncertainty over the course of cultural transformation at The Wrekin District Council. The management team that Roger had assembled developed a strong understanding and commitment to the new approach, providing support and encouragement to each other. Roger also felt that his long-term membership of an Action Learning group,[4] comprised of CEOs from a wide range of businesses and organisations, had been invaluable in helping him maintain a perspective on things. Members of Roger's group offered both challenge and robust support to him in a way that was completely independent of the local politics within the Wrekin. The group helped him to find and sustain his own clarity in the midst of uncertainty and the many pressing operational matters that can crowd in on all leaders. They helped him to reaffirm his resolve and to persevere with his intent. The members of this group served as an important emotional and practical anchor for Roger throughout his seven years as CEO at the Wrekin.

---

[4]Action learning is a group-based method for supporting individual learning in the context of their professional lives. Group members encourage reflection on actions taken in order to elicit insights and to encourage experimentation as part of a continuous learning cycle (Revans, 1982; see also Pedler, 1996).

Structured Processes as Anchor Points

We have discussed how the use of structured processes can serve as a form of loom, or frame that enables what we have described as a 'Meta Conversation'. The cases in this work point to the value of workshops, inquiry processes, and facilitated events, conferences and so on, as providing forums that both legitimate, contain and support different kinds of conversation. Just as a loom holds the warp threads in tension while the weft threads are interwoven, so these events and processes provide sufficient structure to enable a different kind of conversation. They allow time and legitimate space in which to inquire, question, discover, experiment, reflect and formulate new understandings as well as new ways of working.

When well facilitated such processes can provide enormously helpful ways of enabling groups to move beyond previously established patterns and to recognise how they unnecessarily constrain themselves through historically transmitted patterns. The use of such structured approaches and interventions is not without risk however. At their best, such forums and process maps can reduce or contain the daunting uncertainty of unpredictable processes and contain the anxieties generated by charting unknown territory with the comfort of a handrail[5] or rudimentary map. At their worst, these methods can easily become a form of petty tyranny and over-engineered process steps that drive out the spontaneity and the uncertainty of true discovery and joint meaning making. A warning made to a group of facilitators sums up my concern here. It was a spontaneous remark by my friend Frank Barrett who observed:

'All great ideas begin as metaphors and end up as geometry.'

In his insightful reflections on the conventions among jazz musicians (Barrett, 2012) Frank notes that one of the conditions that fosters great jazz improvisation is the use of minimum structures that allow for maximum improvisation. Typically the elements of minimum structure for jazz musicians include agreement over the key, the time signature and the melody. These minimal understandings are sufficient to allow for extraordinary improvisation to unfold as the ensemble explores multiple ways of expressing and configuring the simplest of melodies.

The process looms or frameworks described in the cases here point to the importance of light touch, enabling structures and ground rules that anchor the processes of discovery and exploration in a way that offers a generative balance between safety and uncertainty, between disturbance and comfort and which, like an improvising jazz ensemble, creates an environment in which new patterns can form.

---

[5]My colleague, Alistair Moffat, has used the phrase 'handrail' to describe this phenomenon. It speaks to the need for a sense of reassurance and direction through, what is for many, uncharted territory.

These processes call for a commitment to inquiry from leaders, a willingness to 'lead and let go'; a preparedness to participate without controlling and a readiness to name and endorse emerging clarity. Legitimating these kinds of dialogical spaces provides an important form of process anchor and represents an important role that leaders can play in creating the conditions in which transformative changes can occur.

3. The Construction of a Web Commences with the Weaving of Radial Threads

Once anchored, spiders weave and then reinforce the strength of radial threads. These crucial, structural threads provide the rudimentary, formative elements of the webs' design and their relationship to each other sets the parameters within which the final pattern of threads will form.

In this section we consider the ability of leaders to influence the formation of a cultural web through the advocacy of high-level cultural principles, values or 'beacons'.[6] We liken these high-level expressions of intent and ambition on the part of leaders to the radial threads woven by spiders early in the process of web construction: they describe the definitive elements of the cultural web and set the parameters within which its detail unfolds. We also suggest that the process of strengthening these key, structural, threads is a key aspect of weaving.

The expression of a leader's ambition, their vision or mission to shape or reshape a culture is a common feature of their agenda, especially when newly appointed. This is a legitimate and expected aspect of their role. Leaders are able to capitalise on their role as powerful participants in a culture through the use of advocacy and with the considerable benefits of corporate media support.

In our work with Kent County Council we heard the new chief executive, Paul Sabin, articulate what he termed his three 'cultural tenets'. They were:

> Management, not administration
>
> Close to the customer
>
> Devolution, not delegation
>
> He described these as his 'tenets' and repeatedly spoke to them in the presence of many audiences both inside and outside the authority. They became his leadership mantra. He drew on his extensive experience of local government both as a senior officer and as a consumer

---

[6]We chose the term beacon early in our work supporting the cultural change process in a large UK County Council. Beacons provide guidance and reference points that can be used to chart a course and to navigate, enabling travellers to explore a bounded territory in relation to fixed reference points.

of local authority services to illustrate and enrich his expositions. At first he delivered these tenets in the form of public speeches in which he included vivid examples and, at times, scathing criticism of current practices in the authority. These homilies had little visible impact other than to stiffen resistance and resentment among long serving officers. Inadvertently, the new CEO was building a wall of resistance to his thinking.

Overtime Paul adopted a different approach to how he delivered his message. He began to use much more discursive methods and forums that engaged local authority staff at all levels in small group discussions. During these he explained the background to his choice of tenets and discussed their relevance to the activities of each department. He welcomed peoples' questions and their challenges and grew to thrive on these lively exchanges. His passion came across and formerly hostile groups came to appreciate his willingness to listen to them. The turn around in attitudes toward the tenets was greatly boosted when Paul began to acknowledge the proud legacy of the County Council and to name aspects of the existing culture that he most admired and wanted to safeguard.

The moment when Paul made the shift from presentational advocacy to engaging in local dialogues was the moment when his efforts to influence the culture gained momentum.

While the core content of his advocacy remained constant, he increasingly welcomed and participated in discussions about what they might mean in local settings. What for instance did devolution mean for the management of the accounting function within the authority? How were the roles of School Inspectors affected by his call for a more customer-centred culture? What did it mean for the Highways Department to adopt a more managerial attitude to their responsibilities?

In the first years of his tenure he spent countless hours discussing these questions with Chief Officers and their teams across the authority. In doing this he was weaving; actively, patiently participating in the formation of shared meaning with staff in the local contexts where they would come to life. And this was a reciprocal process of debating, informing and being informed, challenging and being challenged in return. Over the course of these countless conversations and debates, Paul's own understanding of the tenets was both deepened and enriched.

It was through these conversations with local officers, supporting the formation of meaning in local contexts, that Paul Sabin was being a weaver among weavers. All parties were involved in the process of figuring out the meaning of these tenets, these key, radial threads of the KCC cultural web. They were making new meaning together.

In addition to his advocacy through dialogue, Paul reinforced his commitment to the tenets through his actions; through those he appointed and promoted; through the projects that received funding, and those that lost their budgets; through the stories that were featured by the Public Relations Department and by revising the County Council's procedures and accounting methods to more closely align with them. He drastically reduced the head count in the Council Headquarters, devolving staff and budgeting responsibility to senior officers and their staff in local offices while simultaneously requiring them to formulate 12 month Business Plans for their departments.

The intensity of the conversations in which he advocated the tenets and worked with managers to interpret their local meaning was also reinforced by the highly visible strategic initiatives and choices that were made in the County Council chamber. By complementing each other the High and Low Profile gestures strengthened and reinforced the radial threads of the cultural web.

Over time Paul stepped back and encouraged each department to find their own ways of interpreting and observing the spirit of these tenets. This was the moment when the radial threads had acquired sufficient strength to allow for the weaving of circular threads to begin, for the forming of local meaning and action. The Supplies Department for example launched a major initiative aimed at enhancing their responsiveness to customers.

These 'radial threads', are high-level expressions of cultural intent. The reinforcement and strengthening of these threads through strategic decisions and actions is a vital aspect of weaving. If high-profile statements of cultural intent represent key structural threads in the process of cultural formation, then the sustained participation by leaders through dialogue, debate and engaged discussion of them is essential to strengthening the threads and supporting their interpretation in local settings.

The example of Paul Sabin and his leadership in Kent County Council illustrates the key difference between the promulgation of cultural slogans and the development of truly shared meaning in a complex organisation.

Radial threads are developed using a variety of methods. The Kent County Council example is not unusual. The newly appointed chief executive formulated these elemental principles and values based on views he expressed during the selection process. His brief on appointment was to 'change the culture' of what was a flagship authority in the United Kingdom. His three tenets expressed his high-level ambitions for its future priorities and culture.

Many new CEOs formulate similar, high level statements, often unpacking them into detailed statements of strategic priorities and intent. It is common for these to feature prominently during conference calls, global broadcasts, CEO updates and the many other creative forums used by corporate communications to 'broadcast the message'. These are the high-profile symbols of a culture. They express intent, espouse ideals and sometimes prescribe required behaviours. They risk equating the shaping of a culture with the launching of a product and casting employees as passive consumers of others' thinking. The examples in this work indicate that the espousal and communication of these high-profile symbols is not sufficient for them to serve as radial threads. They suggest instead that what counts is the sustained dialogue, debate and engaged discussion that is essential to the formation of new, *shared meaning* throughout a community. This is to see cultural formation as a process, not the delivery of a product.

It also has to do with the extent to which these high-profile espousals are reinforced by the low-profile symbols of organisational life. This calls for careful attention to the story told by the unrehearsed, unheralded, everyday actions and gestures that comprise the mundane routine of a leader's day.

In the informal meaning making forums of all organisations, it is the low-profile symbols and gestures that draw comment, confer credibility and provide an all-important context to the high-profile espousals of leaders.

> We have described earlier how Roger Paine and his team at the Wrekin adopted a different approach to the formation of their radial threads.
>
> 'Being an interventionist authority' was a phrase that Roger coined early in his leadership. It served as one of the first radial threads of what was to become an exceptionally innovative cultural web.
>
> Later radial threads were woven by a cross-section of staff following a process of consultation and debate. They suggested that the principles of Quality, Caring and Fairness were an encapsulation of values that were widely shared among Wrekin employees. These values were endorsed by the elected members (local politicians), and by the management team including the CEO.
>
> The decision by the management team, acting on the advice of their staff, to refrain from a high profile communications exercise to promote these values drew our attention to an apparent paradox. We discovered that relatively few staff were aware of the slogan, 'QUALITY, CARING AND FAIRNESS' that was prominently displayed in the training centre. Our research revealed that the choices they made and the priorities that were evident in their everyday actions were entirely consistent with these values however. They lived them in a matter of fact, self-evident way summed up by the phrase: 'This Is the Wrekin way'. The values undoubtedly pervaded the Wrekin culture but ironically, few people could readily name them. This is evidence to support Clifford Geertz's observation that 'Acts are the said of social discourse' (Geertz, 1973). It also reinforces our view that it is through the low profile symbols, through the

unheralded everyday acts and actions that such radial threads acquire credibility and infiltrate awareness.

Quality Caring and Fairness became enduring, radial threads at the heart of the Wrekin Cultural web. They acquired their strength initially as a consequence of their resonance with the views and values of Wrekin staff and were reinforced as members of the Management team repeatedly demonstrated commitment to them.

In the NSN case (Chapter 6) we saw how Simon Beresford Wylie began with very few guiding principles and aspirations. He wanted to encourage a culture of inclusion and involvement, a pride in and commitment to a shared identity, a community of responsible, grown-up professionals that were highly responsive to customers' needs. By signing up to the extended conversation that occurred through the Culture Square, Simon and his team lived up to these principles and ultimately saw them enjoy exceptional support throughout the globally dispersed business.

The weaving of these radial threads, together with visible, congruent and persevering dedication to them over time is a legitimate role for leaders in shaping cultural change. A key feature of these radial threads is that they allow space for improvisation and encourage local interpretation.

These and other stories in this work suggest that shared meaning only becomes clear and settled over time and as a consequence of debate, questioning, careful listening and reflection. For a leader to play a role in shaping a culture is to commit to intense participation, to sustained engagement in multiple forums over a sustained period of time. It is also to be prepared to embody her advocacy in multiple settings, repeatedly and through the infinite forms that low-profile symbols can take.

The view of organisation cultures explored in this work cautions that however powerful and compelling a leaders' advocacy, there are other factors that limit and constrain their ability to directly 'manage' or 'engineer' a desired culture in accordance with some form of blue-print, mandate or Master Plan.

The formally expressed views and opinions of leaders undoubtedly have a very significant impact on what people take as priorities. Perceptions of a leader's intentions become qualified over time, however, as the content of their advocacy is set in the broader context of their everyday gestures. Radial cultural threads derive their potency from the clarity of their message, by the congruence between high and low-profile symbols, and through the sheer perseverance and engaged dedication of leaders.

It is in the interplay between a leader's high and low-profile gestures that interpretations are made and understandings gradually form. Leaders cannot directly control the interpretations of their followers, or the much more elusive interpretive frames that they invoke in the course of making such interpretations. We have earlier described this process of local meaning making as informal, networked and amounting to what has been described as a shadow conversation. If we add to this the fact that a new leader inherits a pre-existing cultural web with its own characteristic resilience, then we can see that the likely impact of high-profile expressions of intent, and the advocacy of desired cultural changes, are likely to be limited in their impact.

4. Spiders Use Temporary Threads in the Process of Constructing a Web.
Once the web is complete they re-ingest these temporary pathways

The NSN case study described in Chapter 6 is a classic example of using temporary threads in the construction of a web. The values and cultural principles that were arrived at following the JAM[7] were very different from those that were used to frame the Culture Square conversation. The early 'embryonic' expressions of cultural intent (the *five* statements)[8] that emerged from the gathering of the first 300 appointees to the newly merged company were 'good enough', temporary statements that gave focus to the Culture Square conversation, sufficient for it to later become self-organising and emergent. Through the medium of the Culture Square everyone throughout the new business was invited to add thoughts and comments, to join the conversation about a desired culture of the new business. Like the temporary threads used in the early construction of a spider's web, the provisional cultural principles provided temporary pathways that eventually allowed the construction of something more lasting and robust.

Contributors to the Culture Square conversation responded to the five cultural themes endorsing them, questioning them, using them to challenge what they saw as practices that were inconsistent with the spirit of the statements and ultimately holding themselves to account against them. New themes emerged through these conversations and formed the basis for the *four* topic areas that gave focus to the 72-hour virtual conference, the JAM.[9] One of the major outputs from the JAM was a draft of core cultural values and principles. After some editing and review these values were endorsed by the Board and provided the founding principles that informed the design of many formal processes and procedures. The temporary threads had served their purpose and were, effectively, dissolved.

This case suggests that we need to view the formation of cultural threads as a process that unfolds over time and that the ideas and concepts that configure the conversation can iterate and unfold several times before a settled sense of shared understanding and agreement emerges. This reinforces the view of organisations as ongoing conversations that self-pattern over time and reminds us that temporary

---

[7]The Jam was an IBM platform for hosting a three-day, company-wide, virtual conference. See Chapter 6 for details.
[8]Customer focus, open communication, achieving together, being valued, innovation leadership.
[9]Getting close to Our Customers, Enabling our People to flourish, Making NSN different, Becoming ONE great company.

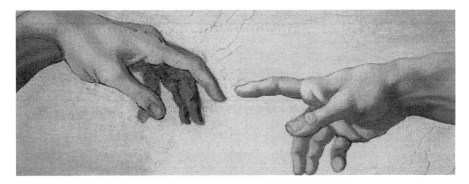

Figure 1:   Detail from Michelangelo's Creation of Adam. C.1511 (in public domain).

threads help to hold open the conversational space long enough for shared understandings to form (Figure 1).

5. Webs are Comprised of Many Interwoven Threads

It is the interconnectivity of threads, where radial and circular threads interlink that provides robustness and distributed strength to a web

'Where the action is' – *Bateson's overlapping ecologies*

'All "Field Naturalists" would know that the largest number of species can be found at the natural boundaries of, for example, say woodlands and grass pastures, swamps and dry land ... that is where the action is.' (Bateson, 1979)

As young boys Gregory Bateson and his brothers shared an avid interest in wild life and especially insects. They combed the Cambridge countryside in search of specimens and acquired an impressive private collection of different species. Reflecting on this later in his career he observed that the diversity of species was greatest at the boundaries between ecologies. It was in the hedgerows between fields, in the borders where scrub adjoined cultivated land and where marshland transitioned to adjacent woodland that the densest and most varied flora and fauna were to be found.

Bateson's observation also informs our understanding of organisation cultures and particularly processes of cultural change. Cultural sensitivities are heightened when members of different cultures come into contact with each other. Opportunities for cultures to change are heightened when they come into contact with other cultures.

The juxtaposition of different worldviews, different assumptive frameworks, different practices and different habits of perception, can provide the spark for generative, insightful reflection and frame-shifting patterns. We have written earlier about the transformative potential when people step outside the boundaries of their thinking, both in the literal sense of being a stranger in a 'foreign' culture but also figuratively, by adopting a different worldview.[10] We have seen many examples of how exposure to the different assumptions and cultural patterns of 'foreign' organisations can provoke imaginations, expose assumptive frameworks, expand the thinking of those who visit them and trigger a reconfiguration of cultural patterns.

Bringing together groups or communities that normally do not interact can be an extraordinarily generative and enlightening experience for both groups. It can also have the opposite effect where both parties reject, judge and distance themselves from the other as mistrust and hostility escalates. For such encounters to be generative the challenge lies in doing this well. It calls for the creation of conditions in which power differences and levels of anxiety on both sides are sufficiently contained such that inquiry and fruitful dialogue can occur. Inter-weaving different cultural traditions and social ecologies can be transformative.

The cases we have described in this work suggest that such cultural interweaving can be understood from three different perspectives:

i.   *Juxtaposing Cultures* — Cultural Safaris
ii. *Working the Weaving*—attending to the practicalities of processing news of difference so as to create the conditions in which it is generative, leads to new understandings and the revision or transformation of an assumptive framework
iii. *Weaving the Social Ecology*—folding in the patchwork of different communities, the different professional and social ecologies that comprise an organisation, into the process of finding new understanding.

i. Juxtaposing Cultures — *Cultural Safaris*

The act of convening groups of people whose organisational worlds do not normally intersect can be an 'eye-opening' experience. The Medic Inn case (see Chapter 5) perhaps is the most extreme and dramatic example of this kind of cultural immersion and its transformative effects. The case offers a powerful illustration of cultural transformation that occurred through juxtaposing two different communities, two different cultural ecologies, and working at finding new understandings, new ways to make sense of their world. The staff of the Medic Inn drew on their inquiries into another hotel with a very different culture in order to fundamentally reconceive their business and its operation. They fashioned a new cultural fabric by interweaving new ways of thinking about the hospitality industry with the new practices they discovered in the course of their visit.

This called for a serious commitment to a process of inquiry, as well as a readiness to question, revisit and revise long-held attitudes and beliefs. It called on those involved to work hard at discovering new meanings and, in the process, to create

---

[10]This is variously described as thinking outside of the box, thinking the unthinkable or 'distorting reality'; see Walter Isaacson's biography of Steve Jobs (Isaacson, 2011).

new frameworks of understanding. The startling transformative effects of this cultural safari owe much to the skilful support of knowledgeable consultants.

We have seen that the value of such excursions is not limited to visits to other organisations. The Magistrate's Courts case (Chapter 5) showed how new thinking and practices were also triggered by inter-court visits, and how this was a source of surprise to staff within the Service. Similarly, when members of the magistrate's Management Team inquired into instances of successfully managed change with each other's staff it was an interweaving of worldviews that proved to be revelatory and transformative. The leaders of the Service saw things through the eyes of their staff and made startling discoveries about parts of the Service than they thought they knew. This 'out of pattern' acting as inquirers not experts, was already disturbing a long established pattern of relations. It signalled their openness to *new ways* of working. The medium expressed the message.

In the same case we described the initial sense of shock and anger felt by mid-level managers following their lunchtime conversations with representatives of the management team. This intervention brought together two co-existing but largely independent communities within the Service. It contrived an overlap in cultural ecologies that normally operated at some remove from each other, two communities that were almost literally worlds apart, and describes the assumptive jolt that this represented. As a result of this encounter long-held assumptions and perceptions were revised in a way that was initially disturbing and unwelcome. The session ultimately proved to be galvanising and key to the participants' decision to be party to formulating new work patterns and practices in the Service.[11] It was the moment when old cultural threads began to unravel and the process of weaving new ones began.

Juxtaposing Cultures – *Café Society as Forum*. One of the catalysing moments during the Kent County Council process of cultural change occurred when middle and senior ranking officers sat down with the counties' politicians, the elected members, in an informal setting designed to resemble a French Café. Over coffee and wine they exchanged ideas about the current and desired cultures of the authority. These were encounters that did not normally occur and certainly the focus of the conversation was unprecedented. While some of the parties to this encounter participated in the formal meetings of the County Council, they had never met and connected in this way before. It was an overlapping of normally separate worlds, or worlds that

---

[11]It was important that this disturbance was contained and 'processed'. This is the *alchemical* principle of containing the energy when different elements are combined and emotional heat is generated. Ultimately the result was a step shift. Similarly in the NSN case, the Culture Square simultaneously permitted and contained the expression of strong feelings; upset, anger, insecurity and confusion as well as excitement. Ultimately this led to a constructive and generative conversation and gave positive impetus to the process.

The secure anchor points (trust in the sovereignty of the forum, the presence of secure political support and commitment, resolute leaders who would not be perturbed by the temporary upset) were crucial in creating a holding container in which the energy generated could be processed and new understandings form.

only ever connected in highly formal contexts and under circumstances constrained by specific agendas and protocols.

We have seen how Danny Chesterman's six-week immersion in the culture of Marks and Spencer turned out to be a watershed moment in the history of The Wrekin District Council. Danny was acting as a modern anthropologist looking to understand how the M&S culture contributed to the consistently high quality standards of their products and services. His reflections sparked a lively conversation among the management team and were key to the reconfiguration of what became a highly innovative culture.

A particular form of cultural interweaving is illustrated by the NSN case (see Chapter 6). In this case, the interweaving occurred between the informal or shadow conversation that gained momentum in the Culture Square, and the officially sponsored discussions that occurred in the 72 hours, pan-global conference known as the JAM. The topics that framed the JAM were based on themes that had formed in the course of conversations occurring in the informal conversations of the Culture Square. One of the outcomes of the JAM was a draft version of cultural principles and values for the newly forming company. At the request of leading participants in the Culture Square this draft was posted into the Culture Square for final comments before receiving the official endorsement of the Board. It was this interweaving, between the official and unofficial discourses that, in my view, contributed to such widespread support for the company values.

Juxtaposing Cultures – *Going off Piste*. The Cultural Inquiry process in the Social Services Department of Omnishire also highlights how exposure to different cultural 'territory' can disturb a settled worldview and provoke a reconfiguration of assumptions.

A collaborative inquiry (Marshall & McLean, 1988) into the department's culture culminated in an event to share the discoveries made by a cross section of department members who had participated in the three-month process. They had concluded that a key feature of the department's culture was that it was highly diversified and more accurately resembled a loose coalition of disparate sub-cultures. Instead of making a lengthy and complex presentation of their findings, the inquiry team invited their senior managers to tour a patchwork representation of the cultural 'clusters' that characterised the department and to engage in discussions with representatives of these sub-cultures around the themes represented in their displays.

The intention was to provide a visual representation of the geographical spread and cultural diversity of this large department. The idea was that visiting senior managers would learn about the discoveries by wandering through this setting and engaging with the displays and their representatives that caught their interest. In this way it was hoped that senior managers would experience the many different cultural ecologies that co-existed under the banner of the Social Services Department.

The format was for three 'rounds' of visits. Managers would go to presentations of their choice. Conversations during the first two rounds were lively and thoughtful. At the last minute it was suggested that, during the third round, each manager might visit a part of the service with which they were least familiar. The idea was for them to go 'off-piste'.

The debriefing of the management team afterwards was dominated by their experiences during the third round. They described themselves as being disturbed by what they had discovered and saw the experience as 'eye opening'. The senior managers had explored what for them was unfamiliar territory and it brought surprising and unsettling news of difference. The experience was later credited with prompting a complete re-evaluation of their service and providing new foundations for its development policy.

All of these cases illustrate Bateson's point. When different cultural ecologies come into contact there is the possibility that something novel will emerge, that taken for granted assumptions will be revised, and that the seeds of a different way of understanding may be sown.

Such encounters can also be counter-productive as people with different ways of understanding their worlds bring different perspectives to bear on a situation, and start from different assumptions and values. When this occurs the risk of misunderstanding, defensiveness, critical judgments and even conflict are heightened.

Clients often describe their organisation as having a 'silo mentality' whereby the orientation of departments is primarily inward and their capacity for cooperation and exchange with other departments is both limited and often compromised.

Cultures that are isolated, 'closed cultures' that do not foster strong connections with other cultures and assumptive worlds, find it hard to change, to regenerate, to adapt to environmental shifts. In a recent consulting assignment I experienced the growing despair and helplessness of senior managers in the fast-moving and fashion-driven world of telecommunications at their inability to persuade the engineers and designers of their products to take seriously the feedback of their, once loyal, customers. Products were developed to meet what the product managers and design engineers perceived to be innovative and leading edge thinking. The audience for their creativity had become other engineers. They were trying to impress each other and not the customer. Senior leaders felt impotent in their efforts to break the conviction of the engineers that the market would follow what they considered to be the last word in 'cool'. The company is currently losing market share at an alarming rate, seeing its share price tumble, shedding staff and beginning to report worrying losses.

In the terms of Bateson's observation, the conceptual ecology of these product managers and engineers, their mind set, was insulated from the adjacent ecologies of their customers and their competitors. As a consequence of this insularity the diversity of their thinking became increasingly impoverished (Table 1).

Bringing together groups or communities that normally do not interact can be an extraordinarily generative and enlightening experience for both groups. It can also result in responses that are defensive, self-justificatory and critical of the 'other'. A recent report on incidents of 'blue on blue' casualties in Afghanistan indicated that much of the hostility between United States and Afghan forces that were officially on the same side, was rooted in harsh judgments about hygiene and personal cleanliness. The judgments led to a breakdown in everyday communications between the troops and an increasing alienation that periodically erupts in acts of extreme violence and death.

Table 1: Introducing a 'tree hugger'.

Andy was a senior HR professional who worked for an energy company. He had just finished his masters degree. To his surprise he had been particularly inspired by one of the modules that entailed a visit to a small college that specialised in environmental studies. There he met an expert on global warming and ecological thinking who introduced him to the science and who led a series of activities, nature walks, meditations and other exercises, that brought Andy into direct contact with some of the phenomena under discussion. Reflecting on his experiences Andy realised that his company had no policy with regard to the environmental impact of its activities. He decided to invite the expert to an upcoming conference for the commercial department of his company. The commercial managers were the dealmakers who oversaw the acquisition of rights to exploitation of energy resources. These were large deals across the globe. Their conferences were highly technical affairs comprising a series of slide presentations and mostly formal sessions. The managers were a mixture of engineers, lawyers and commercial experts.

At first Andy's colleagues welcomed his suggestion to invite the expert to the Commercial Manager's conference. His presence would be unusual and would bring a very different perspective to their somewhat technical world. Before long Andy began to receive expressions of concern from his colleagues. By the conservative standards of the commercial managers the expert was somewhat eccentric. His corduroy trousers, tie-less shirt and hand knitted pullover would immediately set him apart from the smartly suited managers with their crisp shirts and sober ties. Were they setting themselves up for an awkward and embarrassing session with a 'tree hugger'? How would this reflect on the HR department? Andy found himself growing increasingly anxious and feeling that he had gone out on a limb in making the invitation. He spent the bulk of his time responding to his colleague's queries and concerns about the unusual guest, reassuring them and calming their fears.

In the event the experience was a surprising success. The expert was respectfully and thoughtfully received, and he managed to get the managers to participate in some of the exercises and activities that had inspired Andy. What secured his status with the group was his command of the science of global warming.

As a consequence of the experience the board began to consider their environmental impact as a business and began the process of formulating policies to mitigate this.

Reflecting on the experience a much-relieved Andy observed that the hardest part had been managing the anxieties of his colleagues. Containing the emotional disturbance provoked by difference is a key condition that is necessary for it to be accepted rather than rejected. In this instance it was an example of a difference that made a difference.

ii. Interconnecting Threads: Working the Weaving

We have seen that revisions, disruptions and interruptions to assumptive frameworks disturb and unsettle people. The actions of the glass furnace workers in decoupling the monitoring instruments of the new technical director of Dartington Glass (see Chapter 7) is an apt symbol of the rejection of a paradigm, a knee jerk response to something alien and unfamiliar.

This raises important practical questions of interest to those of us concerned with understanding how cultural change occurs. Under what circumstances is contact between cultures likely to be generative as opposed to rejecting and dismissive? As an Organisation Development practitioner I bring a professional interest to this. I am interested in those conditions and processes that support generative, intercultural weaving.

The cases described in this work offer a number of pointers:

Inter-cultural connections are generative:

When there is a serious commitment to inquiry on the part of leaders. When leaders participate in the inquiry process whether as ethnographers, information gatherers, sense makers, or all of these. When leaders are able to bring genuine curiosity and humility and relinquish any attachment to having the answer.

When we embrace 'the gift of difference'. When there is openness to difference, when it is valued as a source of generative provocation, for example: listening to newcomers, actively encouraging those regarded as 'new blood' appointments. Attending to the 'mavericks' and the unheard voices, the unusual suspects. When ongoing support is given to those who experiment.

An example of this occurred during the Culture Square dialogue (Chapter 6). The topic of conversation was attitudes towards competitors:

> 'Respecting our competition is a step towards understanding them, therefore giving us the ability to compete against them. Having worked with or for many of NSN's competitors over the years, I don't believe in simplistic statements of superiority.'

> 'I agree with your idea of valuing or respecting the competition. The Nokia Siemens Merger shows how quickly you can find yourself in the same boat with former competitors. I suspect that as we meet and begin to work with one another, *many of us are starting to throw old pre-conceived notions about the former competition overboard.*'[12]

---

[12]Italics have been used to highlight the discarding of 'inherited conceptions' in favour of a different and respectful view of customers. Here is a specific example of weaving new ways of seeing, new understandings.

'Respecting the competition means acknowledging that our competitors also have great people creating great products and we need to compete and fight hard to take business away from them.'

When the conditions for dialogue and for conversation are encouraged, given expert support and are endorsed by leaders. This includes making opportunities to connect and converse in low threat, informal settings. Good facilitation can be an enormous help with this.

When people are able to tolerate the uncertainty and confusion that accompanies 'not knowing' and the questioning of familiar certainties. When people are able to trust that the emergence of new understandings takes time and cannot be engineered.

When attention and support is given to people's emotional needs during periods of vulnerability and uncertainty. This applies as much for leaders as for anyone else. We have discovered that leaders and senior managers often find such activities unfamiliar and risky. There is a clear role for skilful facilitation here. In so far as it is possible, we have found it helpful to prepare leaders to anticipate feelings of disorientation and to provide them with real time, ongoing support in the face of the unfamiliar and the unexpected. Coaching is another means of doing this.

When emerging clarity is named and endorsed and when new ideas and new practices are legitimated.

When people feel OK about themselves, when they are curious but not defensive.

When there is a genuine desire to learn from other cultures, not copy them.

When there is a willingness to reflect on taken for granted assumptions and framings. When people are willing to reflect on the assumptive sea in which they swim. When people take a step back and gain perspective on their cultural web.

I see these as the conditions in which new connections are woven, new insights surface, existing assumptions are questioned and new practices are adopted. In effect, when new cultural patterns are woven.

These cases remind us that contact between cultures is not by itself sufficient to contribute to a shift of cultural pattern. In each case time and care was taken to dwell in the news of difference that such contact heralded. In each of these cases significant time and resource was committed to processing news of difference, to making new sense of things in light of the information and the assumptive jolts that occurred following excursions into other cultural ecologies.

These examples demonstrate how members of different organisations embraced news of difference in a positive, constructive spirit, setting it alongside the dominant assumptions and interpretations of their existing culture. They show how, through reflection, debate and dialogue, they gradually refashioned that worldview, drawing on new threads of understanding to fashion a new cultural fabric.

In these examples we see senior managers and leaders signalling their support for this as a worthwhile endeavour as well as enduring the discomfort of uncertainty. They saw the value in committing the time and space in which to make new sense in this way. In so doing, they held open a moment of opportunity, a conceptual space, long enough for something new, something novel and unexpected, to take form.

Another term for this, of course, is learning. Gregory Bateson (Bateson, 1972) inspired by Whitehead and Russell's work (1910, 1912, 1913), called it 'second-order' learning. This is learning at the level of the conceptual frames and assumptions that we use to configure our everyday understanding. The revision of these conceptual frames and assumptions is another way of describing cultural change.

iii. Interconnecting Threads: Weaving the Social Ecology

The third sense in which the generative possibilities that arise when cultures interconnect has to do with the interweaving of different professional and occupational groups, people who hold different levels of power, different perspectives, and different preoccupations. All organisations are differentiated into many communities, into groups with varying affinities and loyalties and this differentiation can be defined as much by level and location as occupation. While some organisations are considered to have so called 'strong cultures' other might more readily be seen as a loose coalition or cluster of sub-cultures.

When considerations of cultural change arise, this differentiation, together with the inevitable and necessary interdependence of these different social and occupational clusters, means that there are many and varied attachments to different outcomes and just as many perspectives that are brought to the conversation.

These cases show that efforts to revise long-held assumptions, conventions, and patterns of relating, highlight the importance of using methods that recognise and include the varied perspectives and attachments of these multiple, interconnecting groups and communities. They point to the value of systematically weaving connections across the spectrum of diverse perspectives in a way that reviews, debates and naturally incorporates difference into the everyday fabric of organisational life.

Large group facilitators speak of the importance of getting the 'whole system in the room'. Setting aside the philosophical debate that questions the positivist assumptions of this phrase,[13] the thinking behind this ambition is informed by a systemic view of organisations. This view that holds that changes in any 'part' of a system will impact all parts of the system and that, in the face of disturbance, 'the

---

[13]Many argue that the notion of a 'whole system' is reification. It treats a system as something that exists in the same way as an object separate from the observer and with a more or less identifiable boundary. The social constructionist view is that all perception is an act of punctuation, an act of unconscious demarcation on the part of the describer. So, from a constructionist perspective a 'system' is not and cannot be regarded as an entity or thing having an existence independent of the viewer, but instead is a rhetorical device, an artifact, a way of seeing and making sense of complex phenomena that are in constant state of flux.

Table 2: Membership of the Wrekin District Council Cooperative Inquiry
Group — the 'Culture Club'.

The Wrekin District Council Culture Club members
Joy Bailey — Play Leader
Terry Brookes — Principal Engineer
Danny Chesterman — Personnel Officer
Pam Edwards — Welfare Officer
Anne Hewitt — Employment Development Assistant
Annette Lewis — Print Room Supervisor
Gordon Little — Street Lighting Technician
Mick Paish — Bricklayer
Brian Piper — Senior Estimator/Surveyor
Derek Shaw — Housing Centre Manager
Tony Smith — Area Foreman
Brian Wright — Janitor

whole' system will look to maintain its integrity and ongoing form. Such a view advocates that any approach to change needs to include the views and thinking of as many parties as possible. It looks to enlist the involvement of all (or a representation of) the voices that will be affected by a change and who collectively constitute the broad ecology configured by a particular question, issue or cause. Table 2 (on page 256) describes the departments and hierarchical levels included in the six-month Cooperative Inquiry into the culture of the Wrekin District Council.

This is what I mean by 'weaving social interconnectivity'.

It is not just about getting people into the room for a one-off meeting, but naturally and continuously taking opportunities to fold people into the process of sense making together while exploring the implications for action that arise from new understandings.

We described how The New Ways Programme at the Inner London Magistrate's Courts (see Chapter 5) gradually gained momentum and drew interest. People began to notice the energising effect of the Appreciative Inquiry process. More and more people accepted invitations to attend the events where discoveries from inquiry visits were presented and discussed. Gradually the most senior members of the Service began to show up to these sessions and joined the discussion of implications and possibilities that were stimulated by the visits.

Over time some of the magistrates themselves began to appear and join the discussions. Participants arranged lunchtime briefings for their colleagues in order to share what they had discovered but also to invite their thinking. The informal format of the open sessions was designed to foster small group conversations that considered the findings of different inquiry groups. Specific ideas for new ways of working that had arisen in the course of the inquiry and sense-making process began to show up in routine meetings. Gradually, as momentum and interest was building, more and more people from all parts of the Service joined in this rolling, unfolding conversation. At every opportunity invitations were made for people to join in. There was an organic, emergent quality to this process that interwove an increasingly diverse collection of voices and perspectives. Over the course of eigh teen months and five iterations of the inquiry process, the fabric of a new culture began to take form.

More and more facilitation methods have been developed that look to interweave multiple perspectives in the service of progressing an agenda that touches them all directly or indirectly. Among the more popular are large group methodologies such as Future Search, Appreciative Inquiry Summits, World Café and Open space. These are typically two or three day facilitated gatherings that are designed to progress a chosen topic. They bring together people with diverse perspectives and interest in the topic both across the spectrum of an organisation but also increasingly from the communities in which an organisation or association is located, and can include those with external connections to the company, association or organisation. They combine a mixture of directed facilitation and self-organisation. Much has been achieved through such set piece events although they can be expensive and complex to organise and can inadvertently heighten expectations of a 'result'. Others, such as Bill Critchley and Patricia Shaw (Critchley & Shaw, 1994) for example, advocate approaches that encourage connection and exchange in the more naturalistic context of the everyday activities of organisational life.

The opportunities afforded by the advent of the Internet have opened up new and hitherto unimaginable possibilities for interweaving. The example of the Culture Square conversation and the 72-hour virtual conference in the course of the NSN merger process (JAM) shows how new meanings and understandings can emerge through these virtual conversations.

What these processes have in common is that they are designed to foster connections, to create the conditions in which shared understanding and commitment arises. They interweave the multiple perspectives, orientations and aspirations of large groups and communities, in a way that transcends formal power relations.

The view of organisations as verbs not nouns, as 'organisings' not organisations, suggests that shared meaning emerges over time. It cannot be forced, engineered or controlled. One of the lessons from these cases is that progress is accelerated when leaders roll up their sleeves and get stuck in, when they join in the conversation, invite others to get involved and do not seek to direct or control it. Shared understandings and the assumptive frameworks that gives them coherence are not products to be delivered, or rolled out, but self-forming patterns that emerge gradually and distinctively over time. Participation, thoughtful, deliberate, inclusive participation with mindfulness, replaces control and lies at the heart of cultural weaving.

6. Webs Provide Non-Sticky Pathways by Which a Spider Can Travel
These are in contrast to other, sticky threads, through which they entrap their prey.

This is an interesting property of webs. Spiders are able to navigate their way around a web using non-sticky pathways whereas foreign visitors, those who fly or stumble into the web by mistake and unnoticing, adhere to the sticky threads and become increasingly entangled the more they seek to escape.

Discovering cultural pathways can be painful and can take time but, once learncd, cultural knowledge opens up the pathways that allow ease of access and mobility. We have seen how cultural knowledge enables and finesses movement and transactions between those 'in the know'. To those outsiders, foreigners or newcomers to the culture, many traps await. Many faux pas can be expected, and the likelihood of sanction, scorn, derision or embarrassment is high. To be part of a culture is to know the hidden routes, the unspoken understandings, the tacit prescriptions and proscriptions. It is also to know the limits or boundaries of what is acceptable and what will invite sanction. It is the difference between being a cultural insider and a culturally naive foreigner or visitor.

Fools step in ...

This very naiveté can be of immense value however. Foreigners bring a heightened awareness of cultural difference. Like insects snared in the threads of a web they cause disturbance and draw attention. They bring fresh eyes to what, for others, is so familiar as to be taken for granted and considered normal. In this way, like jesters or fools, they can illuminate what otherwise would remain in the shadows of awareness. Not that raising awareness of cultural threads explicitly is always welcomed or wise. Invisibility is a crucial, and at times jealously guarded property of a web. Those who seek to reveal or illuminate cultural knowledge, without the permission or request of those who have woven it, can expect to be sanctioned, immobilised or worse still, devoured as sustenance for the weavers.

We have noted how newcomers also bring difference, different ways of doing things and different ways of seeing and thinking about things. This makes them anomalies in the broader context of a culture. As such they are likely targets for sanction and ridicule but they also represent an important source of disturbance and disruption to business as usual. As anomalies they are to be treasured, the difference they bring contains the potential to trigger new thinking and to form new cultural pathways. This requires sensitive and enlightened leadership as we discussed earlier.

Cultures create a sense of identity and inclusion. They define a community. Foreigners or outsiders help us to see that which is shared between us. In this sense we can see the symbiotic relationship between members of a culture and nonmembers. Just as spiders depend on insects to become entrapped in their webs for their sustenance, so too, foreigners and outsiders help us to differentiate ourselves from others, strengthening our sense of identity and provoking a shared sense of connection and camaraderie between insiders.

7. Webs Are Hard to See ...
The fish is the last to know about the sea ...

Cultures are about the development of meaning, about ways of comprehending and making sense of the worlds we inhabit. Once developed these frameworks help us to interpret events, statements, gestures, and the circumstances that shape our lives. They serve as guide rails that help us choose how to act or respond in different situations. They help us to map the terrain of our experience, to name it and in so doing to help us decide on appropriate action. Just as maps help us to navigate our way through unfamiliar territory, so too these webs of signification offer pathways that enable exploration and action.

What sets these maps apart is that they are largely hidden from us. They reside in the realm of the taken for granted, in our common sense, unquestioned understandings of reality. We have inherited their routes and pathways from those we like, admire, and aspire to emulate. We have absorbed them through association with our peers, through competition and cooperation, and through the hearing and sharing of stories. In these, and many other ways, we become co-weavers of the rich, dense fabric that is a culture.

Like the filaments of a cobweb, cultural threads are hard to discern. It is only when we experience the disorientation of being part of a different culture, a different ecology of assumptions and conventions, that we begin to notice and perhaps question those that are most familiar to us.

The consequence of participating in daily, weekly, monthly routines and exchanges enables us to operate on automatic for much of the time, to 'sleep walk' through the routines of daily life. Things acquire a comforting familiarity and we accept them without question or reflection for the most part. It is hard for us to notice our assumptions and this is a capability that is rarely called for. We live in a world that has the illusion of normality and permanence. The stories in this work demonstrate that these pathways, these hidden cultural threads, can condemn us to repeat unhelpful patterns and blind us to alternative options that fall outside of our conceptual pathways.

To a fish the sea is always there, pervasive, constant and unnoticed. It provides a medium that enables mobility, gives sustenance and supports all aspects of the life cycle. Like the sea, culture provides a pervasive context that informs action, guides choices and infiltrates the complex patterns of daily activities. And like fish, we take it for granted.

The virtues (and paradoxes) of thinking inside the box

Seeing cultures as hard-to-notice webs offers new insight into the complex and paradoxical business of organisational change. In Chapter 8, we described how cultural understandings and assumptions constrain and shape strategies for change. We hear much about 'thinking out of the box' as an injunction to think unconventionally. Without an awareness of our existing culture these stories alert us to the serious risk of coming up with 'inside the box' change strategies, with what we have also described as 'more of the same' solutions. Without an understanding of what is inside the box we make it much harder to think outside of it.

These stories point to the immense value of a grounded understanding of the threads that inform and guide our current thinking and choices. Simply put, the lesson is as clear as it is straightforward: *know your culture*. Revealing the hidden, tacit assumptions and understandings of daily organisational life can both liberate and energise any change agenda and, as the NSN case illustrates, it can provide an informed platform for dialogue about the future (see Chapter 8).

8. The Spaces Are as Important as the Thread

A web is comprised of threads and spaces between threads. In the West our perceptual habits incline us to focus on an object, a figure, the subject of our interest. In considering a cobweb it is natural for us to look at the threads, the pattern of the weave, and of course, if visible, we are drawn to the creator of the web, the spider. If, alternatively, we were to think of a spider's web as a series of spaces formed and framed by the interwoven filaments of the silk, perhaps we might 'see it' in a different way. The spaces are as necessary as the threads; they define each other and depend on each other for the successful capture of prey.

In a world in which clarity and expertise in communication is highly prized, a world where 'being on message' is considered to be a hallmark of the consummate professional, the importance of communicative 'space', of ambiguity and even uncertainty, can seem alien if not perverse. The stories in this work suggest, however, that when we are concerned with identifying and revising the basic assumptions that inform our behaviour as members of an organisation, when we are looking to encourage a reconfiguration of behaviour around different assumptions and values, then the creation of generative space is a sine qua non. Deliberately embracing uncertainty, tolerating the discomfort of ambiguity and trusting that understanding will emerge through engagement and dialogue, runs counter to prevailing wisdom. It certainly sits squarely in opposition to a view of leaders as all knowing and skilful controllers of communication and definers of a culture.

And yet time and again these cases illustrate that the identification and interruption of long-standing patterns calls for the creation, maintenance and protection of space.

Space to inquire, space to reflect on patterns, space to experiment, to experience difference, space for dialogue to unfold, space to step back, to gain perspective, space to discover, space to process, to make sense, to weave new understanding, to acknowledge and attend to the emotional disturbance that accompanies the turmoil and uncertainty when paradigms shift.

In Chapter 4, we discussed at length some of the more common threads that are available to leaders or senior managers when seeking to foster particular attitudes or values. We noted that, when seen as a collective, these threads amount to a web, an ecology of conceptual invitations. We have seen for example how a leader's choice of language and metaphor can encourage a particular worldview or mind set. We have explored ways in which organisation members closely scrutinise the way in which leaders spend their time, which airline cabin they travel in, where they park their car, who they lunch with, and who they promote, overlook and ignore. These 'low-profile' symbols can take an almost infinite variety of forms. We have seen how settings, the architecture design and furnishing of office buildings, are forms of high-profile symbol that are intended to convey desired values and impressions. These and many other cultural 'threads' are readily available to be managed and fashioned in accordance with a desired intent. This is a natural and legitimate aspect of all leadership. Seeing the chief executive sitting at the front desk receiving visitors is a powerful image and one that accords with a desire to convey the idea of an outwardly focused, community serving local authority.

These stories also suggest however that in the course of a shift in patterns of shared understanding, when conversations come to be configured by different themes within a community, some form of cultural or communicative 'space' often, if not always, plays a part. During such episodes there is a moment, a period, of not knowing, of not controlling the agenda, of letting go and yielding to the unfolding, emerging understanding as it takes form. It is a time of joining with others in processes of discovering and creating new understanding.

These are the spaces between cultural filaments. Spaces in which the outcome is not clear or known, when things stubbornly refuse to fall into place, when there is fierce or intense debate or dissent, when people are puzzling the significance of unexpected information. They are spaces in which unfamiliar voices can suddenly galvanise attention and take people's thinking in an unexpected direction. It is a time of stepping into the unknown, of embracing the spirit of those early explorers who embarked from familiar shores with a sense of adventure mixed with trepidation.

This calls for an uncommon level of tolerance for ambiguity on the part of leaders. It also calls for a trust in the process, for trust in the people, for trust in the power of the collective over the individual. It challenges leaders to let go, to resist the temptation to interfere and to be prepared to be changed by what they encounter. It calls on them to value the seeming contradictions and tensions between different perspectives.

The process of paradigm change is one of disturbance, confusion and disorientation when old certainties dissolve and when everything seems to be in chaos. This suggests that instead of seeing the task of cultural change as *creating* new meaning it may be more helpful to see it as a time of *finding* new meaning together, in the midst of seeming chaos and turmoil. New ideas, new possibilities, new understandings emerge through the gaps between our old sense making frameworks.

At such times leaders need to surrender to this turmoil, like swimmers caught in a whirlpool, trusting that they will eventually emerge the other side into a more tranquil flow.

In our work supporting leaders and organisation members in their ambitions to effect cultural change we have observed that, in those circumstances when something significant has shifted, there is always a moment of surrender, a moment when a leader yields to the uncertain flow of the process. It is in these moments of greatest uncertainty, and often, greatest anxiety, that new possibilities begin to form.

The many stories in this work show that the formation of shared meaning, the development of new understandings, framings and patterns of behaviour, the reweaving of cultural webs, depends as much on the use of 'spaces' as it does on the weaving of cultural threads.

This was illustrated by two large-scale cases and two smaller scale examples of the creative use of space. The Culture Square as part of the NSN merger process and The Medic Inn example demonstrate significant examples of dedicating significant space for cultural transformation. The experiences at The Wrekin District Council and Worth Abbey offer smaller scale examples of the same principle.

Space for Cultural Formation in NSN

We have described in Chapter 6 how the dialogical space represented by the Culture Square allowed for reflection, for the expression and acknowledgment of strong feelings and for the exchange of aspirations, ideas and expertise. Through the course of this expanding conversation participants gradually stepped into an increasingly constructive conversation. In so doing they identified and enacted new norms of behaviour and formulated new principles for configuring future activity in the merged company.

The value of the Culture Square as a safe and constructive space for the exchange of ideas and feelings, for testing and debating ideas and core values, depended on a belief that the forum was not a means of manipulation on the part of 'management'. Its success rested on the integrity of the space as a forum in which people could trust that there would not be retribution for voicing criticism or for expressing strong feelings. Many of the early exchanges in the conversation could be seen as a test of this integrity. As trust grew, so people felt free to take small risks and ultimately engaged in a lively and generative conversation that was sustained for the best part of 12 months.

The Culture Square gradually became a cauldron of debate, cathartic discharge, and the exchange of technical and procedural expertise, where new ideas, new possibilities and principles were slowly fermenting. Importantly, it was for some time, the only medium through which anyone in the new company could participate in the conversation about its future. In the course of this unfolding conversation, certain ideas or phrases became increasingly prominent. As they were repeated and embellished they became part of the new lexicon, part of the emerging culture. To some extent the pan global virtual conference, the JAM, served to officially endorse and bring to clear articulation the shared understandings that had matured in the Culture Square. The Culture Square offers an example of a space in which new cultural threads, new principles, new 'webs of signification' were woven. Above all, it became an increasingly powerful symbol of the NSN leaders' commitment to a culture of inclusion, and participation.

The Medic Inn — space to inquire

The Medic Inn example described in Chapter 5 also illustrates the importance of space in the transformation of what had become a severely dysfunctional culture.

Realising that the management team had become mired in sterile debates and irre-solvable differences the consulting team made the radical proposal that the manage-ment team, together with other key members of staff, undertake an inquiry into the culture of a different hotel in another city choosing to visit an award-winning hotel much admired for the excellence of its service. Acting as anthropologists, the visiting delegation of managers and staff from the Medic Inn engaged in an Appreciative Inquiry into all aspects of their hosts operation, its management and culture.

With the support of two highly skilled facilitators, the group shared with each other what they had discovered in the course of their interviews, their observations and their experience of being guests in the hotel over the course of several days. They had accumulated a rich and complex volume of information.

The many awards showered on the hotel in the years following this work are a measure of the cultural transformation that occurred in the Medic Inn. The decision to commit so much time and resource to this experiment, *to invest in the time and space required to undertake such an intensive inquiry and sense making process*, took courage and can be considered as an enormous act of faith. Its success was in no small measure attributable to the knowledge and skill of the facilitators and their advisers.

Both of these examples illustrate somewhat bold, ambitious and large-scale inter-ventions. Other examples from this work suggest that much can be also be accom-plished by the use of more modest spaces. The two hours spent by Roger Paine and his management team reflecting on the experiences and observations of Danny Chesterman's six-week secondment, for example, proved to be a watershed in how they approached their efforts to transform the Wrekin Culture.

Equally, by posing the question: 'How can we as a management team support you through the merger process?' a senior manager in NSN opened up a space for ideas and comment that proved to be informative and which suggested a respect for the views of staff.

Finally, the delightful story of the 13-year-old pupils at Worth Abbey (see Chapter 4) eagerly garnering accounts of 'exceptional educational moments' from a rich variety of sources, was dependent on the formulation of an inspired question and on the willingness of the headmaster and his staff to sanction an unprecedented journey with an unknown outcome. Approving this experiment by sanctioning the time, resources and space in the curriculum, opened up what turned out to be a very generative organisational space. The educational rewards, as well as the contagious enthusiasm for the process and its outcomes, far exceeded his expectations and con-tinued to ripple through the school in many unexpected ways.

9. Spiders Work with up to Seven Different Kinds of Silk When Weaving a Web

This feature of the formation of a spiders' web, the need to work with many threads, is the focus for the next and final chapter in this work.

References

Barrett, F. (2012). *Yes to the mess: Surprising leadership lessons from Jazz.* Boston, MA: Harvard Business School Publishing.

Bateson, G. (1972). *Steps to an ecology of mind: Collected essays in anthropology, psychiatry, evolution, and epistemology.* Chicago, IL: University of Chicago Press.

Bateson G. (1979). *Interfaces — boundaries which connect.* Gregory Bateson recorded live at Esalen. Big Sur Tapes. Esalen Institute.

Blair, T. (2010). *A journey, my political life.* New York, Toronto: Alfred A Knopf.

Bradbury, R. (1992). *Zen in the art of writing.* New York, NY: Bantam.

Carleton, J. R., & Lineberry, C. (2004). *Achieving post-merger success: A stakeholder's guide to cultural due diligence, assessment, and integration.* Chichester: Wiley.

Cranford, S. W. Tarakanova, A. Pugno, M. N., & Buehler, M. J. (2012). Nonlinear material behaviour of spider silk yields robust webs. *Nature, 482*(7383), 72.

Critchley, B., & Shaw, P. (1994). Lighting up networks. *Leadership & Organization Development Journal.*

Geertz, C. (1973). *The interpretation of cultures: Selected essays.* New York, NY: Basic Books.

Gregory, R. (1971). *Eye and brain.* New York, NY: McGraw Hill.

Griffin, D., & Stacey, R. (Eds.). (2005). *Complexity and the experience of leading organisations.* New York, NY: Routledge.

Isaacson, W. (2011). *Steve jobs.* New York, NY: Simon & Schuster.

Keeney, B. (1983). *Aesthetics of change.* New York, NY: The Guilford Press.

Korzybski, A. (1931). *A non-aristotelian system and its necessity for rigour in mathematics and physics.* Paper presented before the American Mathematical Society. December 1931.

Marshall, J., & McLean, A. (1988). Reflections in action: Exploring organizational culture. In P. Reason (Ed.), *Human inquiry in action. Developments in new paradigm research.* London: Sage Publications.

McLean, A. J., & Marshall, J. (1989). *The wrekin district council: A cultural portrait.* Luton: Local Government Training Board.

Pedler, M. (1996). *Action learning for managers.* London: Lemos and Crane.

Revans, R. W. (1982). *The origin and growth of action learning.* Brickley, UK: Chartwell-Bratt.

Saravanan, D. (2006). Spider silk — structure, properties and spinning. *Journal of Textile and Apparel Technology and Management, 5*(1), 1–20.

Whitehead, A. N., & Russell, B. (1910). *Principia mathematica.* Cambridge University Press, 1910, 1912 and 1913. Second edition, 1925 (Vol. 1), 1927 (Vols. 2, 3). Abridged as *Principia Mathematica to* Cambridge University Press, 1962.

Chapter 10

The Leader's Tale: A Weaver Among Weavers

A recurring observation throughout this work has been that the question of organisation culture poses particular challenges for leaders, especially for leaders who aspire to effect some form of change of culture. It is an elusive concept to define and it is even more difficult to pin down how a leader might make a difference. In this closing chapter I am looking to draw together the main insights that these stories, these weavers tales, bring to the role of leaders in this fascinating field.

It is as if we were to meet with the CEO featured in the opening story sitting at his desk having opened the first two envelopes and pondering whether to open the third. If we were to replace the somewhat bleak and jaundiced message contained in that third envelope with advice drawn from this excursion into the territory of organisation culture and culture change, what would we say? Instead of the injunction to 'prepare three envelopes', what message might serve as a helpful prompt or steer?

I offer these closing thoughts with these questions in mind.

I begin by drawing attention to an irony. Thinking about the role of leaders in relation to the cultures of their oganisations requires them to embrace a relatively unfamiliar view of organisations, processes of change and the role of senior leaders. Efforts to facilitate a reconfiguration of cultural patterns require the adoption of a different view of organisations than one that sees them primarily as structures to be dismantled and reassembled or as machines to be controlled and reengineered. Similarly, we have argued that a view of leaders that casts them as commanding, directing or in some fashion masterminding a change of culture is ill conceived.

In exploring the fascinating territory of organisation culture and questions of cultural change, we have suggested that leaders may be well served on their journey by the insights, assumptions and perspectives offered by different intellectual companions: social anthropologists, social constructionists and writers who draw on ideas from complexity theory.

Before we reprise the major conclusions regarding the role that leaders can play in this arena we offer a reminder of the key assumptions and perspectives, the epistemological 'ground' from which they have grown.

While there are many ways in which leaders participate in the formation of meaning and understandings, the cultural perspective obliges them to come to terms with the view that ultimately, cultural understandings and habits are socially formed.

This way of thinking requires leaders to consider themselves as participants in a culture, as members of a culture who both influence it and in turn are influenced by it. They may be big fish but they swim in the same assumptive sea as everyone else. They are party to the same worldview, they contribute to the cultural narratives, the stories, interpretations, and understandings in the same way as other members, and as we have seen, they can be subject to the same blind spots. As members of a culture they are weavers among weavers, not directors or commanders who are in a position to control or engineer it.

This work proposes a view of organisations that sees them as verbs not nouns, as continuously unfolding processes of organising, sense making and acting. It is a view that sees organisations and cultures as social phenomena, as webs of signification that are woven by all members and which gradually acquire distinctive, yet compelling patterns. Cultures are social phenomena, social accomplishments, interpretative frameworks and shared understandings that unobtrusively shape perception and inform action.

The formation of cultural patterns is something that occurs over time. We have likened them to foot-trodden pathways formed in the lawns that criss-cross between campus buildings. Cultural threads, cultural pathways emerge as expressions of patterned human behaviour and socially held understandings. There is a self-organising quality about cultures that belies control. For this reason we have cautioned against embracing a managerial view of culture as if it is something that can be engineered according to the agenda of any individual or group, however powerful. Rather we have urged a respect for the social nature of cultural patterns and a regard for their resilience, particularly in the face of disturbance.

Once formed these cultural pathways guide thinking, shape habits of perception and inform peoples' behaviour in powerful, yet largely unnoticed ways. The pervasiveness and resilience of these patterns cautions that leaders looking to intervene in some way are well advised to take steps to re-acquaint themselves with these patterns; to appreciate the landscape 'inside of the box' before attempting to think outside of it; to bring back into conscious awareness that which normally and necessarily resides as background information.

Webs, self-evidently, are comprised of multiple threads and their formation is a continuous, never ending process of weaving on the part of multiple weavers. In spite of these notes of caution we have seen that an impressive number of such cultural threads may be readily accessible to leaders.

We know that the formal structures and reporting relationships of an organisation carry messages of status and priorities and that the form and fabric of buildings convey cultural messages that are both intended and unintended. We know that the systems and processes of organisation life shape peoples' behaviour, their perceptions and convey embedded values. We have discussed how leaders exert cultural influences through the metaphors they use, the questions they ask and through the way in which they spend their time and manage their presence. We also know that certain actions and decisions are particularly potent forms of symbol. Appointments, promotions and departures, for example, are especially conspicuous symbols that draw attention and provoke meaning making. Taken as a whole these many and varied forms of invitation might be thought of as an ecology, a web of invitations formed by many threads. And these are cultural threads that are more or less within the control of leaders. They are available to be used as an expression of cultural intent, as ways in which leaders can look to nurture a desired culture.

Leaders provoke stories and meaning making conversations: continuous commentaries that speculate on the significance of their actions, non-actions and statements. We have observed that leaders are continually issuing micro invitations through their choice of language, through their asides and through those events, settings and people that command their time. Their use of high-profile symbols such as speeches, formal announcements and the pronouncements of corporate media is mediated by cultural messages that are carried through the agency of more mundane aspects of everyday leadership, what we have referred to as low-profile symbols. It is through the interplay between high and low-profile symbols, between their carefully tailored and rehearsed, formal gestures and their unrehearsed, unguarded and spontaneous actions and statements that a leaders' cultural impression is formed.

Perhaps one of the more confounding features of organisation cultures is that leaders cannot control how their gestures are interpreted. Shared meaning arises through shared processes of sense making and largely beyond a leader's direct control.

We have also considered the predicament facing all leaders that while they cannot directly control how their gestures will be interpreted, they find themselves under constant and intense scrutiny. We have argued that leaders cannot notcommunicate, that they are constantly sending cultural signals regardless of intent or desire. Leaders provoke stories but they cannot control what meaning others will take from them. They influence but do not control the living complexity that is a cultural web.

The issue for leaders is not whether or not they influence a culture but to accept the inevitability that all leaders are cultural weavers whether they choose it or not. This shifts attention to questions associated with HOW they already participate, knowingly or otherwise and deliberately or inadvertently, and brings into focus important questions regarding their intentionality and agency. Even though a leader cannot engineer or directly fashion a desired culture, as a weaver among weavers, they are important participants in its co-creation.

So the emphasis shifts away from that of control to a consideration of where can they exert influence and exercise informed choices. In addition it points to a facilitative or enabling role for leaders: how can they create the circumstances in which new understandings form, familiar attachments and orientations are relinquished and new cultural narratives, new cultural motifs become figural.

Instead of asking how can a leader engineer or manage a change of culture insights from anthropology and social constructionist perspectives suggest asking the question in different ways: how can leaders create the conditions in which new cultural understandings emerge; how can those assumptions, metaphors and narratives that are instrumental in the emergence of new interpretive frameworks find articulation and enactment? In short: what can leaders do to create and support the conditions in which a change of culture becomes possible?

In seeing cultures as webs we have sought to convey an understanding of the phenomenon of culture as complex, patterned and interwoven and as remarkably resilient in the face of external pressure or interference. We have suggested that this way of thinking about culture however also offers important and helpful signposts for leaders interested in this area.

In this closing section we reprise the implications of our observations for leaders and others who aspire to exercise influence over the dominant narratives within a culture. They are described under the following headings:

- Be the message: leader as living symbol
- Leader as weaver among weavers — work with many weavers
- Leader as cultural caretaker, broker and sponsor
- Ensure secure anchors
- Leader as cultural provocateur
- Look for the pattern that connects — know your culture
- Attend to the message of the medium
- Shine a light — the power of presence
- Create and guard the quality of spaces between threads
- Encourage overlapping ecologies

Be the Message: Leader as Living Symbol

The inevitable visibility combined with the intense scrutiny afforded to leaders' actions and utterances calls for a highly tuned awareness of the immense symbolic significance of their role and power, a realisation that their every utterance, gesture and act either affirms or conflicts with high-profile espousals, long-held beliefs, values and understandings. Leaders may not create meaning directly, but they certainly provoke meaning making among those who are their followers. They continuously issue micro-invitations to others to see the world in a particular way, whether deliberately or unintentionally. In this sense leaders are continuously weaving a culture. We have seen countless examples of the extraordinary interest and sensitivity afforded to the seemingly smallest and most casual of gestures by a leader. Organisation members are highly sensitised to these, low-profile gestures, and equally wary of formal, high-profile proclamations. We have seen, for example, how significance is placed on such seemingly trivial phenomena as which sites leaders visit, how often and which they avoid or neglect. We have described how easily a leader's casual aside can destroy the development of a fragile narrative of change.

We have also seen how much is read into who leaders promote, who they favour and who they overlook; that as much scrutiny is given to the meetings they skip as the ones they attend; that their jokes and the aircraft cabin they use when travelling all draw comment and contribute to an interpretive narrative. In the age of the internet and other social media the scrutiny afforded to leaders' actions and statements, has intensified to an unprecedented level. Similarly, the explosive growth of social media has ensured that the audience for receiving these stories has increased exponentially. The need for leaders to be mindful of what messages their unrehearsed behaviour is signalling has never been greater.

The stories in this work suggest a remarkable sophistication on the part of organisation members in noticing the alignment or disjunction between a leader's high and low-profile gestures. Everything leaders say and do needs to be considered as culturally significant, as conveying meaning, as inviting a worldview. It is a perpetual part of the project of leadership, but has particular valence when leaders are new. Being so figural in initiating the stories and narratives that pulse through the meaning making conversations of everyday, organisational life is an extraordinary opportunity for leaders who are looking to encourage particular attitudes, values and behaviours. It requires, however, an acute feel for this aspect of leadership and calls for a sophisticated level of reflexivity, in the moment self-awareness, as well as clarity of intent. This is beyond being a skill. It is more than an internalised sense of self as symbol. It is a synthesis of awareness, intent and integrity. It is a way of being.

The stories in this work point to the significance of four disciplines or attitudes for leaders as cultural weavers: intentionality, mindfulness, submission and inquiring mind.

Intentionality: Being prepared to advocate beliefs and values clearly and with heart. Openly expressing a broad sense of purpose, a desire to influence or encourage particular attitudes, values or forms of behaviour. We have likened this aspect of their role to the formation of radial threads that occurs early in the construction of a spider's web. Through their advocacy leaders can define the territory, tone and broad cultural intent of their organisation. At the same time they are also setting boundaries that indicate the limits of what is acceptable.

Mindfulness: This is the cultivation of a heightened, in-the-moment awareness of themselves as living symbols that provoke speculation, draw interpretations and generate an unending stream of stories that percolate through the informal, sense making communities of their organisation.

Of equal importance is heightening leaders' awareness of how they participate in the interpretation of others' gestures and, especially how they respond to news of difference.

Another way of describing this capacity for reflexivity, for the in-the-moment ability to select and craft low-profile symbols consistent with a desired invitation is captured by the injunction: be the story.

Submission: In recognition that they cannot directly control processes of interpretation and local meaning making leaders need to be able to both lead and let go, to advocate and to be prepared to follow others. This highlights a role for leaders in nurturing local processes of understanding, of sponsoring, protecting and legitimating spaces in which others can find or develop new ways of understanding. This calls on leaders to be ready to name and endorse emergent understanding and to see themselves as participants in the collective processes of meaning making, not as directing them.

Inquiring mind: As cultural weavers leaders are strategically placed to express an attitude of openness to difference, to anomalies, a regard for the maverick, for the unfamiliar, the strange and seemingly alien. They can set the tone that invites in others a willingness to look twice, to surrender to others' ways of thinking and acting, to hold a reverence for difference and an alertness to faint signals. This calls for a willingness to embark on a journey without knowing the destination; trusting that it will yield unexpected insights.

Work with Many Weavers: Leader as Weaver Among Weavers

We have argued that it is through the iterative cycles of invitation and interpretation that shared meaning gradually forms. These cycles of invitation and interpretation, of gesture and response, are reciprocal and vary in length of time. It can be months, if not years for example, before a leader discovers how a key speech or presentation was received, and how it was interpreted among different groups and communities within an organisation. It follows that by creating conditions that shorten these cycle times the process can be accelerated. Shared understanding grows when people are brought into contact, through the use of dialogue and conversation. Shortening gesture — response cycles and fostering dialogue combine to accelerate the emergence of shared understanding, even, as we have seen, in large, global organisations.

A third theme in our discussion has been the adoption of a systemic view of organisations. We have suggested that any organisation can be understood as a patchwork of interconnecting and interdependent groups and communities. These communities can be professionally based or defined by location or function. Their allegiance to the larger whole may vary. Their sense of commitment to official values and policy may also vary in strength. We have described them as 'subcultures' and occasionally as 'social ecologies' that organise themselves around locally shared understandings, values and leaders.

In the context of efforts to create the conditions for either cultural change or cultural formation this systemic view points to the value of enlisting, including and involving many and multiple voices and perspectives. In the terms of our metaphor of webs and weaving, it is to work with the whole web. This underlines the need for social processes and technologies that are capable of holding diverse perspectives in some form of purposeful and productive conversation. Over the past two decades or so we have seen the growth in popularity and use of methods such as Open Space, AI summits, Global Café and so on. The common feature of these methods is that they are based on the principle of *polyvocality*, of bringing 'all of the voices' into the room and facilitating multiple conversations around a common theme. Recent development in virtual technology have meant that these virtual rooms can host many thousands of voices that speak from just as many perspectives. They are examples of convening many weavers. Their processes encourage inquiry, dialogue, the discovery of shared aspirations and shared understanding.

Cultural webs are the collective accomplishment of many weavers over time. Leaders interested in fostering cultural change are advised to work with many weavers.

Leader as Caretaker, Broker and Sponsor

By virtue of their position and power leaders can do much to create the conditions in which cultural change occurs. This is not the same as being able to exercise direct control over the formation and change of a culture but it is to recognise that the vibrancy and capability of cultures for self-renewal and emergent change can be nurtured and protected. Leaders are uniquely placed to do this. We have seen how cultures that are self-referencing and that insulate themselves from the realities of adjacent ecologies are at risk of extinction. They risk becoming historical anomalies and losing their relevance to others. For commercial organisations this is especially worrying, but it is a concern for all forms of community that need to demonstrate their relevance and ensure their ongoing integrity in the midst of a changing world.

In this section we offer thoughts on how leaders can do this. How they can perform the role of a cultural caretaker, as someone who is attending to and cultivating the regenerative capacity of a cultural web. It is about safeguarding the craft of weaving and ensuring the skills and processes necessary for skilful, accomplished weaving to occur.

Ensure Secure Anchors

Cultural change is an unsettling time for everyone and can trigger irrational and deeply set insecurities and fears. We have seen how cultural patterns have a resilience that is to be respected and that attempts to interfere with them can have perilous consequences for those who disregard them.

We have also seen that when cultural patterns change they reconfigure themselves around new ideas, new principles and practices. We have suggested that the establishment of secure anchors is a key role that leaders can play in supporting the reconfiguration of cultural patterns. We have earlier identified these anchors as demonstrating commitment to the journey and as providing political and emotional support through the inevitable uncertainty of the process. This is particularly so for those organisation members who pioneer new ideas and practices, for those who bring 'news of difference' and for those who experiment. In this regard we have drawn heavily on William Bateson's use of the phrase: 'treasure your exceptions'. We have also spoken of ensuring that leaders safeguard their own robust political support and that they receive external encouragement as well as challenge and support throughout the process.

Finally, we have suggested that by commissioning processes that encourage and support what we have termed 'meta-conversations' leaders can legitimate processes of inquiry, encourage reflection and dialogue and be party to the emergence of new understanding. We likened these devices to a weaver's loom. These looms represent a way of holding or anchoring processes necessary for new understanding and patterns of behaviour to form. They hold open the anxiety provoking space of not knowing long enough for transformative understandings to emerge.

Supporting, sponsoring and participating in these generative spaces, is an important way in which leaders contribute to cultural change. We find Frank Barrett's (Frank Barrett, 2012) vivid phrase 'say yes to the mess'[1] to be a perfect way of capturing this aspect of leadership through cultural change. It underlines the importance of tolerating the mess, confusion, anxiety and uncertainty that often precedes the emergence of a new pattern, a new approach or a new way of understanding. It is an especially challenging part of leadership through cultural change.

Leader as Cultural Provocateur

Part of the importance of ensuring secure anchor points, especially those concerned with political support, is because of leaders' privileged capability to sever old cultural attachments, to signal the end of a cultural era. Releasing those conspicuous players who embody unwanted thinking and behaviour, for example, is more than the reshuffling of personnel; it can be a cultural intervention of seismic cultural significance. It is a form of un-tethering a culture from old and un-needed anchor points. Challenging old habits, acting as a cultural provocateur by questioning sacred cows as well as old stories and routines, is a necessary part of a leader's role in cultural change, and it is bound to alienate her from some as well as endear her to others. This calls for the full use of her power and calls for unshakeable support from those on whom her power depends.

Look for the Pattern That Connects — Know Your Culture

While cultural knowledge, perceptual habits and patterns are necessarily taken for granted and hidden from conscious awareness, we have seen that this can also make things difficult when cultural change is called for. We have seen how cultural patterns can lock us into 'more of the same' thinking and into repetitive cycles of problem construction. We have discussed how easily our 'strategies for change' can, in themselves, be based on the same cultural assumptions that led to a difficulty in the first place. We have talked about this in terms of how 'the solution is the problem' (Watzlawick, Weakland, & Fisch, 1974) and how 'the more things change the more they stay the same'. We have also described how our consulting experiences of helping clients to surface their cultural understandings and knowledge almost invariably

---

[1]See Barrett (2012).

led to spontaneous changes in long standing patterns. It is clear from these stories that taking the time to explicate what are normally implicit understandings unlocks new possibilities and enables new behaviour. It is as if we are prisoners of unquestioned understandings and agreements about how to go about things and the process of cultural inquiry opens the door of the prison cell. The process of bringing cultural contours into relief is both revelatory and galvanising. It opens up new possibilities and reveals new options for future development.

Heightening cultural awareness is a powerful precursor for cultural change. Once cultural patterns have been identified and named, change becomes more possible and often occurs spontaneously.

Leaders can play an invaluable role in legitimating and sponsoring cultural inquiries, in revealing those expectations and understandings that normally reside in the background of everyday organisational life. Just as the focus of a camera can bring into sharp relief objects at a particular depth of field while simultaneously making other objects or settings less distinct, so too with cultural awareness. By bringing into focus the tacitly understood patterns and pathways of a cultural web it becomes possible to appreciate the whole and to openly discuss and assess their current relevance, to question their utility and to begin a process of forming new pathways, weaving new cultural threads.

From a practical point of view this means sponsoring cultural reviews and processes of inquiry as well as encouraging interest and discussion in the discoveries.[2] It can also be achieved in ways that blend more naturally into the everyday rhythms of organisational life. One of the gifts of newcomers and outsiders is that they see things with fresh eyes. Taking the time to discover what they notice, what for them is news of difference, can be culturally illuminating.

We have also seen how visits to other cultures, what we have referred to as Cultural Safaris, heighten awareness of cultural differences. As cultural 'strangers,' as newcomers, or even as 'tourists', we have a heightened sensitivity to difference. While noticing difference elsewhere we are also confronted with our assumptions about what we consider to be 'normal' and 'right'. We are awakened to different ways of thinking and acting by such experiences. Such episodes provide precious, though transitory, opportunities to reflect on our expectations and assumptions as to what is 'normal' and 'right'.

---

[2]Here I must declare a passionate bias. There are many proprietary 'tools' offered by consultants that purport to provide a cultural description. I have reservations about the methods and validity of many of these. My concerns are twofold: firstly they are frequently based on dimensions or discriminators developed by a research/consulting company, essentially using positivistic criteria against which 'cultures' are assessed and compared. My concern is that what these provide is a read out against constructs devised by the researchers/consultants. True ethnography is concerned with discovering the dominant constructs held by members of a culture, understanding things from the 'native's point of view', as Geertz puts it. My second concern is that the products of such expert analyses have a technical, esoteric quality that does not invite understanding or widespread dialogue among members of a culture. The cultural 'understanding' resulting from such studies is limited to a restricted group of experts.

Leaders have the capability to capitalise on the insights arising from these fish-out-of-water experiences, to legitimate, encourage and participate in debriefing such experiences, simultaneously reflecting on the news of difference as well as the 'news of sameness'[3] that they provide.

Attend to the Message of the Medium

We have noted that the term organisation invites us to think in terms of nouns; to consider an organisation as a 'thing'. This in turn invites us to consider how best to manage and to lead "it". In the context of cultures and cultural change we have suggested that it might be more helpful to use a verb instead and to think more in terms of 'organisings'. This perspective draws attention to the active, living exchanges and transactions that are a perpetual feature of what we think of as organisations. It emphasises the dynamic, interactive processes that give order, flow and pattern to everyday organisational life. If we think of organisations as nouns we endorse a product view that emphasises such things as goals and outputs. Leaders, of course, are rightly concerned with ensuring the nature and quality of such outputs. If, instead, we think in terms of organisings our interest is drawn to the quality and significance of processes. How things occur matters. Processes convey cultural information that is just as potent as that expressed through artefacts.

How a meeting is conducted, for example, is often discussed more than its content. The way in which a new initiative is introduced and launched can carry much, culturally coded, information. It can, for example, express assumptions about status, power and reveal attitudes towards inclusion and diversity. And, of course, it will express beliefs about how to run processes. In chapter four we examined this idea using the phrase 'when the medium is the message'. We described the case of an organisation that experienced little success in its efforts to introduce a more strategic mindset through the use of traditional methods of lecturing and case studies. It was only when they adopted an approach to developing strategic thinking and behaviour that required participants to *be strategic in the way in they learned about strategy* that things began to change.

This is an important orientation for leaders to bring to all matters where processes are being discussed, particularly processes that touch significant numbers of people within an organisation but also those outsiders who engage with it in some capacity. The following questions look to provoke this kind of orientation:

What meaning do you want people to take from their experience of participating in this process?

---

[3]'News of sameness' is my shorthand for cultural knowledge that we come to regard as normal, as right and as 'obvious'.

How can these ideas or processes be introduced and managed in a way that conveys desired cultural messages?

How can the medium embody the message?

Shine a Light — the Power of Presence

We have discussed how a leader's presence draws attention. It gets noticed and commented on. It shines a light. How leaders spend their time conveys information about priorities, it signals what matters and what merits attention. We have also seen how a leader's absence can also be heavily symbolic. Quite simply, leaders can influence the formation and strength of cultural threads through the way in which they manage their presence: presence amplifies, absence dampens. Perhaps one of the most striking yet subtle features of Roger Paine's leadership of the culture change at the Wrekin District Council was the thoughtful way in which he managed his presence. His repeated presence on the reception desk each Monday morning sent an unequivocal message about his belief in service to the community. This grand gesture was reinforced by other more subtle, yet equally noticed, uses of his presence. For example, the way in which he would deliberately but quietly show up in the background of those events or meetings which expressed desired cultural values and murmur the barely audible phrase: 'Good 'innit!'

Creating and Safeguarding the Quality of Spaces Between Threads

Clifford Geertz suggests that cultures, like nature, abhor a vacuum. When we are faced with uncertainty, with unfamiliar or confusing situations, we bring familiar and trusted frameworks for making sense of them. This can bring comfort and a sense of control. As we have seen throughout this work, by invoking familiar mindsets at such times, by drawing on familiar explanations and habits of perception, we run the serious risk of recreating old patterns and missing new possibilities. The Glassblowers searching for the cause of their 'bad glass', focused their efforts on the functioning of the furnace, and completely missed the fact that they had been delivered the wrong grade of sand. Their craft culture guided them to trust their instincts when more scientific and systematic measurement procedures would have quickly revealed the source of the problem.

Developing or expanding new ways of making sense, of seeing things in a different way, calls for time and a suspension of familiar perceptual frameworks. It is hard to do this under the pressures and deadlines of business as usual. We have seen from the cases of cultural change explored in this work that the formation of new mindsets, of new ways of thinking and operating, calls for dedicated time and resource. We have also seen that the formation of new interpretive frameworks through the use of inquiry, dialogue and debate is a process that unfolds over time.

Creating the necessary time and space for these new frameworks to form is as important to processes of cultural change and formation as the spaces in a spiders web. We saw especially in the NSN and Medic Inn cases the value of dedicating and protecting time and resource to supporting processes through which new understandings grew. We also saw how important it was to separate them from the pressing, goal driven imperatives of daily operations, and from being used as channels for normal operational communications. They might be compared to the sealed vessels by which, according to legend, alchemists turned base metals into noble ones of silver or gold. We have noted the emotional resilience that this called for, especially on the part of leaders and the extraordinary restraint that it took them to refrain from intervening. Cultural change, the transformation of long-held values, beliefs and traditions is an extraordinary undertaking that calls for extraordinary leadership and extraordinary processes.

Leaders have a vital role to play in creating and protecting the space and conditions in which this can occur.

Encourage Overlapping Ecologies

We have noted on many occasions that cultures, once formed have a self-referencing quality. As explanatory frameworks and systems of belief they serve to help people make meaning of what would otherwise remain a 'blooming, buzzing confusion' (William James, 1890). Cultures help to provide a sense of order and serve as a necessary and invaluable medium through which social behaviour and coordinated action can occur. In the same way as a spider's web can be hard to see, so cultural understandings are part of the 'background expectancies' of our working lives and for most of us, most of the time, happily remain unquestioned and unnoticed. The stories in this work have shown that, at the same time as cultures enable social exchange and coordinated behaviour, they also serve to subtly direct and control how we make sense of things and how we act. Those who deviate from culturally acceptable pathways can expect to be sanctioned or marginalised. The combined consequence of these qualities, taken as a whole, is that cultures are essentially conservative, self-perpetuating, phenomena. Left undisturbed the worldview of a culture is reinforced and tends to an orientation that is predominantly inward. In more common terms, it becomes 'closed'.

We have described how reward and promotion criteria tend to perpetuate dominant beliefs and values. Those in power tend to promote and reward attitudes and behaviours that are culturally defined as desirable. The result is more of the same. The same kind of people migrate to positions of power and influence and, in turn, come to define the criteria by which others succeed. Ultimately these self-referencing and self-justifying communities become increasingly anomalous in the broader social and commercial context, until they experience a crisis or collapse.

We have seen how culturally dissonant understanding and practices are experienced as a jolt, and are received as an unwelcome disruption, an unwanted disturbance. We have described instances of how news of difference is pushed away, marginalised, ignored, ridiculed or coerced into conformity. We have also seen that under the appropriate circumstances news of difference can be regarded more constructively. We have described examples of how sponsored inquiries, such as secondments or 'safaris' into other cultural settings can bring back news of difference that is both provocative and welcomed as generative. We have also seen how cultural visits and exchanges between departments, units or subcultures can prove to be both illuminating and generative. We have also noted the important part played by skilful facilitation in supporting the sense making following such excursions.

Exposure to difference, when combined with serious, thoughtful reflection and questioning and the inclusion of different perspectives, different voices, can lead to a revision of assumptions, assumptive frameworks and often a reconfiguration of values. The possibility for a shift or revision of cultural assumptions occurs when social, cultural ecologies overlap. This is fertile territory for the revision of long-held assumptions, for the introduction of new practices and new interpretive frames.

We have seen that exposure to other cultures more often than not generates some form of collective emotional frisson, the expression and discharge of anxiety that occurs whenever our taken for granted sense of things is brought into question.

There is clearly a role for leaders here. They are well placed to ensure that their organisation or business avoids this kind of cultural inertia, complacency and tendency to self-referencing, self-justification. It calls for courage and determination to see the process through, to not panic when expressions of anxiety and anger surface, to accept the disorientation and confusion that necessarily accompanies a cultural disturbance and the reconfiguration of conceptual frames.

It also calls for the active encouragement of excursions, cultural safaris into other cultural ecologies. It can also mean welcoming those who bring news of difference into an organisation. Showing a genuine and respectful interest in the difference that they bring and that they represent in a way that resembles the spirit of the early social anthropologists.[4] Above all it points to the importance of a willingness to question and revise long-held and cherished beliefs, to dwell in the unfamiliar and seemingly nonsensical, to be part of the process of puzzling out new understandings, developing new explanations and constructs, and to be ready to name new clarity as it forms.

Leaders are well placed to broker these inter-cultural connections, to sponsor safaris, to trust the generative potential of holding adjacent cultural ecologies in contact. They have the power to champion those who bring news of difference and to challenge those who dampen, deny and reject it.

We have observed a restless quality in those leaders who have been party to cultural change episodes in their organisations. In part we see this as a natural desire to continually stretch their staff to reach ever-higher standards and levels of performance, never settling for good enough. Their restlessness might also be seen as a healthy epistemological restlessness. A perpetual inclination to question, to disturb

---

[4]In the same way as we have come to question the arrogance of our assumptions that western cultures were in some ways more advanced or civilised than these 'tribal' societies, we are suggesting that organisation leaders can set a tone of humility and respect for other cultures.

and challenge accepted understandings and orthodoxies, an instinctive mistrust towards the received interpretations of others.

Limits of the Metaphor

This work was inspired by Geertz' (1973) view of cultures as webs of signification. When invoking a metaphor to bring a fresh perspective to a field of human activity there is always a risk of overworking the metaphor, of trying to force fit one's observations into the metaphor. This work is no exception and I find it instructive to consider those aspects of the field of cultural change that do not sit comfortably or naturally into this way of seeing. Webs are largely, though not exclusively, the work of a solitary spider. On occasion apparently, webs are created by a group of spiders working in concert.[5] However, throughout this work I have emphasised that cultural webs are not the products of the solitary endeavours of an individual but, self-evidently, are social creations, the observable patterns formed by the complex interactions and exchanges that come to characterise all forms of human community. They more closely resemble the great tapestries that were woven by many weavers, working in concert. In this sense, cultures might better be thought of as living tapestries.

Individuals working on their own cannot create a pattern of their choice. Cultures are the product of relationships in dynamic interaction over time. Leaders cannot control how their followers will respond to their overtures, their speeches. They cannot control how any single act or utterance or gesture, however well crafted, will be interpreted. What counts is how any such action sits in the broader context of their behaviour.

The stories in this work underline what is widely understood, that leaders need to attend to the nature of the (multiple) invitations they make on a continuing basis and to the many forms that such invitations take. This requires them to take seriously their symbolic power and calls for heightened, in-the-moment, awareness. We have also seen how contradictions, inconsistencies and mixed messages between the high and low-profile symbols draw comment and often judgment in a way that ensures that they too are amplified.

A key conclusion for leaders and their teams looking to encourage a shift of culture is unequivocal: weave with many threads.

And Finally ...

By way of concluding these reflections, and this book, I have found myself recalling that newly appointed chief executive as he progressively opened the envelopes left to

---

[5]There is a famous example was reported at Lake Tawakoni State Park in Texas. It measured 200 yards across and is believed by entomologists to be the result of social spiders.

him by his predecessor. What might constitute a more helpful injunction in that third envelope? What would encapsulate the spirit of the ideas and insights offered by these stories of cultural change?

I find myself recalling a gift from a client offered some ten or so years ago. Among other things she was an impresario and theatre owner. The gift was a T-shirt with a quote from a play that she had produced. The author was Athol Fugard, a highly regarded South African playwright. The quote read:

'Wake up and dream properly!' (Athol Fugard, 1996)

At the risk of sounding somewhat pompous I find an adapted version of this quote speaks to the challenge for those leaders, managers and facilitators who would wish to learn more about the craft and practice of achieving cultural change:

'Wake up and weave properly!'

References

Barrett F. (2012). *Say yes to the mess*. Boston, MA: Harvard Press.

Fugard, A. (1996). *Valley song*. New York, NY: Theatre Communication Group Inc.

Geertz, C. (1973). *The interpretation of cultures: Selected essays*. New York, NY: Basic Books.

James, W. (1890). *The principles of psychology. Classics in the history of psychology, an Internet resource developed by Christopher D. Green of York University*. Toronto, Ontario.

Watzlawick, P., Weakland, J., & Fisch, R. (1974). *Change: Principles of problem formation and problem resolution*. New York, NY: W. W. Norton Page.

Index